Donald Ernest Mansell
Vesta West Mansell

# SURE AS THE DAWN

REVIEW AND HERALD® PUBLISHING ASSOCIATION
HAGERSTOWN, MD 21740

This book was
Edited by Raymond H. Woolsey
Designed by Bill Kirstein
Cover design by Helcio Deslandes
Cover photo by G. Fritz/SUPERSTOCK, INC.
Type set: 11/12 Isbell Book

PRINTED IN U.S.A.

98 97 96 95 94 93        10 9 8 7 6 5 4 3 2 1

**Library of Congress Cataloging in Publication Data**

Mansell, Donald Ernest, 1923—
    Sure as the dawn/Donald Ernest Mansell and Vesta West Mansell.
        p.      cm.
    Includes index.
    1. Devotional calendars—Seventh-day Adventists. 2. Seventh-day
Adventists—Prayer-books and devotions—English. I. Mansell, Vesta
West, 1932-     . II. Title.
BV4810.M36    1993
242'.2—dc20                        93-3782
                                          CIP

ISBN 0-8280-0723-3

# Dedicated to
## our grandchildren:

Donald Ernest Mansell II, Dora Erika Mansell,
Charles Everett Mansell, Elizabeth Lynn Draget,
and Monica Jennifer Draget

# Preface

The most important thing in life is to know God as a personal friend through Jesus Christ, whom He has sent. Once we have obtained this knowledge, the next most important thing is to share it with others. No matter what a Christian's vocation may be, it is his or her privilege to impart to others what has been learned—not in an intrusive, unpleasant way, but winsomely, appealingly. This can be accomplished effectively only as God works through the individual—as self is hidden with Christ in God.

The purpose of this book is to show how Christ has lived out His life in the lives of others who have known God. The authors have endeavored to select practical, positive illustrations of this principle. Occasionally a negative example has been included for contrast. After all, the Christian life is seldom a steady, upward climb. The reason for emphasis on positive illustrations is that the authors believe that it is more important to know how to do what is right than how to avoid doing what is wrong.

In reading this book, may you come to know God still better—whom to know is life eternal.

# About the Authors

Donald Ernest Mansell was born in Rio de Janeiro, Brazil, of missionary parents. When he was 7, his family went to the Madeira Islands, then to the Azores. They were on their way to service in Mozambique when they made a stopover in Manila, where they were caught by invading forces shortly after the bombing of Pearl Harbor. The Mansells were interned in various places on the island of Luzon until they were liberated in 1945.

Mansell graduated from Pacific Union College with a bachelor's degree in theology. One of his early appointments was to Lodi, California, where he met Vesta West. Vesta, born in Daly City, California, had graduated from Lodi Academy and attended La Sierra College.

Shortly after their marriage, the couple went to the Central Amazon Mission. They returned to the United States in 1958, and Mansell enrolled at Potomac (now Andrews) University, graduating with an MA in 1959. After several years as a pastor and Bible teacher, he joined the Review and Herald Publishing Association as an editor. Vesta worked at the Washington Adventist Hospital as a secretary.

From 1975 to 1982 Mansell served as an assistant secretary at the Ellen G. White Estate in Washington, D.C. Then he joined the Pacific Press Publishing Association as an editor. Since his retirement in 1988 he has been aiding several overseas divisions as an editorial consultant. Vesta assists him with her secretarial skills. They have four children and five grandchildren.

*Let us press on to know the Lord; for as certain as the break of dawn He comes to us.*
*Hosea 6:3, MLB.*

# Press On to Know the Lord

Pressing on to know the Lord means more than a superficial knowledge of God. It means an ever deepening acquaintanceship with Him. As surely as day follows night, the consciousness that God exists dawns on every soul who will wholeheartedly "feel after him" (Acts 17:27). But if one goes no further, this realization fades quickly into nothingness. On the other hand, if we are in earnest we will not be content with the mere knowledge that God exists. Having encountered God, having learned to appreciate His character, we long to know Him better and look forward with eagerness to times of communion with our heavenly Friend.

For most people there is no better time for these encounters than the first thing in the morning, after a refreshing night's sleep. It is then that the mind is clearest and least cumbered by the cares of this life. Harriet Beecher Stowe, the American poetess, has captured the experience that may be yours in these memorable lines:

Still, still with Thee, when purple morning breaketh,
　　When the bird waketh, and the shadows flee;
Fairer than morning, lovelier than the daylight,
　　Dawns the sweet consciousness, I am with Thee!

Alone with Thee, amid the mystic shadows,
　　The solemn hush of nature newly born;
Alone with Thee, in holy adoration,
　　In the calm dew and freshness of the morn.

So shall it be at last, in that bright morning,
　　When the soul waketh, and life's shadows flee;
Oh, in that glad hour, fairer than daylight dawning,
　　Shall rise the glorious thought, I am with Thee!

As you commune with God morning by morning throughout this year, may your knowledge of Him be like the "shining light, that grows in brilliance till perfect day" (Prov. 4:18, NAB)—*the day you and I, and all of us, meet God face to face in His eternal kingdom!*

2

*As the deer pants for the water brooks, so my soul pants for Thee, O God. My soul thirsts for God, for the living God. Ps. 42:1, 2, NASB.*

# A Thirst for God

Every human being has experienced thirst at one time or another. The thirstiest I have ever been was during the first days of January 1942. My parents, my brother, and I happened to be passing through the Philippines on our way to Africa as missionaries when Pearl Harbor was bombed and war broke out. On December 29, 1941, we were taken captive by the Imperial Japanese Army and interned in Camp John Hay. During the fighting the pump that supplied water to our camp was destroyed, and for several days what little water we drank had to be lugged in manually and was rationed out in driblets.

God created us in such a way that when our bodies need water they tell us so—we thirst. But in our verse for meditation, the psalmist was not speaking of physical thirst. He was using physical thirst as a figure for a deeper thirst—the thirst of the soul for God. It was to this need that Augustine, an early Church Father, referred when he wrote: "O God, Thou has created us for Thyself, and we are not satisfied until our souls rest in Thee."

There are many who sense a need for something, they know not what. They endeavor to satisfy this soul-thirst by drinking at the "broken cisterns" of the world (see Jer. 2:13)—human philosophy, psychology, drugs—but their craving remains.

He who drinks of the water of life drinks to thirst no more (see John 4:14). This does not mean that because he thirsts no more, he never drinks again. It means that, having found the Source of living waters, his God-created soul-thirst is forever quenched *as he continues to drink this spiritual water.* But this isn't all; as he drinks he in turn becomes to others "a well of water springing up into everlasting life" (verse 14).

The "water" the self-revealing God offers thirsting souls is a knowledge of Himself. When we drink this water, our soul-thirst is quenched, yet paradoxically, we long for more. The heartfelt cry of our soul is "More of Thee, Lord, still more of Thee."

# How to Know God for Sure

Several years ago I approached the old bridge over the Russian River at Healdsburg, California, while it was being painted. As I waited to drive across, I noticed a boy coming from the opposite direction. When he reached a sign that said "Wet Paint," he paused, read it, then dabbed his finger in the still-wet pigment. He wouldn't take somebody else's word for whether the paint was wet. He wanted to know for himself.

Students of the mind tell us there are three ways or combinations of ways by which we acquire knowledge: (1) taking someone's word, (2) reasoning through to a conclusion, or (3) performing an experiment. Of the three ways, the surest and most satisfying is doing an experiment. The probable reason is because we like to know in the surest possible manner whether the knowledge we have acquired is true. If we take someone's word for it, we can be deceived; if we try to use pure reason without knowing all the facts, we may reach the wrong conclusion. But properly done experiments always yield the same results, and we may rest secure in the conclusion reached.

When Paul wrote that he *knew* whom he had believed, he was certain beyond all doubt. He had come to know his Lord, not because of what someone had told him, nor because he had arrived at this knowledge by pure reason. He knew God as a result of firsthand experience—by experiment, if you please.

When I was in high school I had a chemistry teacher named James Thompson. One of the things Mr. Thompson taught us was that water consisted of two gases, hydrogen and oxygen. He also said it contained twice as many hydrogen atoms as oxygen atoms. We had learned something. Later Mr. Thompson had us separate water into its component elements by electrolysis. Now we knew by actual experiment that what he had told us was true. We also found that no matter how many times we performed this experiment, we always got the same result.

Experimental knowledge of God is the surest, most satisfying way to know Him. It is the kind of knowledge you and I must have if we would inherit eternal life (see John 17:3).

*Eternal life means to know you, the only true God. John 17:3, TEV.*

# A Life or Death Matter

Our verse implies that knowing God is an eternal life-or-death matter and that this knowledge must be experiential.

When I attended college, a schoolmate, Allan Schwant, told me about two roommates in a Midwestern university who were arguing about God's existence. We'll call the believer Bob and his agnostic roommate John. Bob insisted that John could find God if he read the Bible. John wasn't so sure, but he finally agreed to the proposition. When he came to the story of Gideon and the fleece, he decided to do the Gideon experiment.

John put out a fleece on the campus lawn one night. That night Bob did some earnest praying. However, when John picked up the fleece next day, *it was wet!*

"I knew it wouldn't work!" he chortled.

What went wrong?

Well, suppose John had gone to the chemistry lab and done an hydrolysis experiment but instead of using an electrolyte he put a nonelectrolyte into the water. If you know anything about chemistry, you know the experiment would fail. Why? Because he didn't use the right method for hydrolyzing water.

Well, then, what is the right method for knowing God?

*We must begin by allowing the possibility that God "exists"* (Heb. 11:6, NIV). But isn't this circular reasoning?

Some years ago an atheist friend said he wanted to believe God exists, but he wanted "reasonable proof." We went over the ground we'd covered thus far. He accepted everything—until it came to accepting the possibility that God exists.

"Stop right there!" he said. "That's circular reasoning."

"Well," I replied, "suppose Thomas Edison had begun his experiments on the light bulb by denying the possibility that such a form of illumination was possible, is it likely he would have been the discoverer of the light bulb?"

My friend got the point. *We must begin by allowing the possibility that God exists.* But when we do, we find "he rewards those who earnestly seek him" (verse 6, NIV).

*When you seek me, you will find me; if you search wholeheartedly. Jer. 29:13, REB.*

 JANUARY

5

# A Wholehearted Search

Before Adam and Eve disobeyed God and ate the fruit of the forbidden tree, they communed with God face-to-face (see Gen. 1:27-30). They knew Him experientially as a friend. However, after they sinned they became alienated from their Creator and hid themselves (Gen. 3:1-8). Sin separates us from God.

But God did not leave man in this condition. He, the omniscient God, is portrayed as going in search of our first parents (see verses 8-10). What unfathomable condescension!

Since man's expulsion from Eden, human beings have had to find God by another method, even "though He is not far from each one of us" (Acts 17:27, NKJV). This method, as we have seen, begins by allowing the possibility that He exists and then continues by searching for Him wholeheartedly.

But there are those who seem determined to find God *their* way. They refuse to follow the method He sets forth in His Word —*and then they wonder why they can't find God!* It is at this point that the one who deceived Adam and Eve, "the god of this world" (2 Cor. 4:4), frequently interposes himself and deceives many (see 2 Thess. 2:4-11). But we need not be deceived, and will not be deceived, if we follow God's method.

Searching for God wholeheartedly means going all out. No halfhearted search will do. Not even an almost wholehearted search will suffice. However, all who earnestly follow God's method of revealing Himself soon discover that He is indeed "a rewarder of those who diligently seek Him" (Heb. 11:6, NKJV).

The third and final step to finding God is to come to Him through Jesus Christ. Jesus, who is "Deity Himself," is the one who makes God "known" to us (John 1:18, Williams; cf. John 14:6). As we read the Bible and study the life of Christ, God becomes to us not some far-off, impersonal being, but a loving, personal friend.

As you follow these simple steps you *will* know God, not theoretically, but experientially—through Jesus Christ, whom He has sent (see John 17:3).

*Acquaint now thyself with [God], and be at peace. Job 22:21.*

# Getting Acquainted With God

What does it mean to acquaint oneself with God? Probably no two people who have come to know God through Jesus Christ will give exactly the same answer to this question. There's a reason for this—no two of us are exactly alike. We are all individuals—and God deals with us as such. Yet there are similarities.

Because of the differences, I hesitate to relate my own experience lest someone say, "That is not the way I came to know God." And yet, unless I relate my own experience, some will say, "How does he know what he is talking about?" I shall, therefore, briefly relate how I came to know God.

I must have begun in early infancy to observe the way my parents lived. Although they would be the last to claim sainthood, what I saw appealed to me, particularly my father's preaching and the private talks he had with me. So at the age of 9, without any prompting by my parents, I gave my life to God. My father baptized me on March 3, 1933, in Funchal, Madeira. God became real to me. But in retrospect, I would have to say I knew Him then "by the hearing of the ear" (Job 42:5).

During my later teen years and into my early 20s, while interned, I strayed away from God and He became unreal to me. I wanted to believe, but I couldn't. At the end of my sophomore year in college, I was ready to give up all religion and join the Army. However, before taking this step, I began reading material on the life of Christ. One morning as I read about the healing of the demoniac son, I came across this statement: "Cast yourself at [Christ's] feet with the cry, 'Lord, I believe; help Thou mine unbelief.' You can never perish while you do this—never" (Ellen G. White, in *Signs of the Times,* Oct. 25, 1905).

The Holy Spirit spoke to me through this biblical incident and said, "That's you. You want to believe, but you can't." I had to agree. "Lord," I prayed, "I believe. Help *Thou* mine unbelief." As the morning sun burns away the fog, my doubts vanished in a moment. Ever since, God has been real to me. Does He sometimes seem more real than at other times? Yes, and in tomorrow's reading I shall explain why.

*Seek the Lord while you can find him. Call upon him now while he is near. Isa. 55:6, TLB.*

# An Acceptable Time

Anyone who has repeatedly searched for God and found Him can testify that there are times when He seems closer than at other times. Is this because God distances Himself from us? Never! His Word assures that He "is not far from each one of us" (Acts 17:27, NASB). Further, He promises, "I will never leave you nor forsake you" (Heb. 13:5, NKJV). Why, then, does He sometimes seem harder to find? Because we have let the "cares and riches and pleasures of this life" (Luke 8:14) crowd out our times of communion with Him! The result? We imperceptibly lose the sense of His presence. The trouble lies with us! Hence the importance of regular times when our thoughts turn to God.

But there is another point to be considered. God never foists Himself upon us, yet throughout every moment of our lives His Holy Spirit is at work, molding circumstances, waiting for the opportune moment to reveal the Divine Presence to us. Although God has set certain times for us to commune with Him, it is usually during times of quiet reflection that the Holy Spirit comes to us revealing the Divine Presence.

In my own experience the times when God seems most real are when I am reading the Bible and the Holy Spirit brings meaning to a certain text that has a marked application to a certain circumstance in my life. At such times it almost seems as if God were speaking to me audibly. Perhaps the most outstanding example was when I came across Mark 9:24, as mentioned in yesterday's reading.

Although God is not restricted to making Himself known to us through the Bible, yet it is His chosen means of communicating with us. The Bible is God's message to us, because "men moved by the Holy Spirit spoke from God" (2 Peter 1:21, NASB). As you read the Scriptures today, let God speak to your heart. Let Him reveal God's presence to you now, in this "acceptable time" (Ps. 69:13).

17

# 8

*Have I not written to you [long ago] excellent things in counsels and knowledge, to make you know the certainty of the words of truth? Prov. 22:20, 21, Amplified.*

# God's Love Letter to Us

In ancient times letters were written on papyrus sheets or scrolls. Papyrus was a reed that grew on the banks of the Nile. This reed was split open and flattened, then laid side by side in parallel fashion and glued to a similar layer placed over it at right angles. After the glue dried, letters were written on these sheets. Sometimes sheets of papyrus were glued or sewed end to end and rolled up to form a scroll.

Many letters and manuscripts written on papyrus dating back 2,000 years and more have been discovered in the trash heaps of Egypt. The dry climate has preserved them. Many of them reveal fascinating things about people of those times! Since most people were illiterate, many of the letters were dictated to a scribe. Some were love letters.

In other parts of the Mediterranean world letters were written on parchment. Parchment was made from the skins of animals. Because of climatic conditions and the perishable nature of this material, few parchments have survived the ruthless tooth of time. The word "parchment," incidentally, is derived from Pergamos, a city in Asia Minor, where these skins were prepared. Interestingly, the church at Pergamos, not far from where John wrote his book of Revelation, was one of the recipients of his letter.

God's prophets were His amanuenses, or scribes. It is not that God couldn't write. We know He could. However, except for the Ten Commandments (see Ex. 32:16), He chose to use prophets as His penmen. The Bible is His love letter to us. Although written centuries ago, it never grows old. On the contrary, it constantly offers new insights into the height and depth, length and breadth, of God's love toward us. We can read and reread its messages as often as we like, yet never exhaust all their meaning.

Unlike any other book ever written, the Bible has the power to change lives for the better. If you let its author, the Holy Spirit, "guide you" (John 16:13) as you study it, it can transform your life. Let it happen! You will never regret it.

*The whole Bible was given to us by inspiration from God and is useful to teach us what is true and to make us realize what is wrong in our lives; it straightens us out and helps us do what is right. 2 Tim. 3:16, TLB.*

JANUARY

9

# The Bible Is the Standard

Several years ago I took my compact disc player to a shop to have it repaired. While I was waiting to check it in, two young men began talking earnestly about religion. One of them mentioned that God had become real to him ever since he had attended a religious meeting. The leader of the meeting had laid his hands on him and healed him of his unbelief. I would have liked to ask the young men some questions, but it would have been rude to jump uninvited into the discussion, so I said nothing. But it set me to thinking.

The danger of depending on supernatural phenomena for gaining a knowledge of God is that it bypasses the Bible, God's chosen means of revealing Himself to humanity (John 5:39). The Bible enables us to ascertain the identity of the spirits behind supernatural phenomena (Isa. 8:20, TLB). It also sets forth doctrine, and tests our experience (2 Tim. 3:16, TLB).

The Bible reveals that behind the scenes of earthly affairs a battle rages between the forces of good and evil (Eph. 6:12). In the Scriptures the veil is drawn aside and we are shown that "the god of this world," Satan, struggles in opposition to the God of heaven, and that he is capable of blinding the minds of those who bypass the Bible and endeavor to obtain a knowledge of God by other means.

Satan has the ability to transform himself "into an angel of light" (2 Cor. 11:14). In this guise he can lead the unwary to believe he is the God of heaven. In the day of judgment, those who have been thus deceived are described as saying, "Lord, Lord, have we not prophesied in thy name? and in thy name have cast out devils? and in thy name done many wonderful works?" But the Lord says, "I never knew you: depart from me" (Matt. 7:22, 23).

Because this is true, how important it is that we search the Scriptures and obtain our knowledge of God through Jesus Christ as revealed in the Bible.

**10**

*O king Agrippa, I was not disobedient unto the heavenly vision. Acts 26:19.*

# Catching a Glimpse of Christ

Johann Heinrich von Dannecker, the celebrated German sculptor who was born in 1758 and died in 1841, gained a reputation early in life for his statues of Greek gods and goddesses. For example, his statue of *Ariadne on a Panther*, sculpted in 1806, was recognized as a masterpiece and brought him international fame.

Not long after this, Dannecker was convicted that he should dedicate his time and talent to Christ. He abandoned the sculpting of heathen goddesses and resolved to devote his time to carving statues of Christ. Twice he felt he had failed, but at last he sculpted a statue of the Saviour that was so exquisitely beautiful he considered it the masterpiece of his life.

It is said that later Napoleon Bonaparte invited him to come to Paris and carve a statue of Venus, but Dannecker turned him down, saying, "Sir, these hands that have carved a statue of Christ can never again carve the likeness of a heathen goddess."

That is the way it was with the apostle Paul. After he caught a glimpse of Jesus Christ on the road to Damascus, he could never forget it. Later when he alluded to this dramatic experience, he wrote: "God, who commanded the light to shine out of darkness, hath shined in our hearts, to give the light of the knowledge of the glory of God in the face of Jesus Christ" (2 Cor. 4:6).

"The face of Jesus Christ!" The face of the Persecuted One was so indelibly impressed on Paul's mind, that, standing before King Agrippa, he could truthfully declare that he had not been disobedient to the heavenly vision.

Paul's life as a follower of Jesus was not an easy one. The persecutor became the persecuted. And yet, in the face of all the hardships he had to endure, he remained faithful and unmoved (see Acts 20:24). Why? Because he had seen "the heavenly vision," and nothing else mattered.

This morning as you read and study your Bible, try to visualize Christ seated by your side. Let His presence capture your imagination—*for when once you catch a glimpse of the heavenly vision, nothing else will matter!*

*If ye do return unto the Lord with all your hearts, then put away the strange gods . . . from among you, and prepare your hearts unto the Lord, and serve him only. 1 Sam. 7:3.*

JANUARY
11

# Strange Gods

Some years ago I heard about an American missionary to India who met a bus driver who worshiped a very strange god.

Buses in India are not built like the conveyances in which people in more developed countries are used to travel. They are built for utility, not convenience. The body of the bus is built as far forward as possible; the driver sits beside the engine, which is housed under a box.

According to the story, the missionary was riding on such a bus. The box seemed a convenient footrest, so he propped his feet on it. Immediately the driver began gesticulating and speaking agitatedly in a dialect the missionary didn't understand. The foreigner was taken aback by all the fuss.

Fortunately a bilingual passenger intervened at this point. He asked the missionary in English kindly to remove his feet from the engine housing. The missionary complied, but asked his interpreter what the problem was. He learned that the box housed the driver's god. By placing his feet on the box, the missionary was showing disrespect for the god within—*the engine!*

Perhaps you smile as I did when I first heard this story. But then, do we really do any better than our Indian friend? Is it not possible that we who profess to know and worship the one true God also worship "strange" gods? I don't mean strange in the sense of something odd or peculiar. I mean strange in the sense that the Bible uses the word—false gods. Is it not possible that we worship such gods in the form of material objects or even mental concepts?

The apostle Paul urges us to examine ourselves (see 2 Cor. 13:5). All of us need to do this periodically. If you find you have been worshiping a strange god, why not cast it out and let the true God have His rightful place in your soul temple. God promises to give you what has been called "the expulsive power of the new affection" to enable you to do this.

21

*Wherefore do ye spend money for that which is not bread? and your labour for that which satisfieth not? hearken diligently unto me, and eat ye that which is good, and let your soul delight itself in fatness. Isa. 55:2.*

# Food for Thought

Some time ago a friend of mine told me about something that happened to him that relates to our text for meditation. He said that one day his wife went to town while he stayed home and did some odd jobs around the house. When it was lunchtime, he went to the refrigerator and looked for some food that didn't require much preparation. Picking up what he thought was some vegetarian meat substitute, he sampled it. It tasted good. He warmed it, then proceeded to eat it with relish. Suddenly he crunched into some sandlike grit. He wondered what it was. When his wife returned from town, the mystery was solved. My friend had been eating dog food!

The meat had undoubtedly been thoroughly sterilized, but this did nothing to settle my friend's stomach. Reading the label on one of the cans, he discovered that it contained "meat by-products," which did nothing to soothe his sense of revulsion.

Amusing? Revolting? *But what a lesson for Christians!* Could it be that some of us are unwittingly devoted to things that "taste good" to our perverted appetites, but are bad for our spiritual welfare—TV and video programs, or magazines that feed the lower nature? What are these "images" but false gods?

A professed Christian recently told me he saw nothing wrong with watching pornography on cable TV, or X-rated videos, or reading salacious magazines, so long as he did it in the privacy of his bedroom—with his wife, of course. But what is the difference between lusting after a woman (or a man, for that matter) in the privacy of one's bedroom and lusting out on the streets? (See Matt. 5:28.)

Instead of feeding our lower nature, shouldn't we rather vow, "I will set no wicked thing before mine eyes" (Ps. 101:3), but feed my soul on that which nourishes my spiritual life—a deeper knowledge of the true God? Think about it.

*You are controlled by your new nature if you have the Spirit of God living in you. (And remember that if anyone doesn't have the Spirit of Christ living in him, he is not a Christian at all.) Rom. 8:9, TLB.*

# All or Nothing

When Mahmud of Ghazni conquered India, he imposed Islam on its people and carried out a policy of destroying all idols. In 1024 he captured Somnath. Outside this city stood a temple dedicated to Siva. The priests of this temple implored him to spare their god. Instead, he smashed it—and out spilled a hoard of treasure!

Something similar happens at conversion. It is as if we said, "Lord Jesus, the temple of my soul is all Yours. Come in and smash the idol of self." We mean this, and Christ takes us at our word. He smashes the idol, and out pours untold treasure. Then, in the joy of our first love we begin taking Jesus from room to room. But unexpectedly we come to a room that houses another god. Although Christ knew about this idol when we turned over the temple to Him, we did not. But now we are aware of it (see John 9:41).

Dr. Frederick Meyer, a noted preacher, found himself one day confronted by just such a situation. He was sitting in his study, wondering why his ministry was so powerless.

Suddenly Christ seemed to be standing by his side. "Let Me have the keys to your life," He seemed to say. The experience was so real that Dr. Meyer says he reached into his pocket and pulled out a bunch of keys.

"Are all the keys here?" Jesus asked.

"Yes, Lord," answered the clergyman. "All except one."

"If you cannot trust Me in all the rooms of your life, I cannot accept any of your keys," said Jesus sadly.

Dr. Meyer said he was so overcome by the feeling that Christ was moving out of his life that he involuntarily cried out, "Lord, come back! Take all the keys to all the rooms of my life."

This experience is repeated in the life of every Christian as the Holy Spirit makes him or her conscious of idols of which he or she was unaware when first converted. If today the Holy Spirit is making you aware of an idol in your soul temple, won't you, by the grace of God, expel it?

# 14

*I will cause a man to be more precious than fine gold, even a son of earth than the finest gold of Ophir. Isa. 13:12, Rotherham.*

# How to Measure Your Self-worth

For many centuries the actual site of Ophir was a mystery to Bible students. Some thought it was situated somewhere in India, others believed it was somewhere along the coast of south Arabia, still others felt it was to be found on the Somali littoral. But recent archaeological findings have indicated that Dilmun, an ancient city situated on an island in the Persian Gulf near Kuwait, where the recent Gulf war was fought, was the site of this fabled emporium.

Fine gold was the most precious substance known in ancient times. To compare a human being to "the finest gold of Ophir" was to give the best accolade possible.

There is a philosophy abroad in the world today called humanism; it encourages people to believe in their self-worth apart from God. Strangely, many Christians unwittingly subscribe to this way of thinking. This subtle philosophy makes man the measure of all things. But those who adopt this criterion are in danger of either overvaluing or undervaluing themselves.

Have you ever met those who in their pride and self-importance overvalued themselves? Conversely, have you ever met those who in thier lack of self-esteem undervalued themselves?

The Bible teaches that human beings should estimate their worth in light of the value *God* has placed upon them. In the words of our verse, "I [God] will cause a man to be more precious" than the gold of Ophir. When we consider the price Jesus paid for our redemption, how can anyone conclude that he isn't worth much?

Never forget that the important thing is not what *we* may think we are worth, or what *others* may think we are worth, but what *God* knows we are worth.

*You . . . must endure hardship as a good soldier of Jesus Christ. 2 Tim. 2:3, NKJV.*

JANUARY
15

# Spiritual Courage

In A.D. 290, during the reign of Roman emperor Valerius Maximianus, Adrian, a 28-year-old soldier of the elite Praetorian Guard, was impressed by the courage of a Christian whom he had been ordered to torture into recanting his faith.

"What gives you such courage to face death?" Adrian asked.

"My belief in the Lord Jesus Christ," replied the martyr.

Although noted for his physical bravery, Adrian realized he knew nothing about this kind of courage. As he pondered the sufferer's reply, he made a decision. Going to the judge who sentenced the martyr, he said, "I have decided to become a Christian. Put my name down as one to be tortured."

But Adrian's Lord had other plans.

Because he belonged to the emperor's elite guard, the judge was reluctant to grant his request. But the story doesn't end here. For the next 23 years, in the face of ostracism and persecution, Adrian showed the kind of courage only Christ can give—courage that the world cannot take away! Finally in A.D. 313 he died a martyr in Nicomedia.

At the present time, in most Western countries and even in the former Eastern Bloc countries, becoming a Christian does not usually result in torture and death. But in some lands it can still cost a person his or her life.

I recently read two books, *The Torn Veil* (London: Marshall Pickering, 1984), by Gulshan Esther, and *I Dared to Call Him Father* (Bromley, Kent: Kingsway Publications, 1978), by Bilquis Sheikh. The books tell how these two women authors, formerly Muslims, faced ostracism, boycott, and even death threats with extraordinary courage after they became Christians.

In our rapidly changing world, who knows what the future holds? Will God's people in Christian lands yet face death for their faith? One thing is certain, so long as "the prince of this world" lives, Christians will be tempted to take the coward's way out. Refuse to go this route. Instead, resolve to endure hardness as a good soldier of Jesus Christ!

25

# 16

*Hold me up, and I shall be safe, and I shall observe Your statutes continually.*
*Ps. 119:117, NKJV.*

# Trusting Christ to Hold You Up

One evening many years ago, Lord Radstock, a celebrated British Christian, stayed so long after a gospel meeting in Woolwich, England, that he almost missed his train. He barely had time to jump on board before the conductor blew his whistle. A young army officer who attended the meeting came running up to the window of the coach where Lord Radstock was sitting and said, "Sir, I heard you speak tonight. I responded to your call and gave my life to Christ. Can you tell me how I can keep from falling?"

Quick as a flash Lord Radstock pulled a pencil from his pocket and laid it on the palm of his hand.

"Can this pencil stand upright?" he asked.

"No."

Then, with a twinkle in his eye, Lord Radstock took hold of the pencil with his free hand and said, "Yes, it can."

"But you're holding it up," observed the young man.

"That's just the point," said Lord Radstock. "Your life is like a helpless pencil. You cannot hold yourself upright—but Christ can!"

By then the train was moving, and the last thing the young man saw was Lord Radstock holding the pencil up.

Twenty-five years later that same officer chanced to meet Lord Radstock in India and told him how his illustration had made an indelible impression on his mind. Said he, "From that day on my life has been in Christ's hands."

Christ is able to keep us from falling (Jude 24). He declares that His hand is so powerful that no man can pluck us out of it (John 10:28). Since this is true, when we fall, it is never Christ's fault—never! The problem lies with us.

When Peter began sinking while walking on the Sea of Galilee, his problem was in looking at the boisterous waves around him instead of at Jesus (Matt. 14:30). In a similar way, only as we continue to look to Jesus and let His all-powerful hands hold us up can we be kept from falling. Can you think of a better time to recommit your life into His hands than right now?

*The eternal God is your Refuge, and underneath are the everlasting arms. Deut. 33:27, TLB.*

JANUARY

17

# Underneath Are the Everlasting Arms

In his vision of the wheels within wheels, Ezekiel saw a resplendent Being, which he describes as having the form of a man seated on a throne (see Eze. 1:26). In a subsequent vision the prophet saw this Being "put forth the form of a hand" (Eze. 8:3, RSV). Although Ezekiel saw only one hand, there must have been two, or the representation would have been less than complete. These hands, then, must have been attached to the everlasting arms our verse talks about, which we are told are "underneath."

Many years ago, during the construction of a bridge across a portion of New York Harbor, the engineers needed to lay a foundation for one of the buttresses. The problem was that just at the place they intended to build this base was an old scow that had sunk years before with a load of stone. The scow was in relatively good condition, so the engineer in charge of the operation decided to raise it.

Divers were sent down and heavy chains were placed under each end of the vessel. They then tried to raise it with derricks, but every effort failed. At last a young engineer had an idea. He had two barges brought to the place where the scow lay, and instructed the men to secure the chains to the barges at low tide. In nine or 10 hours, as the tide came in, the old scow began to shiver and shake, but inexorably to rise! What the derricks couldn't accomplish by brute force, the mighty Atlantic Ocean accomplished with ease!

Something similar happens in our relationship with God. Of ourselves we can do nothing about getting rid of our "load of sin," but the omnipotent God can accomplish through us that which we cannot accomplish of ourselves. Observe that although we are powerless to accomplish anything, there is a part we must play—we must cooperate with divine power.

How thankful we can be that in getting rid of our load of sin the everlasting arms of the eternal God are underneath to lift it from us—*and so long as we continue to cooperate with Him the removal is permanent.*

**27**

# 18

*At the same time [Felix] was hoping that Paul would offer him a bribe, so he sent for him frequently and talked with him.*
*Acts 24:26, NIV.*

# Men Who Cannot Be Bought or Sold

It was Sir Robert Walpole, British politician of the early 1700s, who insinuated that every man has his price. This certainly was true of Felix, but it is not universally true.

In 1896, when Booker T. Washington, founder of Tuskegee Institute in Alabama, learned that a brilliant Black chemurgist and agriculture experimenter, George Washington Carver, was on the faculty of Iowa State College, he investigated. He was so impressed with the scope of Carver's work that he invited him to join the faculty at Tuskegee.

During the negotiations Washington said to Carver, "I cannot offer you a large salary: I cannot offer you fame; but I can offer you immortality." Although the remuneration was not large, Carver accepted after prayerful consideration.

Later, when Carver became famous, Thomas Edison, great American inventive genius, offered him the astronomical salary of $175,000 a year—a fortune in those days. But Carver, who was dedicated not only to his people but to all the people of the South, graciously declined, stating that while he appreciated the offer, he felt God was not through with him at Tuskegee. In 1940, three years before his death, Carver donated his entire life savings, consisting of $33,000, to establish the Carver Foundation to carry on his work.

The world needs more men like Carver.

"The greatest want [or need] of the world is the want of men—men who will not be bought or sold; men who in their inmost souls are true and honest, men who do not fear to call sin by its right name, men whose conscience is as true to duty as the needle to the pole, men who will stand for the right though the heavens fall" (*Education*, p. 57).

What is said here of men is equally true of women.

Christ offers those who stand true to principle, not merely earthly "immortality" but immortality in the world to come. This is an offer well worth the price.

> *I tell you that unless your righteousness surpasses that of the Pharisees . . . , you will certainly not enter the kingdom of heaven.*
> **Matt. 5:20, NIV.**

# Are You a Pharisee Flogger?

Jesus' most scathing denunciations were reserved, not for publicans and sinners, but for the Pharisees. You can read about the woes He pronounced against them in Matthew 23. Now, surely, since Christ denounced these hypocrites, one would think it is all right for us to jump on the bandwagon and flog the Pharisees. When was the last time you heard a preacher express pity for these "poor, pilloried people"?

I recently read an anecdote that sounded apocryphal—apocryphal, that is, until I thought about some of the sermons I've preached against the Pharisees. According to the story, the lesson in a Sunday school class was the parable of the Pharisee and the publican. You remember, they both "went up into the temple to pray," and the Pharisee said, among other things, "I thank thee, that I am not as other men are, extortioners, unjust, adulterers, or *even as this publican*" (Luke 18:10, 11).

At the close of class the teacher asked one of the boys to pray and, according to the story, he intoned: "Lord, we thank Thee we are not like that Pharisee."

Exquisite irony! Can't you just visualize the boy snatching the "measuring stick" the Pharisee has been using to beat the publican and turning on the Pharisee and beating him with it? But wasn't this precisely what Jesus did when He denounced the Pharisees? Not in the least! Jesus "knew what was in man" (John 2:25); you and I do not. When you and I denounce this "much maligned" sect—not to mention *other "sinners above all men"* (Luke 13:4)—we need to ask ourselves: What is my motive? Are my "pharisaical denunciations" spoken in order to boost my own righteousness?—by contrast, of course.

The Pharisees possessed righteousness. The Bible says they did (see Matt. 5:20)—but not the right kind. The kind of righteousness we need does not compare itself with the righteousness—or unrighteousness—of others. It looks to Jesus, and in the light of His righteousness "all our righteousnesses [of whatever kind] are as filthy rags" (Isa. 64:6).

JANUARY

# 20

*" 'When, Lord, did we ever see you hungry or thirsty or a stranger or naked or sick or in prison, and we would not help you?' The King will reply, 'I tell you, whenever you refused to help one of these least important ones, you refused to help me.' " Matt. 25:44, 45, TEV.*

# When God Works Through Us

Shortly after William McKinley was elected president of the United States, a prominent politician was recommended to fill the post of ambassador to a foreign country. As McKinley pondered the recommendation, an incident that had occurred one evening several years before helped him make his decision.

That particular evening McKinley boarded a streetcar and sat down in the last vacant seat. Moments later an old washer-woman entered the far end of the car carrying a heavy basket of clothes. She walked the length of the car looking for a seat. Finding none, she happened to stop in the aisle opposite the man the president was now considering for the position of ambassador. The man obviously saw the elderly woman, but instead of offering her his seat, he shifted his newspaper so as to block her from view. Touched by her plight, McKinley quietly got up, walked down the aisle, picked up her basket, and led her to his seat. The candidate for the ambassadorship probably never realized that his little selfish act cost him what would have been the crowning position of his career.

What would you have done, what would I have done, had we been in this man's position? Suppose we had given the old woman our seat, would we have done it as "eyeservice," in order "to be seen of men" (Eph. 6:6; Matt. 23:5)—or would we have done it because God was working in us "to do of his good pleasure" (Phil. 2:13)?

The kind of good deeds that heaven approves are those that spring from a heart of selfless love—the kind of love that sees a need and performs an act of kindness—*and never seeks recognition!* But, should recognition come, this love graciously gives our heavenly Father the credit and glory and goes right on doing good, unmindful that it has done anything out of the ordinary. And it hasn't done anything unusual—it was simply God doing His good pleasure through us!

30

*My brothers, what good is it for someone to say*
*that he has faith if his actions do not prove it?*
*James 2:14, TEV.*

JANUARY

21

# Do You Really Believe?

In 1859 Jean-Francois Gravelet, famous French tightrope walker and acrobat, better known as "Blondin," crossed Niagara Falls on a rope 1,100 feet long suspended 160 feet above the roaring cataract. He traversed the falls on a tightrope in various ways: trundling a wheelbarrow, sitting down midway while he fried and ate an omelette, in a sack, blindfolded, and on stilts! People by the thousands came from everywhere to watch his breathtaking feats.

After these performances the crowd would cheer, "Blondin! Blondin! Blondin!" On one occasion, after completing one of his famous crossings, he asked, "Do you believe I can carry one of you across on my shoulders?"

"Yes! Yes! Yes!" the crowd roared back.

"All right," said Blondin, "if you believe I can do it, let me carry *you* across."

The cheering stopped. No one stirred. It was one thing to believe Blondin could carry *someone else* across, but it was different to believe he could carry *"me"* across. Finally, one man did step forward—obviously someone who had the courage of his convictions. While the crowd watched, Blondin carried him safely across to the other side.

There are many today who are like the people in the crowd cheering Blondin. They profess to believe that Jesus is able to save—somebody else, but not *"me."* Such "faith" is worthless.

The Bible gives ample evidence that Christ "is able to save completely any and all who come to God through Him" (Heb. 7:25, C. B. Williams). After all, He saved the penitent thief in his extremity, didn't he? Why, then, should anyone question His ability to save *"me"*?

Salvation means taking the initial step of trusting in Jesus for salvation, but it includes more: it includes trusting Him every step of the way. As we do this, He in turn carries us through to the end successfully—just as Blondin did when he carried the man across Niagara Falls on his shoulders. And Jesus does it *far more securely!*

**22**

*"Is it true, O Shadrach, Meshach, and Abednego," [Nebuchadnezzar] asked, "that you are refusing to serve my gods or to worship the golden statue I set up? I'll give you one more chance. When the music plays, if you fall down and worship the statue, all will be well. But if you refuse, you will be thrown into a flaming furnace within the hour." Dan. 3:14, 15, TLB.*

# Standing Up for What Is Right

It is not easy to stand up for the right when you know that you may displease an earthly potentate, on whose whim your life and well-being may depend—especially if he has been your friend and benefactor. Yet the three Hebrew youths in our verse chose death rather than to worship the golden image. It was not merely a matter of worshiping a false god. Bowing to the image would have negated the interpretation God had previously inspired them to give Nebuchadnezzar (see Dan. 2:18, 19, 36).

Similarly, when Daniel was forbidden by Darius's royal decree to pray to the God of heaven for 30 days, he refused to dissemble by ceasing to pray openly, as was his custom.

It takes courage to stand up and be counted as a Christian when your "friends" are persons in positions of power who can do you real harm.

Frederick the Great of Prussia was known for his ruthlessness and contempt for religion. On one occasion the king was making coarse jokes about Jesus Christ, and his guests were roaring with laughter. General Joachim von Zieten, a devout Christian, stood and addressed his king in words to this effect: "Sire, you know I am not afraid of death. I have fought and won many battles for you. Now I am an old man and I shall soon have to appear in the presence of One greater than you, the mighty God who saved me from my sins, the Lord Jesus Christ against whom you blaspheme. I salute you, sire, as an old man who loves his Saviour and stands on the shore of eternity."

The joking stopped.

How can we develop the kind of courage shown by the Hebrew worthies, by Daniel, by Von Zieten? He who has bowed humbly before the Majesty of the heaven need "not be afraid of what man can do unto" him (Ps. 56:11).

*As obedient children, do not let your characters be shaped any longer by the desires you cherished in your days of ignorance. The One who called you is holy; like him, be holy in all your behaviour. 1 Peter 1:14, 15, NEB.*

# Christianity Transforms

World War II press correspondent Clarence Hall related the following syndicated newspaper story:

"[About 1915] an American missionary en route to Japan . . . stopped . . . [at Shimmabuke, a tiny village on Okinawa] just long enough to make two converts—Shosei Kina and his brother Mojon. He left a Bible with them and passed on. For 30 years they had no other contact with any other Christian missionary, but they made the Bible come alive! They taught the other villagers until every man, woman, and child in Shimmabuke became a Christian.

"Shosei Kina became the headman of the village, and Mojon the chief teacher. In the school the Bible was read daily. The precepts of the Bible were law in the village. In those 30 years there developed a Christian democracy in its purest form.

"When the American army came across the island, an advance patrol swept up to the village compound with guns level. Two old men stepped forth, bowed low, and began to speak. An interpreter explained that the old men were welcoming the Americans as fellow Christians!

"The flabbergasted GIs sent for their chaplain. He came with officers of the Intelligence Service. They toured the village. They were astounded at the spotlessly clean homes and streets and gentility of the inhabitants."

I once talked with a minister who declared that "if a man is saved, he can get drunk every day of his life and still be saved, once he has been saved." I am almost certain he couldn't have meant what he said, for Christianity does make a difference for the better in the lives of people. If it does not, the problem is not with Christianity but with those who profess to follow it (see 1 Tim. 3:8).

We can experience what the Bible calls "the power of God unto salvation" (Rom. 1:16)—the gospel—by wholeheartedly permitting it to control our lives.

## 24

*And with all his abundant wealth through Christ Jesus, my God will supply all your needs. Phil. 4:19, TEV.*

# Needs and Wants

My parents, my brother, and I were on our way to Mozambique, East Africa, when our ship docked in Manila on December 4, 1941. Several days later Pearl Harbor was bombed and three weeks after that we were taken prisoners by the Imperial Japanese Army and interned in Camp John Hay in northern Luzon.

After Bataan fell, we were transferred to Camp Holmes (now Camp Dangwa), a few miles away. At the new camp we found various pieces of military equipment that the retreating American and Philippine armies had abandoned. Among these were .3030 caliber rifle bullets. Some of these were what we called "boattail" slugs. These projectiles were greatly prized, and if one managed to inveigle from a Japanese soldier a .27 caliber slug to go with the .3030, he was the envy of everyone in camp.

Ralph Longway, my best friend, had a stash of slugs hidden away among his things. One day 3-year-old Jamie Mather discovered Ralph's hoard and purloined a fistful of them. If I rightly remember, Jamie's 6-year-old brother, Billie, went to Ralph and tattled on the little fellow. Ralph went to Jamie and patiently tried to coax him into surrendering the "precious" items, but Jamie wasn't about to give them up.

Finally Ralph appealed to a higher authority—Jamie's father. I can still see Dr. Bruce Mather holding Jamie in his left arm, patiently coaxing him to return his one last slug, and I can hear Jamie squealing, "But I n-e-e-e-ed it!" In the end father Mather had to pry the slug forcibly from Jamie's little fist and return it to Ralph, amid howls of protest.

We smile at Jamie's confusing his wants with his needs, but don't we do the same thing? Don't we sometimes pray for things we want but which we don't really need? God's Word assures us that "no good thing will he withhold from them that walk uprightly" (Ps. 84:11).

God promises He will "meet all [our] needs according to His glorious riches," but He has never promised to supply all our wants.

*For we are like a sweet-smelling incense offered by Christ to God, which spreads among those who are being saved and those who are being lost. For those who are being lost, it is a deadly stench that kills; but for those who are being saved, it is a fragrance that brings life.*
*2 Cor. 2:15, 16, TEV.*

# The Fragrance of Christ

These verses are better understood when they are set against the practice of the Romans in New Testament times. Paul draws his imagery from a Roman triumph, the highest honor the empire could bestow on one of its victorious commanders. In the triumphal procession marched not only the victors but also the vanquished, the latter in chains, soon to be put to death or into slavery.

At the head of the procession came the priests swinging their censers, the sweet-smelling incense perfuming the air. To the victors the smell of the incense was a fragrance signifying life; to the wretched captives it was nothing less than the stench of death.

Paul's graphic pen picture has some significant parallels when compared with the effect of the gospel message on the inhabitants of this world. Christ's triumphal procession honors His victory over the powers of darkness at the cross (see Eph. 4:8). Every person who has ever lived marches in this procession. To those who have accepted salvation, the victory of Christ is the fragrance of eternal life to come, while for those who have rejected it, it is a stench that signalizes the second death.

But at this point the parallels end. Unlike a Roman triumph, we can choose to march with the victors. Today is still the day of salvation (see 2 Cor. 6:2).

Of all people in the world, Christians ought to be joyful and hold their heads high. Yet the countenances of some professed Christians could be mistaken for the faces of the vanquished. Could it be that in many cases these Christians have chosen to look down at the hellish shadow Satan casts across their path rather than the glorious light shining from the face of Jesus Christ?

*There are those who receive the seed in good soil; they hear the word and welcome it; and they bear fruit thirtyfold, sixtyfold, or a hundredfold. Mark 4:20, NEB.*

# Seed Sown in Good Soil

Kandavalli Rajeshwar Rao, a man in his 40s, was born in Madras, India, and reared a Hindu. About four o'clock one morning, some 15 years ago, while visiting relatives, a voice woke him from a sound sleep, with the words "Mark 4:20." Nothing more. He awakened the others in the room and asked, "Did any of you hear a voice?" No one had. When he dozed off again, the voice repeated, "Mark 4:20." Again no one else heard the words. His curiosity was aroused.

When Rao reached home he asked a Hindu priest what Mark 4:20 meant. The priest did not know, but suggested he ask a Muslim mullah. Rao sought out a mullah. The man said he did not know what Mark 4:20 meant, but thought it might be related to Christians. Rao then asked a Baptist pastor, who read him the verse from the Bible. He bought a New Testament from the minister and read it through twice. A short time after finishing the second reading, some young men gave him a handbill advertising some gospel meetings. Rao and his wife attended. When the evangelist made an altar call, of the 600 present, only Rao and his wife took their stand for Christ.

Following baptism, Rao felt called to the ministry and enrolled at Spicer Memorial College. After graduating he felt a burden to take the gospel to the Gond people, a tribe that had never before heard the gospel. At first they thought he was a police agent and refused to listen to him. Then they kidnaped his son. Fortunately, someone saw this happen and told Rao, who gave chase on his bicycle. When he overtook the men, he asked them why they were taking his son. "We're going to kill him," they replied. "Then kill me, too," said Rao, "but accept Jesus as your Saviour." Impressed, the kidnappers let them both go.

After working among these people for two years, Rao baptized the man who instigated the kidnapping. At the end of two more years 50 people were baptized. My wife and I met Pastor Rao in Pune in 1991. Mark 4:20 is being fulfilled in India!

*Morning by morning, O Lord, you hear my voice; morning by morning I lay my requests before you and wait in expectation.*
**Ps. 5:3, NIV.**

JANUARY

27

# The Beauty of Holiness

The beautiful thoughts expressed by these words were probably first put into verse in a modern language by Dr. Isaac Watts in 1719. They are remembered in the following familiar lines, which are most appropriate for morning devotions:

> Lord, in the morning Thou shalt hear
> My voice ascending high;
> To Thee will I direct my prayer,
> To Thee lift up mine eye.

Dr. Watts, who lived from 1674 to 1748, wrote some of the most beautiful and best-loved hymns sung by Christians. Most hymnals contain a large selection of his compositions. Small of stature (he was but five feet tall), he had a massive head, a hooked nose, small piercing eyes, and a frail body.

Isaac's father, a Dissenter, was jailed for his faith numerous times, once while Isaac was still an infant. Every day during her husband's incarceration Mrs. Watts would take little Isaac to the prison and, seated on a stone mounting-block opposite her husband's cell, feed her baby while conversing with his father. Out of the trying circumstances that marked his life Isaac developed a beautiful Christian character and strong religious convictions.

When he was a young man a beautiful young lady fell in love with him through reading his poetry. When the two finally met she was completely disillusioned—but with Watts it was love at first sight. When he asked her to marry him she graciously declined, adding, no doubt with the best of intentions, "Mr. Watts, I only wish I could say I admire the casket as much as I admire the jewel." Watts took the young lady's social gaffe good-naturedly, and although he never married, the two remained good friends for more than 30 years.

If there is one lesson to be learned from Dr. Watts' life, it is that our physical appearance need not—in fact, must not—be permitted to affect our spiritual experience.

*You will have compassion on us. You will tread our sins beneath your feet; you will throw them into the depths of the ocean. Micah 7:19, TLB.*

# The Depths of the Ocean

I was 6 when our family returned from mission service in Brazil. On the voyage to the States, at a spot off Puerto Rico, Captain Evans, the commander of our ship, the S.S. *Alban*, stood on the ship's upper deck and pointed down. "The ocean is five miles deep here," he said.

That is deep, but there are deeper places. The deepest spot is in the Mariana Trench, off the east coast of the Philippines. It measures 36,204 feet deep—7,176 feet deeper than Mount Everest (29,028 feet) is high!

On January 23, 1960, the bathyscaphe *Trieste,* with Jaques Piccard and Lt. Donald Walsh on board, descended into this awesome chasm. As they neared the bottom they heard a loud cracking noise. Examination showed that one of the small observation windows had fractured under the tremendous pressure of nearly eight tons per square inch. The men had to decide whether to continue or surface. After examining the damage, they decided it was not serious enough to abort the mission and went on down to 35,793.6 feet. They found the ocean floor covered with a layer of soft muck.

When God promises to cast our sins into the depths of the sea (Micah 7:19), He is really saying that, so far as He is concerned, He has put them out of his mind (see Heb. 10:17). Elsewhere the Bible says: "As far as the east is from the west, so far hath he removed our transgressions from us" (Ps. 103:12). No one knows how far that is, for the distance is infinite.

Yet there are some people—many of them professed Christians—who are pretty good divers. I don't know what kind of paraphernalia they put on to get down to the "bottom of things," but these muckrakers seem to enjoy roiling the ooze in the ocean depths and stirring things up that God has "settled."

If God has cast sins that have been confessed, forgiven, and forsaken into the depths of the sea, isn't it best to leave them there, undisturbed?

# Get Moving

I once heard Dwight A. Delafield state that God never guides something that isn't moving. This is true.

My wife was 55 and I was 64 when we learned to ski, and one of the things we learned (the hard way) was that you can't guide your skis unless you're moving. Guidance implies giving direction to something that is in motion.

When I was a small child, my father made me a wheelless "car" out of a kerosene crate. I have a photograph of it. It had a "steering wheel," but for all my steering, the only direction it ever went was somewhere in my imagination.

The other day as I was walking through a shopping arcade I paused to watch a boy guiding a race car on a video screen. His violent maneuverings appeared to invalidate the Delafield truism. But did it? Not really. In actuality the "race car" was going nowhere, except on the video screen. Even though the boy seemed to be guiding something, he was only guiding an illusion.

Some people sit back, do nothing, and then expect the Lord to guide them. Others pray, "Guide me, Lord," and then refuse to move in the direction God has already revealed they should go. Perhaps you have prayed this way. I know I have.

The Lord doesn't reveal to us everything that is going to happen in the future. If He did, we wouldn't need faith. God leads us step by step. When we step out in faith and, by His grace, do what we *know* we ought to do (in other words, *get moving),* He guides us on to the next step.

As you review your life today, is God guiding you? Or is He waiting for you to get moving? I don't mean get moving in the direction that *seems right* for you to go (see Prov. 14:12), but in the direction *God* wants you to go. And never forget: "It is not in man that walketh to direct his steps" (Jer. 10:23).

As in the physical realm, so in the spiritual: God only guides someone who is moving! If you don't seem to be going anywhere spiritually, get moving in the direction you *know* God wants you to go, and He will guide you on to the next step!

*The word of God kept on spreading; and the number of disciples continued to increase greatly. Acts 6:7, NASB.*

# How God Spreads His Word

When I worked as a missionary in the city of Manaus, Brazil, I got to know two English brothers who were Wycliffe Bible translators. They were doing a great work of translating the Word of God into the language of the Indians who live along the Amazon River. All Christians owe a profound debt of gratitude to these faithful people for their good work.

Shortly before World War II, Cameron Townsend, a Wycliffe Bible translator in Mexico, tried to secure permission to translate the Scriptures into the languages of the Indian tribes of that country. However, anticlerical sentiment was high. One official told him bluntly, "So long as I am in this office the Bible will never be translated into the language of the Indians." Townsend tried other ways to secure permission, all to no avail.

Stymied, Townsend and his wife went to live in a little, obscure Indian village. They learned the language, ministered to the people, and waited for God to open the way. One day Townsend noticed that the spring in the center of the village plaza produced an abundance of water but it ran off down the hill and was wasted. He suggested that the Indians plant crops in an area to which the water could easily be channeled. Soon the Indians were growing twice as much food as before. The people were grateful. Townsend published a short article in a Mexican paper about this transformation.

Somehow that article found its way into the hands of Lázaro Cárdenas, president of Mexico. The president was so impressed by what he read that he drove to the little Indian village and interviewed Townsend. In the course of their visit, Townsend asked the president for permission to translate the Bible into the language of the Indians. Permission was granted!

God does not always answer our prayers immediately, or in exactly the way we would like, but if we wholeheartedly submit to His will and follow His leadings, He will open to us avenues of service for Him that will amaze us. Try it!

*You sympathized with the prisoners and you accepted cheerfully the plundering of your property, knowing well that [in heaven] you . . . had better and lasting possession.*
Heb. 10:34, MLB.

JANUARY
31

# Genuine Altruism

If prison conditions today are better than they were two centuries ago, we owe it largely to John Howard, a well-to-do English Quaker. In 1773 he was appointed high sheriff of Bedfordshire and became interested in the conditions of the prisons under his care. He decided to inspect them personally. What he discovered shocked him. The jailers and their underlings were not paid by the civil authorities, but depended for their livelihood on fees extorted from the prisoners or their families. Resolved to put a stop to this practice, he published his findings. As a consequence, Parliament passed two acts: one that provided salaries for prison wardens, and another that set minimum standards for prisoner health care.

Later, Howard's inspection of penal institutions in Europe resulted in prison reform in that area. His philanthropic work was so appreciated that his admirers collected more than 1,500 pounds sterling (a small fortune in those days) to erect a statue in his honor. When he heard about the project, he pleaded—in fact, demanded—that it be stopped, and it was.

In February 1789 Howard decided to visit Russia and other countries in the East, where prison conditions beggared belief. He was 72 when he departed for Russia; he left behind these inspiring words:

"I am not insensible to the dangers that must attend such a journey. . . . Should it please God to cut off my life in the prosecution of this design, let not my conduct be uncandidly imputed to rashness or enthusiasm, but to a serious, deliberate conviction that I am pursuing the path of duty, and a sincere desire of being made an instrument of more extensive usefulness to my fellow creatures than could be expected in the narrower circle of a retired life."

Within a year Howard was dead of camp fever. Here was a man who counted heaven's reward for selfless service more important than ease or earthly possessions.

What an example for us!

*Oh that my words were now written! oh that they were printed in a book! That they were graven with an iron pen and lead in the rock for ever! For I know that my redeemer liveth. Job 19:23-25.*

# Printed in a Book

Printing and books as we know them today were, of course, unknown in Job's day. The New International Version translates these words in our passage: "written on a scroll," which is certainly more correct, for printing from movable type did not come into general use until the latter part of the fifteenth century.

However, this was not the first time movable type was used. As early as the ninth century of our era, the Chinese were printing from blocks. A book so printed was discovered in the province of Kansu in 1900 and contains the following intriguing statement: "Printed on May 11, 868, by Wang Chieh, for free general distribution, in order in deep reverence to perpetuate the memory of his parents" (*Encyclopedia Britannica,* [1954], vol. 18, p. 499). A couple of centuries later, Pi Sheng, a Chinese compatriot, was printing from movable type. Yet this extraordinary invention was abandoned and apparently lost until about the middle of the fifteenth century, when it was reinvented in Europe.

Printing from movable type has been rated one of the greatest, if not *the* greatest, inventions of all time. The reason for this is that it not only preserves the intellectual achievements of the past and present, but makes those achievements available to the rest of the world.

Curiously, alphabetic writing, another great innovation from the past, was apparently invented by Semitic slaves, using what is known as the "acrophonic principle." Such an alphabet was found etched into the wall of a copper mine on the Sinai Peninsula in 1906 by Sir Flinders Petrie—not far from where Job lived—and dates back to a time not long before that of Moses, the writer of Job.

In his lament, Job wanted the world to know that, although he was suffering without apparent cause, yet he steadfastly maintained his faith in the coming Redeemer, who would restore his disease-ridden body to health and vigor.

Job's ringing testimony should be an encouragement to us today, when we are undergoing pain and suffering.

*Put off your old nature which belongs to your former manner of life . . . and be renewed in the spirit of your minds, and put on the new nature, created after the likeness of God in true righteousness and holiness. Eph. 4:22-24, RSV.*

FEBRUARY

2

# Victory Over the Old Nature

One day as Hudson Taylor, celebrated missionary to China, was traveling, he came to a river and contracted with a boatman to ferry him across. As he waited, a mandarin in silks and satins arrived at the landing and tried to rent the boat from under him. The boatman protested that he had already rented his craft to the missionary, but the mandarin was insistent. Then, without a word, he turned and struck the "foreign devil" a powerful blow between the eyes and strutted off toward the boat.

Taylor was momentarily stunned. Naturally hot-tempered, his first impulse was to push his assailant into the river. In fact, he raised his hand to do just that, then dropped it.

Instead, he said, "Sir, I was tempted to shove you into the river just now, but the Jesus I serve kept me from doing it. As you know, I rented the boat before you came, but I gladly invite you to share it with me."

The mandarin didn't expect this kind of a reaction, and although he offered no apology, the smitten look on his face and his acceptance of Taylor's invitation were apology enough.

Sometimes victory over a sin is gained in a moment. Many, for example, have gained instant victory over drugs. Others have struggled on for days, or even years, before the habit was conquered, and some, sad to say, never gain the victory.

We may not always know why we cannot seem to gain the victory over a besetting sin. But could it be that deep down we really do not want to give up a cherished sin? If we are not sure, we need to pray David's prayer in Psalm 139:23, 24.

One thing is certain: when we fail, it is *never* God's fault. But what can we do to gain victory? First, we must acknowledge that we are powerless to change ourselves; second, we can ask God to do for us that which we cannot do for ourselves; third, we are to resist by God's grace *at the moment of temptation;* and fourth, by faith we may thank God for answering our prayer. Try it. It works!

*[Christ] has forgiven us all our sins; he has cancelled the bond which was outstanding against us . . . ; he has set it aside, nailing it to the cross. Col. 2:13, 14, REB.*

# Canceled Debts

The word "bond" in our verse, *cheirographon* in Greek, is frequently used in the ancient papyri to mean a certificate of indebtedness signed by the debtor and canceled (*exaleiphō,* "wiped out") only when the debt was paid.

During one of the lulls in the siege of Plevna, Bulgaria, in the summer of 1877, Nicholas II, the last czar of Russia, was making the rounds of his camp when he came across a young officer who had fallen asleep at a table while writing a letter to his wife. Peering over the young man's shoulders, Nicholas read about the officer's distress over his inability to pay his financial obligations. "Who will pay my debts?" he had written in despair. Nicholas picked up the pen that lay on the table and wrote, "I will pay—Nicholas." We can imagine the officer's surprise when he awoke and read that promise. We can also imagine the thankfulness he must have expressed, to his sovereign, not only in words but also in deeds and deepened loyalty.

The Sovereign of the universe, the Captain of our salvation, has done for us something similar to that which Czar Nicholas II did for that young officer. He has canceled our debt of sin. In return, we express our heartfelt gratitude in words and also in an ever-deepening commitment to the One who redeemed us.

Some seem to think that, the debt having been canceled, they can go on sinning with impunity and still be saved. If this were true, Christ would be the minister of sin, would He not? (See Gal. 2:17.) And Christ's words to the woman taken in adultery, "Go, and sin no more" (John 8:11), would be a senseless mockery. But does this mean that this woman lived, or at least could have lived, a sin-free life forever after? On the answer to this question turns the whole issue of righteousness by faith.

Why not daily commit all that you are to God and let Him be the judge of whether you have achieved such perfection? One thing is certain, Christ offers not only pardoning grace; He also offers overcoming grace—power to "sin no more."

*Whatsoever thy hand findeth to do, do it with thy might; for there is no work, nor device, nor knowledge, nor wisdom, in Sheol, whither thou goest. Eccl. 9:10, ARV.*

FEBRUARY

4

# Serve God Wholeheartedly

Kagawa Toyohiko was born into a well-to-do Buddhist home in Kobe, Japan, on July 10, 1888. At age 4 he was orphaned and taken in by relatives. In 1905, at the age of 17, he enrolled at Presbyterian College in Tokyo and converted to Christianity under the ministry of Dr. Myers, an American missionary. When he told his uncle he had become a Christian, he was disowned and driven from home penniless. Dr. Myers took him in, and he continued his education, graduating in 1908.

While in college, Kagawa was diagnosed as having tuberculosis and told he did not have long to live. When he heard this, he decided to spend what remained of his life helping those less fortunate than himself—telling them about the Jesus he had found. He chose as his mission field the outcasts of Shinkawa.

For six years, in spite of the pronouncement that there was "not a sound organ in his body," Kagawa labored for Christ with burning zeal—*and survived!* In 1914 he went to America and studied for three years at Princeton Theological Seminary, graduating with a divinity degree. Returning to Japan in 1917, he became involved in evangelism and humanitarian work. In time he became known as the most influential Christian in Japan.

When Japan declared war on the Allies in 1941, Kagawa was arrested and imprisoned. He survived the war and was influential in democratizing Japan. He died in Tokyo April 23, 1960, after an inspiring life of total dedication to the cause of the Jesus he loved.

Most of us do not live under the dark shadow of knowing we have a short time to live. But whether we do or not, every life has its limits. An accident, disease, even old age, can terminate it quickly. So the question is: What are we going to do with our lives, our talents, in the time that remains?

Why not search inside yourself and discover how you can best employ your God-given talents in service to others? Then, with all your might, do that which your "hand" finds to do.

**5**

*The Lord fills me with his spirit and power, and gives me a sense of justice and the courage to tell the people . . . what their sins are. Micah 3:8, TEV.*

# The Secret of Spiritual Power

Dwight Lyman Moody was born in East Northfield, Massachusetts, in 1837. He lost his father when he was a young child. At 17, while a shoe salesman in his uncle's store in Boston, Dwight was converted. Not long after this he moved to Chicago, where he established a successful shoe business of his own. While still a young Christian, Moody heard a minister declare that the world had yet to see what could be accomplished by one man who wholly consecrated himself to Christ. Moody accepted these words as a personal challenge and resolved to be that man.

One Sunday morning in 1856 the 19-year-old shoe salesman walked into church followed by a motley group of tramps, alcoholics, and street people whom he had invited. He continued to do this until God called him to a larger ministry.

In 1860 Moody quit his shoe business and devoted himself to missionary work, helping Civil War soldiers spiritually. Eleven years later Ira D. Sankey, a musician, joined him, and they held a series of fruitful revival meetings. From then on, Moody conducted successful evangelistic campaigns in Great Britain and America. According to one of his friends, before his death in 1899, he "reduced the population of hell by a million souls."

The secret of Moody's power lay in a life wholly dedicated to God. Although he never graduated from high school, never received any theological training, and was said to be deficient in grammar and syntax, his sermons were colorful, dramatic, and powerful. Above all, they were accompanied by intense personal conviction.

The same was true of Christ's first disciples. They were uneducated fishermen, but they dedicated themselves wholly to God. The Holy Spirit took possession of them, and within a relatively short time they, like Paul and his companions, "turned the world upside down" (see Acts 17:6).

This same spiritual power is available to you and me today.

*I thank God, whom I serve, as my forefathers did, with a clear conscience, as night and day I constantly remember you in my prayers.*
**2 Tim. 1:3, NIV.**

# Obeying the Voice of Conscience

I have always held the Scotsman Eric Liddell in high regard. Like me, he was imprisoned in a Japanese civilian-prisoner-of-war camp. Unfortunately, he did not survive the experience. The reason I esteem him so highly is that he had the courage to live up to his convictions.

As a young man, Liddell, a ministerial student in his native Scotland, trained for the 100-meter dash in the 1924 Olympics. He was a fast sprinter and stood an excellent chance of winning a medal. However, he learned that the race was scheduled for a Sunday, and he felt he could not in good conscience run on his day of worship. True to his convictions, he withdrew from the competition. His fans were stunned. Some praised him, while others thought him a fool.

Then a runner dropped out of the 400-meter race, a contest that was to be held on a weekday. Liddell offered to fill the slot, even though the race was four times longer than the one for which he had trained. To everyone's surprise, he ran the race in an astonishing 47.6 seconds—a world record—and won a gold medal!

Later, Liddell served the Lord as a missionary to China. It was there that he died in an internment camp in 1945.

Conscience is not something to be trifled with, for it is the mental faculty through which the Holy Spirit speaks to us. Some have supposed that conscience per se is the voice of the Holy Spirit. This is incorrect, and here is an illustration of my point: Among certain African tribes, twins are considered taboo. When twins are born, the infants are exposed to die. Strangely, parents who go against this evil practice suffer "pangs of conscience"— and this is certainly not the work of the Holy Spirit.

In order for conscience to be a safe guide, it needs to be educated by the Word of God. When it is, we should obey it, for it is the vehicle through which God speaks to us.

*If you forgive men their trespasses, your heavenly Father will also forgive you. But if you do not forgive men their trespasses, neither will your Father forgive your trespasses. Matt. 6:14, 15, NKJV.*

# The Meaning of Forgiveness

It is said that when Moravian missionaries first went to preach the gospel to the Eskimos, they found no word in their language for forgiveness, so they coined one. The word they coined is *issumagijoujungnainermik*. Now, you probably can't pronounce this word any more than I can, but it has a beautiful significance. It means "not-being-able-to-think-about-it-anymore." The best way to stop holding a grudge is to look for ways to do the offender good.

In 1946 Czeslaw Godlewski was a member of a young outlaw gang that ransacked the German countryside. On one occasion the gang gunned down nine members of the Hamelmann family in cold blood. Wilhelm, the father, was the only survivor. He bore the scars of four bullet wounds.

Eventually the gang was arrested, and Godlewski was tried, convicted, and sentenced to 20 years in prison. At the end of his term the state didn't know what to do with him. He had no kin and nowhere to go.

When Hamelmann, a Christian, heard about this, he went to the civil authorities and asked that Godlewski be released to his custody. He wanted to adopt him as a son. In his request, he wrote, "Christ died for my sins and forgave me. Should I not then forgive this man?"

What a magnanimous spirit! Would that more Christians manifested it.

Have you ever heard anyone say "I can forgive, but I can't forget"? Perhaps you've even said this yourself, or at least thought it. I know I have.

How does one overcome these feelings? The best way is to actively seek the good of those who wrong you, not in an ostentatious, obnoxious way, but quietly, lovingly, unobtrusively, being "wise as serpents, and harmless as doves" (Matt. 10:16).

Paul laid down an excellent principle when he said, "Be not overcome of evil, but overcome evil with good" (Rom. 12:21).

*If you show snobbery, you are committing a sin and you stand convicted by that law as transgressors. James 2:9, NEB.*

FEBRUARY
8

# What You Can Do About Prejudice

Snobbery is a common manifestation of prejudice. But prejudice is not limited to snobbery. Frequently it manifests itself in other ways.

There was a time I disliked red hair. Now I love it. The change came about suddenly. How? Well, one day I was given a grandson, named after me, who has the most beautiful red hair you ever saw. You know, of course, what made the difference.

When you think about it, prejudice is one of the most stupid activities in which human beings can engage. Frequently it is directed against something over which the object of the prejudice has no control. Take the matter of hair. Why should I, or anyone for that matter, be prejudiced against those who have red hair—or black hair, or blond hair, or curly hair? Who had anything to say about the kind of hair—or color of skin—they were born with? Or, to go a bit further: Who ever chose the race into which they were born?

But if prejudices are wrong, does this mean that a person should have no preferences? Of course not. When one marries, he or she expresses a preference—and that preference had better be permanent, or there is trouble ahead for that marriage! Where, then, is the line that divides prejudice from preference? It is drawn at the point where a "preference" is directed *against* another person or persons. Christians may have legitimate preferences, but they will not have prejudices.

The problem is that some professed Christians have prejudices that they label "preferences."

Is there something you and I as Christians can do when prejudice is directed against us? There is. We cannot demand love and acceptance, but respect, even love and acceptance, can be *engendered* by one who is gracious in the face of prejudice.

Christian graciousness doesn't mean making yourself a doormat. It does mean letting divine grace work in and through you. When others are prejudiced against you, let this God-given attribute manifest itself in your life.

*Christ . . . left behind an example, so that you might follow on in His footsteps.*
**1 Peter 2:21, MLB.**

# Following Footsteps

Years ago I read about an incident that happened in Chicago before the days of Prohibition. A young husband and father—we'll call him John—was having a struggle with the drinking habit.

One snowy winter evening John told his wife he was going to visit friends. His wife knew that that would mean worrying for hours over whether or not he would get home safely. In spite of her pleas, John put on his hat, coat, and boots, and walked out the front door toward the family car. As he crunched through the snow he heard the front door open and his little son's voice calling, "Daddy, I'm coming in your footsteps! Daddy, I'm coming in your footsteps!"

Turning around, John saw little John struggling toward him, placing his small feet in the impressions of his father's big feet. I have often wondered if the little fellow's mother put him up to this ploy. Whether she did or not, it made John consider seriously the example he was setting for his son. He waited until little John reached him, then, picking him up in his arms, he returned to the house, determined never to touch another drop of liquor.

Following the example of another human being can be hazardous, because not one of us is perfect. However, as our verse recommends, it is always safe to follow in Jesus' footsteps. He lived a perfect life and thus set a perfect example.

In his First Epistle to the Corinthians, the apostle Paul says, "Follow my example as I follow Christ's" (1 Cor. 11:1, NEB). When Paul wrote this, he was encouraging the Corinthian Christians to follow his example, *but only insofar as he followed Christ's example.*

I don't know about you, but I've always felt uneasy about encouraging other people to follow my example. Of course, with Paul it was different. After all, he was writing under inspiration. However, whether or not we like it, whether or not we encourage it, some people may follow our example. How important, then, that we walk as Jesus walked.

# Faithful to the End

On January 12, 1992, more than 200 people gathered at Fort Benton, Montana, to celebrate the fiftieth anniversary of the death of Shep, a sheepdog that waited five and a half years at the local train station for his master to return.

Shep's vigil began in August 1936, when he watched the baggage men load his master's casket onto a train for burial in a distant cemetery. From that day until his death, Shep met each of four daily Great Northern passenger trains that arrived at the Benton station. Kind friends supplied old Shep with food. The vigil ended January 12, 1942, when the faithful dog slipped and fell beneath the wheels of an arriving train.

Steve McSweeney, 63 years old, attended the anniversary ceremony. He said as a boy he watched Shep's vigil. He stated that the dog never went to meet a train unless it was the type of train that had borne his master away.

These days such faithfulness appears to be far more common among members of the canine species than among human beings. And this lack of constancy, this lack of steadfastness to persons as well as to principles, is not improving as time goes on. If anything, it is getting worse, and we may expect it to get even worse as we near the time of Christ's return; for He asked, "When the Son of Man comes, will He find faith on the earth?" (Luke 18:8, NASB). The answer to this rhetorical question will generally be negative.

But there is a bright side to this gloomy picture. Listen to these words of encouragement: "Among earth's inhabitants, scattered in every land, there are those who have not bowed the knee to Baal. Like the stars of heaven, which appear only at night, these faithful ones will shine forth when darkness covers the earth and gross darkness the people. . . . The darker the night, the more brilliantly will they shine" (*Prophets and Kings*, pp. 188, 189).

By practicing steadfast faithfulness today, it will be our privilege to be numbered among the faithful few when Christ returns.

**FEBRUARY**

# 11

*Play joyous melodies of praise upon the lyre and on the harp. Compose new songs of praise to [the Lord], accompanied skillfully on the harp. Ps. 33:2, 3, TLB.*

# The Power of Music

In its simplest terms, music is made up of three basic components: melody, harmony, and rhythm. Few things have greater power for good or evil than this art form. At its best, melody predominates; at its worst, rhythm predominates.

Two famous Scandinavians, Ole Bornemann Bull, a distinguished Norwegian composer-violinist, and John Ericsson, a celebrated Swedish-American inventor and marine engineer, were close friends in their youth, but eventually they drifted apart. However, the two met again on one of Bull's American tours.

Bull tried several times to interest Ericsson in attending one of his concerts. Ericsson, who had never been interested in music, declined. After several more invitations Bull finally said half seriously, "If you won't come, I'll bring my violin to your shop and play."

"If you do," Ericsson responded, probably just as seriously, "I'll smash it to pieces."

Aware of the strange power music can have upon the human spirit, Bull decided on a ruse. One day he arrived at Ericsson's shop with his violin disassembled. He pointed out certain difficulties he was having with the instrument and asked Ericsson about the scientific principles involved. Ericsson's interest was aroused, and they discussed the various effects of sound in relation to wood. Finally, to illustrate what he meant, Bull reassembled his instrument, and drawing the bow across the strings, played a few bars of familiar Scandinavian music.

Long-forgotten memories were revived in Ericsson's heart. He was stirred to the depths of his soul. Tears welled up in his eyes, and when Bull paused for a moment, he pleaded, "Play on! Don't stop! I never before realized what was missing in my life. Now I know."

Ellen White says that music, "*rightly employed*, . . . is a precious gift of God, designed to uplift the thoughts to high and noble themes, to inspire and elevate the soul" (*Messages to Young People,* p. 291; italics supplied). Choose your music carefully.

*"If your enemy is hungry, feed him; if he is thirsty, give him a drink; by doing this you will heap live coals on his head." Do not let evil conquer you, but use good to defeat evil.*
**Rom. 12:20, NEB.**

FEBRUARY
12

# Overcoming Evil With Good

After his assassination, President Abraham Lincoln came to be regarded as one of the greatest chief executives America ever had. But it was not always so. Many of his contemporaries despised him because of his physical appearance and his humble origin. (He was a gangling six feet four inches and was born in a log cabin.)

No one treated Lincoln with greater contempt than Edwin M. Stanton. He not only denounced Lincoln's policies as those of a "low, cunning clown," but also lampooned him as "the original gorilla." He joked that explorer Paul du Chaillu was a fool for trying to capture a gorilla in Africa when he could have found one so easily in Springfield, Illinois, the capital of Lincoln's home state.

Lincoln did not respond to these barbs. Rather, he chose Stanton as his secretary of war because of his superb organizational ability. The years wore on. On the night of April 14, 1865, Lincoln and his family were attending a play at the Ford Theater in Washington, when John Wilkes Booth, one of the best-known actors of the day, shot him from the back of the presidential box. The president died the next morning, surrounded by his family and high government officials. Among the the latter was Stanton, who said with deep emotion, "There lies the greatest ruler of men the world has ever seen."

Lesser men would have fired Stanton because of his personal attacks; not the wise and patient Lincoln. By applying the principle of returning good for evil, he gained the respect and admiration of his enemies.

The American poet Edwin Markham encapsulates the outworking of this precept in these words:

> He drew a circle that shut me out—
> Heretic, rebel, a thing to flout.
> But love and I had wit to win;
> We drew a circle that took him in.

*Finally, all of you be of one mind, having compassion for one another; love as brothers, be tenderhearted, be courteous.*
*1 Peter 3:8, NKJV.*

# Christian Courtesy

The word "courtesy" comes from the age of chivalry when behavior in the king's court was marked by deep respect, proper deportment, and gracious concern for the sensitivities of others. These, incidentally, are also the marks of a true Christian.

From 1990 to 1992 my wife and I served as missionaries in Thailand. Some of the things we appreciated in the Thai people were their courtesy and generous spirit. It therefore came to us as no surprise to learn that in 1862, when King Rama IV heard about the American Civil War, he wrote President Lincoln offering to send him some elephants to help put down the Southern rebellion and free the slaves.

Lincoln had enough to keep him busy just conducting the affairs of a nation at war and could reasonably be excused for ignoring the king's letter, since the use of elephants in the conflict then in progress was impractical. But Lincoln did not ignore the missive. Instead, he drafted a reply himself, thanking His Majesty for his thoughtfulness and explaining that climatic conditions in America ruled out the use of elephants in warfare. He ended the letter with, "Your good friend, Abraham Lincoln."

How thoughtful!

As a boy I remember hearing about a woman who was deeply embarrassed when she accidentally tipped over her wineglass during a banquet given by Queen Elizabeth I, I believe it was. All eyes focused on the unfortunate guest. Some even cast reproachful glances in her direction. Just then the queen's wine goblet tipped over—and not by accident. The reproachful looks suddenly changed to fawning solicitude as attention shifted from the guest to the queen.

What a clever way to save someone from embarrassment!

But while Christian courtesy seeks to save others from embarrassment, it goes further. It manifests itself in sensitivity to the rights of everyone, whether his or her station in life is deemed high or low. A Christian is courteous because "all are to be treated with refinement and delicacy, as the sons and daughters of God" (*The Ministry of Healing*, p. 489).

*Many waters cannot quench the flame of love, neither can the floods drown it. If a man tried to buy it with everything he owned, he couldn't do it. S. of Sol. 8:7, TLB.*

FEBRUARY
14

# A Song of Love

As I write, it will soon be 40 years that Vesta and I have been married. Ours has been an exceptionally happy, heaven-blessed union—and we are the first to admit that it is the Lord's doing, not ours.

After our heavenly Father, my earthly father deserves a large measure of credit for our happiness. He did not have the advantage of being born into a happy home. His father and mother were divorced when he was a babe in arms. But one day Dad gave his heart to God—totally. He resolved to serve God, nothing more, nothing less, and nothing else! As a consequence God was able to lead him to my mother, and because Mom had committed her life completely to God, He could lead her to Dad.

Not once in all the years did I ever see them quarrel. After I grew up I asked Dad, "Didn't you ever have any disagreements?"

I was surprised at his answer, "Oh, yes, but we never disagreed in front of you children. No problem ever arose between us that was so great but what we could resolve it by humbly kneeling at the foot of the cross."

As we children grew up, Mom and Dad openly demonstrated their affection for each other. Even in their dotage, when we took them into our home, their courtship continued, as our children well know.

Vesta and I have endeavored to emulate their example in our marriage. After all, life is uncertain. If something should happen to one of us, we want our last memory of the other to be a happy one.

We are aware that in a sinful world things could change overnight. And because this is so, we put "no confidence in the flesh" (Phil. 3:3). We know that "except the Lord build the house, they labour in vain that build it: except the Lord keep the city, the watchman waketh but in vain" (Ps. 127:1). We know that only as we commit our lives totally to God moment by moment are we safe—but this we are determined to do. May this also be your resolve.

*Do not put yourself forward in the king's presence or take your place among the great; for it is better that he should say to you, "Come up here," than move you down to make room for a nobleman. Prov. 25:6, 7, NEB.*

# Rudeness Versus Love

On February 26, 1844, President John Tyler and other government dignitaries went on an inspection tour of the recently constructed *Princeton,* the most powerful warship in the U.S. Navy at the time. For entertainment, Captain Stockton had a crew fire the ship's giant cannon called, ironically, "The Peacemaker."

Just before the gun discharged a second time, a friend tapped one of the observers, Missouri senator Thomas Benton, on the shoulder. When Benton stepped back to speak to his friend, Secretary of the Navy Gilmer rudely elbowed his way past him and took his place on the front row. Extremely annoyed, Benton was about to express some rudeness himself when the gun went off—and *burst,* killing Gilmer and several others. Benton was spared.

Up to this time Benton had had a reputation for being cantankerous and downright rude. For example, he had recently made an insolent speech directed at Daniel Webster, then secretary of state. But after his narrow escape, Benton became a changed man. This is what he wrote Webster after the gun blew up:

"It seems to me, Mr. Webster, as if that touch on my shoulder was the hand of the Almighty stretched down there, drawing me away from what otherwise would have been instantaneous death. That one circumstance has changed the whole current of my life. I feel that I am a different man; and I want, in the first place, to be at peace with all those with whom I have been so sharply at variance."

Rudeness never pays. Solomon puts it this way: "Pride goeth before destruction, and an haughty spirit before a fall" (Prov. 16:18). Even when arrogance seems to pay, there is always a day of reckoning—if not in this life, in the judgment to come.

"Love," on the other hand, "is very patient and kind, . . . never haughty or selfish or rude. Love does not demand its own way" (1 Cor. 13:4, 5, TLB). May your life and mine always reflect this Christian virtue.

*Though I am free and belong to no man, I make myself a slave to everyone, to win as many as possible. 1 Cor. 9:19, NIV.*

FEBRUARY

16

# Slave of Slaves

The same ship that brought John Wesley to America also carried a Swiss family named Bininger. Both the father and mother died on the voyage, but their son, Abraham, survived. When he grew to manhood, he asked to be sent as a missionary to the slaves on St. Thomas island in the Caribbean, then a Danish possession.

When Abraham Bininger arrived there, he found that it was against the law for anyone but a slave to preach to the slaves. So he wrote the governor of the island asking to be made a slave in order that he could preach the message of salvation to the slaves.

Perplexed by the strange request, the governor forwarded his letter to the king of Denmark. The king was so touched by it that he sent a royal rescript empowering Bininger to tell the story of Jesus to whomever he chose—to Black or White, bond or free.

This is real commitment!

This is the kind of commitment the apostle Paul had. So dedicated was he to the salvation of souls that he declared, "Woe is unto me, if I preach not the gospel!" (1 Cor. 9:16). In fact, in one of his letters he was so burdened for the salvation of his own persecuting people that he wrote, "Oh, Israel, my people! Oh, my Jewish brothers! How I long for you to come to Christ. My heart is heavy within me and I grieve bitterly day and night because of you. Christ knows and the Holy Spirit knows that it is no mere pretense when I say that I would be willing to be forever damned if that would save you" (Rom. 9:1-3, TLB).

God may not have called you or me to do the work that Bininger and Paul were called to do, but He calls us to have the same commitment and dedication they had.

If you cannot cross the ocean and the heathen lands explore,
You can find the heathen nearer, you can help them at
    your door;
If you cannot speak like angels, if you cannot preach like
    Paul,
You can tell the love of Jesus, you can say He died for all.
                                        —Daniel March

57

*Whenever I am afraid, I will trust in You. In God (I will praise His word), in God I have put my trust; I will not fear. What can flesh do to me? Ps. 56:3, 4, NKJV.*

# Trust That Conquers Fear

On June 14, 1985, the news was broadcast that TWA Flight 847 had been hijacked by Palestinian terrorists with 147 passengers and a crew of eight aboard. A day or two later Captain John Testrake was shown on television poking his head out the window of his plane. He wore a couple of days' growth of beard, and a terrorist, pistol in hand, was waving the cameramen away.

The hijackers were desperate. They threatened that if there was just one false move, they would blow up the plane with the people on board—themselves included. As you may remember, they demonstrated that they meant what they said.

The ordeal lasted 17 harrowing days. But all through it, Captain Testrake, who long before had made his peace with God, remained calm. After the trying experience, he said he felt the presence of Jesus with him throughout the entire episode, that it was He who had kept him from being afraid.

I can empathize with victims of hijackings. During the 37 months I was a captive of the Imperial Japanese Army, there were many times I was sure I would not survive the war. I had just turned 18 two months before my family—my parents, my brother, and I—were captured. Looking at the prospects of survival from the human point of view, I concluded that before the Americans took over our camp, the last thing the Japanese would want was one more potential American soldier to fight them, and they would do away with me. Yet when the turnover did come, God delivered us in a remarkable way. Not one internee lost his life during the fighting!

No one relishes the thought of living under the constant threat of imminent death at the hands of evil men. However, as Christians we have the assurance that God is with us in every trial, for He has promised, "I will never leave you nor forsake you" (Heb. 13:5, NKJV). The psalmist trusted God to keep His promise; so did Captain Testrake; and so can you and I!

*Out of the depths have I cried unto thee, O Lord. Lord, hear my voice: let thine ears be attentive to the voice of my supplications. . . . My soul waiteth for the Lord more than they that watch for the morning. Ps. 130:1-6.*

FEBRUARY

18

# Cry From a Cave

Although the superscription of this psalm does not tell us who composed it, some scholars believe it was written by David while he was hiding in the cave of Adullam. Some of the sentiments it expresses certainly could support this conclusion.

Hunted down like a wild animal by the jealously insane Saul, David finally sought solace and safety in the cave of Adullam, situated some 15 miles south of Jerusalem. Caves, as we all know, are normally dark. The pathos of the refrain, "more than they that watch for the morning," is touching. Some believe it suggests that David composed this psalm in the early-morning hours. If so, the darkness preceding the dawn doubtless heightened his mood of despair.

Many have felt as David did. So if this includes you, you are not alone. Most of us have felt that way at one time or another in our lives.

Many years ago a young lawyer in the Midwest suffered such deep depression that his friends feared for his life. In order to prevent him from committing suicide, they took away from him everything that might contribute to this possibility. During this time the young attorney wrote, "I am now the most miserable man living. Whether I shall ever be better, I cannot tell. I awfully forebode I shall not." *He was wrong!* In time circumstances changed, and the young lawyer—Abraham Lincoln—went on to become one of America's best loved and greatest presidents.

And David, of course, went on to become king of Israel. I'm glad that in spite of the dark, foreboding future, the psalmist concluded his composition with these triumphant words: "Hope in the Lord! For with the Lord there is steadfast love, and with him is plenteous redemption" (verse 7, RSV). So never let the darkness get you down, rather, "hope thou in God" (Ps. 42:5)—who answers the cry of His faithful ones in the cave of despair.

*I am reminded of your sincere faith, a faith that dwelt first in your grandmother Lois and in your mother Eunice and now, I am sure, dwells in you. 2 Tim. 1:5, RSV.*

# Artists for Eternity

I was 6 years old the first time I saw the Statue of Liberty in New York Harbor. It left an indelible impression on my young mind as our ship, the S.S. *Alban*, sailed past and Captain Evans pointed it out to us. It was almost exactly 50 years later, however, before I visited Liberty Island and stood beside the "lady" who lifts her "lamp beside the golden door" and climbed the stairs leading up to the lookout windows in her brow.

The statue was designed by French sculptor Frédéric Auguste Bartholdi, who spent nearly 20 years in conceiving, designing, building, and installing it. He personally superintended the collection of 1 million francs from the French people toward the project. In 1884, when subscriptions lagged, he pledged his own fortune to defray expenses, practically bankrupting himself. The statue was dedicated on October 28, 1886, by President Grover Cleveland.

It is said that when Bartholdi began his work, he searched for a subject whose form and features best fitted the concept of "liberty" that he had in mind. He studied many possibilities but finally modeled his work after the likeness of his mother—not an altogether surprising choice.

Whether mothers realize it or not, their children tend to fashion their lives after them. Parents, especially mothers, by virtue of their closeness to their children during their first months of life, have a unique privilege. Speaking of this role, someone has written:

"No other work can equal hers in importance. She has not, like the artist, to paint a form of beauty upon canvas, nor, like the sculptor, to chisel it from marble. She has not, like the author, to embody a noble thought in words of power, nor, like the musician, to express a beautiful sentiment in melody. It is hers, with the help of God, to develop in a human soul the likeness of the divine" (*The Faith I Live By*, p. 264).

May parents, especially mothers, always seek divine guidance in their important work.

# Soldiers, Stand Your Ground!

The context in which our verse appears compares the Christian to a soldier who, having put on the whole armor of God, resolutely stands his ground.

One day many years ago an English farmer noticed a party of fox hunters about to cross one of his fields. Having recently planted wheat in that plot, he knew that his crop would be ruined if trampled by the horses. Calling one of his young field hands, he instructed him to go to the gate and refuse to let the party enter the field. No sooner had the young man arrived at the gate than one of the horsemen rode up and ordered him to open the gate. The lad respectfully refused, explaining why.

At last a horseman of commanding bearing trotted up and said in a tone of stern authority, "Young man, I am the duke of Wellington, and I am accustomed to being obeyed. I order you to open that gate at once!"

Without flinching, the young man tipped his cap and answered respectfully, "Sire, I am sure the duke of Wellington would be the last person in the world who would want me to disobey my master's orders."

There was a moment of silence as the duke pondered how to react. Then turning to his friends, he said, "I honor any man who cannot be threatened into disobeying his orders. If I had an army of soldiers like that, I could conquer the world."

A Christian should always obey those in authority, whether it be a "king, as the supreme authority, or . . . governors, who are sent by him" (1 Peter 2:13, NIV). This includes all duly constituted authority. But there is a limit. When those in authority demand that we disobey God or commit acts clearly contrary to His revealed will, we must humbly but respectfully decline to obey.

This is what Peter and John did when the Jewish leaders demanded they stop preaching the gospel. They replied firmly yet respectfully, "Judge for yourselves whether it is right in God's sight to obey you rather than God. For we cannot help speaking about what we have seen and heard" (Acts 4:19, 20, NIV).

*As for you, O man of God, flee from all these things; aim at and pursue righteousness—that is, right standing with God and true goodness; godliness (which is the loving fear of God and Christlikeness), faith, love, steadfastness (patience) and gentle-heartedness.*
*1 Tim. 6:11, Amplified.*

# Shun Evil, Pursue Goodness

Many professed Christians aim at the lowest possible standard and still hope to make it into heaven. Such an attitude is presumptuous. The true Christian aims at perfect conformity to the will of God. Does this mean that a true Christian never falls, never makes a mistake? No, but it does mean that his obedience to Christ is wholehearted. The nominal Christian, on the other hand, is like the drayman who boasted he liked to drive his wagon as close to the precipice as possible without going over. According to the story, if you remember, he lost his bid.

Some activities are admittedly so "borderline" that it is difficult to argue against them or point out their danger. In and of themselves they may be innocent, but carried to extremes they turn out to be injurious to our spiritual welfare. First Corinthians 6:12 says: "I can do anything I want to if Christ has not said no, but some of these things aren't good for me. Even if I am allowed to do them, I'll refuse to if I think they might get such a grip on me that I can't easily stop when I want to" (TLB). This is a good principle to live by.

Susanna Wesley, the mother of John Wesley, the founder of Methodism, laid down a practical definition of what is proper and what is improper for a Christian to do. She told her famous son, "If you would judge the lawfulness or the unlawfulness of pleasure, then take this simple rule: Whatever weakens your reason, impairs the tenderness of your consciousness, obscures your sense of [the presence of] God, and takes off the relish of spiritual things—that to you is sin." This is excellent advice.

Putting this rule into practice begins with a mind-set—a resolve to serve God with your entire being, making "no provision for the flesh, to fulfill its lusts" (Rom. 13:14, NKJV). Having done this, if you discover you haven't quite attained sainthood and have fallen, get up, and by God's grace press toward the mark!

*The man who is reliable when very little is involved is just as reliable when a great deal is involved; and when a man is dishonest when very little is involved, he will be just as dishonest when a great deal is involved.*
*Luke 16:10, Barclay.*

# Faithfulness in Small Matters

In Treasure Valley in Idaho where I live, the main county roads are laid out in a square, gridlike pattern, about a mile apart. I say "about" a mile because at some intersections, where one expects to go straight he must jog. I inquired about this and was told that some of the early surveyors made minute mistakes in their work. Today our roads reflect their mistakes. Some of these jogs are as much as 70 or 80 feet. Apparently, a very small discrepancy can become quite significant when a line is projected a considerable distance. Fortunately, not all surveyors are careless.

As a young man, George Washington, later the first president of the United States, did quite a bit of surveying in the Virginia wilderness for Lord Fairfax. In 1913, in preparation for purchasing some of this region for the Appalachian forest service, government surveyors resurveyed the area. The surveyors found that the marks made by Washington were as perfect as it was possible for human beings to make them in his day.

This same fidelity carried over into his leadership of the Colonies during the Revolutionary War and into his subsequent administration of the infant nation.

The reward for faithful service is increased responsibilities. Often this recompense comes in this life. But Jesus refers in Luke 16:10 to rewards in the world to come. This means that, while Christians do not scorn honors that may come to them in this life (they accept them graciously), they do not perform their duties to the best of their ability in order to achieve worldly honor.

Whatever your lifework in this world, resolve by God's grace to do it so well that coming generations will know you did your best. Make sure the boundary lines of your conduct are so absolutely true that the landmarks of your successes, when compared with the principles of honor, measure square.

FEBRUARY

23

*Although my father and my mother have forsaken me, yet the Lord will take me up [adopt me as His child]. Ps. 27:10, Amplified.*

# Unwanted

I was about 9 when my father told me I was not a "mistake," I was wanted. This assurance gave me a feeling of security that is hard to describe. My brother was told the same thing. It is a tragic truth that many children not only are denied this assurance, but are plainly told they were not wanted.

In his book *Come Before Winter* Charles R. Swindoll tells of a telephone call he received late one night. It was from a throwaway girl. She was a "mistake." Her parents didn't want her when she was born, so they placed her in a foster home and tried to walk out of her life. When she reached her teens, she somehow managed to locate her father and mother and went to meet them—only to discover they weren't eager to have her around.

One day they informed her that they were going to adopt a baby boy and start a new life—and made it plain that she was not a part of their plans. She was heartbroken. Pathetically, she offered to leave, perhaps hoping they would change their minds. They didn't. Her father's callous reaction was to offer to help her pack. Putting his words into action, he stuffed some clothes in a backpack, gave her a sleeping bag, slipped her a $10 bill, and waved her goodbye!

Swindoll tried to draw more information from the poor girl so he could help her, but she would say no more. When she said goodbye and hung up, he wept. Who wouldn't? Well, apparently, some parents wouldn't. Someday God will bring such parents into judgment (see Eccl. 12:14).

How can parents treat children, who didn't even ask to be born, the way this girl was treated? Is this not what Isaiah is talking about when he speaks of people who "turn away from . . . [their] own flesh and blood" (Isa. 58:7, NIV)?

We live in an age when fathers, and even mothers, throw away their children. But there is hope! These children can take comfort in the fact that, if they are disowned by their parents, *the Lord will adopt them as His children!*

*Cry aloud, spare not, lift up thy voice like a trumpet, and show my people their transgression, and the house of Jacob their sins. Isa. 58:1.*

FEBRUARY
24

# Cry Aloud, Spare Not

Rowland Hill, an evangelist renowned for his earnestness and powerful voice, was preaching at Wotton-under-Edge, England, one evening when some mischievous boys began mocking his fervor. After the meeting, some of the sobersided pillars of the church took Hill to task over being "intoxicated with the exuberance of his own verbosity" (see Acts 26:24).

Unfazed by the criticism, Hill cried out in a loud voice at his next meeting, "Beware! I am in earnest. You may laugh at me and call me an enthusiast, but I am not. Mine are words of truth and soberness. One day, when I first came to this part of the country, I happened to be walking by the gravel pit on the outskirts of town just as the sides of the pit caved in and buried three of your fellow citizens. I shouted for help so loudly that I was heard in town a mile away. Help came, and thank God, two of the three unfortunate men were saved from certain death.

"No one then called me an enthusiast. Why, then, do some of you charge me with being too much in earnest when I see poor sinners bound for perdition, point out their sins, and plead for them to flee to Christ and abandon their evil ways?"

The mocking and criticism stopped.

People usually can tell the difference between someone who is truly in earnest about the salvation of sinners and a haranguing hypocrite who rants against sin but who is either blind to, or glosses over, his own character defects.

When the Lord calls people to cry aloud and spare not, He does not commission them to assume a holier-than-thou attitude. To the contrary, God detests such posturing (see Isa. 65:5). Those called to the office of pointing out sin will reflect Christ in their own lives. Their focus will be on Christ, the sinner's only hope. Instead of pretending to be above sinning, they will humbly acknowledge by their actions, if not their words, that they are merely sinners in the process of being saved.

# 25

*The Lord looks down from heaven upon the children of men, to see if there are any that act wisely, that seek after God. They have all gone astray, they are all alike corrupt.*
**Ps. 14:2, 3, RSV.**

# What Fools We Mortals Be

During the years my parents were missionaries in the Azores archipelago, Mr. George Hayes was the British consul in those islands. Occasionally he or his wife would invite my brother and me to his home to read and play games with Yvonne, his daughter, who was about our age. Sometimes we would spend hours looking at magazines. One magazine, called *Punch,* always captured my attention. It carried on its masthead an etching of a character with a long hooked nose and wearing a sly grin. Under his picture appeared these words: "What fools these mortals be."

According to our verse for this morning, this is true of all of us. Sometimes the seemingly most intelligent people do some of the most foolish things. Solomon is a prime example of this. Endowed with superior intelligence, this mighty monarch came to the point of forgetting that his towering talents were gifts from God. For a time, he lost sight of the Giver of his gifts.

This was the same trap into which Lucifer fell (see Eze. 28:12, 15, 17)—and into which many of us are prone to fall (see 1 Tim. 3:6, NIV). Many upon whom God has bestowed exceptional abilities act as if they had earned or somehow deserved these gifts. Frequently this attitude is demonstrated in the high-handed way they treat those less fortunate or less gifted. What fools we mortals be if or when we act this way!

If God has endowed us with special abilities, that in no way justifies our being proud or looking down on those less gifted. Rather, we should recognize that these blessings are gifts to be employed in bringing honor and glory to the Giver—and to benefit our fellow human beings.

God has bestowed in varying degrees talents and gifts on every person—and this includes you and me (see 1 Cor. 12:4). Let us show by our actions that we recognize the true Source of our gifts, and use them to the glory of God and the good of others.

*The Lord does not see as man sees; for man looks at the outward appearance, but the Lord looks at the heart. 1 Sam. 16:7, NKJV.*

FEBRUARY
26

# Character Is What Counts

Few of us are completely satisfied with our physical appearance. Given a choice, most of us would rather look different from what we do. But some people go so far as to let their looks, good or poor, spoil their life. In either case, self is central.

Charles William Eliot was born in 1834 with a serious facial disfigurement. Back in those days people didn't know how to correct such deformities. One day, when he was old enough to understand, his mother took him aside and said, "My son, it is not possible for you to get rid of this handicap, but it is possible for you, with God's help, to grow a mind and soul so big that people will forget to look at your face." What a wise mother!

Charles took these words to heart. Instead of dwelling on his misfortune and wishing he had better looks, he developed his intellectual and spiritual gifts. He became an educator and leader in public affairs. At the age of 35 he was elected president of Harvard University, a position he held for 40 years. When he retired, he had elevated Harvard to world renown.

He is reputed to have exercised on his countrymen an influence far beyond that of the usual academic dignitary. During his later years he was looked up to not only in educational matters but in political, industrial, social, and spiritual questions as well.

There is nothing intrinsically wrong with wanting to improve our physical appearance. Today many of these disfigurements can be corrected by plastic surgery. However, if our looks are not repugnant and yet we seek cosmetic improvement, perhaps we should ask ourselves, What is my motive? Is it pride?

On the other hand, if we are good-looking, this is nothing about which to feel smug. Accidents can destroy good looks in a trice. So the important question is: Is "the hidden person of [my] heart" (1 Peter 3:4, NKJV) drawing the attention of others to Christ?

*My kinsmen who went up [to spy out the land of Canaan] with me disheartened the people, but I followed the Lord my God wholeheartedly. Joshua 14:8, MLB.*

# Wholehearted Dedication

Ellen White seldom commented on the soul-winning activities of other churches, but she did about the Salvation Army. This is what she said: "The Salvation Army workers are trying to save the neglected, downtrodden ones. Discourage them not" (*Welfare Ministry,* p. 251).

William Booth (1829-1912) founded the Salvation Army in 1878 and is remembered for his successful efforts in uplifting the downtrodden, especially alcoholics. Apprenticed at an early age to a pawnbroker, Booth witnessed the misery caused by alcohol, and he was roused to a lifelong passion against the poverty and degradation associated with intemperance.

Within 10 years of the founding of his organization many in England were stirred against him and his followers.

Salvationists were knocked down, kicked, or brutally assaulted. Many were sent to prison for preaching the gospel. But Booth and his adherents persevered. In time the world came to recognize his efforts to better society. Before his death he was made a freeman of London, Oxford University gave him an honorary doctorate, and he was invited to the coronation of Edward VII. Yet none of these honors deflected him from his dedication to God.

Asked by Dr. Wilbur J. Chapman what the secret of his success was, Booth replied, "God has had all there was of me. There have been men with greater brains than I, men with greater opportunities; but from the day I got the poor of London on my heart, and a vision of what Jesus Christ could do for the poor of London, I made up my mind that God would have all of William Booth that there was."

Later Dr. Chapman remarked: "The greatness of a man's power is the measure of his surrender."

Another Christian put this truth thus: "There is no limit to the usefulness of one who, by putting self aside, makes room for the working of the Holy Spirit upon his heart, and lives a life wholly consecrated to God" (*The Desire of Ages,* pp. 250, 251).

This is the kind of dedication God desires from you and me.

*Salvation is found in no one else, for there is no other name under heaven given to men by which we must be saved. Acts 4:12, NIV.*

# The Name That Saves

In 1727, fresh out of Oxford divinity school, John Wesley, one of the founders of Methodism, was perplexed over England's social problems—slavery, the exploitation of the poor, drunkenness, and prostitution. He became a minister of the established church and in 1735 went as a missionary to the American Indians along the coast of Georgia.

On his voyage to America, his ship was nearly swamped in a raging storm. Many of those on board, including Wesley, unashamedly feared for their lives. Wesley noticed, however, the calmness of a group of Moravian missionaries. Later he asked one of them why he was not afraid.

"Why should I be afraid?" the Moravian questioned. "I know Christ." Then he asked pointedly, "Do you know Christ?"

Wesley knew in his heart that his answer would have to be negative, and he did not respond. His subsequent efforts in Georgia were a dismal failure, and in 1738 he boarded ship and returned to his homeland.

Back in England he met Peter Boehler, a Moravian missionary to the Carolinas, who invited him to a prayer meeting service. That night, May 24, 1738, Wesley was converted, and later, referring to this experience, wrote: "About a quarter before nine . . . I felt my heart strangely warmed. I felt [that now] I did know Christ, Christ alone for my salvation."

Heretofore, by his own account, Wesley had depended on his upright character for salvation. Now, converted and on fire for God, he launched the mighty Methodist movement.

There is power in Christ's name. Not that a name per se has any power, but faith in the personality and power of the possessor of that name effects change. When we by faith open our hearts in total surrender to Christ, a change for the better takes place. It may be cataclysmic, like the change Paul experienced on the road to Damascus, or it may be a dawning experience, such as Timothy had. *But a change will take place*—if our commitment to Christ is total and unreserved. Nothing less is acceptable to God.

69

*Let us then approach the throne of grace with assurance, so that we may receive mercy and find grace to help us in time of need.*
*Heb. 4:16, MLB.*

# Approaching the Throne of Grace

In the ancient Near East someone approached the throne of a king in a posture of submissiveness. In those days coming uninvited into the presence of an earthly potentate could mean death (see Esther 4:11). But times have changed. For many years it has been Saudi Arabian custom for any subject, even the lowliest citizen, to come before higher authorities—whether a tribal chief, a governor, or the king himself—and present his petition. However, not until 1952 when King Abdul Aziz issued a decree did the custom officially become a right. Even so, although the Saudis have this right, I am confident that no citizen comes before the king without showing him due respect.

Some translations render the Greek word *parresia* as "boldly" rather than "with assurance," as our text has it. While boldly is an allowable rendering, it may connote "brazen impudence," and this certainly is not the attitude with which we should approach the throne of the King of the universe.

Yet I have heard some Christians almost give the impression that they have a right to approach God with demanding audacity—because Jesus died for them. This, I feel, is a mistake.

One of the many meanings of grace (Greek, *charis*) is "unmerited favor." This seems to suggest that the proper attitude for approaching the throne, from which unmerited favor is dispensed, is humility rather than brazen temerity. On the other hand, this does not mean we are to approach God cringingly, wondering whether or not He will receive us; for He receives all who come to Him by faith, humbly seeking His undeserved favor (see James 4:6).

But grace also has another meaning—divine power to accomplish God's will. Paul refers to grace in this sense when he says that the grace God bestowed upon him "was not in vain; but I laboured more abundantly than they all: yet not I, but the grace of God which was with me" (1 Cor. 15:10).

We all need grace—not only grace for the forgiveness of sin, but grace that enables us to overcome sin when we are tempted.

*Ye have condemned and killed the just; and he doth not resist you. Be patient, therefore, brethren, unto the coming of the Lord.*
*James 5:6, 7.*

MARCH

2

# The Vulnerability of the Just

Aristides the Just, an Athenian statesman and general, is believed to have earned his nickname from his equitable distribution of the tax burden on the members of the Athenian alliance known as the Delian League.

In 483 B.C., because he opposed the policies of Themistocles, another Athenian general, the *ecclesia,* or assembly of Athenian citizens that met on the Areopagus, voted to banish Aristides from the country.

During the procedure, an illiterate citizen, not knowing who Aristides was, is said to have asked him to write "Aristides" on an *ostrakon* (a shell or pottery fragment), meaning he was voting for his exile. Aristides did as the man asked, then inquired if he knew Aristides, and if so, what he had against him.

"I know nothing about Aristides," the man replied, "but I am tired of hearing people call him Aristides the Just."

(Our word "ostracism," incidentally, comes from *ostrakon.* Many years ago archaeologists actually found a potsherd with Aristides' name scratched on it; it is believed to be a vote cast for his exile.)

One would think that because Aristides' fellow citizens banished him, he would have turned against his ungrateful country, but he did not. In 480 B.C. he returned to Athens and played an important role in the victory at Marathon. A few days later, at the Battle of Salamis, he rendered loyal service to none other than Themistocles, his political opponent.

Although Aristides was descended from a wealthy Athenian family, he died poor; so poor, in fact, that there wasn't enough money to pay for his burial.

It frequently happens that, like Aristides, "whoever shuns evil becomes a prey" (Isa. 59:15, NIV). But Christians have the consolation of knowing that God is aware of injustice, for Isaiah goes on to say, "the Lord looked and was displeased" (verse 15, NIV). While we should be "wise as serpents" (Matt. 10:16), let us never become cynical. Rather, let us keep on loving and doing all the good we can to those who may not like us.

71

*Kind and upright is the Eternal . . . , guiding humble souls aright, teaching humble souls his way. Ps. 25:8, 9, Moffatt.*

# Divine Guidance

Adoniram Judson, American Baptist missionary to Burma and the first missionary to leave American soil, felt God's call to mission service in the early 1800s. In February 1810 he dedicated his life to that end. Two years later he and his bride, Ann Hasseltine, sailed for Calcutta, India, arriving there on July 17 — the day before the outbreak of the War of 1812.

Relations between England and America had been strained for some time, so it was not surprising that the British East India Company ordered the couple to leave the country. With sad hearts they went to the island of Mauritius, south of India.

Four months later they returned to India (this time to Madras), intending to go on to Polo Penang, an island in the Malaca Straits, where they hoped to establish a mission. Once again the British East India Company ordered them out of India; this time the order was to leave immediately.

Because there were no ships bound for Polo Penang but one was going to Rangoon, Burma, the Judsons took passage on it. Burma was the last place in the world they would have chosen to go to, yet they felt that God was leading them there. They disembarked in Rangoon on July 13, 1813, and God began to open up the way for them to bring Christ to that country.

In spite of persecution, imprisonment, serious sickness, and the successive deaths of three wives, Judson worked on in the certain knowledge that God was guiding — and he continued to serve the people of Burma for the next 37 years. In spite of all the hardships he endured, he managed not only to learn Burmese well enough to preach in it, but to complete a translation of the Bible into that language, in 1834. Later he compiled a Burmese grammar as well as a Burmese dictionary.

The Lord blessed Judson's efforts with a rich harvest of souls. "Subsequent history," wrote his son Edward, years later, "had proved that the hand which led . . . [him] so strangely and sternly was the hand that never errs."

That same hand is ready to guide you and me, if we are humble and teachable.

*My people have been as lost sheep; their shepherds have caused them to stray. . . . All who found them have devoured them, and their adversaries said, "We are not guilty," because they have sinned against the Lord.*
*Jer. 50:6, 7, MLB.*

# Two Lost Sheep Found

The late Dr. P. W. Philpott, pastor of a church in Hamilton, Canada, used to tell how a stranger awakened him at 3:00 one morning and asked him to come and pray for a dying prostitute. He got up, dressed, and followed the stranger to the "red light district." There he found a young girl, still in her teens, dying. He studied her features for a moment to see if he could recognize her. He didn't.

"My name is Mary," she said. "You don't know me, but I know you. I called you because I was sure you would come and pray for me. You see, I know I'm going to die. The girls don't think so, but I know I am."

While Dr. Philpott thought of what to say, Mary asked him to read the parable of the lost sheep. After reading it he added the verse that says that the Good Shepherd gives His life for His sheep (see Luke 15:3-7; John 10:11).

As Dr. Philpott knelt and prayed, the other girls, sobbing, knelt around Mary's bed. When he finished, Mary said, "I'm glad the Good Shepherd found me before it was too late!"

Confident that Mary would recover, Dr. Philpott went home. When he returned the next morning, one of the girls came out crying and told him Mary had died.

Years later in another city, a woman came up to Dr. Philpott after a service and said, "You don't remember, but I was the girl who came out and told you Mary had died. But there was something I didn't tell you. The day the Good Shepherd brought Mary in on one shoulder, he brought me in on the other."

That was an interesting way to put it.

Society condemns harlots but often condones the men responsible for initiating and perpetuating harlotry. The Good Shepherd does not condone prostitution, but He looks beyond the sin and sees in these women and men souls to be saved. Shouldn't we do the same?

*You are the light of the world. A city on a hill cannot be hidden. . . . In the same way, let your light shine before men, that they may see your good deeds and praise your Father in heaven. Matt. 5:14-16, NIV.*

# Unwitting Witness

Many years ago a violent storm leveled a little church on the south coast of England. The congregation was too poor to replace it. One day a representative from the admiralty called on the pastor and asked him when his parishioners planned to rebuild the church.

"Probably never," replied the pastor. "The congregation is too poor."

"Well," said the government representative, "if you cannot rebuild it, the admiralty will have to. Your congregation may not realize it, but the spire of your church used to be one of the landmarks by which ships steered their course up the Channel. Since its disappearance we have had many enquiries about it."

Sometimes unconscious lifestyle, little unremembered deeds of kindness, and encouraging words spoken without premeditation can be vehicles through which the Holy Spirit reaches souls and engenders in them a desire to let Christ take control of their lives. Such acts are like the unwitting witness of that little church.

While my wife and I were missionaries in Boa Vista, capital of Roraima (then the Territory of Rio Branco), Brazil, a woman asked for Bible studies. Unbeknownst to me, she had a grown son who was mentally retarded. One day in the midst of a study he burst into the room in a state of undress, uttering gibberish. I was stunned; his mother was embarrassed and quickly ushered him out. I tried to appear unruffled, but I know I didn't succeed.

A few days later our term of service ended, and I never completed the studies with that woman. I lost track of her and considered my witness a failure. But apparently it wasn't. Four years later a fellow missionary brought word that she had accepted Christ! Thank God for that! My friend also said she claimed I was instrumental in her conversion, but I claim no credit for it.

Could it be that some of our witnessing is unwitting?

*A certain Samaritan, as he journeyed, came where . . . [the wounded man] was: and when he saw him, had compassion on him, and went to him, and bound up his wounds.*
*Luke 10:33, 34.*

# Unnamed Samaritans

One winter during the latter part of the eighteenth century, Johann Friedrich Oberlin, a pastor in Alsace, France, was traveling afoot through the mountains near Strasbourg, when he lost his way and fell into a snowdrift. He was rescued from almost certain death by a wagoner who happened by. After he revived, Oberlin offered his benefactor a reward. The man politely refused to accept anything.

"Well," said Oberlin, "at least tell me your name."

"All right," replied the stranger with a smile, "tell me the name of the good Samaritan."

"His name is not recorded," answered Oberlin.

"Then let me withhold mine," the stranger insisted.

Sinful human nature usually isn't so modest. It craves recognition, even when it turns down a reward. Jesus spoke in regard to this weakness in some of His discourses.

It was customary among the Jews to levy assessments on members of the community to provide for the necessities of the poor. These funds were augmented by freewill offerings. In addition to these, appeals for contributions were made from time to time in open-air meetings on the streets. It was on these latter occasions especially that people were tempted to contribute large sums in order to gain the adulation and praise of their fellowmen. Jesus pointed out that such giving violated the true spirit of charity.

This is one extreme, but there is danger in shifting to the opposite extreme—making a big fuss about not being recognized and thereby actually drawing attention to what we have done!

We do not know what the wagoner's reasons were for refusing to even give his name. From this distance it would appear that to have said who he was would have been the gracious thing to do. However, we must not judge his motives, for we do not know all the circumstances. One thing is certain, a Christian's motive for doing good is to bring glory to God, not himself.

*I, even I, am He that blotteth out your transgressions for My own sake, and I will not remember your sins. Isa. 43:25, NKJV.*

# Remembering to Forget

Time is a great healer. As it passes, things of lesser importance tend to fade into insignificance. The things that are hard to forget are usually those things that have injured our egos or our consciences. We all know people who never forgive and never forget. We also know people who forgive (or at least say they do), but never forget. But with God it is different. When our sins are confessed, pardoned, and given up, He treats us as if we had never sinned. The only way they can ever be revived is if we take them back (see Eze. 33:8-16).

Why anyone would want to take back his sins when God has put them out of His mind so completely that He treats us as if we had never sinned is a mystery. We may never understand how God does His part, but by faith we can accept the fact that He has the power to do this.

Clara Barton, the founder of the American Red Cross, was talking to a friend one day when her friend asked her if she remembered an especially cruel injury someone had inflicted on her years before. Miss Barton said she could not recall the incident.

"Surely you must remember," insisted her friend.

"No," replied Miss Barton, "I do not recall it, but I do distinctly remember forgetting it."

A mild rebuke? Probably. After all, how can one forget something one distinctly remembers forgetting? Paradoxical, is it not? It seems like a contradiction of terms, but actually it is not. Some things can be so painful, for instance, that one can no longer remember them.

Normally people have a hard time doing this. But in the spiritual realm we can do it when we become partakers of the divine nature. If we consent, God, who is a perfect forgetter, will impart to us this special ability so that we too can remember our sins no more. The reason is, of course, because Jesus has taken these sins upon Himself and they are no longer ours.

*Do not use any vow when you make a promise.
. . . Just say "Yes" or "No"—anything else you
say comes from the Evil One.
Matt. 5:34-37, TEV.*

MARCH
8

# Their Word Was as Good as an Oath

Our Quaker friends take this command of Jesus quite literally. Although we may think they take Christ's words too far—after all, He Himself answered under oath (Matt. 26:63, 64), and Paul repeatedly invoked God as witness that what he said was true (2 Cor. 1:23; 11:31; cf. 1 Thess. 5:27)—we honor them for their conscientiousness.

In the mid-1600s a group of Quakers was thrown into New Gate Prison in London for refusing to take a judicial oath. "The law demands that you swear that your statements are true," thundered the officers of the court, to which the Quakers replied, "Nay, a man's word is as binding as any oath can be." So to prison they went.

Conditions at the prison were so vile that one of the Quakers died within a few months. In 1662 a coroner's jury was sent to the prison to hold an inquest over the man's death and was so horrified by conditions that the panel wondered that more hadn't perished. A sheriff was sent to the prison with orders to transfer 30 of the Quakers to Bridewell prison to relieve the crowded condition of their cell at New Gate.

It was then that a strange thing happened. The porter, who had had occasion to observe the Quakers' behavior and was supposed to escort them to their new quarters, said, "You who are to go to Bridewell Prison know your way. Your word is trustworthy. There is no need for me to accompany you."

As the people of London gazed on the ragged, undernourished prisoners walking two by two through their streets, carrying their belongings on their backs, someone asked Thomas Elwood, the Quaker leader, why they didn't escape. His reply is memorable. Said he, "Because our word, which we have given, is our keeper."

We can all learn a lesson from these faithful, fearless Christians. May God help us to be so faithful to the promises we make that our word will be better than any kind of judicial oath.

**9**

*God said, "Take your son, your only son, Isaac, whom you love, and go to the region of Moriah. Sacrifice him there as a burnt offering on one of the mountains I will tell you about."*
Gen. 22:2, NIV.

# Is God First in Your Life?

Abraham must have blanched when he heard this awful command. Isaac was not His only son. He had Ishmael. But Isaac was uniquely born to be the "seed." We do not know how Abraham knew it was God's voice he heard; we only know he knew that God had given the command. The old man must have ached to talk things over with Sarah. But no, she would try to keep him from obeying.

The place designated for the sacrifice, Mount Moriah, was three days walking distance from Abraham's camp. His decision made, the old man rose up early in the morning and saddled an ass. Taking Isaac, two servants, and wood for the sacrifice, he trudged off on what must have been a melancholy journey. During those three days everything inside Abraham must have died—except his faith!

Upon arrival on Mount Moriah, Abraham and Isaac prepared an altar for the sacrifice. All the while Isaac asked heartbreaking questions. When he learned he was to be the sacrifice, he must have been horrified. Who wouldn't be? But he had learned to trust and obey his father, and above all, he had learned to trust and obey the God of his father. He believed God could restore him to life (see Heb. 11:17-19).

Obediently climbing up and laying himself on the altar, he awaited the stroke that would end his life. (Was this God's way of letting Abraham know the heartrending agony *He* would experience when on behalf of us all He delivered up His own beloved Son to the demands of justice?)

With trembling hands the old man unsheathed the knife and raised it above his head. As his hand began to descend, the angel of the covenant cried out, "Abraham, Abraham!"

"Here I am," he answered.

"Lay down the knife; don't hurt the lad in any way, . . . for [now] I know that God is first in your life" (Gen. 22:12, TLB).

It is unlikely that God will ever call upon you or me or anyone else to undergo the ordeal Abraham went through, but the question is: Is God first in your life, in my life?

*"This is the covenant I will make . . . ," declares the Lord. "I will put my law in their minds and write it on their hearts." Jer. 31:33, NIV.*

MARCH

10

# The New Covenant

When William Penn took up his duties as chief magistrate of the colony of Pennsylvania, he called a conference of the Indian chiefs of the region. At the appointed time Penn, accompanied by a few unarmed friends, all of whom were clad in the simple garb of the Quakers, arrived at the agreed-upon meeting place.

Speaking through a translator, Penn said words to this effect: "My friends, we have met on the broad pathway of good faith. We are all one flesh and one blood. Since we are brothers, neither of us will take advantage of the other. When disputes arise, we will settle them peaceably in council. Between us there will be nothing but openness and love."

The spokesman for the chiefs replied: "While the rivers run and the sun shines we will live in peace with the children of William Penn."

A record of the treaty was never made. Its terms were written, not on decaying parchment, but on the hearts of men. During the 70 years that the colony remained under the control of the Quakers, not a drop of blood was shed in war within the borders of Pennsylvania. The treaty written in the hearts of earnest, sincere men proved to be far more effective than any legal document, the terms of which the parties do not take to heart.

When God gave Israel His ten-commandment law, He wrote its precepts on stone. These principles served as a basis for the covenant, or agreement, He made with them. There is no question but that these commandments were "holy, just, and good," or that God could keep His part of the contract. But in less than 40 days the Israelites had broken their part of the bargain and worshiped the golden calf (see Ex. 32). Why? Because they failed to allow God to write the principles of His law in their hearts.

When we allow God to write His ten commandments in our hearts (that is, in our minds), we "delight to do [His] will" (Ps. 40:8). Why not let God write His law in your mind this morning?

*If we say that we have fellowship with him [God], and walk in darkness, we lie, and do not the truth: but if we walk in the light, as he is in the light, we have fellowship one with another, and the blood of Jesus Christ his Son cleanseth us from all sin. 1 John 1:6, 7.*

# Momentum in the Christian Life

We have all watched a ball roll along the ground and seen its direction and speed changed by a pebble. This phenomenon is known as Newton's first law of thermodynamics. According to this principle, "a body remains in a state of rest or of uniform motion in a straight line unless acted upon by an external force." In the case under consideration, the inertia of the pebble is the external force exerted on the ball.

The Bible sometimes uses walking to describe a person's way of life, whether good or bad. For example, Colossians 1:10 speaks of walking "worthy of the Lord" whereas Job 34:8 speaks of walking "with wicked men." When the momentum of our way of life increases, it is described as running. Thus Psalm 119:32 speaks of running in the way of God's commandments, and Isaiah 59:7 speaks of feet that run to do evil.

Conversion, as the Bible uses the term, literally means "a turning around." When a person is converted under the influence of the Holy Spirit, he turns from his evil ways and begins moving toward God. Implicit in this change of direction is the idea of *momentum*—the tendency to continue moving in a certain direction.

According to this analogy, if a person is moving toward God and falls under temptation, his progress is slowed, *not necessarily* stopped. In other words, he is not immediately "lost" only to be "saved" if he confesses and repents. But if a person *continues* to yield to temptation, at some point his progress slows and finally a retrograde motion sets in. If we conceive of the Christian life as an upward climb, what is this but backsliding?

But the analogy need not end this way. If, instead of being overcome, we overcome temptation by God's grace, our heavenward momentum actually increases. May this be your experience as you walk in the light of Christ's presence!

*Remember this: whoever turns a sinner back from his wrong way will save that sinner's soul from death and bring about the forgiveness of many sins. James 5:20, TEV.*

MARCH

12

# Saving a Soul From Death

One evening in the fall of 1989, not long after our 4-year-old granddaughter, Monica, her 6-year-old sister, Elizabeth, and their parents came to live with us, the girls were playing quietly in their room—perhaps too quietly. Suddenly I heard Elizabeth shout, "Come quick! Monica is about to fall off the roof!" (She meant the window.) I was reading in bed when I heard the commotion and jumped up to look out our bedroom window onto the only roof she could possibly be referring to. I saw nothing to alarm me.

However, Elizabeth kept screaming, "Come quick! Come quick! She's about to fall!" I then rushed down the hall to the girls' bedroom on the second floor. Tore, their dad, who had been studying in his bedroom across the hall from them, got there first. But I arrived in time to see Monica clinging to the window sill by her fingertips and Elizabeth hanging on to her arms for dear life.

In no time Tore grabbed Monica and pulled her to safety. Drained of energy, he sat on their bed with his face buried in his hands. When we had all calmed down, we knelt and thanked God for sparing Monica—and for giving Elizabeth the presence of mind to hang on.

How did it happen? The girls had been playing at the window sill and had unlatched the screen. Then, leaning out the window, Monica lost her balance and began to fall. Elizabeth managed to grab her arms and held on until her father ran in and rescued her. Had Elizabeth not helped her sister, it is quite possible, even probable, we would not have Monica with us today. She would almost certainly have been impaled on some jagged nails that were sticking up from some old railroad ties on the ground directly below.

Most people show great concern for someone whose physical life is in jeopardy. Few, however, show as much concern when it comes to saving someone in danger of losing eternal life. But those who succeed in saving such a soul from death also "bring about the forgiveness of many sins"—the sins of the soul saved.

*[God] commanded the clouds above and opened the doors of Heaven, and He rained down upon them manna to eat and gave them Heaven's grain. Ps. 78:23, 24, Amplified.*

# Bread of Heaven

In early 1931 a region in north China where a mission station had been established was experiencing severe famine because of a drought. The missionaries had fed many of the destitute Chinese from their own food supplies, but the time came when they had nothing left even for themselves. In the crisis that followed they tried to assure their Chinese friends that the God of heaven was a prayer-hearing and a prayer-answering God. But they did more than merely assure. They invited the Chinese to join them in prayer each afternoon.

On the fourth day after these seasons of intercession began, someone interrupted the meeting by calling attention to something unusual going on outside. When the people went out, they saw a very dark cloud far to the north. It was coming their way. As it passed overhead, it began to rain heavily—but not ordinary rain! What fell were millions upon millions of dark seeds—a kind of grain. These proved to be edible, and the supply that fell was sufficient to tide the people over until the harvest.

Later the missionaries learned that a violent storm in Mongolia had wrecked some granaries where such seeds were stored. These seeds had been carried some 1,500 miles and dropped in the very district where prayer was being offered.

Was this a miracle or just a coincidence? Was this an answer to prayer or "just one of those things"? I happen to believe it was a miracle performed in answer to prayer—even though it may have a natural explanation! God is sovereign. He is not bound to work His wonders in the ways that man prescribes.

Although something occurring in the physical world that deviates from the known laws of nature is called a miracle, it is not the greatest of miracles. The greatest of miracles is the transformation that takes place when God turns a vile sinner into a saint. This is a miracle you and I can let happen.

*The angel of the Lord said to Satan, "May the Lord condemn you, Satan! . . . This man is like a stick snatched from the fire." Zech. 3:2, TEV.*

MARCH

14

# A Brand From the Burning

Samuel Wesley, the father of John and Charles Wesley, the founders of Methodism, was rector of Epworth Parish in Lincolnshire from 1697 to 1729. The two boys were born in the Epworth parsonage in 1703 and 1707, respectively. In 1709, when John was 6, the rectory and everything in it burned to the ground. The Wesleys had many children. All were taken to safety except John. (Charles, incidentally, was carried out by his nurse.)

Little John was apparently overlooked until the roof was about to collapse and he was heard crying. His father ran to the stairs, but they were so nearly consumed that they could not bear his weight. In an agony of despair he dropped to his knees and pleaded with God to save his son. God heard that prayer!

As his father prayed, John climbed up on top of a chest of drawers where some of the neighbors could see him. One brave man hoisted on the shoulders of another pulled the boy through the window just before the roof came crashing down. This experience so impressed itself on John's mind that years later he wrote these words under a portrait of himself: "Is not this a brand picked out of the burning?"—a paraphrase of our text.

The background to Zechariah's words is the return of the Jews from the Babylonian captivity. Both the visible and invisible forces of good and evil were struggling for supremacy. In 538 B.C. Cyrus had issued a decree permitting the Jews to return to their homeland and rebuild their Temple. But Satan opposed it through an edict forbidding any restoration of Jerusalem or the Temple.

In the vision of Zechariah 3, Joshua the high priest represents God's penitent people whom Satan opposes with his accusations. He points to their former sins as the reason they should not be restored to divine favor. But these returning Jews had repented of their sins, and therefore, God could rebuke Satan and rescue them as brands from the fire.

In a sense, each one of us who repents and accepts salvation is a brand plucked from the burning.

*The Lord is our defence; and the Holy One of Israel is our king. Ps. 89:18.*

# We Have a King

In the early days of August 1557 an army of Spaniards under Emmanuel Philibert of Savoy invaded France. They besieged the little town of St. Quentin, where Admiral Gaspard II de Coligny had taken refuge with his army. After weeks of resistance, the ramparts of the French army were in a shambles, fever and famine had decimated the ranks of the defenders, and treason was in the air.

One day the Spaniards shot an arrow into the city with a message attached. It promised that if Coligny would only surrender the city and his army and pledge allegiance to Philip II of Spain, the lives and property of the defenders would be spared.

Coligny read the message and, without a moment's hesitation, rejected its terms. Taking a piece of parchment, he wrote his answer, tied it to a javelin, and hurled it into the enemy lines. His reply consisted of two Latin words: "*Regem habemus*" ("We have a king"). He referred to Henry II of France. It takes courage to be loyal.

A couple of weeks after I had been liberated from Japanese internment, I decided to go down to the fighting front. Fierce battles were still raging in Manila, south of the Pasig River, so I had to be careful as I went down Rizal Avenue. I was stopped by some GIs within a block of Jones Bridge. Across the river I could see the top of the post office building, which was being shelled with mortars and raked by machine-gun fire.

Suddenly I saw a Japanese soldier calmly climb a metal scaffolding on top of the building and tie a Japanese flag to a metal post—in defiance of the enemy and in the face of almost certain death! That, to me, was loyalty. (Incidentally, he made it down unscathed, but I doubt he survived the battle.)

We too have a King. Are we as steadfastly faithful to Him as we are to earthly governments? The Bible commands Christians to be loyal to "the powers that be" (Rom. 13:1). We should be the best of citizens, but our supreme loyalty should be to the "King of kings, and Lord of lords."

*You have heard that it was said, "An eye for an eye and a tooth for a tooth." But I tell you not to resist an evil person. But whoever slaps you on your right cheek, turn the other to him also. If anyone wants to sue you and take away your tunic, let him have your cloak also.*
*Matt. 5:38-40, NKJV.*

# Gain Through Loss

Around the turn of the twentieth century some of the great powers of Europe attempted to partition China into zones of influence. These efforts were deeply resented by the Chinese. Eventually, they sparked a popular movement to drive out the "foreign devils," called the boxer Rebellion. This uprising, started by a secret society called the Righteous and Harmonious Fists, began in Shandong province and spread to the northeast of the country. From January to August 1900, mission compounds were besieged and frequently looted. Scores of missionaries and thousands of Chinese Christians lost their lives at the hands of angry mobs. In order to stop the bloodshed, the great powers intervened militarily. The uprising was quelled, peace was restored, and reparations were exacted from an embittered Chinese government.

During the rioting a hospital belonging to the China Inland Mission and administered by Dr. Frank A. Keller was looted by the rebels, with great loss. After the uprising, Keller, a young man, felt that the mission should be indemnified for damages. But before taking action he decided to seek counsel from Hudson Taylor, the aged founder of the mission. He arrived at Taylor's home while the old missionary was engaged in prayer— *for him!* While waiting to speak to Taylor, Keller was impressed that the best course to follow was to waive all claims to indemnity.

When Keller returned to his mission station, he informed the local mandarin of his decision. His Christian attitude so impressed this government official that he and Keller became fast friends. Subsequently, this mandarin was instrumental in opening up Hunan province to Christian missions.

Instead of demanding our rights when we suffer injury or loss, "let us pursue the things which make for peace" (Rom. 14:19, NKJV). Such an attitude always turns out to our eternal advantage—and sometimes to our temporal advantage as well.

*I will set a sign among them, and I will send those that escape of them unto the nations . . . to the isles afar off, that have not heard my fame, neither have seen my glory; and they shall declare my glory among the Gentiles. Isa. 66:19.*

# The Emerald Isle

William Drennan, in his poem "Erin," was the first to call Ireland the Emerald Isle. Christianity was first introduced into Ireland by Palladius around A.D. 431, but it was Patrick, his successor, who led the Irish to convert to Christianity. Ancient records indicate that Patrick many have been an observer of the seventh-day Sabbath and that he believed in the second coming of Christ.

Although several centuries later the Irish converted to Roman Catholicism, the original form of Christianity they espoused under Patrick was far closer to the teachings of Jesus and His apostles than that which prevailed elsewhere in Christendom at the time. During the Dark Ages these Celtic Christians preserved the light of truth and civilization largely lost in other parts of Europe.

From their centers of learning the Irish Christians sent forth missionaries to Europe and other parts of the world, thus fulfilling Isaiah's prophecy mentioned in our verse. For instance, Columba, the great missionary to Scotland, began the evangelization of that land in 563. Later he founded a school for training missionaries on the island of Iona. Columbanus, who went to France as a missionary about 585, founded an abbey at Luxeuil.

The Irish have strong family ties. Although many of them have emigrated to America and other parts of the world, the celebration of St. Patrick's Day binds them together. When my family and I were in a Japanese internment camp, Father Robert Sheridan, the camp's Roman Catholic priest, urged anyone with Irish blood to "wear the green" on St. Patrick's Day. I asked my father if we had any Irish in us. He said his grandmother came from Belfast. Later research showed it was Belfast, Maine, not Belfast, Northern Ireland, which is Protestant.

One of the admirable qualities of the Irish is their tenacity in the face of adversity. Even if we do not have Irish ancestors, we can all emulate their admirable spirit in the ongoing conflict between the forces of good and evil.

*When they say to you, "Seek those who are mediums [channelers] and wizards, who whisper and mutter," should not a people seek their God? Should they seek the dead on behalf of the living? To the law and the testimony! If they do not speak according to this word, it is because there is no light in them.*
*Isa. 8:19, 20, NKJV.*

# Our Spiritual "Metal Detector"

Anyone who has done any traveling by plane in the past few years has had to pass through a metal detector before boarding the plane. The most thorough search my wife, our youngest daughter, and I have ever had to go through was at the Manila airport during the Gulf war. We had to be at the air terminal four hours before flight time and, in addition to three baggage inspections, were each subjected to two body searches. We didn't complain.

We usually think of metal detectors that show up concealed weapons as a modern concept. They are not. While we were living in Thailand we visited the ancient capital of Ayutthaya, not far from Bangkok. We learned that centuries ago the royal palaces had metal detectors—not the sophisticated metal detectors we have today, but they were good enough for that age. The palace gates were made of lodestone, a natural magnet. If a would-be assassin tried to come through such a gate with a concealed weapon, the magnetite would pull on the hidden weapon like an invisible hand. Startled, the killer would involuntarily reach for his knife, and trained guards, watching every movement of palace visitors, would seize and dispatch him before he could do the royal family any harm.

The great "metal detector" in the spiritual realm is the ten-commandment law that God wrote on tables of stone with His own finger. The "testimony" our verse talks about is that which God inspired His prophets to write: in other words, the Bible.

The finite human mind is incapable of detecting all error. This is especially true when it comes to spirit phenomena. Spirit entities exist in a state normally invisible to human eyes. This means that if they are evil they possess incalculable powers to deceive. Our only hope in detecting them is to compare their teachings, not their appearance (see 2 Cor. 11:14, 15), with the Word of God, the "metal detector" of error.

*[God] the Father did not spare his own Son, but gave him up for us all; and with this gift how can he fail to lavish upon us all he has to give? Rom. 8:32, NEB.*

# What Eternal Life Cost

One summer day in 1937 John Griffith, controller of a railroad drawbridge across the Mississippi, took Greg, his 8-year-old son with him to work. About noon John raised the bridge to let some ships pass while he and Greg ate their lunch on the observation deck. At 1:07 p.m. John heard the distant whistle of the *Memphis Express.* He had just reached for the master lever to lower the bridge for the train when he looked around for Greg. What he saw made his heart freeze. Greg had slipped and fallen into the massive gears that operated the bridge. His left leg was caught in the cogs of the two main gears!

With lightning speed John's mind searched for options. There were only two: sacrifice his son and spare the 400 passengers, or sacrifice the 400 passengers and spare his son. John knew which alternative he would have to choose. Burying his face in his left arm, he threw the master switch with his right hand. The bridge lowered into place, and the train sped safely across, but Greg lost his life.

When it came to the human race, God faced the same terrible alternatives: sacrifice His Son and spare the human race, or sacrifice the human race and spare His Son. He chose the former.

One of the most difficult duties of a pastor is to visit parishioners who have just lost a son or a daughter. During World War II a minister went to visit a couple who had just been notified their only son had been killed in action. When the pastor reached the home the father was pacing up and down the floor, asking again and again, "Where was God when my son was killed?"

"The same place He was when His Son was killed," the pastor answered.

The reply is ingenious, but it really does not answer the father's question. We seldom know why God permits one person to die and spares another, but one thing is certain: He who spared not His Son to save us "does not afflict willingly, nor grieve the children of men" (Lam. 3:33, NKJV; cf. Isa. 63:9).

# Risking Life for Others

Our verse is taken from the song of Deborah and Barak, after the defeat of Sisera. Sisera, you will recall, was the commander of a Canaanite army that had oppressed Israel for 20 years. He was killed by Jael, a courageous woman, after the battle. In the encounter that led to Sisera's defeat, the soldiers of Zebulun and Naphtali played a conspicuous part, risking their lives for the good of others.

While the men of these two tribes laid their lives on the line to liberate their fellow Israelites, they made no demand for recognition. God, however, saw fit to make honorable mention of their selfless and heroic deed in His Word.

One day many years ago, a woman started to cross a New York City street. She became confused and stepped directly into the path of an oncoming streetcar. The people who happened to be watching saw a tragedy in the making, but they were too horrified to act. One man, however, had the presence of mind to do what needed to be done. Powerfully built, he rushed forward and, at the risk of his life, picked the woman up bodily and whisked her to safety.

A police officer who witnessed the courageous act said to the hero, "I have to report this incident, sir, and I would like to recommend your name for valor and quick thinking."

"There's no need to mention my name," said the stranger.

"But I'll have to put down something," insisted the policeman.

"Then simply put down that a Black man did it." The hero smiled and disappeared into the crowd.

Later it was established that the Black man was Dr. Robert R. Moton, president of Tuskegee Institute. (This school, to which Dr. Moton had dedicated his life, was founded by Booker T. Washington and was one of the first colleges to provide adequate education for Black Americans.)

God does not usually ask us to risk our physical lives for others, but He does ask us to dedicate our lives to Him in service to others.

*In all things you yourself must be an example of good behavior. Titus 2:7, TEV.*

# The Power of Example

James H. McConkey tells how late one winter the ice on the river near his boyhood home began breaking up unexpectedly early. Freshets began to pile up large chunks of ice, damming sections of the river. A few miles from the McConkey home an enormous ice gorge isolated 11 men, women, and children. Word spread quickly that these people were doomed by the rising waters. Spectators gathered from every direction.

James's older brother heard about the perilous plight of these unfortunate people and was moved to action. Stuffing a $50 bill in his pocket, he hurried to the place where the tragedy was about to occur.

When he arrived at the scene, scores of people were standing around on the riverbank watching—doing nothing! Stepping up to a group of men, McConkey offered to give any one of them $50 to rescue the imperiled families. Not a man stirred.

Finally McConkey sent a boy to a store nearby to buy a rope. When he returned, McConkey secured one end of the rope around his waist, then challenged all who had the courage to tie themselves to the line and go with him to the rescue. By this time the situation was extremely critical. Now, however, without hesitation, four men joined him, securing themselves to the rope. With McConkey taking the lead, they picked their way over the slippery ice and brought every man, woman, and child to safety.

When McConkey offered money, the bystanders were not willing to risk their lives, but when he laid his own life on the line and challenged others by his example, he found people willing to follow. Courage is contagious!

In the moral realm the same is true. The natural human tendency is to follow "a multitude to do evil" (Ex. 23:2), but when one person shows courage and stands up for principle, others are inspired to follow.

Today you may find yourself in a situation that calls for standing up for what is right. Have the courage to show your convictions—and others will be inspired to follow your example!

*As [Jesus] was speaking, the Jewish leaders and Pharisees brought a woman caught in adultery and placed her out in front of the staring crowd. "Teacher," they said to Jesus, "this woman was caught in the very act of adultery. Moses' law says to kill her. What about it?"*
*John 8:3-5, TLB.*

# The Ex-adulteress

Nowhere in the Bible is the application of a double standard more clearly shown than in the case of the woman taken in adultery. If this woman had been caught in the very act, her partner must have been caught too, yet apparently he was allowed to get away scot-free! And this in spite of the fact that the very law to which Jesus' enemies appealed clearly specified that both parties were to be stoned to death (see Deut. 22:22).

Can you imagine the embarrassment of this poor woman at being thrust in front of the staring crowd while her accusers kept demanding that Jesus answer them? But Jesus said nothing. He simply stooped down and began to write. After a bit He stood up and said, "Let the sinless one among you throw the first stone at her" (John 8:7, MLB).

Then He stooped again and wrote some more—their sins. As He did so, the woman's accusers silently slipped away until only she and Jesus were left. It was then that Jesus uttered those wonderful words, "Neither do I condemn thee: go, and sin no more" (verse 11).

Ellen G. White gives us a fascinating sequel to this story. She says: "This penitent woman became one of the firmest friends of Jesus. She repaid his forgiveness and compassion with a self-sacrificing love and worship. Afterward, when she stood sorrow-stricken at the foot of the cross, and saw the dying agony on the face of her Lord, and heard His bitter cry, her soul was pierced afresh" (*Signs of the Times*, Oct. 23, 1879).

Because Mary Magdalene was at the cross and watched Jesus die (Matt. 27:56), and formerly she had been an unchaste woman (see *The Desire of Ages*, p. 566), some have conjectured that she and the woman taken in adultery were one and the same person—and they may be right! But the important point is that regardless of the sin, there is hope—if sinners repent, are converted, and let the Lord deliver them from their sinful ways.

**23**

*Bear one another's burdens, and so fulfil the law of Christ. Gal. 6:2, RSV.*

# Helping One Another

Birds and animals can teach us many lessons. Job 12:7 says: "Ask now the beasts, and they shall teach thee; and the fowls of the air, and they shall tell thee."

Every spring and fall I see geese flying in V-formation over our home in Idaho. Perhaps you have seen geese fly this way also. If you watch them long enough, you may notice that at certain intervals the lead bird will drop off and fly at one end of the formation and another will move up to take his place.

Scientists have discovered that geese fly in this particular configuration because, energy-wise, it is much more efficient than flying spread out. It has been found that the flapping of the wings of the lead goose, followed by similar action by the birds behind him, creates an uplift of air that gives an extra boost to those farther back in the formation. It has been estimated that by flying in this particular pattern the geese expend up to 60 percent less energy than they would otherwise.

The point position is the most energy-consuming because of wind resistance, so the geese rotate this position every few minutes. The easiest flying is experienced by the rear sections of the formation. It has also been observed that the stronger birds permit the young, the weak, and the older birds to occupy these advantageous positions.

Christians should "uplift" one another with words of encouragement and with prayers for those less strong, whether their weakness is in the physical, mental, social, or spiritual realm.

The application of this principle in personal relationships —in the home, in the community, in the church, in the nation, in the world—would solve many of humanity's problems. Human solutions are not the answer. Only the grace of Christ working in us as individuals can make the application of this principle succeed.

As Christians we need to look around us and discover who within our ambit of life is less fortunate than we are and apply this lesson from the birds of the heavens.

*[Elijah] came and sat down under a juniper tree: and he requested for himself that he might die; and said, It is enough; now, O Lord, take away my life. 1 Kings 19:4.*

MARCH

24

# Beyond Discouragement

Have you ever felt so discouraged you reckoned life wasn't worth living? Well, if you have, you're not alone. In our verse for meditation, that mighty servant of God, Elijah, came to the point of deciding that life wasn't worth living.

After his mountaintop experience on Carmel, during which he was outnumbered by hundreds of false prophets, Elijah ran ahead of Ahab's chariot some 20 miles in the pelting rain, until they reached the royal palace at Jezreel. Instead of inviting his servant in out of the rain, the callous king left him standing outside the city gate.

It was then that something happened to Elijah. He began feeling sorry for himself. Here he was, sopping wet, hungry, and miserable, and above all, his efforts unappreciated. Sound familiar?

At this critical moment Satan instigated wicked queen Jezebel to send a messenger with word that by the next day Elijah would be a dead man. Cold and famished, his blood sugar doubtless low, Elijah forgot who had stood by him on Mount Carmel. He took to his heels. When he reached Beersheba he left his servant and went a day's journey into the wilderness and begged God to let him die. Instead, God sent an angel with food and water to show him He cared. Please notice that God did not permit His servant to be tried above what he was able to bear.

Like Elijah, most of us have times when we feel utterly discouraged. It seems that our trials are more than we can bear. It is hard to believe that God is the kind benefactor we had always believed Him to be. At such times death almost seems preferable to life, and many of us lose our hold on God. *But we shouldn't! Listen!*

God will not permit you to be tried above what you are able to bear any more than He did Elijah. Hidden from view, His angels are nearby, seeking to save you from yourself (1 Kings 19:5-7). Let them do the work they have been commissioned to do.

*You were not redeemed with perishable things like silver or gold from your futile way of life inherited from your forefathers, but with precious blood, as of a lamb unblemished and spotless, the blood of Christ.*
*1 Peter 1:18, 19, NASB.*

# Precious Blood

Several years ago the International News Service published an interesting story about a Mrs. Rose L. McMullin. This woman had been traveling back and forth across America, donating blood everywhere she went. At the time the story was run she had just arrived in New York City to give blood to a 25-year-old mother. Not long before that she had been in Salt Lake City, where she had given a transfusion. At the time of the news release she had supplied more than 400 blood transfusions in 40 states!

Mrs. McMullin has been recognized as a phenomenon by the medical world. She is one of those very rare individuals whose blood contains a factor that resists *Staphylococcus aureus,* a bacterium that can cause serious complications when it enters the bloodstream. In addition, she is also one of those rare individuals whose body quickly recoups from blood loss, so she could give two transfusions in succession with a brief rest in between.

As much as we can marvel at the qualities of Mrs. McMullin's blood, it could never accomplish what the blood of Jesus Christ has done for us. His "blood . . . cleanses us from all sin" (1 John 1:7, NKJV). But how can blood cleanse from sin? We usually think of blood as soiling things, not cleansing them.

The reason is because in the Bible blood symbolizes life. Leviticus 17:14 declares: "The blood . . . represents the life" (Amplified). But blood does not merely stand for the vital life force present in all living things, it also represents the life lived. This is an important point often overlooked by theologians.

Jesus lived a sinless life, and His blood, representing both His life force and the life He lived, stands in place of our sinful lives. It is in this sense that His "blood . . . cleanses us from all sin."

But to be effective, you and I must, by faith, accept His blood shed on our behalf. When we do this, we are not only *forgiven* every sin, but are *given* power to overcome sin.

*"Martha, Martha," the Lord answered, "you are worried and harassed about putting on a meal with a whole lot of courses. One will do perfectly well. Mary has chosen the best dish, and it is not going to be taken away from her."*
*Luke 10:41, 42, Barclay.*

# The Worried Woman

Imagine the scene with me. It took place in one of the better-off homes of Bethany, where Mary and Martha and their brother, Lazarus, lived. The fact that they had to prepare a meal after their guest arrived seems to suggest that Jesus had arrived at their home unannounced. From this we can probably infer that He had been invited to drop in at any time.

After welcoming Jesus (verse 39), Martha began to busy herself preparing a sumptuous meal—the "many things" (Greek, *polla*) about which she was worried. Mary is next mentioned. The Greek word *kai*, usually translated "and," in this context can be rendered "also." This latter usage would imply that Mary at first helped her sister while at the same time listening to Jesus, but that eventually she stopped helping and sat down, captivated by Jesus' words.

Finally, in exasperation Martha interrupted, asking (perhaps demanding) that Jesus order Mary to come back and help prepare the multicourse meal. It is interesting to note that Jesus did not ignore the importance of the meal. However, Jesus suggested that only one thing was necessary. And Jesus went right on and identified the instruction He was imparting to Mary as the best; this, He said, would not be taken from her. Mary had her priorities straight.

Just as physical food is important for the maintenance of physical life, so spiritual nourishment is important for maintaining spiritual life. *No, the latter is more important!* Job understood this when he declared: "I have esteemed the words of his mouth more than my necessary food" (Job 23:12). The world would be a better place if more people worried less about physical food and were more concerned about spiritual nourishment.

# 27

*I looked on my right hand, and beheld, but there was no man that would know me: refuge failed me; no man cared for my soul.*
**Ps. 142:4.**

# A Burden for Souls

In Hebrew the expression rendered "my soul" often simply means "me." That's what it means here. However, in some instances, such as James 5:20, soul refers to people in need of salvation. For the present let us think of the soul in this latter sense. How much concern do you and I have for the salvation of those around us?

When renowned American evangelist Dwight L. Moody was a young teenager, he got a job as a clerk in his uncle's shoe store. A few weeks before this he had enrolled in a Sunday school class in which a Mr. Edward Kimball was the teacher. Mr. Kimball was not just an ordinary Sunday school teacher; he was concerned about the spiritual welfare of his students. One day he felt impressed to appeal to young Moody to commit his life to Christ.

On April 21, 1855, Mr. Kimball went to the store where Moody worked and asked to see him. He found the young clerk at the back of the store, wrapping shoes in paper and putting them on shelves. Laying his hand on Dwight's shoulder, he said, "Dwight, I'm concerned about you." His lips trembled and he could not go on. When he regained his composure he told Moody about Christ's love for him and appealed for him to respond to that love.

After his teacher had left, Moody said to himself, "Isn't this strange? Here is a man who has only known me for a short time and yet he cares for my soul. I guess it's time I got concerned about it myself." Going down to the basement, he knelt behind some boxes and committed his life to Christ. His life took a new direction. The rest is history. Moody became one of the greatest soul winners of his generation.

What if Mr. Kimball had not cared for souls?

All about us are people in need of Christ. How concerned are you and I about their salvation? If the Holy Spirit should impress you today to speak to someone about being saved, would He find that you cared?

*We have many parts in the one body, and all these parts have different functions. In the same way, though we are many, we are one body in union with Christ. Romans 12:4, 5, TEV.*

# Unity in Diversity

The Christian hymn "Blest Be the Tie That Binds," often sung at partings, was written by John Fawcett, a Baptist minister of a small congregation in England. In 1772, after serving as pastor for seven years, he was called to serve as pastor to a large church in London. The day after preaching his farewell sermon his household goods were loaded onto a wagon. Many of his parishioners came to see him off. Some of them, weeping, expressed sorrow at his departure and pleaded for him to stay.

He was so moved by their love that he had his goods off-loaded and sent word to the big city church that he had changed his mind. He remained with his little church for the rest of his life. Soon after his decision to stay he wrote the hymn for which he is noted. Christ's love, of course, as our verse tells us, is the tie that binds.

Jesus' disciples often showed a lack of unity as they selfishly strove to occupy the highest positions in His coming kingdom. This spirit of status-seeking dominated them right up to the final day before He was crucified. It was because of this division-causing attitude that, just before they left the upper room to go to Gethsemane, Jesus prayed for unity—not only unity among His disciples, but among those who would believe on Him through their witness. And that includes you and me, doesn't it? (See John 17:20, 21.)

Unity is not the same thing as uniformity. God does not expect every Christian to speak and act in exactly the same way as every other Christian. Diversity is not only permissible among Christians, it is desirable. However, there should be agreement with respect to fundamental beliefs—and it goes without saying, these beliefs must be Bible-based. Richard Baxter, English preacher, put it this way: "In necessary things, unity; in doubtful things, liberty; in all things, charity."

In the judgment the great question you and I will be asked will not be "What did you believe?" important as this is, but "How did you treat others?"

# 29

*[Jesus] said, Of a truth I say unto you, that this poor widow hath cast in more than they all. Luke 21:3.*

# How God Estimates Your Offerings

The incident of the widow casting in two mites probably occurred Tuesday afternoon of Passion Week. Imagine the scene: All morning long, first the Pharisees and Herodians, then the Sadducees, and finally the scribes had been plying Jesus with tricky questions, doing everything they could to trip Him up. Now it is early afternoon, and Jesus is "standing opposite the Temple treasury" (Mark 12:41, NEB) teaching the multitude. Presently, "He looked up and saw the rich people dropping their gifts into the chest of the temple treasury" (Luke 21:1, NEB). With what fanfare some of them made their contributions!

In another context the Bible tells us that when some people of Christ's day did an "act of charity," they announced it "with a flourish of trumpets . . . to win admiration from men" (Matt. 6:2, NEB). So it is possible that some of the rich people referred to in the story of the widow actually drew attention to their generosity by having a trumpet blown before them. Note that the context immediately preceding the widow's act tells us that Jesus warned His audience against those "who eat up the property of widows, while they say long prayers for appearance sake" (Mark 12:40, NEB). These people were hypocrites.

People today don't have trumpets blown to attract attention to their generous contribution to the church—at least, not in the same way. And yet we have all heard the expression "blowing one's own horn." Sometimes horn-blowing is done when we overprotest that we do not want to draw attention to our contribution, *all the while attracting the very attention our subconscious mind craves, by the big fuss we are making!* Think about it.

But here is another point to consider: How could Jesus say that the widow who "threw in [only] two mites"—the smallest coin in circulation at the time—"cast in more than they all" (verse 42)? Have you ever considered that because of the widow's selfless example, many people since Jesus' day have contributed to God's cause with greater faithfulness and in the same modest spirit? Could it be that it was in this way that she "cast in more than they all"?

*The blood shall be a sign for you, upon the houses where you are; and when I see the blood, I will pass over you, and no plague shall fall upon you to destroy you. Ex. 12:13, RSV.*

MARCH
30

# There's Power in the Blood

During the sixteenth century the Dutch revolted against Philip II of Spain, who, by one of those quirks of succession, had also become king of the Netherlands. In an effort to regain control of the Low Countries, Philip sent the infamous Duke of Alva with an army to crush the Hollanders.

The city of Rotterdam held out for a time, but finally capitulated. The victorious soldiers went from house to house, massacring their occupants without regard to age or sex. In one instance several families had taken refuge in one home and were praying for deliverance, all the while wondering how they could cooperate with God to save their lives.

Suddenly one of the young men had an idea. The owner of the house had a goat. Quickly he fetched the animal, slit its throat, and swept the blood under the front door with a broom. From there it trickled down the steps and into the street.

When the soldiers reached that particular house, their commanding officer, seeing the blood, said, "Our men have already been here. Let us go to the next house."

Have you ever wondered how the blood of Jesus Christ saves us today? It is because, whereas the "wages of sin is death" (Rom. 6:23), "blood . . . makes atonement, because it is the life" (Lev. 17:11, TLB).

The Hebrew word *nephesh*, here rendered "life," means not only life present in all living things—the universal life principle—but *the life lived*. Christ gave up His life. In so doing, He paid the wages of sin in our stead. But it was because He had lived a sinless life that His life could be substituted for our sinful lives. This life He will live out in us, if we will let Him.

The wonderful thing about the plan of redemption is that we do not need to understand all its intricacies. The important thing is to "take the cup of salvation" (Ps. 116:13) and allow Christ to live out His life within us.

*Since I, the Lord and Teacher, have washed your feet, you ought to wash each other's feet. I have given you an example to follow: do as I have done to you. John 13:14, 15, TLB.*

# Servant of Servants

One of the titles the Roman pontiff has taken to himself is that of "servant of servants." In harmony with this title, each year the pope washes the feet of 12 common priests. They are brought from the Italian capital into Saint Peter's Basilica for this rite.

Some time ago I edited a book entitled *Missions: A Two-way Street*, by Jon Dybdahl. In the book the author tells of a taboo observed among the Thais that may seem strange to some of us. In the West certain bodily functions are never mentioned in polite company. Not so in Thailand. The Thais speak unashamedly of these matters, yet they regard the feet as unmentionable appendages. To point at someone with one's foot is a marked sign of disrespect.

Dybdahl learned the hard way how seriously the Thais take this taboo. One day he sat in a courtroom, one ankle resting on the knee of the other leg, waving his size 13 shoe at no one in particular. The bailiff told him in no uncertain terms to keep his feet flat on the floor!

Some time later Dybdahl met a Buddhist monk who was making cement reliefs in his monastery. The reliefs depicted significant incidents in the world's great religions. Would Dybdahl suggest a motif that best represented Christianity? After reflecting on the request, Dybdahl suggested the foot-washing scene preceding the Last Supper.

"Do you mean that Jesus washed the feet of His disciples?" the monk inquired in astonishment.

"Yes," Dybdahl replied simply.

After a few moments the monk responded with reverent awe, "I think I now understand what Christianity is all about. I will portray Jesus washing the feet of His disciples."

Did this realization lead the monk to accept Christ? Dybdahl didn't know. But the important question for us is Shouldn't you and I follow more faithfully the example of humility manifested by the original Servant of servants?

*Peter said unto [Jesus], Although all shall be offended, yet will not I. And Jesus saith unto him, Verily I say unto thee, That this day, even in this night, before the cock crow twice, thou shalt deny me thrice. But [Peter] spake the more vehemently, If I should die with thee, I will not deny thee in any wise. Mark 14:29-31.*

# Don't Be Cocksure

The expression "cocksure" has been defined as "given to or marked by overconfidence." Some believe it is derived from Peter's overconfident boast that he would never deny his Lord, even when Jesus prophesied that before the cock crowed twice Peter would deny Him three times. However, others dispute this origin.

In his second vehement assertion, Peter stated that he was willing to follow Christ not only to prison but also to death—*and he meant it!* (See Mark 14:46, 47; Luke 22:49, 50.)

He showed that he was in earnest by drawing his sword when the disciples were vastly outnumbered by the mob that came to arrest Jesus. Peter struck off the ear of Malchus, the high priest's servant. Yet, moments later, this "brave" man turned and fled for his life. Later that night he denied his Lord three times, the last time with cursing and swearing. Why this sudden, unexpected change?

The reason is quite simple. In spite of the fact that Jesus had repeatedly warned His disciples that He would be betrayed, condemned, and crucified, they refused to believe it would happen. They were steeped in Jewish misinterpretations of the Messianic prophecies of the Old Testament that depicted the Messiah setting up a glorious kingdom. But they overlooked the prophecies that showed that before the glorious kingdom, the Messiah would come as a suffering servant.

So when Jesus, who had never before allowed Himself to be arrested, let the mob take Him prisoner, the disciples' hope for an earthly Messianic kingdom was shattered and they decided to abandon ship—including cocksure Peter.

It never pays to put our "confidence in the flesh" (Phil. 3:3), for God's Word admonishes us: "Let him that thinketh he standeth take heed lest he fall" (1 Cor. 10:12). If you are going to do any boasting, let it be "in the Lord" (Ps. 34:2).

*We are the ones who strayed away like sheep! We, who left God's paths to follow our own. Yet God laid on him the guilt and sins of every one of us! Isa. 53:6, TLB.*

# Big Enough to Take the Blame

When William Ewart Gladstone, one of the great British prime ministers of the nineteenth century, was chancellor of the exchequer, he asked for the treasury to send him certain statistics upon which he intended to base his budget proposal. The statistician made a mistake, but so sure was Gladstone of this man's accuracy that he did not take time to verify his figures. He went before the House of Commons and made his speech, basing his appeal on the incorrect figures. No sooner had his speech hit the newspapers than someone exposed the error.

Although this revelation was extremely embarrassing, Gladstone shouldered the blame. Then, going to his office, he sent for the statistician. When the man appeared, he was certain he was going to lose his job. Instead, Gladstone said, "I know how you must feel over what has happened, and I have sent for you to put you at ease. You have been busy handling the intricacies of the national accounts for a long time, and this is the first mistake you have made. I congratulate you on your accomplishment and wish to express my appreciation for your faithful service."

You can imagine the man's relief. It takes a big man to take the blame for the failings of others.

Every human being has failed when it comes to sin. The Bible states, "There is none righteous, no, not one" (Rom. 3:10). When one fails, the natural tendency is to lay the blame on someone else. That is what Adam did after the Fall—he blamed Eve. That is what Eve did—she blamed the serpent. But that is not what Christ did. He took upon Himself "the iniquity of us all" (Isa. 53:6).

When there are misunderstandings, individuals usually feel that they are right and the other person is wrong—and they expect the other person to come around and make amends. But this doesn't usually happen. We need to take Christ as our model and be big enough to take the "blame" if necessary, even when we are actually in the right. It takes a big person to do that.

*All I want is to know Christ and to experience the power of his resurrection. Phil. 3:10, TEV.*  APRIL

3

# Resurrection Power

The same power that resurrected Jesus from the dead is needed to bring life to the soul that is "dead in trespasses and sins" (Eph. 2:1). Elsewhere Paul declares that one who lives "in self-indulgence is dead while [he or] she lives" (1 Tim. 5:6, MLB). Such a person may be alive physically but spiritually he or she is dead. People in this condition need "resurrection power," for, to know Christ personally means not merely to experience bodily resurrection at the Second Coming (see 1 Thess. 4:15-17) but to experience spiritual resurrection in this present life.

We have all met people who fit the category of being physically alive but were spiritually dead. Elsewhere in his writings Paul describes such a person as a "natural man." Talk to such a person about spiritual things and "they are foolishness" to him or her (1 Cor. 2:14). You might just as well talk to a corpse.

While working as a missionary on the Amazon, I studied the Bible in the home of a Mr. Moraes, who qualified as a "natural" man. He worshiped a god called Intellect. He caviled at Christianity and belittled his believing wife. It's a wonder he permitted me to study the Bible in his home, let alone listen himself. But he did, and yet he seemed to be totally unresponsive. But then the Holy Spirit did something I couldn't do. In His own mysterious way He reached into this man's mind and brought to life a soul dead in trespasses and sins. And what a difference it made! I had the privilege of baptizing Mr. Moraes.

In this life it is not enough to experience resurrection power once. Just as getting to know Christ better is an ever-deepening acquaintanceship with Him, so experiencing resurrection power is an ever-deepening process. As we gain a deeper knowledge of Christ through His Word and open our hearts to His Spirit, those areas of our minds that are still spiritually dead are "quickened"—brought to life. Today as you get to know God better through the study of His Word, open the doors of your mind to the Holy Spirit and experience that power that raised Jesus from the dead (see 1 Peter 3:18, NIV).

*He will kindle a burning like the burning of a fire. So the Light of Israel will be for a fire, and his Holy One for a flame. Isa. 10:16, 17, NKJV.*

# Keepers of the Flame

In 1790, more than 200 years ago, John and Sarah Morris of Philadelphia emigrated to Saluda, North Carolina, now part of the Great Smoky National Park, and kindled a fire by using a flintstone and a piece of steel. So far as I know, this fire has been kept burning to this day. Times have changed, wars have come and gone, from time to time new cabins have replaced old ones, and the fire has been moved from one abode to another, but generations of Morrises have carefully tended the fire and kept it burning.

This flame is reputed to be the oldest man-made, continually burning fire in America, perhaps in the world. Keeping it going has been no easy task, for it consumes about a cord of wood a month and must be carefully watched lest it die out.

God's Word is compared to a fire—a fire that burns in the hearts of men and women. You remember the story. As Cleopas and his companion (some think it was his wife) walked to Emmaus on Sunday afternoon following Christ's resurrection, they were approached by a Stranger. After they told Him about their crushed hopes, Jesus, who was the stranger, "began with Moses and all the prophets, and explained to them the passages which referred to himself" (Luke 24:27, NEB). Subsequently, when they realized they had been talking to Jesus Himself, they said, "Were not our hearts burning within us while he talked with us on the road and opened the Scriptures to us?" (verse 32, NIV). But note, *they were not satisfied to keep the good news to themselves.* That very night they hurried back to Jerusalem to tell their friends the wonderful message!

Like the Morrises, you and I are keepers of the flame—the gospel flame. That flame of hope, now committed to us, has been kept alive for almost 2,000 years. Sometimes it has burned low, but it has never gone out, thank God!

Do you ever feel as if at times the flame in your heart is burning low? If you do, let the Spirit of God fan it into a blazing fire that is not satisfied until it has ignited hope in the hearts of others.

*Can a mother forget the baby at her breast and have no compassion on the child she has borne? Though she may forget, I will not forget you! See, I have engraved you on the palms of my hands. Isa. 49:15, 16, NIV.*

APRIL

5

# Scarred Hands

Many years ago William Dixon, of Brackenwaithe, England, lost his wife and only son. One day he passed a neighbor's house and noticed it was on fire. A crowd gathered. Friends rescued the aged grandmother, but her orphaned grandson was trapped in an upstairs room. Risking his life, Dixon climbed hand over hand up a hot iron pipe on the side of the house. He reached the boy and lowered him to safety, but his hands were badly burned.

Not long after the fire, the grandmother died and the town council met to decide what to do with the boy. Three people, one of whom was a father who had lost a son, appeared before the council offering to adopt the orphan. After the first two claimants had made their pleas, Dixon stood. Too full of emotion to speak, he simply held up his scarred hands. When the vote was taken, the boy was given to him.

Is it any wonder? The first two claimants in all probability had good reasons and the best of motives for wanting to adopt the boy, but Dixon had something the others didn't have. He had paid the price.

In the great hereafter there will doubtless be many who have lived up to all the light they had but who have never known about the price Jesus paid for their redemption. Zechariah says that in that day someone will ask, "What are these wounds in thine hands? Then he shall answer, Those with which I was wounded in the house of my friends" (Zech. 13:6).

Your sins, my sins, have wounded the Saviour, yet He has inscribed our names on His nail-scarred hands. But this isn't all. He assures us no one can "pluck [us] out of [His] hand" (John 10:28). His hands are powerful. Habakkuk says, "Rays flashed from his hand, where his power was hidden" (Hab. 3:4, NIV).

Thank God that these hands possess all power and that our names are inscribed on them.

**6**

*I am crucified with Christ: nevertheless I live; yet not I, but Christ liveth in me: and the life which I now live in the flesh I live by the faith of the Son of God, who loved me, and gave himself for me. Gal. 2:20.*

# The Crucifixion of Self

I had heard about the *flagellantes* of the Philippines long before I saw one. But on Friday, March 29, 1991, I saw some of these penitents when I attended a reunion of former internees in Luzon. It was a pathetic sight to see these men lashing their backs with flails until the blood ran. Others in later stages of penance trudged along the side of the highway bearing heavy crosses, simulating Christ's painful trek to Golgotha.

These penitents were unquestionably sincere in what they were doing. However, in Isaiah 1:12 the Lord asks pointedly, "Who has required this from your hand"? (NKJV). Does God require it? Is this what He asks us to do to gain His favor? A thousand times No! What God calls for is clearly set forth in Micah 6:8, where the prophet asks, "What does the Lord require of you?" He answers, "To act justly, to love mercy, and to walk humbly with your God" (NKJV).

One of the problems we sinful human beings have is that we tend to be either unmercifully just or unjustly merciful. This is true, whether it has to do with our treatment of others or our treatment of ourselves.

Have you ever known individuals who, figuratively speaking, were still beating themselves for some wrong they had committed long ago? On the other hand, have you ever known those who did something positively wrong who were altogether too merciful on themselves?

One thing is certain; neither self-flagellation nor being too merciful is the solution. There are some things for which amends can never be made—murder, for instance. In such instances all we can do is put the matter in God's hands, seek His forgiveness—and let Him direct us in making whatever restitution is possible. This principle applies to all sins against others. It is only as we walk humbly with God that He can show us *what* to do to make things right, and *how* and *when* to do it.

*God has already placed Jesus Christ as the one and only foundation, and no other foundation can be laid. 1 Cor. 3:11, TEV.*

APRIL

7

# Salvation Only in Christ

One afternoon in 1965 Daniel Waswa, a Christian in Kenya, trudged up a hill not far from his home and was crucified by his wife. She did it on his instructions—he instructed her step by step. As he hung on the instrument of self-imposed torture, he told the crowd that had gathered, "I am dying for the sins of all Kenyans."

After nailing her husband to the cross, his wife collapsed and died, apparently from shock.

Waswa's neighbors knew that being crucified was no spur-of-the-moment decision on his part. For years he had talked about dying by crucifixion, and claimed he had been especially called by God for this purpose.

After he had been hanging for several hours, his neighbors pleaded with him to let them take him down. At first he refused, but after a while he relented and was taken down still alive. However, he died not long after the ordeal, from infection of the nail wounds.

How a professed Christian could conceive that his self immolation could save anyone is hard to understand. Perhaps Waswa got the idea from misreading Galatians 2:20. If so, how tragic that he didn't understand the Bible better. The Bible plainly says that "salvation is to be found through [Christ] alone" and that "in all the world there is no one else whom God has given who can save us" (Acts 4:12, TEV). Further, Hebrews 10:10 declares that Christ made this sacrifice "once" and "for all" (Jerusalem). So, sincere as our friend may have been, his sacrifice could provide salvation for no one—not even himself.

Only the sacrifice of the Creator could suffice to satisfy the demands of justice and provide salvation of the beings He created. This is "the one and only foundation" of the Christian religion. How grateful we can be that God so loved us that He made this sacrifice on our behalf in the person of His Son.

*Thou wast slain and by thy blood didst ransom men for God from every tribe and tongue and people and nation. Rev. 5:9, RSV.*

# Ransomed by the Blood

Back in the days when the Barbary coast of North Africa was noted for its piracy, before United States Marines cooperated with the British and Dutch navies to put the pirates out of business, the cashier of a Liverpool merchant received a small-denomination Bank of England note and held it up to the light to see whether or not it was authentic. It turned out to be genuine. But as he looked at the note, his curiosity was aroused, for he saw some brownish markings on the front of the note as well as its margins, which looked suspiciously like handwriting. Scrutinizing these markings with a magnifying glass, he was able to make out the following message: "If this note should fall into the hands of John Dean, of Longhillmar, he will learn thereby that his brother is languishing in prison in Algiers."

A search was immediately made in Longhillmar, Wales, for Mr. Dean. When he was found and shown the note, he immediately set about raising money to secure his brother's release. At the same time he enlisted the services of the British government. After the unfortunate man was freed, he told how he had been held prisoner for 11 long years. Soon after his imprisonment, he had written the message on a bank note with his own blood, drawn by cutting his hand with a sharp instrument. Then, using a sharpened piece of wood as a pen, he had dipped it in his blood and written the note in the hope that someone, someday, would notice it and contact his brother.

In the same way that the unfortunate man in the Algerian prison was utterly unable to redeem himself in a physical sense, so we, in a spiritual sense, cannot ransom ourselves from the prison house of sin. As the psalmist says: "Truly no man can ransom himself, or give to God the price of his life, for the ransom of his life is costly, and can never suffice" (Ps. 49:7, 8, RSV).

The only way any of us can ever be ransomed from our sinful predicament is by the blood of our Elder Brother. This blood is able to ransom men and women from every tribe and tongue and people and nation—and this includes you and me, thank God!

*Jephthah['s] . . . mother was a prostitute. His father . . . had several other sons by his legitimate wife, and when these half brothers grew up, they chased Jephthah out of the country. "You son of a whore!" they said. "You'll not get any of our father's estate."*
*Judges 11:1, 2, TLB.*

# Illegitimacy

For some perverse reason, human beings tend to blame illegitimacy not so much on the parents of the misbegotten child as on the child itself. This is what happened to Jephthah.

Several years ago I read a book by Sidney Stewart titled *Give Us This Day,* in which he tells about the hardships he and a group of soldiers passed through during the Battle of Bataan and in various prisoner-of-war camps.

In one poignant passage he tells how one night he and his buddy, Rass, heard a wounded soldier moaning about 25 feet from their dugout. Risking their lives, they crawled over to the man and dragged him to their shelter. He looked more like a boy than a man, and was obviously mortally wounded.

"I'm so scared of dying," he said. "I don't know what's going to happen after I'm dead."

"Kid," said Rass tenderly, "don't you know anything about God and heaven?"

"I don't know about God," he moaned, staring with wide, frightened eyes. "I've never been to church in my life. I never had a dad. Just me and Mom."

Rass, a Christian, took the boy's hand and told him the story of salvation. By the time he finished, dawn was breaking and Stew could see the boy's face more clearly. The boy never took his eyes off Rass. Stew studied his face. He was smiling faintly now as though someone had showed him something for the first time.

"I'm not afraid anymore," he said at last. He closed his eyes. His head fell to one side, and he was gone!

How thankful we can be that salvation and what we can make of ourselves do not depend on being legitimate. God accepts us just as we are. We do not have to answer for our parents' mistakes (see Eze. 18:4). But how much easier it would be for those less fortunate if we showed them more acceptance and understanding.

*Mephibosheth said unto [King David], Yea, let [Ziba] take all, forasmuch as my lord the king is come again in peace unto his own house.*
*2 Sam. 19:30.*

# Loyalty in Spite of Loss

The story of Mephibosheth is one of the finest examples of loyalty in spite of loss found anywhere in the Bible. Crippled at the age of 5, when his nurse dropped him as she fled after the catastrophic defeat at Mount Gilboa, he not only lost the use of his legs, but he also lost his father, Jonathan; his uncles; and his grandfather, Saul. A new dynasty now took over, and Mephibosheth grew up fearing David would take his life.

Mephibosheth had good reasons for being afraid. It was the practice in those days for an ascendant king to put to death all potential rivals, and Mephibosheth, a possible pretender, could pose a threat to the throne. However, because of his friendship with Jonathan, David not only spared Mephibosheth's life but also restored to him his father's property and invited him to come to Jerusalem and be a permanent guest of the royal family.

All went well until Absalom, David's son, revolted against his father and forced him to flee Jerusalem. In his crippled condition, Mephibosheth could not accompany his royal benefactor. Later, when David returned, having quelled his son's rebellion, he failed to take Mephibosheth's condition into consideration and accused him of disloyalty. Then with uncharacteristic high-handedness, he expropriated half of Mephibosheth's patrimony and gave it to Ziba, the man who bore false witness against him.

Instead of becoming bitter and turning against David, Mephibosheth said in effect, "Let Ziba take it all. The important thing is that my lord the king has returned in peace." Mephibosheth not only accepted his loss gracefully, but he remained loyal to his king. With him, the loss of material things had nothing to do with loyalty.

God is not high-handed, but He sometimes permits us to lose our material possessions for our eternal good. When this happens, some professed Christians turn against their heavenly Benefactor. A true Christian, however, remains loyal to God, even if this means "the loss of all things" (Phil. 3:8).

*One day the little girl said to her mistress, "I wish my master would go to see the prophet in Samaria. He would heal him of his leprosy!"*
*2 Kings 5:3, TLB.*

APRIL

11

# The Little Captive Maid

We don't know her name nor do we know exactly how old she was, but we know she was a young Jewish girl, perhaps just a child, for the writer of 2 Kings 5 speaks of her as a "little maid" (verse 2, RSV). She may very well have been the daughter of one of the so-called "sons of the prophets" (cf. 2 Kings 2:3; 4:1), because, unlike many of her countrymen at the time, she believed in the true God.

We also know that she had been kidnapped by a band of marauding Syrian soldiers and had been taken to a strange land, and that she was a slave to Mrs. Naaman, the wife of one of the leading generals of Syria.

In spite of having been forcibly abducted from her country, she had within her something no one could take away—faith in the true God. Because of this faith, she could make the best of her situation and actually love those who had deprived her of the earthly things she loved most. Here was a Christian long before Christ was born.

After telling about Naaman's greatness, the writer of the narrative adds one terrible phrase, "but he was a leper" (2 Kings 5:1). In those days there was no cure for this dread disease, yet the captive maid believed that Jehovah, through His prophet Elisha, could heal Naaman. And this in spite of the fact that there were "many lepers . . . in Israel in the time of Elisha, . . . [yet] none of them [had been] cleansed" (Luke 4:27, NKJV).

By her courageous faith and goodwill, this captive girl enriched the household in which she lived. She enriched the people of Syria. But most important of all, she has enriched all who have lived since her time and have read her story, including you and me.

We may never be captives in a strange land, as was this maid, but no one is immune to sudden and unexpected change. I, for instance, never dreamed I would be taken prisoner in World War II, but I was. So whatever happens, we can thank God for the faithful example of the little captive maid.

# 12

*Do not rejoice at the fall of your enemy; do not gloat when he is brought down, or the Lord will be displeased at the sight.*
*Prov. 24:17, 18, REB.*

# Never Gloat Over an Enemy's Defeat

Although America has engaged in greater wars, none has been bloodier than the Civil War, in which a half million men lost their lives. Abraham Lincoln was president of the United States of America and Jefferson Davis was the chief executive of Confederate States of America during this terrible bloodbath.

After the Northern forces captured Richmond, the capital of the Confederacy, Lincoln ordered that "there be no triumphant entry" into the city. A few days later he went to Richmond with a small entourage and made his way to Davis's empty executive office. Bidding two officials accompanying him to step outside, he remained alone in the room. After a little while one of the officials became curious and peeked in to see what Lincoln was doing. What he saw, he never forgot. Lincoln was sitting, his head bowed over Davis's desk, his face buried in his hands, tears streaming down his face.

This was the way it was with this great man. Although he stood firm as a rock as commander in chief of the Union armies, he took no pleasure in the defeat of his enemies. The world would be a better place if it had more people like that.

In his second inaugural address, spoken only a few days before his assassination, Lincoln appealed, "With malice toward none; with charity for all; with firmness in the right, as God gives us to see the right, let us strive to finish the work we are in; to bind up the nation's wounds." Had he lived, it is quite likely that bitterness between the North and the South would not have continued after the war as long and as fiercely as it did.

You and I can learn much from Lincoln's magnanimity toward his enemies. Have you, for instance, ever "earnestly contend[ed] for the faith . . . once delivered unto the saints" (Jude 3)—and won—only to let your sinful human nature take over, and you gloat over your opponent's discomfiture? I have. God is not pleased by such behavior. If we have indeed won a victory for the faith, let us be magnanimous and remember that the glory belongs to God, not us.

*We have this assurance: Those who belong to God shall live again. Their bodies shall rise again! Those who dwell in the dust shall awake and sing for joy! For God's light of life will fall like dew upon them! Isa. 26:19, TLB.*

# The Dead Shall Live Again

A few weeks ago, as I write, the body of a prehistoric man was discovered near Hauslab Pass in the Tyrolean Alps on the border between Austria and Italy. On September 19, 1991, a German couple, Helmut and Erika Simon, were walking along the Similaun glacier when Erika suddenly stopped and shouted, "There's something here in the snow. It's a man!" The "man" had strange tattoo markings on his back. Helmut stopped and took some pictures and reported the find.

Two days later Rheinhold Messner, hearing about the discovery, decided to make his own investigation. When he saw the corpse, he realized it was an archeological discovery of great importance.

Several days after that, Rainer Henn, a forensic specialist at the University of Innsbruck, Austria, took a crew with him to recover the corpse. After carefully packing it in ice, he took it, together with some artifacts found near the body—a bronze ax, a bow, a leather shoe, a quiver with 14 arrows, etc.—back to Innsbruck by helicopter.

Scientists have tentatively dated the man as having lived about 2000 B.C., around the time of Abraham. They are hoping to learn from his remains, the artifacts found with him, and the place his body was found, how the man died, what kind of food he ate, and the genetic makeup of the people that populated Europe at that time.

How interesting that a glacier should hold this secret until our day. Could this be significant? I believe it could be. But, significant or not, the time is coming when not only glaciers but the earth, and "the sea" as well, will give "up the dead which [are] in them" (Rev. 20:13, NASB).

Our curiosity is piqued. When this time comes, will the prehistoric man from the Hauslab Pass be found among the redeemed Isaiah talks about, or among the lost? We cannot tell. But you and I can decide which group we will be in.

# 14

*I will go home to my father and say, "Father, I have sinned against both heaven and you, and am no longer worthy of being called your son." Luke 15:18, 19, TLB.*

# Prodigal Restored

You've probably sung the hymn "Come, Thou Fount of Every Blessing" many times, but do you know who composed it? Not many people do. It was written in 1758 by Robert Robinson; it breathes the spirit of one who loved God yet was struggling with his carnal nature. This is evident when he speaks in the last verse of being "prone to wander . . . [from] the God" he loves.

It is said that later in life Robinson lost his way spiritually and decided to travel, hoping to find enjoyment in worldly pleasures. One day while traveling in a stagecoach, he apparently became enamored with a lovely young woman and struck up a conversation. She was a Christian, and when she learned his name, she remembered it was the same as that of the hymn writer. As they chatted, she handed him her hymnal, open to this hymn, and asked him what he thought of it. He was taken aback to see it was his own composition. He tried to evade her question, but she gently persisted.

Suddenly he began to weep, and with tears running down his cheeks, said, "I was the one who wrote that hymn many years ago. I'd give anything to experience the joy I then knew." The young woman assured him that the "streams of mercy" he spoke of in his hymn still flowed, and appealed for him to come back to "the fold of God."

The story has a happy ending. Then and there Robinson recommitted his life to God and once again experienced the peace that had been his.

Do you love the Lord yet find that you are prone to "leave the God" you love? Who in this world of sin has not felt that way? Most of us have. What's the solution? Frequent and ever-deepening commitments to God.

Can you think of a better time to renew and deepen your commitment than right now? As you do this, you will be bound "closer still" to the God you love and will be less prone to wander away from Him.

*It is rare that anyone should lay down his life for a just man, though it is barely possible that for a good man someone may have the courage to die. It is precisely in this that God proves his love for us: that while we were still sinners, Christ died for us. Rom. 5:7, 8, NAB.*

# "I Can Die Better"

Self-preservation is the first law of nature; ordinarily a person will give anything or do anything to preserve his or her life. However, there are examples of people who have actually given their lives for others.

When the *Empress of Ireland* went down with 130 Salvation Army officers on board, 109 of their bodies were recovered—and not one had on a life jacket. Many of the surviving passengers told how, when the Salvationists discovered that there were not enough life preservers for everyone, those who had them removed them and strapped them on other passengers, saying, "I can die better than you can."

In July 1942 Sergeant Franciszek Gajowniczek was selected for execution by the Nazi guards at Auschwitz extermination camp. As he pleaded for his life, a Franciscan priest, Maxmillian Kolbe, stepped forward and volunteered to die in his place. This must have taken real courage. A short time later Kolbe died from starvation and a dose of carbolic acid administered to him by his captors.

Now, it isn't very often that God inspires an individual to literally lay down his life for someone else. But He does present us with a similar challenge in the spiritual realm. First John 3:15-18 says: "Anyone who hates his Christian brother is really a murderer at heart; and you know that no one wanting to murder has eternal life within. We know what real love is from Christ's example in dying for us. And so we also ought to lay down our lives for our Christian brothers. But if someone who is supposed to be a Christian has money enough to live well, and sees a brother in need, and won't help him—how can God's love be within *him?* Little children, let us stop just *saying* we love people; let us *really* love them, and *show it* by our *actions"* (TLB).

*Where is God my Maker, who gives songs in the night, who teaches us more than the beasts of the earth, and makes us wiser than the birds of the air? Job 35:10, 11, RSV.*

# Songs in the Night

In northeast Brazil, where I lived as a child, I remember my mother waking us children up one night and taking us outside in the backyard to listen to the singing of a sabia, a species of song thrush that sings at night. I do not know, but it is possible that these birds sing in the daytime, too.

Mockingbirds sing at night as well as in the daytime. Perhaps you have heard them. Where I live in Idaho, I have occasionally heard one singing during the night hours. It is said that no other bird can rival its "operatic skill"—although some seem to try. This delightful mimic not only copies the songs of other birds, it even mimes instrumental music—and improves on it, so I am told. But the mockingbird is more than an imitator; it also creates. Sometimes it composes its own original renditions. Heard on a moonlit night, its song is filled with trills, swells, tremolos, and pure liquid melody that thrills those who hear it.

On occasion all of us pass through "nighttimes" of discouragement, and "the birds of the heavens" can teach us important lessons. Instead of giving in to sorrow, let us lift our voices in songs of praise to God. In our verse for meditation, the question is asked, "Where is God my Maker, who gives songs in the night?" And the encouraging answer is "He is not far from each one of us" (Acts 17:27, NKJV). How precious, then, the thought that it is *God Himself* who gives us these songs.

Paul and Silas had learned this lesson. The record says that at "midnight," after they had been severely beaten and "thrust . . . into the inner prison," they "sang praises unto God: and the [other] prisoners heard them" (Acts 16:23-25).

In the midnight of the soul, when the future seems black, it is not easy to sing joyful hymns of praise to God. But such songs have an undeniable power to lift our spirits. So when you feel down, sing *in spite of your feelings.* It will completely alter your emotions and sweep away the clouds of despondency. Try it!

*[Mine enemies] are around me now, wherever I turn, watching for a chance to pull me down. They are like lions, waiting for me, wanting to tear me to pieces. Ps. 17:11, 12, TEV.*

# Lions Are Never Tamed

Psalm 17 is a "prayer of David" for deliverance from his physical enemies, whom he compares to lions. As he later learned, these adversaries were not nearly as treacherous as the "lions" that attacked his spiritual life and almost destroyed it.

Lion trainers tell us that there is no such thing as a tame lion. A lion whelp raised as a pet may feed out of your hand, it may seem to be under your control, it may even let you put your head in its mouth, but given the right circumstances it will turn on you when you least expect it and tear you limb from limb.

Baron Richard d'Arcy, a French aristocrat, raised a pet lion from a baby and kept it around his house. At night he locked it in a bathroom. One evening in 1977 when he led his pet to its quarters it refused to enter. He prodded it. Suddenly it turned on him and in a matter of seconds clawed him to death. The police were summoned. When they arrived, they had no choice but to shoot the beast. Although for a long time it had appeared to be docile, it revealed its true nature when least expected.

Cherished sins are like untamable lions. These sins originate with sinful thoughts that, unless brought "into captivity . . . to the obedience of Christ" (2 Cor. 10:5), sooner or later turn on us and destroy us.

A few years ago Robert J. Spangler wrote in *Ministry* magazine about a pastor friend he once visited. During one of their conversations the pastor mentioned that his secretary had been making improper advances. Spangler implored the man to put distance between himself and this woman, but the pastor laughed and said he could handle the situation. It wasn't long before the man turned in his credentials because he had broken the seventh commandment.

When sinful thoughts seek to insinuate themselves into your mind, cry out with all your heart, "Arise, O Lord, confront them, overthrow them" (Ps. 17:13, RSV). God will do His part if you and I will do our part.

# 18

*We have a more sure word of prophecy; where unto ye do well that you take heed, as unto a light that shineth in a dark place, until the day dawn, and the day star arise in your hearts.*
**2 Peter 1:19.**

# Our Guiding Light

One stormy, pitch-black night during World War II, six American pilots returning from a combat mission in the southwestern Pacific got lost some 200 miles from their home base. Because of the danger of the enemy's locating their airfield, they had no radio beam on which to home in. As they approached the vicinity of their airfield, their friends on the ground could hear them break radio silence as they talked to one another, trying to find a landing place. The conversation went like this: "Jim, do you know where we are?"

"No, but we should have gotten there by now."

"How much gas do you have left?"

"Getting low . . ."

The men on the ground knew that the pilots were closer home than they realized. And, of course, they could also sense the mounting tension as the planes began to run low on fuel. Finally the men on the ground turned on searchlights. Immediately they heard over the radio the pilots say, almost in unison, "I see a light! I see a light! We're OK, thank God." Minutes later they landed their planes safely.

Peter, who wrote our verse for meditation, was a witness to Christ's transfiguration (see Matt. 17:1, 2; 2 Peter 1:17, 18). To him this was incontrovertible evidence of Christ's deity. But you and I were not there. Thus it is not coercive evidence to us. But prophecy is far more incontrovertible evidence than having personally witnessed the Transfiguration. How can this be? Because we can experience the change the Bible can accomplish in our lives, as well as see Bible prophecy fulfilling before our eyes every day!

Prophecy, God's ability to predict the future, is the acid test of the reliability of His Word. In Isaiah 46:9, 10, He declares unequivocally, "I alone am God; there is none like Me, declaring the end from the beginning" (NKJV).

Yes, the Bible, God's prophetic Word, is a reliable guiding light. May its rays guide us even to the end.

*The fool has said in his heart, "There is no God." They have corrupted their behavior and made it abominable. There is none who does right. Ps. 14:1, MLB.*

# Atheist Confounded

Charles Bradlaugh, a noted British atheist, once challenged Hugh Price Hughes, a gospel minister in a London slum, to a debate on the validity of Christianity. Hughes accepted, on the following condition:

"I propose that we each bring some concrete evidence for the validity of our beliefs in the form of men and women who have been redeemed from lives of sin and shame by the influence of our teachings. I will bring 100 such men and women, and you bring the same number. If you cannot bring a hundred, bring 50. If you cannot bring 50, just bring 20. If you cannot being 20, I will be satisfied with 10. In fact, Mr. Bradlaugh, I challenge you to bring just one."

Bradlaugh, unable to meet the condition, withdrew from the debate.

The most incontrovertible evidence for the validity of Christianity is not found in philosophy, nor psychology, nor drugs, but in the power of the gospel to transform lives. The apostle Paul speaks of this transformation as "the power of God unto salvation to every one that believeth" (Rom. 1:16).

Some years ago an alcoholic from Chicago's skid row staggered toward Lake Michigan to end his miserable life. As he stumbled past Pacific Garden Mission someone noticed him and helped him through the door and into the meeting hall. There he collapsed on the floor in front of the preacher and fell asleep.

Workers at the mission put him to bed and cared for his needs. Next day the superintendent told him about the power of God that could change his life. The derelict, Harry Monroe, accepted that power, and was transformed from a hopeless bum into a sober citizen. Later he became superintendent of the very mission where he was converted.

The same transforming power is available to you and me today. Let us accept it into our lives. The change it can bring about is an argument no unbeliever can gainsay.

*He who has a beautiful eye will be blessed, for he gives of his bread to the poor.*
*Prov. 22:9, NKJV.*

# Windows of the Soul

Our faces, especially our eyes, tend to reveal what is hidden in our minds. Some have called the eyes the windows of the soul. The following anecdote may be apocryphal, but it illustrates a point.

A farmer in financial straits was obliged to apply for a bank loan. He presented his request to the president of the local bank, a man reputed to be tightfisted and cynical. The president, who had two perfectly good eyes, said sarcastically, "I'll grant the loan if you can tell me which of my eyes is a glass eye."

After carefully scrutinizing the bank executive's visage, the farmer replied, "Your left eye, sir."

"Wrong!" exulted the bank executive. "Why did you guess my left eye?"

"Because," returned the farmer bitterly, "it seemed to have a gleam of kindness the other one didn't have."

One day a group of friends were out horseback riding. At length they came to a swollen creek. On the bank sat a poor man who looked disconsolate; he was unable to cross the creek. As the riders passed, the man scrutinized their faces but said nothing. Just as the last rider was about to enter the water, the lone man asked if he would be so kind as to take him across. Not only was the horseman quick to accede to the request, he even helped the stranger onto his mount.

When they reached the other side, one of the riders took the poor man aside and quietly scolded him for asking Thomas Jefferson to ferry him across when he could have asked any one of the other men. The man's reply is enlightening: "There are some faces on which is clearly written 'No' to a request you intend to make, and there are other faces on which is written 'Yes.' "

If today someone were to ask you a reasonable favor and it was within your power to grant it, what kind of answer would he or she find written on your face?

*Fight the good fight of faith, lay hold on eternal life, to which you were also called and have confessed the good confession in the presence of many witnesses. 1 Tim. 6:12, NKJV.*

APRIL

21

# Fight the Good Fight of Faith

Philip Henry Sheridan, major general of the Union Army during the Civil War, is generally recognized as the Union's most able cavalry commander. My wife's great-grandfather, First Lt. William Sanders, fought under Sheridan and is said to have once saved the general's life. After the war Sanders dedicated his life to saving souls for God's kingdom.

Early in April 1865, during the Battle of Richmond, one of the raw recruits under Sheridan became separated from his company. He began running here and there in a futile effort to find his fellow soldiers to join them in the fighting. About this time he saw Sheridan riding up and diffidently asked him what he should do. "Why, step in anywhere," snapped the general. "There's fighting all along the line."

The church militant fights in a spiritual war far fiercer than any physical conflict fought by earthly armies. Ellen White describes it this way: "In vision I saw two armies in terrible conflict. One army was led by the banners bearing the world's insignia; the other was led by the bloodstained banner of Prince Immanuel" (*Testimonies*, vol. 8, p. 41).

In this cosmic conflict all of us are combatants. "Our contest is not with human foes alone, but with the rulers, authorities, and cosmic powers of this dark world; that is, with the spirit-forces of evil challenging us in the heavenly contest" (Eph. 6:12, Williams).

Thus, part of this conflict is fought in the realm of the invisible—but part of it is fought on the firm green field of reality. There are yet many objectives that the church militant must take, but many of its soldiers seem to be running around accomplishing nothing—like the raw recruit in Sheridan's army.

There's fighting all along the line. Step in wherever you see a need and fight the good fight of faith to the best of your ability.

APRIL

# 22

When you give a feast, invite the poor, the maimed, the lame, the blind. And you will be blessed, because they cannot repay you; for you shall be repaid at the resurrection of the just. Luke 14:13, 14, NKJV.

# Payment Deferred

In yesterday's reading I mentioned that William Sanders, my wife's great-grandfather, served in the Union calvary in the Civil War. On one occasion he was with a body of reconnoitering cavalrymen when the group was surprised by the enemy. The commanding officer told his men to scatter.

Sanders spurred his mount and dashed off, galloping as fast as his mare would go. Coming to a gate, he tried to open it with his foot. The mare shied, bolted through the opening, and landed on its side in a ditch, pinning Sanders' leg under her and knocking him out momentarily.

When he regained consciousness, he was staring up the barrel of a Confederate cavalryman's rifle. Instead of shooting Sanders, the rebel asked him if he was hurt. Sanders said he was not. The rebel soldier dismounted, helped Sanders put the mare on her feet, and assisted him in mounting. Sanders thanked his benefactor. Then the rebel said, "Now, get out of here as fast as you can." Sanders needed no prompting.

There were other good Samaritans in that brutal war. During one battle a Union officer was wounded and lay on the battlefield calling for water. A Confederate soldier came to his aid at the risk of his life and gave him a drink. In gratitude the officer took out his gold watch and offered it to his benefactor. The man refused to take it.

"Then give me your name and address," said the officer.

The soldier said, "My name is James Moore. I'm from Burke County, North Carolina."

The officer survived the war and soon after wrote the Confederate soldier, saying, "I have settled on you $10,000, to be paid in four annual installments of $2,500 each."

Payment for an act of kindness in time of war is not unheard of, although it may be rare. The Christian, however, does not do deeds of kindness in the hope of getting paid back. He shows compassion, even to enemies, because it is the Christian thing to do. His real recompense will be received at Christ's coming.

*The number of those who lapped, putting their hand to their mouth, were 300 men; but all the rest of the [10,000] bowed down upon their knees to drink water. And the Lord said to Gideon, By the 300 men who lapped I will deliver you, and give the Midianites into your hand. Judges 7:6, 7, Amplified.*

# The Faithful Few

When I was 6 years old, I visited my maternal grandparents for the first time. One of their sons, my uncle Carl, was an engineer on one of the trains that passed through Huntington, West Virginia, where my grandparents lived. I was always fascinated by the steam engines that pulled the cars back in those days. I especially liked to watch the engines being filled with water from a large overhead tank in the marshaling yard. My uncles tried to explain to me how fire caused water to boil, and boiling water made the trains move. I remember the words, but it was years before I clearly understood what they were talking about.

In those days, across the river in Ohio, and not far from where my grandparents lived, ran the tracks of the Baltimore and Ohio railroad. One B&O train, said to be "limited," unlike the trains uncle Carl drove, never stopped to take on water. Instead, it scooped up water from a trough nearly a half mile long that ran between the tracks. This trough was kept filled, and when the "limited" came through, the stoker pressed a lever. This caused a scoop to drop down and take on water as the train raced along—a bit like the actions of Gideon's 300.

In the story of Gideon, the 10,000 who were led to the brook apparently expected immediately to attack the enemy some distance on the other side. Most of the 10,000, apparently dubious of the the outcome, knelt down on the bank of the stream and leisurely drank their fill, reluctant to meet the enemy. Not so the 300. These latter soldiers were so eager to engage the Midianites that they scooped up water with their hands and put it in their mouths as they crossed the brook.

Today the Lord of hosts is looking for soldiers with the mettle of the 300. May you and I by our readiness to meet the forces of evil as God directs, show that we are worthy to be numbered among the faithful few.

*Come, let me put it thus, the Eternal argues: scarlet your sins may be, but they can become white as snow, they may be red as crimson, and yet turn white as wool. Isa. 1:18, Moffatt.*

# Let Me Put It This Way

As I think of the boundless condescension of our heavenly Father in offering to cleanse us of our sins, it is beyond my comprehension that anyone would turn down His gracious offer. Why, oh why, must He plead with us in order to persuade us to accept a proposal too good to be turned down?

David, himself a forgiven sinner, describes the blessing of one who accepts the divine offer. He exclaims, "Oh the bliss of him whose guilt is pardoned, and his sin forgiven! Oh the bliss of him whom the Eternal has absolved, whose spirit has made full confession" (Ps. 32:1, 2, Moffatt). And yet, most human beings reject God's offer of pardon and eternal life (see Matt. 7:13).

Why do so many seek renown and the honor of men when God offers them a place of highest honor in the royal family of heaven (see Rev. 3:21)? Why do they choose earthly real estate instead of the "eternal inheritance" (Heb. 9:15)? Why do they choose death rather than life (Eze. 33:11)? Why do they insist on retaining the filthy rags of their own rectitude when the King of kings holds out to them His own royal robe of righteousness (see Matt. 22:11, 12)? Why are they satisfied to travel within the confines of this wretched, sin-sick planet, when, if they accept His offer, they might one day "wing their tireless flight to worlds afar" (*The Great Controversy*, p. 677)?

All these questions add up to the sad reality that sin has so confused man's reasoning powers that he cannot think straight. All who fail to accept Heaven's gracious, most reasonable offer will someday sadly confess, "What a fool I've been!"

Our heavenly Father has made every provision to meet us in our fallen condition. Sin has weakened our powers of reasoning. So He lays before us His offer in terms the simplest mind can understand. He goes further. He promises to any who lack wisdom to "bring forth thy righteousness as the light, and thy judgment as the noonday" (Ps. 37:6).

Why not accept God's offer now—this minute?

*When Simon saw that the Spirit was bestowed through the laying on of the apostles' hands, he offered them money and said, "Give me the same power too, so that when I lay my hands on anyone, he will receive the Holy Spirit." Peter replied, "Your money go with you to damnation." Acts 8:18-20, NEB.*

APRIL

25

# Trusting in Uncertain Riches

Simon Magus's endeavor to obtain the gift of the Holy Ghost by purchasing it with money has given rise to the term "simony" —the practice of buying or selling a church office or ecclesiastical preferment. Peter didn't fall for Simon's proposal, but material gain seems to cast a hypnotic spell over many minds.

Many years ago the ship *Shanunga*, on her way from Liverpool to New York, collided with a smaller vessel, the *Iduna.* The latter, a Swedish bark, was carrying 206 passengers and crew. The *Iduma* began to sink rapidly. Captain Patten, of the *Shanunga*, immediately launched his lifeboats and sent them to the rescue. But only 34 persons were saved. The remaining 172 people, including the captain, were lost. One reason so few were saved was that many tied money belts filled with gold and silver around their waists and the weight dragged them to the bottom.

A similar tragedy with a different twist happened to the ship *Valencia.* Among those who drowned in that accident was a Mr. J. B. Graham. A few days before he took passage on the ship he sold a mine in Alaska for $60,000. Part of the proceeds from the sale was a bagful of gold. As the ship was sinking, he frantically offered the gold to anyone who would save him. But his pleas went unheeded. Material things had lost their value, and the bag of gold lay on the deck, kicked here and there by those who were anxious to save their own lives.

The Bible speaks of a time when people "will throw away the gold and silver idols they have made, and abandon them to the moles and the bats" (Isa. 2:20, TEV). What a tragedy that people should cling so tenaciously to "uncertain riches" (1 Tim. 6:17) that they lose their temporal lives. But far greater is the tragedy of those who value uncertain riches so highly that they lose eternal life.

*Put Me to the test, says the Lord of hosts, if I will not open the windows of heaven for you and pour out for you a more than sufficient blessing. And I will rebuke the devouring locust for you, and it shall not destroy the fruit of your ground. Mal. 3:10, 11, MLB.*

# Locusts Rebuked

Have you ever seen locusts so thick they were a menace to life? I remember traveling through South Dakota in the summer of 1940 when the highways were so littered with slime from the crushed bodies of these insects that they made driving extremely dangerous.

One day in the spring of 1877 the farmers of Minnesota woke up to the fact that unless God intervened, a plague of locusts would destroy their wheat crop, spelling ruin for many families. John S. Pillsbury, governor of the state, proclaimed a fast to be held on April 26. He urged every man, woman, and child to pray for divine help. Next morning, as if to mock their pleas, the sun rose in a cloudless sky, temperatures soared—and the dreaded insects began to hatch in alarming numbers. The heat wave persisted for three days. Some feared God had turned His back on them.

However, the next day a cold wave swept down from the north, temperatures plummeted, and the locusts were destroyed more effectively than if sprayed with insecticide. After the harvest the farmers' granaries were filled to overflowing with wheat, and April 26 went down in Minnesota history as the day the Lord kept His promise to rebuke the devourer.

God does not always fulfill His promises in tangible ways, as He did in the foregoing incident. Were He always to answer our prayers the way *we* want them answered, our service to Him would be based on selfishness, and He desires service that springs from gratitude and appreciation of His character of love. So He permits the sun and the rain—and the locusts—to fall on the just and the unjust, and more often than not, His promises are fulfilled in the form of spiritual blessings.

When you pray and God does not seem to answer your prayers just the way you think they should be answered, see if He hasn't answered them as unexpected spiritual blessings.

*If you had a hundred sheep and one of them strayed away and was lost in the wilderness, wouldn't you leave the ninety-nine others to go and search for the lost one until you found it? Luke 15:4, TLB.*

APRIL

27

# Seeking the Lost

When my daughter Marjorie and her husband, Tore, left Norway in 1988 and came to America, Monica, their youngest daughter, was only 3 years old. Her sister, Elizabeth, had just had her fifth birthday a couple months before.

One day when their mother was at work and Tore had to go to Boise, I was left at home alone with the girls. I heard Monica whimper a bit when her father left, but I was busy and didn't pay much attention to it. After about a half hour I decided to check on the girls. I found Elizabeth in the girls' bedroom but saw no sign of Monica. I asked Elizabeth if she knew where her sister was. She did not. I checked everywhere inside and outside the house, but she was nowhere to be found. Becoming concerned, I told Elizabeth to come with me to look for her sister.

We started down the gravel road from our house that leads to the county road, searching the open fields on either side as we went. We saw no sign of the child. By this time I was getting more than concerned. When we got to the main road I asked old John Ronfelt, one of our farmer neighbors, if he had seen Monica. He must have detected worry written all over my face, because he asked, "Did you lose a kid?" I said I had.

Almost as soon as I said this I heard a wail a few hundred yards up the county road and turned to look. It was Monica! You can imagine my relief. Elizabeth and I ran all the way to where she was. As I picked her up in my arms, I thanked God she was safe. I asked her why she had left the house. She said through her sobs, "I wanted to tell Daddy goodbye."

My heart was touched and I thought, *Am I as concerned for souls that are spiritually lost as I was for my grandchild who was physically lost?* If all Christians had greater spiritual concern, isn't it possible that our soul-winning efforts would be more successful?

*Love keeps no score of wrongs; does not gloat over other men's sins, but delights in the truth.*
*1 Cor. 13:5, 6, NEB.*

# Love Is Vulnerable

Roberto de Vicenzo, an Argentine golfer, might not have been the world's greatest, but one day he surprised everyone (himself included) by winning a tournament. At the eighteenth hole a PGA official handed him a check. As he walked to his car, a sad-eyed young woman approached him. "It's been a good day for you, hasn't it?"

Vicenzo nodded.

The woman continued, "Could you help me? I have a baby with an incurable blood disease, and the doctors say she doesn't have long to live."

Moved by this plea, Vicenzo paused, pulled out his pen, endorsed his winning check, and pressed it into her hand. "Make some good days for the baby," he said.

The look of surprise on the girl's face was thanks enough.

A week later Vicenzo was having lunch at the country club when one of the PGA officials approached him. "I heard that you turned over the check you won last week to a young mother with a sick baby."

Vicenzo nodded affirmation.

"Well, let me tell you, friend. That woman was a phony. She doesn't have a sick baby. She isn't even married. She fleeced you, old boy."

"You mean to say there's no baby dying without hope?"

"Right!" the official chortled.

"That's the best news I've heard all week!" exclaimed the golfer.

What a beautiful attitude!

This is the way it is with agape (ah-GAH-peh) love. It never gloats over other people's misfortunes. Like Vicenzo, it rejoices in good news. Because it attributes good motives to others, it is vulnerable, but it never becomes cynical.

This does not mean that Christians must be fall guys or doormats. It does mean that while they are "harmless as doves," they are "wise as serpents" (Matt. 10:16); that while they are prudent, they never become paranoid.

*God hath chosen the foolish things of the world to confound the wise; and God hath chosen the weak things of the world to confound the things which are mighty. 1 Cor. 1:27.*

APRIL
29

# Handicap Advantage

Some decades ago the Harvard University faculty proposed that all applicants for scholarships undergo a physical examination and that funds be made available only to those applicants who might be expected to produce an adequate return for the investment.

Since a vigorous mind usually goes with a healthy body, you would think that the winners of the scholarships would be those in the best physical condition, wouldn't you? So did most of the faculty.

During the debate over the proposal, someone suggested that the faculty members themselves be tested to see if a strong mind invariably accompanied a strong body. The survey was made, and it was discovered that the majority of the faculty had some kind of physical disability, yet every one had a vigorous mind—at least they didn't try to deny it. End of debate!

Frequently people whose bodies are frail turn their efforts to mental activity. Take Harriet Martineau (1802-1876), an enormously popular English author. "Never," she wrote concerning her physical condition, "was a poor mortal cursed with a more beggarly nervous system." Besides this, she was totally deaf. So she turned to writing and authored numerous books. During one period she wrote one story a month for 34 successive months. The scene in each episode was laid in a different part of the world. This required research, and a special knowledge concerning the conditions in that region as well.

The apostle Paul is another example. The physical description that comes down to us from ancient times in no way flatters him. He certainly was no Adonis. In 2 Corinthians 12:9 he speaks of a physical weakness from which he suffered. And yet no leader of the early church was more active, won more converts, or left a greater legacy to later Christians than he did.

Listen to his testimony: "Most gladly therefore will I . . . glory in my infirmities, that the power of Christ may rest upon me." Are you physically weak? Let Christ's power rest on you!

*Lord, who may abide in Your tabernacle? Who may dwell in Your holy hill? He who walks uprightly . . . ; He who swears to his own hurt and does not change. Ps. 15:1-4, NKJV.*

# Keeping Pledges

Many years ago, while the duke of Burgundy was presiding over the Cabinet Council of France, one of the ministers proposed that a certain treaty be broken, since it would result in important economic advantages for the country. Many "good" reasons were put forward to justify this action. The duke listened silently. After everyone had spoken, he rose and, placing one hand on a copy of the agreement, said with firmness, "Gentlemen, we have a treaty!" That ended the matter.

I once had a couple in my church who pledged a considerable sum of money for the Lord's work—then went back on their word. After this they vowed never to make another pledge. I don't know what their motive was in pledging so much in the first place. Was it ostentation? I do not know. But I do know what the Bible says about keeping our word. Ecclesiastes 5:5, 6 says: "Better is it that thou shouldest not vow, than that thou shouldest vow and not pay. Suffer not thy mouth to cause thy flesh to sin; neither say thou before the [recording] angel, that it was an error."

The Lord has no need of our money to carry forward His work on earth. After all, "everything [we have] is a gift from [Him], and [when we give,] we have only given back what is [His] already" (1 Chron. 29:14, TEV). We are merely His stewards—managers of the things with which He has entrusted us. But let us never forget—"it is required in stewards, that a man [or woman] be found faithful" (1 Cor. 4:2).

God longs for us to be faithful. This is why He entreats us to bring to His storehouse a faithful tithe and generous offerings (Mal. 3:8-10). These are His tests of our love and fidelity.

So when we give—*or fail to give!*—let us examine our motive for doing so. Is self involved—ostentation or avarice? If it is, let God replace it with His love. Then, recognizing that we are merely stewards, let us pledge generously—and fulfill our pledges faithfully!

*Fear not, for I am with you, be not dismayed, for I am your God; I will strengthen you, I will help you, I will uphold you with my victorious right hand. Isa. 41:10, RSV.*

MAY

1

# Help From the Commander

When I attended college, I used to get my haircuts at a barbershop run by a Mr. Beyers in St. Helena, California. One day as he was cutting my hair, he mentioned that he was a former marine and had been stationed for a time in Shanghai. He began telling me about his experiences.

As he was talking, an elderly gentleman walked in, sat down, and listened quietly to our conversation. When there was an appropriate pause, the old man said that he too had spent several years in the Orient. He was a " '98er"—a veteran of the Spanish-American War. I had known several '98ers while I was interned, so I was more than casually interested in what the old man had to say.

I have forgotten all the stories Mr. Beyers told, but one that the old '98er related was indelibly impressed on my memory. I think I remember it because it illustrates the Christian life so well.

The old soldier said he was in the first wave that stormed ashore in Manila Bay at dawn on May 1, 1898. He had never before been under fire, and he was scared. Shells sent up geysers of water all around, and bullets whizzed over his head as he leaped from the landing boat into the surf.

As he waded toward the beach, he stumbled and fell. At almost the same instant, he felt a strong hand grab his arm and lift him back up onto his feet. When he turned around to see who had helped him, he saw it was Brigadier General Arthur MacArthur, the commander of his brigade and the father of General Douglas MacArthur of World War II fame!

As a soldier in Christ's army, you need never lose your footing, for He "is able to keep you from falling" (Jude 24). And yet there are times when, because of our carelessness, the tempter entices us and we slip and fall. When this happens, "the commander of the Lord's army" (Joshua 5:15, RSV) stands ready to lift us up and encourage us to renew the battle against the enemy. Now it is up to us: Will we let Him help us?

*Peter and the other apostles replied: "We must obey God rather than men!" Acts 5:29, NIV.*

# The Courage of Your Convictions

Early in life Thomas Ken (1637-1711) was orphaned and brought up by Izaak Walton, his stepbrother-in-law by marriage and famed author of *The Compleat Angler.* Short of stature but possessed of a fearless spirit that belied his size, Ken was sent to Winchester College at 14; he later attended Oxford. After graduating, he returned to Winchester, where he became chaplain to the Anglican bishop.

When Charles II came to the throne he was impressed by "little Ken who tells me my faults," and appointed him royal chaplain. On one of his visits to Winchester, the king selected Ken's manse as the abode for his mistress, Nell Gwyn. But Ken would have none of it—even if it meant displeasing his royal benefactor! Said he, "A woman of ill repute ought not to be endured in the house of a clergyman, least of all in that of the king's chaplain. . . . Not for his kingdom will I comply with the king's command." That took courage for it was a rebuke of the king's way of life as well as that of the woman in question.

In order to make it impossible to carry out the king's request, Ken had the roof of his house removed for repairs. Back in those days displeasing a king could mean losing one's life, but Ken was more concerned with displeasing the King of heaven than displeasing any earthly monarch. However, instead of displeasing Charles, Ken's courageous stand gained the king's admiration. Not long after, when the king was being urged to appoint this or that clergyman bishop of Bath, Charles waved aside all arguments with: "Who shall have Bath and Wells but little Ken who would not give poor Nelly lodging."

"The greatest want of the world is the want of men—men who will not be bought or sold; men who in their inmost souls are true and honest, men who do not fear to call sin by its right name, men whose conscience is as true to duty as the needle to the pole, men who will stand for the right though the heavens fall" (*Education,* p. 57).

The world needs more men and women with the strength of character shown by "little" Ken.

*There were many widows in Israel in Elijah's time. . . . Yet Elijah was not sent to any of them.*
*Luke 4:25, 26, NIV.*

MAY

3

# Only God Knows the Heart

You remember the story: The people of the kingdom of Israel had backslidden terribly. In an endeavor to bring them back to the worship of Jehovah, God had sent a three-and-a-half-year drought on the land (see 1 Kings 17). After the brook Cherith dried up, "the word of the Lord came" to Elijah, instructing him to go "to Zerephath, which belongeth to Zidon," because He had "commanded a widow woman there to sustain" him (verses 5-9).

We know very little about this woman. We don't even know her name. When Jesus spoke to His listeners about her, she had been dead for more than 700 years. Why, then, mention this nameless, virtually unknown woman? Because she was the kind of person who would do *anything* God asked her to do.

It is evident that there wasn't a home in Israel where Elijah would have been welcomed—either because its residents feared reprisals by the king, or because they hated Elijah for causing the drought. At the time these events occurred, you will recall, Ahab and Jezebel were, respectively, king and queen. Ahab was a weak-willed wicked man; Jezebel, a strong-willed wicked woman.

Strangely enough, God sent Elijah to Sidon, the very stronghold of heathendom, to find refuge. Don't forget, Ethbaal, king of Sidon, was Jezebel's father (see 1 Kings 16:31), and in all probability an idolater too. Yet, in this Baal-worshiping country lived a widow whom God could use to care for His servant. I think that sometimes we are prone to imagine that God's true followers are found only in Christian countries—we forget that "in every nation whoever fears Him and works righteousness is accepted by Him" (Acts 10:35, NKJV).

Some years ago I sat at the feet of a professor who insisted that, with rare exception, only those who heard about Christ had a possibility of being saved—otherwise there would be no purpose in Christ commanding His followers to "preach the gospel to every creature" (Mark 16:15). He *may* have had a point, but maybe we'll all be surprised when we get to heaven and find some people there we didn't expect to see—perhaps that will include you and me!

*The prophet [Elisha] answered, "As surely as the Lord lives, whom I serve, I will not accept a thing [for the miracle]." And even though Naaman urged him, he refused.*
**2 Kings 5:16, NIV.**

# Integrity

The dictionary defines integrity as strict adherence to a moral code. History offers examples of people who lived by this principle. The three Hebrew youths, Hananiah, Mishael, and Azariah, for instance, are outstanding examples of this. They could have rationalized that they were not actually worshiping an idol when Nebuchadnezzar commanded everyone to bow to his golden image on pain of death. After all, they were not worshiping the image "in their hearts." But to have done so would have been a violation of the second commandment.

It would also have been a denial of the interpretation of the dream of a golden image that Daniel had earlier given the king. In the dream the image was not entirely of gold, only the head (see Dan. 2:32-43)—a small point, perhaps, but an important one.

In 1884, following the death of both his wife and his mother, Theodore Roosevelt left politics and spent the next three years on his cattle ranch in western Dakota Territory. One day as he rode over the range with several of his cowboys, they came across a 2-year-old steer that had never been branded. One of Roosevelt's ablest cowboys lassoed the animal, built a fire, and prepared to brand the steer. But there was a problem. The property on which the maverick was found belonged to Gregor Lang. Hence, the animal legally belonged to Lang, not to Roosevelt.

Roosevelt watched the procedure but said nothing—until the cowpuncher reached for the hot iron to brand the animal.

"Hold on!" cried Roosevelt. "That's Lang's steer, not mine."

"That's all right. I always put your brand on the mavericks when I find them," said the ranch hand.

"Drop that iron," said Roosevelt quietly. "Go to the ranch and get your pay. I don't need men like you."

"Hey! What have I done wrong?" exclaimed the shocked cowboy.

"A man who will steal *for* me will steal *from* me," answered Roosevelt. "I don't need men like you. Go get your pay."

The world needs more men and women who have the integrity to say no to wrongdoing. "When sinners tempt you, don't give in" (Prov. 1:10, TEV).

*Blessed be the God and Father of our Lord Jesus Christ, the Father of mercies and God of all comfort, who consoles us in our every trouble, so that we may be able to encourage those in any kind of distress, with the consolation with which we are divinely sustained. 2 Cor. 1:3, 4, MLB.*

# The God of All Comfort

During some gospel meetings held in Omaha, Nebraska, G. Campbell Morgan, a celebrated preacher, tried to comfort Salvation Army commander Booth-Tucker. The latter had recently lost his wife. He confessed to Morgan that he could not understand why God permitted Mrs. Booth-Tucker to die, but he asked, "Don't you know that the cross can only be preached by tragedy?" Then he related to Morgan the following incident.

"When my wife and I were in Chicago, trying to lead to Christ a man who had recently lost his wife, I seemed to be getting nowhere. At last the man said, 'It's all very well for you to talk the way you do. But I lost my faith in God when my wife was taken from me. You speak of my loss as a divine providence, but if that beautiful woman by your side were to be taken from you, how would you feel about God?' "

Within a month Booth-Tucker lost his wife in a tragic railway accident. At her funeral, conducted in the hall in Chicago where he preached, he gave this testimony: "I still believe in God. I love Him, and I know Him."

I wish I knew whether or not the man to whom Booth-Tucker spoke was present at the memorial service and what his reaction was, if he was there. I do know of a similar case. A minister had been unable to comfort a widower in his congregation, but after losing his own wife he was able to speak acceptable words of encouragement.

God understands bereavement. Having lost a Son to an unjust and cruel death, He has earned the right to be called the "God of all comfort." When we are bereft of loved ones, He knows what we are going through, and He sends His Holy Spirit to console us. Never forget that one of the titles of the Holy Spirit is "the Comforter" because He gives us strength.

*Abstain from all appearance of evil.*
*1 Thess. 5:22.*

# Avoid the Appearance of Evil

Although he never gambled, Charles Haddon Spurgeon, famous British evangelist, occasionally stopped in Monaco, famed for its casinos and lovely gardens, the latter of which he once declared to be the "most beautiful in the world."

One day a friend of the evangelist told him about a conversation he had recently had while traveling in the French Riviera with the manager of one of the gambling houses in Monte Carlo.

"Why don't you visit our gardens," inquired Monsieur Blanc.

"Well," answered Spurgeon's friend, "I don't gamble, and since my presence at your gardens would yield no return for your business, I hardly think it would be fair for me to avail myself of the opportunity to visit them."

"Oh, but you are mistaken," countered the manager. "Although you do not gamble yourself, your presence would be indirectly profitable to me. You see, people who know you would feel at home in my casino, and for many, from there to the gambling tables would be just a step."

After hearing that, Spurgeon vowed never again to go near the gardens of Monte Carlo.

Some people think they are exercising their "Christian liberty" when they frequent places and engage in activities that are borderline, never considering the evil influence they may have on others. They plead that they are not responsible for what others do, and, of course, this is true. But the matter doesn't end there. We are responsible for our influence.

The apostle Paul recognized this principle when he wrote, "We know that an idol is nothing . . . , and that there is none other God but one" (1 Cor. 8:4). However, even though there may be nothing intrinsically wrong with a certain practice, yet Paul vowed that if engaging in this activity made his "brother stumble," he would never do this again (verse 13, NKJV).

Frequently when it comes to Christian standards the question is not Is this intrinsically wrong? but What direction am I going and what influence will it have on others?

136

*Because [Jesus Christ] himself suffered when he was tempted, he is able to help those who are being tempted. Heb. 2:18, NIV.*

MAY
7

# What It Means to Empathize

It is said that a person who has always enjoyed good health has a hard time empathizing with someone suffering physically. I once read about a nurse, obviously in excellent health, who told a patient who was moaning loudly after an operation to "please shut up" because he was disturbing the entire ward. Another patient, who overheard her, asked if she had ever had an operation.

"No," she answered curtly, and started to leave.

"Well," suggested the questioner, "I think it's about time you did. Maybe you'd understand."

While physical suffering is the most obvious kind of pain, it is not the only kind. Psychological and spiritual pain seem just as agonizing, perhaps more so. Empathy means entering mentally into a sufferer's experience.

Because Jesus endured spiritual, mental, and physical suffering (see Heb. 2:17 and 5:7), He can empathize with us. But He does more than just enter mentally into our sufferings. He offers us help. Notice, because He was "tempted in every way, just as we are—yet without sin" (Heb. 4:15, NIV), "he is able to help those who are being tempted."

One would think that because every human being (Christ excepted) has "sinned, and come short of the glory of God" (Rom. 3:23) every one of us would empathize with and help those who have fallen under temptation. But all too often we don't.

I once sat on a church board and listened to a board member rail against a brother who had been "overtaken in a fault" (Gal. 6:1). No one knew it at the time, but later it was discovered that the railer was guilty of the very sin for which he so severely condemned his brother.

But does empathizing with a sinner mean condoning his sin? No! But it does mean that when we must discipline, we should remember "the pit from which [we] were dug" (Isa. 51:1, NKJV). From this worm's-eye view (see Job 25:6), we can look beyond the sin and see in the sinner a soul to be saved!

## 8

*Blessed are the dead which die in the Lord from henceforth: Yea, saith the Spirit, that they may rest from their labours; and their works do follow them. Rev. 14:13.*

# Mother's Works Follow Her

The words of our text appear on my paternal grandfather's tombstone in Dyas, Alabama. However, they might far more appropriately have been inscribed on a grave marker in Brownville Junction, Maine, where my father's mother lies buried. Her headstone simply gives her name, the years of her birth and death—and the one word "Mother."

Married to Grandpa at age 14 (he was 27), Grandma's life was one of hardships. Grandpa didn't always act the Christian he professed to be. My father was a babe in arms when Grandma finally divorced Grandpa. But now she was left with four little boys, the oldest 10 years, and no means of support. (There was no welfare in those days.) At this point the state of Minnesota stepped in and placed the two older boys in a poor boys' home, promising to return them to her when she could care for them.

For a time Grandma's plight can be described only as desperate. Then a young Irishman, George Hart, fell in love with her and married her.

For the next 10 years Grandma tried to get her two older boys back, as she had been promised. We learned about her valiant efforts 60 years later while I was doing some research on the family and discovered her heartrending letters. She finally succeeded in getting one boy back, but not the other.

As I was growing up, Dad told me more than once about how diligently Grandma tried to rear her boys "in the nurture and admonition of the Lord" (Eph. 6:4). She taught her boys to treat women with deference and respect. Not once did my father ever hear her speak one unkind word against her ex-husband. Yet she died at age 40, considering her life a failure—*but it wasn't a failure!* In time, her sons showed that they had learned well the lessons she taught them—even the son she never got back!

I have often thought how pleasantly surprised Grandma will be when she awakes on the resurrection morning and realizes how faithfully her works have followed her.

Yes, the works of mothers follow them.

*Her children arise up, and call her blessed; her husband also, and he praiseth her. Many daughters have done virtuously, but thou excellest them all. Prov. 31:28, 29.*

MAY

9

# A Tribute to Mothers

At one time or another most of us have eaten food advertised as one of "Heinz 57 Varieties." I'm not sure how Henry J. Heinz arrived at the figure 57, but I do know that when his last will and testament was read, it contained the following tribute:

"Looking forward to the time when my earthly career will end, I desire to set forth at the very beginning of this will, as the most important item in it, a confession of my faith in Jesus Christ as my Saviour. I also desire to bear witness to the fact that throughout my life, in which there were unusual joys and sorrows, I have been wonderfully sustained by my faith in God through Jesus Christ. This legacy was left me by my consecrated mother, a woman of strong faith, and to it I attribute any success I have attained."

Others have paid similar tributes to their mothers. John Ruskin, a great English essayist, critic, and reformer, wrote:

"All that I have ever taught of art, everything that I have written, whatever greatness there has been in any thought of mine, whatever I have done in my life, has simply been due to the fact that, when I was a child, my mother daily read with me a part of the Bible, and daily made me learn part of it by heart."

The other day, before I wrote this reading, I happened to mention to my wife that Bible texts come easily to my mind because of my mother's training. It was she who taught my brother and me while our family was in the mission field, and her emphasis on Bible knowledge left an ineffaceable impression.

Someone has written: "When the judgment shall sit, and the books shall be opened; when the 'well done' of the great Judge is pronounced, and the crown of immortal glory is placed upon the brow of the victor, many will raise their crowns in sight of the assembled universe and, pointing to their mother say: 'She made me all I am through the grace of God' " *(Messaages to Young People,* p. 330).

Today we honor our mothers, but only God can bestow on them the honor they really deserve.

139

# 10

*I will send you Elijah . . . before the great and terrible day of the Lord comes. And he will turn the hearts of the fathers to their children and the hearts of the children to their fathers. Mal. 4:5, 6, RSV.*

# Reconciled—Almost Too Late

Sue Kidd, a nurse in a South Carolina hospital, wrote a poignant story for *Guideposts* a few years ago. She had just checked the vital signs of a Mr. Williams, who had had a slight heart attack a few hours before. All indications seemed good. As she was leaving his room, he asked her to call Janie, his only daughter. She promised she would. He also requested a piece of paper and a pencil, which Sue placed on the table beside his bed.

When Sue reached Janie and told her about her father, there was a scream. "No! It can't be. He's not dying, is he?"

Sue assured her he wasn't, but suggested she visit him without delay.

"I'll be right there," Janie promised. Then, before hanging up, she confessed, "My daddy and I haven't spoken to each other for almost a year. We had a terrible argument over my boyfriend and I ran out of the house saying, 'I hate you.' I've wanted to ask forgiveness, but . . ." Then she hung up.

When Sue returned to check on Mr. Williams, he was no longer breathing. All efforts to resuscitate him were futile. When Janie arrived and heard the terrible news, she was inconsolable. "I never hated him," she sobbed. She insisted Sue take her to her father's bedside. Seeing his lifeless form, she burst into tears and buried her face in the bed sheets.

Just then Sue noticed the piece of paper she had given Mr. Williams. He had written on it: "My dearest Janie, I forgive you. I also pray you will forgive me. I know you love me and I love you too. Daddy." She handed the note to Janie, who read it over and over, whispering as she did so, "Thank God!"

How wonderful to see the heart of a parent "turned" to his child—and vice versa—but how much more wonderful if this reconciliation had taken place while Mr. Williams was still alive!

Perhaps there is a lesson here for us.

*In Joppa there was a disciple named Tabitha . . . , who filled her days with acts of kindness and charity. Acts 9:36, NEB.*

MAY

11

# Selfless Service

As a general rule, women have a way of dealing with sickness and misfortune that men usually lack. As a teenager Florence Nightingale, the founder of modern nursing, believed she heard the voice of God calling her to service. When her parents learned of her decision to become a nurse, they bitterly opposed her. She was beautiful and intelligent, and her mother had plans for a brilliant marriage. One of her suitors, Richard Monckton Milnes, later an English lord, begged her many times to marry him, but she declined.

In 1850, at the age of 30, her parents finally allowed her to go to Kaiserswerth, Germany, to gain nursing experience. In 1854 she was able to put her training into practice, when Britain became involved in the Crimean War. Sidney Herbert, the secretary of war in the British cabinet, invited her to go to Crimea and care for the wounded. She accepted, and sailed from England with 38 other women nurses.

When she reached Scutari (opposite Constantinople, now Istanbul), she found hundreds of uncared-for wounded who had just arrived from the Battle of Balaclava. Many of these men were members of the unit made famous by Alfred, Lord Tennyson's poem "The Charge of the Light Brigade."

Some of those in the government opposed Miss Nightingale's efforts on behalf of the soldiers, claiming she was "spoiling the brutes," but she went right on with her work of mercy. To the wounded she was known as "the lady with the lamp" because of her custom of going through the wards at night with a lamp in her hand.

When the war ended in 1856 and she returned to England, honors were heaped upon her, but she waved them all aside and dedicated the remainder of her active years in service for others, retiring in obscurity. In 1907, when she was awarded the British Order of Merit, the announcement came as a surprise to most people. They thought she had died half a century earlier.

God may not have called you or me to the nursing profession, but He has called every Christian to render selfless service to others in one way or another.

141

*If you give, you will get! Your gift will return to you in full and overflowing measure, pressed down, shaken together to make room for more, and running over. Whatever measure you use to give—large or small—will be used to measure what is given back to you. Luke 6:38, TLB.*

# Recompense

Two students working their way through Stanford University in California were having a hard time paying their expenses. Then one of them had a bright idea. Why not engage Ignace Paderewski, the celebrated Polish pianist, to give a piano recital? With the profits they could pay off their debts to the school. The young men approached Paderewski's manager with their proposal and the manager agreed, on condition that they guarantee Paderewski $2,000.

The young men were sure they could easily raise more than this amount and proceeded to stage the concert. But when the proceeds were totaled, they amounted to only $1,600. Going to the great pianist in great embarrassment, the young men handed him the $1,600 with a promissory note for $400. They gave their word that they would redeem the note at the earliest possible moment.

"No, boys," said Paderewski, "that will never do." Tearing up the note, he returned the money to the young men and said, "Take out of the $1,600 all of your expenses, keep for each of you 10 percent of the balance for your efforts, and let me have what is left."

The young men couldn't believe what they were hearing.

Years passed. At the end of World War I Paderewski, now premier of Poland, found himself struggling to feed millions of his starving compatriots. He appealed to Herbert C. Hoover, who at the time was in charge of America's relief effort, and soon tons of food began to pour in to feed Poland's starving population. Soon after, Paderewski traveled to Paris to thank his benefactor.

"You're more than welcome, Mr. Paderewski," replied Hoover. "You probably don't remember me, but you once helped me when I was a poor college student at Stanford University."

Yes, kindness pays. But in some cases we shall have to wait and be "recompensed at the resurrection of the just" (Luke 14:14).

*The kind of fasting I want is this: . . . Share your food with the hungry and open your homes to the homeless poor. Give clothes to those who have nothing to wear. . . . Then my favor will shine on you like the morning sun, and your wounds will be quickly healed.*
*Isa. 58:6-8, TEV.*

MAY

13

# Best Medicine for Mental Healing

Many psychological problems manifest themselves as food addiction (overweight) or revulsion (anorexia), some as nervous ticks, and still others as mental breakdowns.

Dr. Karl A. Menninger, renowned psychiatrist and founder of the world-famous Winter General Veterans Administration Hospital in Topeka, Kansas, once gave a lecture on mental health. During the question period that followed he was asked, "What would you advise a person to do if he felt a nervous breakdown coming on?" Many expected Menninger to reply, "Consult a good psychiatrist." But to his audience's surprise, he answered, "Lock up your house, go across the railroad tracks, find someone in need, and then do something to help that person."

The expression "across the railroad tracks," or "the other side of the tracks," comes from mid-nineteenth-century America, when the railroad companies in the United States were constructing the great lines of travel across the continent. As they moved across the land, it was common for towns to spring up here and there along the tracks. The more affluent members of the community usually lived on one side of the tracks, while the less fortunate lived on the other side of the tracks.

Are you depressed? Does everything seem dark and gloomy? Would you like God's favor to shine upon you like the morning sun? Then go over to the "other side of the tracks." Observe, inquire around if need be, but find someone who is in greater need than you and minister to that person.

It may be that that person's greatest need is not food or shelter or clothing. It may be that his or her greatest need is for friendship. Showing this individual Christian love and concern will not only help him or her, but it will also help you; for, as you do this, you will find that "the Sun of righteousness [will indeed] arise [upon you] with healing in his wings" (Mal. 4:2).

# 14

*Even though our physical being is gradually decaying, yet our spiritual being is renewed day after day. And this small and temporary trouble we suffer will bring us a tremendous and eternal glory, much greater than the trouble.*
**2 Cor. 4:16, 17, TEV.**

# Renewed Day by Day

In one of his books, Kagawa Toyohiko, a renowned Japanese Christian, tells the thrilling story of one of his countrymen who was struck with a pemphigus-like skin disease that was slowly sapping his life away. Medical science had only one palliative—a chemical solution that alleviated but did not cure his ailment. In order for the treatment to be effective, his body had to be immersed (except for his head, of course) in this solution. With the stoicism typical of the Japanese, the sufferer stepped into a bathtubful of the solution. There he remained, except for brief excursions, for seven long years!

As the days dragged slowly by, a ray of light pierced into the man's pain-racked brain—the gospel story. He opened the gates of his soul to its message, and a surge of hope and power flooded his consciousness. At his request, a New Testament was suspended at eye level so he could read it. Day by day, month by month, year by year, he drank in the life-giving words from the Book. He almost forgot the pain in his wasting body; in its place an abiding peace came over him. As his strength ebbed, his spiritual life enlarged. His bathtub became a kind of altar to God.

Whether medical science has found a cure for this particular disease, I do not know. But there are other incurable afflictions today that are just as dreadful, perhaps more so.

The world is nothing but a pesthouse, and sooner or later this lazaretto claims every victim. But the situation is not hopeless! No matter how slowly or rapidly our physical bodies are degenerating, we can renew our spiritual natures day by day as we study the Word—and look forward to the day we shall all have new, immortal bodies.

*Why worry about your clothes? Look at the field lilies! They don't worry about theirs. Yet King Solomon in all his glory was not clothed as beautifully as they. And if God cares so wonderfully for flowers that are here today and gone tomorrow, won't he more surely care for you? Matt. 6:28-30, TLB.*

# The Ministry of Flowers

One of the most precious memories I have of my boyhood is of going out into the country for a family picnic. While Mom set out a delicious dinner Dad would take us children to a nearby field to look for wildflowers. When we found one, he would open his coin purse and, taking out a small, folding magnifying glass, would hold the little flower under it and let us marvel at its beauty.

As I write, flowers are blooming everywhere. In response to the genial rays of the sun that is just now peeping over the mountains to the east, the flowers are gradually opening their lovely petals. Human efforts to open them, however careful, would only ruin them. Only the hand of the Creator can perform this miracle and increase the beauty of the opening bud.

Beautiful flowers are the result of beautiful thoughts dreamed up by the Master Gardener. In a sense, we are flowers planted in the garden of the Lord, and it is our privilege to respond to the life-giving rays of the Sun of Righteousness. Unaided by our gracious God, all efforts on our part to better ourselves can only result in ruin. Only the hand that made us can bring out in us the true beauty of holiness.

"God is a lover of the beautiful, but that which He most loves is a beautiful character. . . . It is beauty of character that shall not perish, but last through the ceaseless ages of eternity. The great Master Artist has taken thought for the lilies, making them so beautiful that they outshine the glory of Solomon. How much more does He care for man, who is the image of the glory of God. He longs to see His children reveal a character after His similitude. As the sunbeam imparts to the flowers their varied and delicate tints, so does God impart to the soul the beauty of His own character" (*My Life Today*, p. 270).

May you and I experience this transformation.

*I said in my haste, "I am cut off from before Your eyes"; nevertheless You heard the voice of my supplications when I cried out to You. Ps. 31:22, NKJV.*

# What if, or Nevertheless

Marion Bond West hit rock bottom when the doctors told her that Jerry, her 47-year-old husband, had a highly malignant brain tumor. Questions crowded into her mind, each beginning with the words "what if." What if the doctors couldn't remove all the tumor? What if Jerry lingered on and suffered for months? What if he should die? The future seemed dark and hopeless.

And then, on May 11, 1983, seven months after receiving the terrible news, Marion was driving home from the hospital after visiting Jerry when something dramatic happened. She was praying as she drove along. Suddenly a single word surfaced in her consciousness: "nevertheless." She knew it was a Bible word, but for a moment she had no idea what message God had in it for her. And then the thought struck her. Here she was alone in her car, *nevertheless,* God was with her. Looking out the window at the sunset, she murmured, "Thank You."

No, Jerry didn't get well. In spite of fervent prayers for healing, God did not see fit to restore him to health. In fact, two and a half months later he died. Marion was left alone—nevertheless, God sustained her. He sustained her not only then but also in the days that followed. Although she faced new problems and perplexing situations without Jerry, nevertheless God helped her to cope, and the "what ifs" became easier to handle.

As Marion discovered, the word "nevertheless" occurs more than 90 times in the Bible and is always used with tremendous power. One of these occurrences is found in Luke 5:5. You remember, the disciples had fished all night without success. Now it was daylight, the worst time of day to try to fish, but Jesus urged them to launch out into the deep and cast their nets, and Peter answered, "Master, we have toiled all night, and have caught nothing: *nevertheless* at thy word I will let down the net." You know the rest of the story.

When everything looks hopeless and forbidding, don't dwell on the "what ifs" of doubt, but on the "neverthelesses" of faith.

*It is to you who believe in [Christ] that he is precious, but to those who do not [believe] he is "a . . . stumbling-block." 1 Peter 2:7, 8, TCNT.*

MAY
17

# The Most Important Discovery

In 1847 Sir James Y. Simpson, a medical doctor in Edinburgh, Scotland, discovered that chloroform could be used as an anesthetic. This discovery made it possible for people to undergo surgeries that otherwise would have been excruciatingly painful. Although chloroform is no longer used, at the time it was considered a great discovery; some even claim it was one of the most important discoveries in medical history. It seems that Dr. Simpson made some other lesser discoveries as well.

Some years later, while Dr. Simpson was lecturing to a class of young medical students at the University of Edinburgh, one of them asked, "What do you consider to have been the most important discovery you ever made?"

"The most important discovery I ever made," replied Dr. Simpson thoughtfully, "was when I discovered that I was a sinner and that Jesus Christ was my Saviour."

It is a sad fact, but nevertheless true, that many people go through life without ever making this twofold discovery. Most of us, of course, make the first part of this discovery quite early in life, but many never discover the second part. This is apparently true even of some professed Christians. This happens, not because God is far removed and inaccessible, for we are assured that "He is not far from each one of us" (Acts 17:27, NKJV), but because He never foists His love upon us.

When I was a callow youth, I thought I was in love with a young lady and tried the "direct approach." I told her forthrightly that I loved her. Fortunately she had better sense than I. Today, of course, I'm glad it didn't work out.

God woos us indirectly through the study of the life of His Son and through the testimony of those who have experienced His Son's salvation. He leaves it up to us to respond to His love.

The most important discovery you and I can make is not merely that we are sinners, but that Jesus is a wonderful Saviour.

# 18

*Everyone knows that two sparrows can be bought for one farthing, and yet death does not come to one of them without your Father knowing about it. . . . So, then, don't be afraid. You are more valuable than a whole collection of sparrows. Matt. 10:29-31, Barclay.*

# Worth More Than Many Sparrows

James H. McConkey, a writer of sermon illustrations, tells how one day he was sitting on a hotel veranda, enjoying the beauties of nature, when his attention was drawn to a rush of sparrows flying past. Suddenly he heard a dull thud. The next moment, there on the ground not 10 feet away lay a little bird on its back. Its tiny feet clawed frantically for a few moments, as if appealing to heaven. There was a convulsive quiver, as if the little creature were in pain. Then it was all over.

McConkey went over and examined the little sparrow. A drop or two of blood on its breast told the story. Apparently the little bird had struck a pane of glass in its flight. To all appearances, said he, no one, except himself sitting there alone, noticed or cared about the death of the little bird. Just then the thought flashed into his mind: *Not a sparrow falls to the ground but what your heavenly Father takes notice, and you are of more value than many sparrows.* How true.

The word in our text translated "farthing," by William Barclay, is *assarion.* This was a small copper coin worth one sixteenth of a Roman denarius; it was one of the smaller coins in circulation in Christ's day. Two sparrows were worth one of these little coins. In Luke's account, five sparrows were sold for two *assaria.* Some might quibble over a seeming discrepancy of Scripture. Others, however, might insist that these statements were made on two different occasions, and that on the Lucan occasion Jesus was simply emphasizing the "worthlessness" of these little birds, because in buying four, one could get an extra one free—and they might just be right.

What gives us value is not what we may think we are worth, or what others may think we are worth, but what our heavenly Father thinks we are worth—and He valued us so much that He gave His only begotten Son to die in our place (see John 3:16).

*Agrippa said to Paul, "You almost persuade me to become a Christian." Acts 26:28, NKJV.*

MAY

19

# The Saddest Words of Tongue or Pen

Most New Testament translations suggest that Agrippa was saying something like, "Do you think that in such a short time you can persuade me to be a Christian?" (NIV; cf. RSV, TEV), or "You think it will not take much to win me over and make a Christian of me" (NEB). However, other translations disagree. Without attempting to resolve this problem, the fact remains that there are some who almost surrender to Christ but ultimately don't.

During World War I British and French naval forces were given the task of opening the Dardanelles to enable the Allies to secure much-needed grain while at the same time delivering arms and ammunition to their Russian allies. After fighting partway up the straits and suffering moderate but not excessive losses, the Allies reached the principal Turkish fort and fought an artillery duel with it. But then they pulled back, and although the Gallipoli campaign dragged on for another year, it ended in a humiliating withdrawal by the Allies.

After the war the Allies learned that when they pulled back, the main Turkish fort was on the point of surrender. It had been reduced to fewer than 30 shells. Had the attack been pressed the next day, the fort would have fallen, and the war would have taken an entirely different course.

Hebrews 10:38 speaks of those who, instead of pressing the attack in the spiritual warfare until victory is won, "draw back" and are lost.

Paradoxically, victory in this war means surrender—the total surrender of self to Christ. What a tragedy that many professed Christians will be lost because they failed to press the attack to final victory. In this war, almost but not wholly saved means to be not almost but wholly lost.

I am glad that the next verse, Hebrews 10:39, ends on a positive note. This verse goes on to say, "But we are not of them who draw back unto perdition; but of them that believe to the saving of the soul." May this experience be yours and mine in the spiritual warfare in which we are all engaged.

# 20

*Thou wilt keep him in perfect peace, whose mind is stayed on thee: because he trusteth in thee. Trust ye in the Lord for ever: for in the Lord Jehovah is everlasting strength.*
*Isa. 26:3, 4.*

# How to Be Kept in Perfect Peace

One of the first things Charles II did when he ascended the throne of England in 1660 was to arrest Archibald Campbell, eighth earl of Argyll, for collaborating with Oliver Cromwell's commonwealth. The king had the earl condemned to death; the execution was set for May 27, 1661.

A painting by E. M. Ward that hangs in the House of Commons is captioned "The Last Sleep of Argyll Before His Execution." It depicts the earl, a devout Christian, dressed in black, sleeping peacefully on a rough couch on one side of his cell. The privy councillor, who has come to lead him to the gallows, stands at the door opposite the condemned man, wearing a red cloak. The privy councillor's perturbed, awestruck appearance contrasts sharply with the peaceful look on the earl's face.

A historian of the period recorded that "on the very day he was to die, . . . [the earl] dined with appetite, conversed with gaiety at the table, and after his last meal lay down, as he was wont, to take a short slumber in order that his body and mind might be full of vigor when he should mount the scaffold."

How many of us would be able to sleep, let alone sleep peacefully, if we knew we were going to be executed in the next few hours? Yet here was a man who lived so close to God that he could sleep in perfect peace while awaiting death.

Incredible as it may seem, facing life can sometimes be harder than facing death. But the God who gave the earl, the apostle Peter (see Acts 12:1-6), and countless martyrs fortitude to face death, offers you and me "perfect peace" to face life. So no matter what lies ahead, God assures us we can have this serenity.

The secret of having this peace is in keeping our minds "stayed" on God. I like the way *The Living Bible* paraphrases Isaiah 26:3: "He will keep in perfect peace all those who trust in him, whose thoughts *turn often to the Lord!*"

Turn your thoughts often to the Lord today and experience this peace that "passeth all understanding" (Phil. 4:7)!

*Why should the sufferer be born to see the light? Why is life given to those who find it so bitter? Job 3:20, REB.*

MAY
21

# Why Me, Lord?

On October 26, 1981, two murderers forced their way into the Weicht home in Conroe, Texas, and shot Craig Weicht, his wife, and their 8-year-old daughter, Karen, leaving them for dead. Mrs. Weicht survived, but was left to suffer the emotional agony of losing those dearest to her.

Once in a moment of rage, she shook a fist at God and shouted, "God, why did You let them kill my husband and my baby! You've taken away everything I loved!"

After the outburst, God spoke to her in a still small voice that seemed to say, *When those murderers killed your loved ones, you didn't have the power to stop them. But when they took My Son's life, I had the power to stop them, but I didn't—because I loved you so much.* (See John 3:16 and Rom. 8:32.)

When she considered the implications of these words, she cried out, "O God, forgive me!"

This is how one Christian handled the loss of loved ones. Here is how another handled it:

Eric Barker, a British missionary who spent more than 50 years in Portugal and was there when World War II began, decided to repatriate his wife and eight children. Barker stayed behind to tidy up some important mission business before leaving. The next Sunday, moments before standing up to preach, someone handed him a telegram with the terrible news that the ship on which his family was traveling had been sunk and all on board had been lost.

Without mentioning the tragedy, Barker announced simply, "I have just received word that my loved ones have arrived home safely," then he preached his sermon dry-eyed. Only later did the people learn about the enormity of his loss. (His announcement reflected his understanding of 2 Corinthians 5:8.)

The "God of all comfort" understands by personal experience the grief we go through when we lose a loved one, and because He does, He is able to comfort "us in all our tribulation." As we are comforted by Him in our tragic losses, we in turn are "able to comfort them which are in . . . trouble" (2 Cor. 1:3, 4).

*By faith Abraham obeyed the call to go out to a land destined for himself and his heirs, and left home without knowing where he was to go. Heb. 11:8, NEB.*

# Stepping Out in Faith

If we would have our prayers answered, we must step out in faith, as did Abraham, obeying what we know to be God's will; for "without faith it is impossible to please him" (Heb. 11:6).

The first time Hudson Taylor, founder of the China Inland Mission, went to the Orient, he traveled in a sailing vessel. As his ship passed some cannibal islands, the ship was becalmed and began to drift inexorably toward shore. As it neared the beach, everyone on board, except Taylor, became extremely apprehensive. They could just imagine the cannibals heating up their caldrons in anticipation of a toothsome feast.

Knowing that Taylor was a man of God, the captain approached him and urged him to pray for divine help.

"I will pray," responded Taylor, "but first you must set the sails."

The captain demurred. He was afraid that the prayer might not be answered and he would be laughed at. "Can't you pray first?" he pleaded.

"I cannot pray unless you first raise the sails," replied Taylor.

The sails were set and Taylor began to pray in his cabin. While he was on his knees, there was an insistent knock at his door. When he asked "Who is there?" the captain inquired, "Are you still praying for wind?" When Taylor answered he was, the captain said, "I think you'd better stop. We already have more wind than we can manage."

Have you ever wondered what the difference is between presumption and stepping out in faith? Consider this: George Müller, who received many answers to prayer, said that the secret to successful prayer is to first ask, Is this the Lord's work? With an affirmative answer to that, the next question is, Is this the Lord's way? And last: Is this the Lord's time?

Abraham, Taylor, and Müller learned the secret of prevailing prayer. It is our privilege to learn it too.

> *You have seen me tossing and turning through the night. You have collected all my tears and preserved them in your bottle! You have recorded every one in your book.*
> *Ps. 56:8, TLB.*

# Tears Recorded

One of the surprises I encountered on a tour I made to the Bible lands were lacrimatories—small vessels used by the ancients for collecting mourners' tears. These small flasks had been removed from burial chambers and placed on display in the great museums of Europe and the Middle East. Some of these tear bottles were fashioned from common clay, others from glass, and still others from costly chalcedony. I especially remember the lacrimatories found in King Tut's tomb. He was only 18 when he died, and the tears placed in these bottles were those of his young widow—poignant reminders of her grief.

Lacrimatories were used in Palestine in David's time, for he mentions them in our verse for this morning. The superscription to Psalm 56 says that this psalm was a "michtam of David, when the Philistines took him in Gath." Some scholars think that *michtam* is a term derived from the Akkadian word *katamu*, "to cover," and thus suggests that this was an atonement psalm. One thing is certain, David surely needed atonement after he fled to Gath.

You remember, David had been anointed as the Lord's king-in-waiting. All through the years God had miraculously preserved him from Saul's murderous designs. But now, with his archenemy in hot pursuit, David's faith faltered and he erred grievously. First he lied to Ahimelech, the priest of Nob, by falsely claiming he was on business for the king. Second, he erred by fleeing to Israel's enemies in Gath. And finally, having gotten himself into a serious predicament, he feigned insanity to escape from the Philistines.

David didn't deserve God's mercy, yet when he cried unto the Lord in heartfelt penitence, God in mercy delivered him. In recognition of such amazing grace, David composed Psalm 56.

So with us. When our faith fails and we fall, we may not deserve God's mercy, yet when in tearful and heartfelt penitence we come to Him, seeking forgiveness and strength to overcome, we can take comfort in the fact that He forgives, and that our tears are preserved in heaven's tear bottles.

*Who [is] so blind as the one who has my trust, so deaf as the servant of the Lord? You have seen much but perceived little.*
*Isa. 42:19, 20, REB.*

# Turning a Blind Eye

British naval hero Horatio Nelson was born at Burnham Thorpe, England, September 29, 1758, the son of an Anglican clergyman. He entered His Majesty's service at the age of 12, and at 35 lost his right eye during the Battle of Calvi on the northwest coast of Corsica. He gained fame six years later at the Battle of Copenhagen while serving under Admiral Parker. In the midst of the melee, Nelson's attention was called to Parker's signal to withdraw. Knowing victory was in sight if he pressed his attack, he decided to disregard his commander's order. Raising his telescope to his blind eye, he professed to be unable to see Parker's signal. He continued to attack and won a signal victory for British arms.

In moral matters Nelson was not so perceptive. For instance, he would have done better to turn a blind eye to the seductive charms of Lady Emma Hamilton, wife of the British ambassador to Naples. In 1800, when Admiral Keith ordered Nelson to leave Naples for Minorca, he disobeyed, claiming his presence in that city was "needed" for political reasons. The truth was, he was infatuated with Lady Hamilton; within a year he divorced his wife and continued his illicit relationship.

It is said that love is blind. It might be more accurate to say that lust is blind. Sexual gratification seems to exert a hypnotic spell over people who ordinarily manifest good judgment. However, love that is of heavenly origin is not blind.

In the history of ancient Israel, Balaam got Balak to seduce Israel through forbidden sex when they were on the very borders of the Promised Land (read Num. 25). We who stand on the borders of the heavenly Canaan face the same temptation. Every day, on every side, our senses are stimulated by sights and sounds that suggest illicit sex. We need to turn a blind eye to all such seductive influences. But we can do so only as we keep our spiritual eyes fixed on Jesus, the Servant of Jehovah and our great Exemplar—and "take hold of [His] strength" to overcome (Isa. 27:5).

*Now Elisha was fallen sick of his sickness whereof he died. And Joash the king of Israel came down unto him, and wept over his face, and said, O my father, my father, the chariot of Israel, and the horsemen thereof.*
2 Kings 13:14.

MAY

# 25

# When God Doesn't Heal

As a child you probably heard stories about Elisha's miracles—the resurrection of the Shunammite's son, the healing of Naaman the leper, the opening of the eyes of Elisha's servant to behold "the mountain was full of horses and chariots of fire round about Elisha" (2 Kings 6:17). But did you ever hear about how God didn't perform a miracle when Elisha was old and was suffering his last illness? Probably not.

In our text Joash, king of Israel, came to see Elisha for the last time. Having inherited a kingdom that had virtually no cavalry (2 Kings 13:7), he knew he needed more than human help against his enemies. As he entered the room where Elisha lay dying, he bent over the aged prophet and wept, "O my father, my father, the chariot of Israel, and the horsemen thereof."

This lament alludes to the angelic deliverance at Dothan, when God sent "horses and chariots of fire" to deliver His prophet from the Syrians who were besieging Dothan. Joash feared that with Elisha gone, the angels that had delivered the man of God at Dothan would no longer be around to deliver Israel. What Joash failed to understand was that angels of God are ever at the side of those who put their trust in Him.

Just because God did not raise up Elisha from his sickbed did not mean that He had abandoned His faithful servant—*or Israel!* Listen to these comforting words: "It was not given Elisha to follow his master [Elijah, to heaven] in a fiery chariot. Upon him the Lord permitted to come a lingering illness. During the long hours of human weakness and suffering, his faith laid fast hold on the promises of God, and he beheld ever about him heavenly messengers of comfort and peace" (*Prophets and Kings,* pp. 263, 264).

What a comfort this realization must have been to the dying prophet! What a solace this *could* have been to Joash! What a consolation it *can be* to us when God doesn't see fit to heal!

*[The Lord] may punish, yet he will have compassion in the fullness of his unfailing love; he does not willingly afflict or punish any mortal. Lam. 3:31-33, REB.*

# Relating to Death and Suffering

A few years ago a child sent the following letter to the popular advice columnist Abigail Van Buren:

"Dear God: Why did You let my brother die? When he was hit by the car, my mother prayed to You to let him live, but You wouldn't. My little brother was only 2 years old, and he couldn't have sinned so bad that You had to punish him that way. Everyone says You are good and can do anything You want to. You could have saved my little brother, but You let him die. You broke my mother's heart. How can I love You?"

The question of death and suffering is a hard one to answer satisfactorily in all cases. In some instances the answer is obvious. The smoker who suffers and dies from lung cancer is reaping the natural results of his violation of the laws of health. We all understand that. But when the innocent suffer and die through no fault of their own, answers are harder to come by.

Death and suffering were never a part of God's original plan. They are the result of disobedience—and not necessarily our own disobedience. In some cases, a newborn with AIDS, for instance, we can trace the cause back to parents. In other cases, we must go farther back to our first parents, Adam and Eve. In still other cases, we must go clear back to Satan, the originator of sin with its attendant suffering and death.

But the wonderful thing is that God's grace is sufficient for every trial. He can change the bad things that happen to us to our eternal good.

Today I took part in an anointing service for a young man who has been paralyzed from the neck down for the past 17 years—the result of an accident while driving under the influence of alcohol. His health is failing fast. Apparently God has not seen fit to heal him, but his dying testimony has been inspiring. He is resigned to God's will. He acknowledged that his accident was probably the only way God could have saved him. But best of all, he confessed that God's grace is indeed sufficient.

*Though by this time you ought to be teachers,*
*you need someone to teach you again.*
*Heb. 5:12, NKJV.*

MAY
27

# Learn in Order to Teach Others

We have a birch tree in our front yard; each spring a pair of robins builds a nest in its branches. Within a few days the bluish eggs hatch, and before long the nestlings are ready for their flying lessons.

By the time the young robins leave the nest, they can manage to fly reasonably well, but usually they require a lot of help in finding food. The young fledglings seem to take pride in their new independence, but their first trial flights are quickly followed by cries that obviously mean "Feed me! Feed me!" and the parent birds are always ready with some food—to begin with.

If you are a bird-watcher, you have probably observed that as the young birds mature, the pattern changes. The young birds learn to feed themselves and eventually become parents themselves and teach their young to fly and find food.

My wife and I have watched this developmental process many times, and you may have too. But have you ever seen birds that forgot what they had learned? Probably not.

Unlike the birds, the recipients of the Epistle to the Hebrews had forgotten what they had once been taught and needed to learn all over again. Maybe they had reverted to the stage in which they were crying, "Feed me! Feed me!"

Have you ever seen church members who complained because they felt they were not being spiritually fed? My wife and I observed this phenomenon while we were doing pastoral work. Now, it is possible, even probable, that these individuals had a valid complaint. Doubtless we, as their spiritual parents, had failed to teach them how to dig into the Word of God and find spiritual sustenance for themselves. But in some instances it seemed to be a case of arrested (even regressive) development, for we never saw them produce spiritual offspring.

Shouldn't believers come to the point where, instead of being merely consumers of spiritual nourishment, crying "Feed me! Feed me!" they learn to "scratch" for themselves, produce spiritual offspring, and in turn teach them to fly and feed themselves?

**MAY 28**

*Do you not realize that as many of us as were baptized in union with Christ Jesus were baptized in union with His death? So we are buried with Him in death through baptism in order that, just as Christ rose from the dead through the Father's glorious power, so we too shall conduct ourselves in a new way of living. Rom. 6:3, 4, MLB.*

# Baptism and a Way of Life

Baptism has been described as an outward sign of an inward change. This inward change manifests itself "in a new way of living." Unfortunately, not all who are baptized experience the inward transformation that should precede this rite. Such persons continue to live the same old life of sin they lived before they were baptized.

About A.D. 500, Clovis, king of the Franks, won a victory over the Alamanni, after which he accepted Christianity and was baptized. After his baptism he offered a tunic to any of his warriors who accepted his new religion. Gregory of Tours says that 3,000 accepted tunics and were baptized. However, as these men went down into the water many of them held their right hand high. That was so that later they could say "This hand was never baptized," and consequently they could swing their battle axes as freely as before.

One cannot help wondering how much of an inward change these men experienced. Fortunately, not all baptismal candidates are like these Frankish warriors. A Canadian railroad engineer was about to be immersed in baptism when his pastor noticed a bulge in his hip pocket. The pastor asked him if he hadn't forgotten to remove his wallet.

"No," the baptismal candidate replied, "I didn't forget. I purposely left it there. I want it to be baptized, too."

What a commendable attitude!

The inward change that precedes baptism does not mean that henceforth the candidate is sinless, any more than a newborn infant is fully developed. What it does mean is that when we are born again our life moves in a "heavenward" direction. So long as we continue progressing in this direction we are walking "in a new way of living."

*Be filled with the Spirit; speaking to yourselves in psalms and hymns and spiritual songs, singing and making melody in your heart to the Lord. Eph. 5:18, 19.*

MAY
29

# Saved by a Song

Doris Paulson had come to the "end of her rope," as the saying goes. Her son had been killed in Vietnam, her doctor had recently told her she had diabetes, and to top it all, her marriage was falling apart. Deciding that life was no longer worth living, she went to her medicine chest, poured out an overdose of pills, and said to herself, *This is the last time I'll see this miserable face.*

Just then she heard someone singing. She listened:

"God of my life, whose gracious power

Through varied scenes my life hath led,

Or turned aside the fatal hour,

Or lifted up my sinking head."

Never were words more timely. Doris recognized the voice as that of Mrs. Smith, her new neighbor next door. Although Mrs. Smith seemed pleasant enough, Doris hardly knew her. But after listening to the words of the song, she decided to get better acquainted with her neighbor. Returning the pills to the bottle, she went next door and rang the doorbell.

"I'll be right there," Mrs. Smith called out cheerily, then, "Hi! Oh, it's you, Mrs. Paulson. Please come in and sit down. Is there anything I can do for you?"

"Would you please sing that song again, the one you were singing just now?" pleaded Doris.

As Mrs. Smith sang, tears streamed down Doris's face. When the song ended, she told her neighbor how it had saved her from suicide.

This song was a turning point in Doris's life. The two women studied the Bible together, and a few weeks later, Doris accepted Jesus as her personal Saviour and was baptized.

Have you ever considered that singing can be a powerful way of witnessing? In Doris's case it saved a soul from physical death—perhaps eternal death as well.

*Though I walk through the valley of the shadow of death, I will fear no evil: for thou art with me. Ps. 23:4.*

# Light in the Valley

This verse, from the most beloved of all the psalms, has ever been a comfort to those facing imminent death—soldiers mortally wounded, sufferers of a terminal illness, people condemned to be executed. But the promise in this verse is not only for those whose days are clearly numbered. It is for every human being, for, whether we like it or not, we are all sojourners on the road to that "undiscover'd country, from whose bourn no traveler returns" (Shakespeare, *Hamlet*).

Our verse for meditation speaks of "the shadow of death." A shadow is cast by light falling on an object. So, to the Christian, the shadow in the valley of death is actually an evidence that Jesus, "the light of the world" (John 8:12), is not far away. How precious, then, is the thought that although we may not see our Saviour with our natural sight, He is nevertheless close by us.

This means that although at times we may feel that we are all alone as we trudge along the road of life, we are not alone. He who promised "I will never leave thee, nor forsake thee" (Heb. 13:5) is "not far from every one of us" (Acts 17:27).

Feelings of loneliness are not limited to you and me. Most people have experienced them at one time or another. Jesus Himself experienced these feelings. He felt abandoned in the Garden of Gethsemane, when "all the disciples forsook him and fled" (Matt. 26:56). He felt even more abandoned on the cross; when surrounded by darkness, it seemed as if even His Father had forsaken Him (Matt. 27:46). But had God forsaken His Son? Never! And neither will Jesus forsake us.

Simply because clouds blot out the light of the sun does not mean that the sun isn't shining beyond the clouds. Similarly, even though at times "the Sun of righteousness" (Mal. 4:2) is obscured by clouds of trouble, remember that beyond the clouds the Sun shines! And never forget, the very shadow that seems so ominous is in reality proof that the Light of the world is nearby!

*[A person] must not say, "I am nothing but a barren tree." For these are the words of the Lord: [They] . . . shall receive from me something better than sons and daughters, a memorial and a name in my own house and within my walls. Isa. 56:3-5, NEB.*

MAY

31

# Better Than Sons or Daughters

My brother always wanted to have a son as an heir to his name. Unfortunately, it didn't work out that way. Instead, he had two lovely daughters, Marjorie and Elizabeth. When my oldest son's wife, Gladys, had their third child, they decided to name him Charles, after my brother. I have always thought that this was a gracious gesture on their part.

So now my brother has a "son" to carry on his name. But far more important than having a son to carry on one's name is being a son or a daughter of God and having one's name inscribed on the walls of God's house, as our verse suggests. This means more than having our names written on the books of some church here on earth, important as this may be, for being a church member does not guarantee an entrance into heaven.

When the 70 disciples whom Jesus sent out returned from their missionary tours rejoicing that "even the demons obey us when we use your name" (Luke 10:17, TLB), Jesus tempered their overenthusiasm by saying, "Do not rejoice so much in the fact that the devils are subject to you as that your names are inscribed in heaven" (verse 20, NAB). This, when all is said and done, is the important thing.

In order for our names to be inscribed in heaven's books we must be adopted as sons and daughters of God (see 2 Cor. 6:17, 18). There is nothing mysterious or difficult about this transaction. It simply means accepting salvation through Christ's sacrifice, and His rulership in our lives instead of our own.

The opportunity to be adopted as a son or a daughter of God is limited. A time will come when it will "cease forever" (Ps. 49:8, NKJV). If you have never accepted God's terms but wish to do so, right now is the time. Tomorrow could be too late. Becoming an adopted son or daughter of God and having your name inscribed in heaven is far more important than having an earthly namesake.

*Adapt yourselves no longer to the pattern of this present world, but let your minds be remade and your whole nature thus transformed. Then you will be able to discern the will of God, and to know what is good, acceptable, and perfect. Rom. 12:2, NEB.*

# Metamorphosis

The word "transformed" comes from the Greek verb *metamorphoo,* "to change, to transfigure, to alter in appearance." Our word "metamorphosis" is derived from this Greek root. One of the definitions of metamorphosis is "a marked and more or less abrupt developmental change in the form or structure of an animal (as a butterfly or a frog) occurring subsequent to birth or hatching."

My wife and I enjoy gardening, but unless we are careful, certain creatures that "metamorphose" ruin our crops. This is their nature. They are called caterpillars. Most people despise these destructive crawling creatures. However, when a caterpillar metamorphoses, its nature is changed and it emerges from its chrysalis as a beautiful butterfly.

In the early centuries of the Christian era, the butterfly was used as a symbol of the resurrection. The thought was that as the caterpillar's nature is changed by the process of metamorphosis, so those who die in Christ will be changed from mortal to immortal by the resurrection at the Second Coming (see 1 Cor. 15:51-53).

There is an exclusive club in America known as the Caterpillar Club. It admits only people who have survived a fall from an airplane *without a parachute and lived to tell about it.* Its members feel they have been given a second chance to live. Not surprisingly, the caterpillar is the symbol of their "new life."

The Bible teaches that God's people will undergo a metamorphosis at the Second Coming. But if we are to experience this change, we must first experience the metamorphosis of conversion—the transformation that takes place when the Holy Spirit comes into our lives and makes us new creatures in Christ. In both instances God's power is at work. Some have called this transforming energy "resurrection power" (see Phil. 3:10).

We all need it in our lives today!

*Fret not thyself because of evildoers. . . . For they shall soon be cut down like the grass, and wither as the green herb. Trust in the Lord, and do good. Ps. 37:1-3.*

JUNE
2

# How to Handle Injustice

Some years ago in Africa a group of inhabitants of a certain land were crossing a road when one of their number was struck by a car and killed. The motorist sped away. The survivors gave chase, but were unable to overtake him.

Returning to the scene of the accident, the bereaved group expressed their anger, grief, and frustration with loud cries and wild gesticulations. Instead of continuing on their journey, they set up a vigil by the body of their fallen comrade.

Later that same day the guilty motorist returned by the same road he had traveled earlier. Recognizing his car, the mourners hurled well-aimed rocks at his vehicle. This time the culprit had to stop. His windshield was smashed so badly he couldn't see the road. The vigilantes then proceeded to break the windows of his car. Luckily he was able to lock the doors, or he would have been torn limb from limb.

Who were the avengers? A band of baboons!

Now, while some might argue that the life of a baboon cannot compare with the life of a human being, who can gainsay that, from a baboon's point of view, at least, the hit-and-run driver received the justice he richly deserved.

In human relationships it often happens that the wrongdoer does not get his just desserts. He may even seem to "get away with it." The thief who is never caught, the man who gets away with murder, and the adulterer who enjoys his or her illicit liaison and is never found out may *think* they have gotten away with it, and they may have—for the time being.

The problem is that these individuals forget that a day of reckoning is coming, when the "Lord, the righteous judge" (2 Tim. 4:8), "shall bring every work into judgment, with every secret thing" (Eccl. 12:14).

Have you ever been wronged and the culprit did not receive full justice? Our verse has some good advice: "Fret not thyself because of evildoers." After you've taken appropriate action in a Christian spirit, leave the injustice in God's hands.

# Presumptuous Sin

Some time ago an old friend stopped by my office. In the course of our visit he said he had recently done something that was contrary to the policy of his employing organization. I must have registered surprise, for he reacted by saying, "It was easier to ask forgiveness than to ask permission."

Policies are man-made rules. There is nothing sacrosanct about them, unless, of course, they involve ethical and moral issues. Let us grant that when these latter are not involved there may be justification for acting contrary to human policies and subsequently asking forgiveness. But now let us ask another question: Is it possible that there are "Christians" who *knowingly* act against God's revealed will—*with the intention of later asking His forgiveness?* I believe most everyone would agree that this is entirely possible.

We all know individuals who *seemed* to act knowingly against clear divine *and human* laws that involve morality. Motives are hard to judge, but from outward appearances such persons frequently strike out on a course of action that clearly violates moral law, apparently heedless of consequences—*until they get caught.* Then, penitent, they plead for forgiveness—and who is to say they aren't sorry, that they don't merit forgiveness? But what if such persons *turn right around and repeat the same offense at their first opportunity?* If some doubt that there are people who act in this manner, they probably haven't heard of recidivism. That a person who acts this way *toward God* could be called a Christian is highly questionable.

To sin presumptuously because God is a forgiving God (see Ps. 130:4; Ex. 34:6, 7) is dangerous. It can lead to the unpardonable sin (see Matt. 12:31, 32). It isn't because this sin does something to God, for He never changes, but because *it does something to us.* Hence, we need to avoid premeditated sin. We need to pray David's prayer: "Keep back thy servant also from presumptuous sins; let them not have dominion over me: then . . . I shall be innocent from the great transgression" (Ps. 19:13).

# Sow Beside All Waters

On May 7, 1946, Roger Simms, recently discharged from the U.S. Army, was hitchhiking home when a businessman in a new Cadillac picked him up.

"Going to Chicago?" the driver of the car inquired.

"Not quite that far," Simms replied as he got in. "Do you live in Chicago?"

"Yes, my name is Hanover, and I own a business there."

As the two drove along, Roger, a Christian, felt impressed to witness to his benefactor, but he kept putting it off. Finally, within 30 minutes from his drop-off point, he could resist the impulse no longer.

"Mr. Hanover," he said, "I would like to talk to you about something very important." He then presented to his friend in a quiet, winsome way his need for a personal commitment to Christ. He ended with an appeal for Mr. Hanover to receive Christ as his Saviour and Lord.

Mr. Hanover, who had said little during Roger's witness, pulled his car over to the shoulder of the highway and stopped. Then and there he committed his life to Christ. "This is the most wonderful thing that has ever happened to me," he said with tears in his eyes.

A few miles down the road Mr. Hanover dropped Roger off.

Five years passed. One day Roger decided to call on the man who had given him a ride. Going to Hanover Enterprises, he asked to see the boss. Instead, he met Mrs. Hanover. When he inquired about her husband, he learned that Mr. Hanover had been killed in an auto accident a few miles from home *on the very day Roger led him to Christ.* For years Mrs. Hanover had prayed for her husband's conversion. What a comfort it was to her to know that he had accepted Christ before he died.

A Christian should always be ready to witness for Christ. "Proclaim the message," says Paul, "press it home on all occasions, convenient or inconvenient" (2 Tim. 4:2, NEB). Today as you go about your work and meet people, let the Holy Spirit show you ways of witnessing winsomely for Christ.

*Cast all your anxiety upon [God] because he cares for you. 1 Peter 5:7, NIV.*

# Put Down Your Whole Weight

The following anecdote may be apocryphal, but it illustrates a point. According to the story, when a West Virginia mountaineer celebrated his seventy-fifth birthday, an airplane pilot offered to fly him over the "hollers" where he had lived all his life. Apprehensive at first, the old man finally accepted the invitation. Back on the ground, one of his friends asked, "Weren't ya scared, Uncle Dudley?"

"No-o-o, not exactly. Ya see, I never put my whole weight down!"

We smile, but isn't this the way it is with many of us? We don't trust God completely. We may be like the man trudging along a country road carrying a heavy bundle on his back. A farmer came along with his wagon and offered him a ride. The man accepted. After a while the farmer noticed the man had picked up his bundle. When the farmer urged him to put it on the floor of the wagon, he allegedly replied, "I don't think the horse should do all the work."

But when it comes to salvation, this is exactly what *is* right. "Salvation belongeth unto the Lord" (Ps. 3:8). It doesn't belong to us. All we can do is accept it; we can do nothing to earn it. This includes both trying to "support" our own weight or trying to "help" God carry our burdens.

Now, to the "natural man" it may seem only reasonable that a person must do something to earn or deserve salvation, but this is not God's way. We must trust Him completely; we must lay our burdens on Him. Then *He* works in us "both to will and to do of his good pleasure" (Phil. 2:13)—and these works are not our own; they are His.

Today as you examine your life, do you find you have never "cast your burden on the Lord" (Ps. 55:22, NKJV), or that, having cast it on Him at some time in the past, you have taken it up again? His gracious invitation is "Come unto me, all ye that labour and are heavy laden, and I will give you rest" (Matt. 11:28). Put down your whole weight. You can trust Him to "sustain you" (Ps. 55:22, NKJV), for "he cares for you."

*Now to [God] who can keep you from falling and set you in the presence of his glory, jubilant and above reproach, to the only God our Saviour, be glory and majesty, might and authority, through Jesus Christ our Lord, before all time, now, and for evermore. Amen.*
*Jude 24, 25, NEB.*

# You Can Be Kept From Falling

Perched atop a 100-meter cliff in Portugal stands an old monastery. In 1946 my parents visited this impressive structure while waiting for visas to enter Mozambique, then a Portuguese colony. To reach the top, Mom and Dad were strapped into a large wicker basket. Several monks hoisted them by a pulley and rope attached to the basket.

It is said that one day a tourist, having settled himself comfortably in such a basket for the precarious ride, asked one of the brothers how often the rope was replaced. "Every time it breaks," the monk answered tongue-in-cheek.

If our life depends on something or someone, we want to be sure that that person or thing is not going to let us down at a critical moment. This is human nature. Those who have studied human instincts tell us that fear of falling is one of the few automatic reflexes with which human babies are born. Although I have never tried it, I am told that if a person holds a newborn infant and makes a sudden move as if to drop it, the baby will instinctively throw out its arms as though to break its fall.

Fear of falling is often the experience of one who has undergone the new birth—or at least it should be (see 1 Cor. 10:12). When we are born again we stand before God as if we had never sinned. But sinful human nature being what it is, there is always the possibility of falling. A Christian fears this, not because the One holding him cannot be trusted, for nothing can take us out of His hand (see John 10:28) unless we remove ourselves. But rather, because we still battle the tendency to fall into sin, even after conversion.

Nothing of human devising can hold you up forever. However, in the spiritual realm there is One who can—if you let Him. The promise is sure: "The eternal God is thy refuge, and underneath are the *everlasting* arms" (Deut. 33:27).

*Both [Christ] that sanctifieth and they who are sanctified are all of one: for which cause he is not ashamed to call them brethren. Heb. 2:11.*

# Not Ashamed

Some years ago a young person from a Third World country came to the United States as an exchange student and quickly adopted American ways. After completing his education he returned to his home country. On hand to meet him were his peasant parents. Also on hand was a coterie of dignitaries and government officials. Ashamed of his poorly clad, humble, illiterate parents, the student pretended not to notice them and passed them by. You can imagine how they felt.

Embarrassment over being recognized as a member of a social or religious group that is looked down upon or is considered to be "off brand" is not a peculiarity of people of Third World countries. Such people can be found almost anywhere.

Several years ago I worked for a Christian institution with a man who was ashamed of being known as a Christian. It happened this way. One day he had to undergo minor surgery and was admitted to a nearby hospital. The hospital was run by a religious organization other than his own. While recuperating, a friend of mine, a minister, paid him a visit.

When the visit was over, the minister began to bow his head to offer prayer for our friend's rapid recovery. But before he could get a word out, the man waved his arms frantically and interrupted. "Shhh! I don't want the folks here to know I'm a _____ [here he gave the name of his denominational affiliation]."

Later it came out why this man was ashamed of being known as a member of that church. His unbecoming conduct toward the nurses belied his religious profession and the standards of his church!

How thankful we can be that Jesus is not ashamed to call us poor, weak, struggling sinners "brethren." But there is a condition, and the condition is that we do not deny Him before others (see Matt. 10:33).

No, a Christian who is walking as Jesus walked has nothing for which to be ashamed.

*God is not unfair. He will not forget the work
you did or the love you showed for him in the
help you gave and are still giving to your fellow
Christians. Heb. 6:10, TEV.*

# Reward for Doing Well

One hot summer day a little more than 100 years ago, a young medical student was going from house to house in a farming community in Maryland, selling books to earn money to pay for his education. Late one afternoon he called at a farmhouse where the only one at home was a teenage girl. After he made his presentation, the girl said, "I'm so sorry, but my mother is a widow and we can't afford to buy books."

The young man then asked, "Would you be so kind as to give me a drink of water?"

"Sure. But we have plenty of milk in the springhouse. Wouldn't you rather have a glass of cold milk instead?"

"I would be most grateful," the young man replied.

Years passed. The medical student became a skilled physician. One day while making his rounds he thought he recognized a patient as the person who, as a girl, had been kind to him. She, however, was too sick to recognize him. Things began to happen. The young woman was moved to a private room and given the finest care medical science could offer.

One day a nurse said to her, "Tomorrow you're going home."

"I'm glad," said the patient, "but the bill worries me."

"Let me go get it, and we'll see how much it is."

The nurse returned with the treasurer of the hospital, who presented the bill to the patient. She glanced at the bottom line. She was shocked at the high amount! But then she noticed these words written across the statement: "Paid in full by a glass of milk. Howard A. Kelly, M.D."

Kindness pays sometimes, but not always, in this life.

A Christian shows kindness to others, not because he or she is looking for a reward in this life or in the life to come, but because the "love of Christ controls" him (2 Cor. 5:14, RSV). A Christian allows Christ to work in him to will and to do of His good pleasure (see Phil. 2:13). His acts of kindness are simply a manifestation of the love of Christ that fills his heart.

*As the bird by wandering, as the swallow by flying, so the curse causeless shall not come. Prov. 26:2.*

# No Curse Without a Cause

Have you ever heard of certain places or people or things that were under a curse? In 1959 when I visited King Tutankhamen's tomb, I was told that it had been cursed. Twenty years earlier I had listened to a radio broadcast in which Howard Carter, the discoverer of the tomb, stated that virtually every person associated with the opening of the royal sarcophagus had died tragically or prematurely, beginning with Carter's patron, Earl Carnarvon. Carter, incidentally, died the very year I heard his broadcast.

Some curses are doubtless of satanic origin, but most of them appear to be nothing more than superstition or mere coincidence. Not so with the curse of sin. The curse pronounced on this earth after Adam and Eve ate of the forbidden tree was real, and it had a cause—not of divine origin, as some seem to suppose, but because of man's deliberate disobedience.

Although our verse for meditation is somewhat enigmatic, its general idea is clear: evil doesn't happen without a cause. The problem is that we do not always know what the cause is. In many instances we can clearly trace a cause-effect relationship between sin and suffering, but in others we cannot.

In the latter instances we tend to chalk up the "curse" to the fact that we live in a world of sin. This is true, of course, but somehow this answer does not leave us entirely satisfied, and we continue to ask "But why?"

In some cases we shall never know the answer in this life. But, if faithful, we shall know in the hereafter. Job's suffering is a case in point. *We* know he suffered because he was a test case in the great controversy between God and Satan, but he did not know that at the time and may not know until he is resurrected by his Redeemer (see Ps. 17:15).

We are assured that in the world to come all the suffering caused by sin will be removed, for, thank God, "there shall be no more curse" (Rev. 22:3). I want to be there to get some satisfying answers, don't you?

*Jesus said to [Martha], "I am the resurrection and the life; he who believes in me, though he die, yet shall he live." John 11:25, RSV.*

JUNE
10

# Plus Ultra

Carthaginian coins dating back some 200 years before the time of Christ have been found in the Azores Islands, where I lived as a teenager. These coins support the belief that Phoenician mariners discovered these islands long before they were claimed for Portugal by Gonçalo Velho Cabral in 1431.

In the twelfth century A.D. Arabian geographers mentioned the existence of nine islands in the Western, or Atlantic, Ocean. However, this knowledge apparently was lost during the Middle Ages. Thus, Portugal, lying along the western coast of the westernmost peninsula of Europe, for many years had as its motto *"ne plus ultra"* ("nothing more beyond").

In those days many believed that anyone sailing beyond the horizon would drop off the edge of the earth. However, as fishermen and others ventured farther and farther out into the Atlantic, they came to realize that their fears were unfounded. Then as daring navigators such as Bartolomeu Dias, Vasco da Gama, and others discovered more land beyond the horizon, Portugal changed its motto to *"plus ultra"* ("more beyond").

To many people there is nothing beyond the sea of life, this present existence. Their motto, in essence, is *"ne plus ultra."* Robert Ingersoll, well-known American agnostic, put it this way: "Life is a narrow vale between the cold and barren peaks of two eternities." To believe this makes life rather meaningless.

This, however, is not what Christians believe. The Bible plainly teaches a life beyond this present life, through the resurrection of the body (see Rom. 8:23). Resurrection, in fact, is the enduring theme of the New Testament. This is the "blessed hope" that will be realized at "the glorious appearing . . . of our Saviour Jesus Christ" (Titus 2:13).

*"Plus ultra!"* "No eye has seen, no ear has heard, no mind has conceived what God has prepared for those who love him" (1 Cor. 2:9, NIV)!

*The king . . . said, "You evil-hearted wretch!
Here I forgave you all that tremendous debt . . .
shouldn't you have mercy on others, just as I
had mercy on you?" Then the . . . king sent the
man to the torture chamber until he had paid
every last penny due. So shall my heavenly
Father do to you if you refuse to truly forgive
your brothers. Matt. 18:32-35, TLB.*

# Pardon Revoked

Some years ago a man from Kentucky named Lucien Young learned that Samuel Holmes, an old friend, was in the penitentiary and had eight more years to serve. Going to the prison, Lucien asked to talk to his old chum. Permission was granted. For two hours the two talked and laughed about their youthful escapades.

Later Lucien, who was a good friend of Governor Blackburn, called at the executive mansion and asked the governor to pardon his friend. The governor asked for a week to think the matter over. When the week was up, Lucien returned to the governor's office.

"Here's the pardon," said the governor, handing Lucien the document. "But before you give it to Sam, I want you to talk to him another couple of hours. If at the end of that time you think he should be pardoned, I will parole him in your custody."

"Fair enough," said Lucien.

Lucien hurried over to the prison and again secured permission to talk to his friend. In the course of their visit, Lucien casually asked, "Sam, when you get out of here, I'd like you to go into business with me. Will you? I may even be able to get you out of here a little early."

Sam stood and walked around awhile. When he resumed talking to his friend, he said, "All right. But before anything else, I have some other business to attend to."

"What's that, Sam?"

"First, I'm going to kill the judge and then the witness who put me in here."

Lucien left the prison and returned the pardon to the governor. Do you blame him?

If we are unforgiving of others, is it any wonder that God will revoke the pardon He has granted us?

# Can You Feel the Tug?

When I was a boy and lived in the Madeira Islands, I used to enjoy flying kites. Whenever the trade winds were blowing, the sky seemed filled with these colorful "birds."

Have you ever flown a kite on a day when a gentle breeze was blowing and paid out more string than the kite needed and then watched it oscillate back and forth in danger of getting tangled up with its lead string? I once lost a kite this way.

Just as a kite flies best when you pull against its "yearning" for freedom, so Christians do their best when they willingly submit to the Master's "reins of kindness," His "leading-strings of love." God knows just how much freedom to give us in order to guide us in the right way. He knows just when to pull in the string to keep us from becoming entangled in sin.

Some 40 or 50 years ago there was a child-rearing philosophy adopted by many parents that taught that a child was happiest and grew up most naturally when it was allowed to develop without parental restraints. According to this theory, restraints could damage a child's psyche. Today many child authorities have pronounced this philosophy bankrupt.

It is true, of course, that harsh, inconsistent, unreasonable restraints are unhealthy. But recent studies have demonstrated that a child is happiest and develops best when parental restraints are reasonable, consistent, and enforced with love. Even the chief promoter of the laissez-faire philosophy of child rearing finally admitted that his method of bringing up children was not best. By this time, however, it was too late to reverse the bad results.

Do you sometimes feel God's restraining "leading-strings" tugging at your heart? Remember, that which is true of kites and children is also true of Christians. The restraints God places upon us are not intended to hurt us, but have as their goal our present and eternal good. The Word of God assures us that "no good thing will he withhold from them that walk uprightly" (Ps. 84:11).

# 13

*As far as I am concerned, God turned into good what you meant for evil, for he brought me to this high position I have today so that I could save the lives of many people.*
**Gen. 50:20, TLB.**

# Blessings in Disguise

Our verse refers to the experience of Joseph. When he was sold into slavery, his brothers were sure his prophetic dreams would never be fulfilled. But they failed to consider that God can take a bad situation and turn it into something good. He has done this for His faithful children countless times.

Wallace Johnson was 40 years old in 1939. He felt that his job at the sawmill where he worked was secure. Then one day his boss called him into his office and told him he was fired. It couldn't have happened at a worse time. America was just coming out of the Great Depression, and Johnson had a wife and children to support. How, he wondered, could the family survive financially now?

Johnson left the sawmill with the feeling that his little world was caving in on him. But on his way home he prayed for divine guidance. By the time he reached home and told his wife what had happened, his spirits were lifting.

"What are you going to do now?" his wife asked.

"I'm going to mortgage the house and go into the building business," he announced.

His first venture was the construction of two small structures. Within five years the Johnsons were multimillionaires. He was the founder of Holiday Inn motels and became known as "the innkeeper of America."

Subsequently he stated, "If I could find the man who fired me, I would thank him. When I was laid off I couldn't see God's hand in it at all, but later I came to realize that He allowed it to happen so I could contribute financially to the support of His work here on earth, while at the same time enabling me to provide jobs for over 100,000 people."

When we seek God in faith, submissive to His will, He can transform the most hopeless, discouraging situation and make it a wonderful opportunity for us to bring glory to His name.

*Every man is tempted, when he is drawn away of his own lust, and enticed. Then when lust hath conceived, it bringeth forth sin: and sin, when it is finished, bringeth forth death.*
*James 1:14, 15.*

# Never Play With Sin

Several years ago Burt Hunter, a reporter for the Long Beach *Press Telegram,* was asked to write a story about a local woman who handled poisonous snakes. When he called at her home, a veritable mansion, he discovered she was young and stunningly beautiful.

When Burt expressed surprise that she should engage in such a hazardous hobby, she laughed.

"I guess I enjoy the element of danger. One of these days I'll get tired of snakes and go on to something else."

As Burt set up his photographic equipment, the woman brought out wicker baskets containing various venomous reptiles and set them on the floor. After handling several, she said, "Be especially still now. This is my newest snake. He is very poisonous and isn't quite used to me yet."

While Burt watched, the woman lifted a so-called two-step snake from its basket. Suddenly she stopped. "Something's wrong," she said. "I don't know what it is, but I'm going to have to put him . . ." She never finished the sentence. Suddenly she stiffened. The snake had struck!

"Quick!" she gasped. "Run upstairs to the bathroom. In the medicine cabinet you'll find a vial of antivenin. Please hurry!"

When Burt returned with the precious serum, the woman told him how to withdraw the antivenin into a syringe. In his nervousness he squeezed the vial too hard. It broke! The precious liquid dripped through his fingers.

"Do you have another vial?" he asked anxiously.

"That is the only one I had," the woman answered in quiet desperation. In minutes her life ended in an agonizing death.

Many who play with the deadly serpents of sin manifest the same daring disregard for their eternal welfare as was manifested by the Long Beach snake handler. When it comes to these serpents, the only safe course is "Touch not; . . . handle not" (Col. 2:21).

**15**

*Ye have heard that it hath been said, Thou shalt love thy neighbour, and hate thine enemy. But I say unto you, Love your enemies, bless them that curse you, do good to them that hate you, and pray for them which despitefully use you, and persecute you. Matt. 5:43, 44.*

# Love Your Enemies

During the American Revolutionary War a man named Wildman, of Ephrata, Pennsylvania, earned a bad reputation for his verbal abuse of Peter Miller, pastor of the Dunker church in the same town. Subsequently Wildman enlisted in the Continental Army. While he was still in the service he was discovered to be a spy. He was tried, convicted, and sentenced to be hanged.

Miller heard about the sentence. His heart was touched. He walked 60 miles to Philadelphia to intercede on Wildman's behalf. When he made his plea before General George Washington, the general replied, "I am sorry, but I cannot grant your request to spare your friend's life."

"But sir, he's not my friend," explained Miller. "He's my worst enemy."

"You mean you walked 60 miles to plead for the life of your enemy? That puts the matter in a different light. Your request is granted."

Washington signed a pardon and gave it to Miller, who walked another 15 miles to where Wildman was awaiting execution. When Wildman saw Miller coming, he sneered to some of his fellow convicts, "There comes old Pete. He came to see me hanged."

Hardly had Wildman said this than Miller pushed his way through the crowd and handed the condemned man the pardon. We can imagine Wildman's surprise. Did Wildman have a change of heart, and did he become Miller's friend? I do not know. But I know that Miller behaved like a Christian.

It is natural to love our friends and hate our enemies, for this is the way the "natural man" behaves (see 1 Cor. 2:14). But this is not how the "spiritual man" acts—because the spirit of Christ, which is in him, enables him to see in every human being, friend or enemy, a soul to be saved.

*The Spirit of Jehovah will come upon thee [Saul], . . . and thou shalt . . . be turned into another man. . . . And it was so, that when he had turned his back to go from Samuel, God gave him another heart. I Sam. 10:6-9.*

# Conversion Works Continuing Change

Conversion means change; without change there is no conversion. When the Spirit of God came upon Saul, the future king of Israel, God gave him a new heart, and he was changed into another person; in other words, he was converted. Unfortunately, he later permitted self to control his life, another spirit took over (see I Sam. 16:14), and he negated his conversion experience. But it need not have happened this way.

At the age of 29 Charles Grandison Finney was a rising young lawyer in New York State. Ministers who tried to interest him in becoming a Christian gave up, concluding he was beyond hope—"a hardened case," they claimed.

Up to 1821 Finney had never owned a Bible, but in order to make his collection of books more complete, he added one to his library. But he did more than that. He began to read the Book. Unlike Saul, who experienced instant conversion, the Bible gradually began to replace Finney's interest in Blackwood's *Commentaries*. Finney was converted, bade goodbye to his clients, and told his lawyer friends he "had a retainer from the Lord Jesus Christ to plead His cause."

In the years that followed, Finney experienced phenomenal success as a revivalist in both America and England. In 1834 he established the Broadway Tabernacle in New York City and later became the second president of Oberlin College. His life was one of ever-deepening commitment to his Lord. And all this happened because a "Reference Book" found its way into a library and subsequently into a man's heart.

The Bible can have the same effect upon your life and mine if we allow its Author, the Holy Spirit, to do His work. Conversion is more than a once-for-all-time experience. To be truly effective, it must be an ever-deepening commitment to God, as His Spirit reveals to us as yet-uncommitted areas in our lives.

*Let us lay aside . . . the sin which doth so easily beset us, and let us run with patience the race that is set before us, looking unto Jesus the author and finisher of our faith. Heb. 12:1, 2.*

# Besetting Sins

The Greek word translated "beset" in our verse is a military term that literally means to surround, as in a siege. This is the way it is with some sins. They have become so habitual that they seem to surround us like an army laying siege to a city.

The story is told of a monk who had the habit of flying into a rage and blaming his fellow monks when things went wrong. He decided to get away from the cause of his problems by transferring to a desert monastery where he had virtually no contact with other human beings.

One morning after settling into his new location, he accidentally bumped his pitcher of water and spilled its contents. He ranted and raved, but there was no one around to blame. He refilled the pitcher. A while later the same thing happened again. In a fit of passion he smashed the pitcher to pieces.

After he calmed down he began thinking, and truth dawned on him that his bad temper lay not in others, but in himself.

Most of us have besetting sins. How does one overcome them?

Suppose you have a clock that doesn't keep accurate time. You set it one night, but the next morning it has lost so much time that you are late for work. Is the solution to take the hands of the clock to a repair shop? What a foolish question, you say, and of course you are right. What a person needs to do is have the inner workings of the clock corrected.

Just so with those "armies" that lay siege to the city of Mansoul (apologies to John Bunyan). The way to conquer them is to recognize that thoughts precede actions. It follows, then, that what we need to do is bring "every thought into subjection to Christ" (2 Cor. 10:5, MLB).

Can you think of a better time to do this than right now?

# For Such a Time as This

The book of Esther contains the dramatic story of how God used a courageous, young, and beautiful Jewish maiden to save her people at a time of grave crisis. The book opens with a great feast put on by Ahasuerus (Xerxes), probably about three years before his ill-fated expedition against Greece in 480 B.C. Before leaving on this campaign, he chose Esther to replace Vashti, his ex-queen, who had embarrassed him before his nobles and consequently had been banished.

On September 23, 480 B.C., Ahasuerus's forces suffered a catastrophic defeat in the naval battle of Salamis, not far from Athens. Continued reverses at the hands of the Athenians may have influenced him to look with favor on a plan advanced by Haman, his prime minister, to exterminate the Jews. At any rate, a death decree was issued by Haman, and signed with the king's signet ring.

Realizing that the Jews' only hope for deliverance was for Esther to go in before the king and plead for the life of her people yet knowing that Persian law forbade her from going in unbidden, Mordecai, her foster father, urged her to go before the king anyway. In support of this suggestion, he asked, "Who knows whether you have not come to the kingdom for such a time as this?" (Esther 4:14, RSV).

With a prayer to her heavenly Father, Esther courageously risked her life and went before the king unbidden. As a result, she saved the lives of her people and thwarted Haman's wicked plan.

The story of this brave queen stirs us to the realization that when crises arise, God can turn them into glorious victories—if we lay self aside and seek His solution to our problems. Today you and I may face problems that from a human standpoint seem insoluble. Why not seek God in prayer with a submissive heart and be ready to apply His solution to our problems? Who knows, perhaps *we* have "come to the kingdom for such a time as this."

*I am leaving you with a gift—peace of mind and heart! And the peace I give isn't fragile like the peace the world gives. So don't be troubled or afraid. John 14:27, TLB.*

# The Peace Christ Gives

High in the Andes mountains of South America stands a bronze statue of Christ. Its base is granite. The figure was cast from old canons. Engraved in Spanish are these memorable words: "Sooner shall these mountains crumble into dust than will Argentines and Chileans break the peace sworn at the feet of Christ the Redeemer."

Since the 1840s, people of these two countries had been warring over their mutual boundary. In 1900, when one of the disputes was at its height, some citizens implored their leaders to ask Edward VII, king of England, to mediate the quarrel. Both governments agreed, and as a result, Chile and Argentina signed a treaty ending the conflict on May 28, 1903.

During the celebration that followed, Señora Costa, an Argentinean woman of distinction, conceived the idea of a monument commemorating the treaty and suggested that the cannons that had been used to make war be melted down and cast into the figure of Christ, the Prince of Peace. At the dedication ceremony the statue was presented to the world as a testimonial to the desire for peace by the citizens of both countries.

Today throughout the world, nations and individuals continue to search for peace—not mere temporary tranquility, but permanent peace. But they search in vain. Why? Because the human heart is innately selfish, and it is selfishness that spawns strife and war.

A few hours before His crucifixion, at the very time the forces of evil threatened to overwhelm Him, Jesus promised His disciples the seemingly impossible—peace. In so doing, He did not promise them a trouble-free life. Quite the contrary; He warned them that in the world they would have tribulation (see John 16:33). But more important, He promised inner peace in the midst of tribulation.

The apostle Paul calls this "the peace of God, which passeth all understanding" (Phil. 4:7). This is the kind of peace you and I can have—peace that the world cannot give and cannot take away!

*[Some] preach Christ out of selfish ambition, not sincerely. . . . But what does it matter? The important thing is that in every way, whether from false motives or true, Christ is preached. And because of this I rejoice.*
**Phil. 1:17, 18, NIV.**

JUNE
20

# Not the Man, but the Message

My father was born in Minneapolis, Minnesota, in 1889, but his ancestors came from New England. Mansells had lived there for the previous 150 years. In 1960 Dad and I decided to go to Maine and do some research on our forefathers. While delving into some interesting source materials in the city hall of Brewer, we found a book containing some fascinating notations. One preacher (not an ancestor or relative, I'm glad to say) had the following comment after his name: "He preached so well when in the pulpit that it was a shame he should ever come out of it; and, when out of the pulpit, he lived so illy that it was a shame he should enter it." I have never forgotten that scathing commentary. (Later I learned that these words were a paraphrase of a statement by John Wesley, a founder of Methodism.)

What a sad commentary on professed servants of God. Such hypocrites existed in Paul's day, they exist today—and, unfortunately, they are not limited to preachers. And yet, in spite of such hypocrisy, Paul rejoiced, as our text indicates! Why? Perhaps an illustration will explain the reason.

During the early 1850s Elisha Kane, husband of Margaret Fox, one of the founders of modern Spiritualism, led several attempts to reach the North Pole. On one of these trips Kane cut a crystal-clear piece of ice, shaped it into a kind of lens, held it up to the sun, and focused its rays on a pile of dry wood. The wood ignited. The Eskimos were mystified by his magic. How could cold ice produce hot fire? The answer, of course, was that the coldness of the ice had nothing to do with the rays of the sun passing through it.

So if unworthy men or women whose lives are not models of virtue are used by God to convert sinners, let us not be discouraged. Rather, let us thank God that the Sun of righteousness has reached hearts with His healing beams.

*Judgment also will I lay to the line, and righteousness to the plummet: and the hail shall sweep away the refuge of lies. Isa. 28:17.*

# Exposing Fraud

When Margot O'Toole tried to duplicate the findings of fellow scientist Dr. Thereza Imanishi-Kari, which indicated beneficial responses of mice bred with an extra immune system gene from another species, she could not come up with the same results. Eventually, while searching through laboratory records, O'Toole came across the data that had been used as the basis for an article published in the April 1986 issue of *Cell*, coauthored by Drs. Imanishi-Kari and Nobel laureate David Baltimore. Suddenly, everything became clear. Much of the lab data had been falsified!

What should she do? One friend advised O'Toole to "walk away" from her discovery. Instead, she chose to present her findings to the authors of the article—who were her superiors. She naively assumed they would be glad to have the "mistake" pointed out and would rectify it. She could not have been more mistaken.

Wrapping himself in a mantle of scientific sanctity, Baltimore flew to the defense of Imanishi-Kari, accusing O'Toole of being a "discontented postdoctoral fellow." O'Toole lost her job, was refused employment by scores of scientific institutions, and finally had to take a job at her brother's moving company to make a living.

But the story doesn't end there. An investigation by the National Institutes of Health uncovered the fraud and vindicated O'Toole. Is she bitter? No, but she admits that "one of the hardest things about telling the truth is being called a liar for it."

Exposing fraud is delicate work requiring sound, balanced judgment and careful self-examination. Many factors must be prudently considered: Are we absolutely sure it is fraud? If it is, what is our motive in exposing it? Is it to boost our ego by embarrassing someone else? Is the matter major or minor? Are we willing to accept the consequences? And so on.

In matters involving eternal life the issue is simpler. As Christians we must stand for truth though the heavens fall. And never forget, in some cases we may not be vindicated until God Himself sweeps away the web of lies.

*Jesus answered, "My kingdom is not of this world: if my kingdom were of this world, then would my servants fight." John 18:36.*

JUNE
22

# What Might Have Been

Christians of the first centuries refused to bear arms because of these words of Jesus. Adolph Harnack (1851-1930), probably the greatest New Testament scholar of his day—and no pacifist, by the way—once stated: "War can never be reconciled with the gospel, nor can we believe that Christ would ever countenance it."

In the early centuries Christians refused induction into the Roman army because it meant killing others. Justin Martyr, a second-century apologist, stated that Christians preferred death to participating in war. As late as March 12, 295, for instance, Maxmillian, a 20-year-old Christian, declined to accept the Roman badge of service, saying, "I have a sign already, the sign of my Lord Jesus Christ." As punishment he was executed.

In more recent times some Christians have justified killing in "just wars," because God's people in Old Testament times fought battles and killed their enemies—and God appeared to approve of what they did. Granted that this appears to be so, let it never be forgotten that this was not God's first or best plan. Thus, in Psalm 81:13, 14, God laments: "O that my people would listen to me, that Israel would walk in my ways! I would soon subdue their enemies, and turn my hand against their foes" (RSV). We may be sure that He would have done this in a just and merciful way.

In one instance, when Israel trusted God, it was not their swords or their bows that drove out their enemies, but God who "spread panic before" them (Joshua 24:12, REB). But Israel chose to be like the surrounding nations; for, as God says through the psalmist, "But My people would not heed My voice, and Israel would have none of Me. So I gave them over to their own stubborn heart, to walk in their own counsels" (Ps. 81:12, 13, NKJV).

In mercy God did not reject His faithless people at once, but the result was "leanness" of soul (Ps. 106:15)—and this eventually led to their rejection of the Messiah.

Rather than following their example, let us not presume on God's mercy, but choose His best way first.

*Go and get all the Jews in Susa together; hold a fast and pray for me. . . . My servant girls and I will be doing the same. After that, I will go to the king, even though it is against the law. If I must die for doing it, I will die.*
**Esther 4:16, TEV.**

# Courage Before Earthly Powers

In former times, rulers had the power of life and death over their subjects. In modern times, although their authority may be limited, they still wield power not to be trifled with. To stand up against such power requires courage. Esther, mentioned in our text, is a prime example of this kind of courage.

Another example of such courage occurred when Kaiser Wilhelm II went on a yachting trip to Norway. To show his authority (he was probably a bit under the influence of alcohol), the Kaiser went up to the bridge and rang the bell to the engine room, ordering full speed ahead. The pilot, a man named Nordhums, promptly countermanded the order. When the Kaiser insisted on repeating his senseless command, the old sailor thundered, "Leave the bridge!" Then, grasping the helm firmly, he continued, "This ship is under my charge, and I will brook no interference from the Kaiser or anyone else!"

The next day the sobered Kaiser decorated Nordhums for his courage, and appointed him his pilot for life—"in Norwegian waters."

A few months ago my wife and I learned of an incident that happened in Thailand that illustrates a similar kind of courage. A Karen government official ordered a Christian school to relocate, for political reasons, to an area where there was fighting against the central Burmese government. The male teachers proceeded to obey the order, but one young Karen woman instructor, realizing the danger this move would pose to the students, stood up to the authorities. When an overzealous Karen soldier threatened to kill her unless she complied, she said, "If you kill me, I'll go to heaven. Where will you go?" The soldier backed down.

The Christian should respect the powers that be. But when these powers come between him and God's clear commands, he must have the courage to draw a line.

# The "Red Cross"

In his history of the Boer War, Sir Arthur Conan Doyle tells how a small contingent of British soldiers was surprised by an enemy force twice its strength. The British were driven back, and the Boers occupied a commanding height from which they were able to enfilade the English lines with cannon shot to deadly effect. The British who had been wounded early in the action lay out in the open; they were in a desperate situation.

A British corporal of the Ceylon Mounted Infantry realized that unless something were done quickly the helpless men would be slaughtered like cattle. He seized a pillow and, with his own blood and that of another soldier, painted a cross on it. He hoisted this as a flag in view of the Boers. The enemy respected the "red cross" and ceased firing, saving the lives of many of the wounded.

The ancient Israelites had six cities of refuge in which someone who inadvertently killed a person could find sanctuary from an avenging relative. These cities were situated strategically so that no Israelite lived more than 30 miles from one of them. A fugitive claiming the protection of one of these cities could count on a fair trial, and if found innocent, could remain in the city until the death of the high priest.

These ancient cities of refuge typified Christ; for Christ, who is God, "is our refuge and strength, a very present help in trouble" (Ps. 46:1). He shelters us when we flee to Him in faith. Solomon was probably alluding to this symbolism when he said: "The name of the Lord is a strong tower; the righteous runs into it and is safe" (Prov. 18:10, NASB).

When we sin and repent and turn to Christ for refuge, He defends us from the attacks of Satan, our enemy. This was exemplified when "the angel of the Lord" defended Joshua the high priest from the accusations of the archdeceiver (see Zech. 3:1-7). But Christ does more: He also gives us the "shield of faith" with which we can "quench all the fiery darts of the wicked" (Eph. 6:16). Only beneath His bloodstained cross can we find sure refuge from the enemy of souls.

*Every one helped his neighbor and said to his brother, "Take courage!" The craftsman encourages the goldsmith, and he who polishes with the hammer encourages him who strikes on the anvil, saying of the soldering, "That is good!" Isa. 41:6, 7, MLB.*

# Cooperation

The weaver ants of Southern Asia build their nests by a most ingenious method. A column of these insects lines up on the edge of a leaf, clinging to it with their hind legs while reaching for another leaf with their front limbs. With consumate cooperation they draw the two edges together. Meanwhile, another team of ants lines up in readiness on the underside of the leaves. Each of these latter ants holds in its pincers a live ant larva, which at the right moment spins a thread and fastens it to the two leaves, holding them fast together. Continuing in this manner, these ants work together until a nest is completed.

Another remarkable example of cooperation is that of the pseudomyrmus ant and a kind of acacia tree that grows in Central America. This particular tree is covered with thorns that grow in pairs like the horns of a bull. Near the tip of one of the horns of each pair is a tiny hole that serves as an entryway to the interior of the thorn, where an ant colony lives.

In return for living quarters, the pseudomyrmus ants protect the acacia tree from leaf-cutting ants. These latter can quickly strip an unprotected tree. The acacia tree in turn provides the pseudomyrmus ants with a sweet nectar, upon which they feed.

Nature offers many other interesting examples of symbiosis, and in some cases this cooperation is absolutely essential to life. However, in the spiritual realm, God, who is infinitely powerful, does not "need" our cooperation in the work of saving sinners. In the words of John Milton, "God doth not need either man's work, or his own gifts" (from the sonnet "On His Blindness").

God could accomplish this work much more quickly and efficiently through the ministration of angels, but in His infinite wisdom—*and for our good*—He invites us to cooperate with Him and with one another. As we do this, let us encourage one another like the people in our verse for meditation.

*These people draw near to Me with their mouth, and honor Me with their lips, but their heart is far from Me. And in vain they worship Me, teaching as doctrines the commandments of men. Matt. 15:8, 9, NKJV.*

JUNE
26

# Following Tradition

The context in which Christ spoke the words of the above passage was a discussion with the scribes and Pharisees over the failure of His disciples to observe the tradition of washing one's hands before meals. Jesus turned the tables on His critics by pointing out that their practice of allowing a child to violate the spirit of the fifth commandment by denying assistance to a needy parent in declaring that his property was *corban* ("devoted to God") "transgress[ed] the commandment of God for the sake of . . . tradition" (Matt. 15:3, RSV).

Dr. Harry Emerson Fosdick, longtime pastor of the Riverside Church in New York City, once related a story that illustrates how misguiding traditions can be. For generations the members of a certain Lutheran church in Denmark always genuflected whenever they passed a certain spot in their cathedral. When asked the reason for this practice, they could give no better explanation than that it was a "tradition."

Finally, in the early 1800s the walls of the church were stripped down for repainting and the mystery was solved—underneath was discovered a painting of the virgin Mary. You see, before Denmark converted to Lutheranism, the church had been a Roman Catholic cathedral and the people were in the habit of bowing to this picture of the Madonna. For more than 300 years these Protestants had been observing a tradition contrary to the teaching of the Ten Commandments (see Ex. 20:4, 5).

But going back to our text: there is nothing intrinsically wrong with the "tradition" of washing hands before meals. As a matter of fact, in the light of modern scientific knowledge, it is an excellent practice. What Jesus was talking about was traditions that lead away from God's Word. Here we need to be discriminating. A tradition is bad if it is inconsistent with the plainly revealed will of God. Examine your "traditions" this morning in this light and see whither they are leading you.

*Moab will spread out his hands as a swimmer spreads out his hands to swim, but his pride will be sunk with every stroke of his hands. Isa. 25:11, REB.*

# Don't Let Fog Obscure Your Goal

Swimming is not a new sport. It goes back to at least the time of Isaiah and probably long before that. Our text may even hint that the ancients knew the stroke we call the Australian crawl. I had to practice this stroke when I took lifeguard training in college.

Ever since 20-year-old Gertrude Ederle became the first woman to swim the English Channel on August 6, 1926, women have been competing to set world swimming records. Thus, on the morning of July 4, 1952, 32-year-old Florence Chadwick waded into the waters off Catalina Island, determined to be the first woman to swim the 21 miles to Long Beach, California. (This was not her first stint at long-distance swimming. Previously she had outdone Ederle by being the first woman to swim the English channel in both directions.)

But Chadwick didn't reach her latest goal. The water was cold that morning and the fog so thick she could hardly see the boats accompanying her. But neither cold nor fatigue caused her to quit. As the hours ticked by, she swam on. Just before reaching shore, she gave up and asked to be taken on board, even though her mother and her trainer begged her to go on. She insisted she could go no farther.

Minutes after quitting, she discovered she was within a mere half mile from shore. She said afterward, "I'm not excusing myself, but if I had been able to see the shore I might have made it." She was defeated, not by the cold nor by fatigue, but by the fog.

There is something in the spiritual realm like fog. It is called unbelief, and it goes under various names. Paul speaks of those whose minds "the god of this age has blinded," who do not believe (2 Cor. 4:4, NIV). Many allow unbelief, skepticism, and pride of opinion to blind them. Don't let this happen to you. By faith let your spiritual eyes pierce through the fog—the fog with which the god of this world obscures the heavenly goal—and press on.

*Get Mark and bring him with you, because he is helpful to me in my ministry. 2 Tim. 4:11, NIV.*

JUNE

# 28

# From a Hindrance to a Help

Mark's mother, Mary, owned a house in Jerusalem (see Acts 12:12). From this we infer that his family was better off than most of the early Christians. He and his uncle Barnabas accompanied Paul on his first missionary journey. All went well, apparently, until they came to Perga in Pamphylia; there the pampered rich boy "departing from them returned to Jerusalem."

When it came time for the next missionary journey, Uncle Barnabas wanted to give Mark a second chance. But Paul said no. In fact, the veteran missionaries "had such a sharp disagreement that they parted company" (Acts 15:39, NIV).

But this wasn't the end of the story. For a while we lose sight of Mark, but in Colossians 4:10 we catch a glimpse of him as Paul urges the believers in Colossae to "receive" him, and in his Epistle to Philemon, Paul refers to Mark as one of his "fellow labourers." Finally, in his last Epistle, Paul instructs Timothy to bring Mark with him to Rome, because "he is helpful to me in my ministry." Clearly Mark had changed from a hindrance to a help.

But would this change have come about without the stick-and-the-carrot treatment Mark received? Possibly not. Mark appears to have needed Paul's "stick" approach to make him realize his shortcomings; on the other hand, he needed Barnabas's "carrot" approach to keep him from giving up in discouragement.

God balances justice and mercy perfectly, and that combination is necessary for our salvation. It is difficult for humans to be so balanced. But sometimes a father and mother, working in concert, can exercise a close proximity to God's mercy and justice that can effectively train a wayward child.

But note: to assure success, the players in this drama must learn to walk humbly with their God (see Micah 6:8).

189

*Hold fast what you have, so that no one may rob you and deprive you of your crown.*
*Rev. 3:11, Amplified.*

# Don't Let Yourself Be Robbed

Many years ago a North Carolina couple moved to Oklahoma in search of a better life. They bought a little farm there. It turned out that the soil was less productive than expected and the water tasted foul. However, in time they got used to the flavor of the water.

One day two thirsty travelers stopped by and asked for a drink. While the farmer talked to them, his wife drew some water from the well and gave a glassful to each of them. One of them poured some of the water into a bottle. For a moment the wife wondered why the man had done that, but she soon dismissed it from her mind.

Months passed. The same two men dropped by again. This time they offered to buy the farm. The offer seemed very reasonable. After all, the farm's yield hardly justified the work put into it. Convinced they were making a shrewd deal, they agreed to sell the miserable place. Only later did they discover that under their feet was a rich deposit of petroleum that would have made them millionaires for the rest of their lives. That glass of water was the clue to the two strangers of the oil beneath the ground.

The Bible is like that farm. Within its covers lies a vast deposit of truth (see John 5:39). The problem is that many who possess this Book never dig deep enough to understand its message and appropriate it to themselves. Like the Oklahoma couple, they barely scratch the surface. Is it any wonder that such people, like the wayside hearers in the parable of the sower (see Matt. 13:4), allow Bible critics who profess to be "beyond what is written" (1 Cor. 4:6, NKJV) to come along and rob them of the most precious thing in the whole world—eternal life?

If you and I want to discover the rich deposits of truth hidden in the Bible, we need to dig into it, not merely scratch its surface. As we do so prayerfully and in the spirit of learners, the Holy Spirit will guide us to rich deposits of truth (see John 16:13 and 1 Cor. 2:10).

*What is man, that thou shouldest magnify him?
and that thou shouldest set thine heart upon
him? And that thou shouldest visit him every
morning, and try him every moment?
Job 7:17, 18.*

# Why God Visits Man

While I was hoeing the pole beans in my garden this morning, I noticed that now and then there were tendrils that were trailing on the ground instead of climbing the reinforcing rods I had placed in the ground. I paused whenever I came to one of these to help it get started ascending the support I had provided for it. This had to be done with the gentlest touch because the tendrils are easily injured and bruised.

This set me to thinking. Just as I helped the tendrils trying to take hold of the support I provided for them, so the heavenly Husbandman saw His fallen, earthly family trying vainly to lift itself by its own strength and wisdom. In His infinite compassion He sent His only begotten Son to assume our human nature in order to give us the help and guidance we so desperately needed.

Previously He had sent an "Instruction Book," but now He came personally to show us how our uplifting could be accomplished. The Instruction Book admonishes us: "Trust in the Lord with all thine heart; and lean not on thine own understanding. In all thy ways acknowledge him, and he shall direct thy paths" (Prov. 3:5, 6).

How glorious are the possibilities set before the fallen race! Through His Son, God has revealed the heights man is capable of reaching. Through the merits of Christ, man can be lifted from his depraved state, purified, and made more precious than the golden wedge of Ophir. "Higher than the highest human thought can reach is God's ideal for His children. Godliness— godlikeness—is the goal to be reached" (*Education*, p. 18).

"We have the privilege of being directed by a wise Counselor. God can make humble men mighty in His service. Those who obediently respond to the call of duty, improving their abilities to the very utmost, may be sure of receiving divine assistance. Angels will come as messengers of light to the help of those who will do all that they can on their part, and then trust in God to cooperate with their efforts" (*Gospel Workers*, p. 79).

*Where can I go from your Spirit? Where can I flee from your presence? If I go up to the heavens, you are there; if I make my bed in the depths, you are there. If I rise on the wings of the dawn, if I settle on the far side of the sea, even there your hand will guide me, your right hand will hold me fast.*
**Ps. 139:7-10, NIV.**

# The Persevering Pursuer

The Royal Canadian Mounted Police have a reputation for "getting their man." They seldom fail. I once read a story of a Canadian farmer who thought he had a sure way of stealing without getting caught. One winter day, while one of his neighbors was away visiting relatives with his family, this scheming farmer drove a wagon over to his neighbor's granary and loaded it with corn. He then headed into town through the snow to sell it. Taking the proceeds from the sale, he headed for the United States, where he intended to enjoy the fruits of his ill-gotten gain. He almost made it.

Unfortunately his victim returned home early and noticed a trail of corn kernels leading from his barn. He became suspicious. He followed the trail to a store in town, where he made inquiry and learned the identity of the thief. The RCMP were notified, and he swore out a warrant for the man's arrest. When the thief reached the border, the Mounties arrested him.

Because of their efficiency the Mounties seem ubiquitous, but they are not omnipresent and hence they do not always get their man. Not so the Holy Spirit. He is present everywhere. How He can be omnipresent and still be a person is beyond our comprehension. To our finite minds a person must be located in a specific place, not present everywhere, with everyone.

The Holy Spirit is the one who prompts us to a better course when we are tempted. It is He who speaks to our consciences when we do wrong. It is He who gives us power to overcome when we decide to break with sin. He is, in fact, our friend.

Someday I believe we shall meet the Holy Spirit. When we do, I want to ask Him about some things that have mystified me. Perhaps you too have some questions you would like to ask Him. I am looking forward to some satisfying answers. Aren't you?

*My eyes pour out tears to God. I want someone to plead with God for me, as a man pleads for his friend! Job 16:20, 21, TEV.*

# How to Seek for Hidden Treasure

Although gold nuggets are found in many parts of the world, the largest nuggets have been found in Australia. One of the largest ever discovered was found at Hill End, New South Wales, on May 10, 1872. Of special interest is the fact that the men who found this prize were on the point of giving up when they found it. Their food was gone, their money spent, their credit nil, *but they persevered*—and suddenly they came upon this mammoth lump of gold. It weighed approximately 640 pounds; it measured 57 inches by 38 inches, and had an average thickness of about four inches. After it was assayed, the miners sold it for the equivalent of US$148,800—a respectable fortune in those days.

In Isaiah 13:12 God says, "I will make a man more precious than fine gold; even a man than the golden wedge of Ophir." I wonder if in our search for souls, on whom God places such great value, we are as persevering as those Australian miners. Do we persist in our search for these spiritual nuggets with as much zeal as miners do for earthly gold?

L. A. Banks, pastor of the First Methodist Episcopal Church of Cleveland, Ohio, once had a parishioner confess to him that he had been a Christian for many years and had labored diligently to win a person for Christ, without success. The pastor encouraged him not to give up but to plead with God, with tears, if necessary. The man tried it. Within six weeks he was instrumental in leading seven people to accept Christ as their Saviour.

Do you suppose that if we searched for souls with tears and as much zeal as gold miners do for gold, we would see many more conversions than we do? Listen: "All over the world men and women are looking wistfully to heaven. Prayers and tears and inquiries go up from souls longing for light, for grace, for the Holy Spirit. Many are on the verge of the kingdom, waiting only to be gathered in" (*Christian Service,* p. 143).

If we are lacking success in soul winning, could it be that we need to plead with God for a soul as a man pleads for a friend or neighbor?

*The words of the Lord are pure words; as silver tried in a furnace on the earth, refined seven times. Ps. 12:6, NASB.*

# God's Words Are Like Pure Silver

On July 3, 1990, the state of Idaho had its one hundredth birthday. To celebrate the event, it struck a series of silver medallions. I purchased one of these as a memento of the centennial. On the obverse side is an inscription that reads: "One troy ounce: Celebrate Idaho: 1889—Centennial—1990: .999 fine Idaho silver." On the reverse side is a bas-relief of two miners at work, and the caption: "Mining in Idaho."

Perhaps you wonder, as I did, what the expression ".999 fine" means. It means that such silver contains no more impurity than one part per thousand of the precious metal. In its natural state silver is usually found in combination with other elements such as chlorine, sulfur, arsenic, antimony, tellurium, gold, lead, etc.

Probably the largest solid lump of "native," that is, pure, silver ever found was taken from Smuggler's mine in Aspen, Colorado, in 1894. It weighed 1,840 pounds! It was in such a pure state that it was unnecessary to subject it to the refining process. Instead, it was put directly into a crucible and melted down. The silver bars cast from it were far purer than the metal in the American silver dollar of the period.

In our verse God's words are compared to silver refined seven times. Seven in the Bible, as most everyone knows, denotes perfection or completeness. The psalmist contrasts the lies of the wicked mentioned in verses 2 to 4 with God's words, which contain no trace of falsehood. Like that lump of native silver found in Colorado, His words are perfectly pure.

Although our words will never attain the perfection of our heavenly Father's words, this does not excuse us from striving toward that goal. I once saw in an office a plaque that suggested that before we open our mouths to speak, we should make our words pass through three gates: Is it true, is it kind, and is it necessary? Today you and I will have opportunities to put this rule into practice.

*Proclaim liberty throughout all the land unto all the inhabitants thereof. Lev. 25:10.*

JULY

4

# The Price of Liberty

The price of liberty is usually high. Not many Americans are likely to reflect that this day, the day that commemorates the freedom of their country, cost some of the signers of the Declaration of Independence dearly. That document concludes with these memorable words: "And for the support of this Declaration, with a firm reliance on the protection of divine Providence, we mutually pledge to each other our Lives, our Fortunes, and our sacred Honor."

Even fewer Americans are likely to remember that a number of the signers of this document paid for their freedom with their lives. Many lost homes and fortunes. Thomas Nelson, one of the delegates from Virginia, directed the bombardment and destruction of his own home in Yorktown, which at the time was occupied by enemy forces. He also assumed personal responsibility for raising $2 million to pay for the assistance the French fleet rendered the forces of George Washington. When he redeemed the note after the war, it cost him his fortune and he died in poverty.

Francis Lewis, a wealthy New York trader and signer of the declaration, lost everything he possessed. His wife was thrown into prison and died soon after she was released.

Richard Stockton, a delegate from New Jersey and a Princeton graduate, lost his wealth, his property, and his priceless library. He was imprisoned during the war and died shortly after peace was concluded.

Yes, the price of political freedom is usually high, but the price of your spiritual freedom and mine cost infinitely more. This price was paid on Calvary, not to appease an angry God, "for the Father himself loveth you" (John 16:27), but to satisfy the demands of justice before the unfallen universe. Only by so doing could God "be just, and [at the same time be] the justifier of him which believeth in Jesus" (Rom. 3:26).

"Eternal vigilance is the price of [political] liberty." It is also the price of spiritual freedom. "Stand fast therefore in the liberty wherewith Christ hath made us free" (Gal. 5:1).

**5** *May the God of peace, who brought up from the dead our Lord Jesus, . . . make you perfect in all goodness so that you may do his will; and may he make of us what he would have us be through Jesus Christ. Heb. 13:20, 21, NEB.*

# Christian Perfection

Many years ago the Foulises, celebrated publishers of Glasgow, Scotland, attempted to publish a "perfect book"—one without a single, humanly discernible error. The manuscript was edited and copyread, after which six experienced proofreaders carefully read each page, eliminating mistakes. After this, a galley proof of each page was posted on the Glasgow University bulletin board for a two-week period. The students were challenged to find typos and were offered a reward of 50 pounds sterling for each mistake discovered. In spite of every precaution, several errors were found after the book was published—*one in the first line of the first page of the book!*

Human perfection on the physical level is an impossibility. But what about the spiritual realm? Is sinless perfection possible? Some insist that it is, while others deny it. I have heard theologians "split hairs" over this issue—and, apparently, lose their perfection while so doing!

All Christians agree that Christ imputes His sinless life to one who is born again. There is no question about this. Salvation could come no other way. Where the disagreements arise is over what happens *after* the new birth. Theologians take opposing views on the matter, some claiming a born-again person can live without sinning, others insisting such a thing is impossible. And so the argument seesaws back and forth.

It is highly unlikely that a debate that has gone on for ages is going to be resolved in the space of a single devotional reading. But perhaps a suggestion is in order: Why not let "the Lord, the righteous judge" (2 Tim. 4:8), decide whether or not a born-again person can *continue* to live without sin? When someone is allowing the Lord "to will and to do of his good pleasure" in his life, is it not best to leave that person in God's hands to "work out [his] own salvation with fear and trembling" (Phil. 2:13, 12)? Why try to do God's work for Him?

*[Jephthah] captured the fords of the Jordan behind the army of Ephraim, and whenever a fugitive from Ephraim tried to cross the river, the Gilead guards challenged him. "Are you a member of the tribe of Ephraim?" they asked. If the man replied that he was not, then they demanded, "Say 'Shibboleth.' " But if he couldn't pronounce the H and said, "Sibboleth" instead of "Shibboleth," he was dragged away and killed. Judges 12:5, 6, TLB.*

# Shibboleth

Our scripture relates an incident that took place in the time of the judges, when a man's life hung on the pronunciation of a word. Not a fighting word, mind you, but a harmless word, *shibboleth*. It simply means "a flowing stream"—hardly something to fight about, let alone deprive a man of his life.

On this occasion, the Ephraimites were the enemies of the men at the ford. The pronunciation of the word was used as a test to identify their tribal origin. When the Ephraimites couldn't pronounce the word "just right," 42,000 of them were put to the sword. From this incident, the word "shibboleth" has passed into other languages meaning a capricious test used to distinguish those who hold a certain belief or opinion from those who do not.

Is it possible that today Seventh-day Adventists have "shibboleths"—beliefs or opinions by which they figuratively "put to the sword" their brethren who happen not to believe exactly as they do?

A generation or two ago the question Who is the "king of the north"? was a shibboleth among us. This was not a matter critical to one's salvation, but some church administrators refused to hire ministerial graduates who did not hold the then prevailing interpretation of Daniel 11:45. Since then the church's interpretation of this prophecy has changed.

Everyone agrees that on matters affecting our salvation—righteousness by faith, for instance—there must be a clear dividing line. But even on this subject, is it not more important to live righteousness by faith and leave certain matters to God, rather than make our particular view a shibboleth?

*Among you there must not be even a hint of sexual immorality, or of any kind of impurity, . . . because these are improper for God's holy people. Nor should there be obscenity, foolish talk or coarse joking, which are out of place, but rather thanksgiving. Eph. 5:3, 4, NIV.*

# The Invisible Line

"It all began innocently, and before I realized it, I found myself involved in an affair with a married man," sobbed the young parishioner who came to me for advice.

How do such things happen? In this case it began with an off-color joke her boss told. She thought it was funny and laughed. But by allowing the invisible line of propriety to be crossed, she opened a door that became easier and easier for her boss to overstep. Repeated familiarity led to rationalization. She began to reason that it would be rude not to laugh at her boss's "witty" remarks. Rationalization led to infatuation, and infatuation led to sexual involvement—and painful regrets.

Whenever one crosses the line of propriety, it is impossible to know where it can lead.

What can one do to prevent such a situation from developing? First of all, determine *beforehand* you will never cross the line. At the first hint of familiarity, ignore the witticism and lift the tone of the conversation, and, if necessary, walk away from the scene.

Polite society usually sets limits to what is proper and what is improper. True, some areas may be nebulous and ill-defined, but ordinarily, when we comport ourselves circumspectly, others do not overstep the bounds set. And it goes without saying, we should not transgress the limits either.

Today many professed Christians scoff at "Victorian prudery." What they forget is that the Bible, long before the time of Queen Victoria, admonished the followers of Christ to avoid "any kind of impurity," including "obscenity," "foolish talk," and "coarse joking." Although some today "glory in their shame" (Phil. 3:19, NEB) on TV talk shows, as a true Christian, determine you will "gird up the loins of your mind" (1 Peter 1:13, NKJV) and set your "affection on things above" (Col. 3:2).

*I will lead the blind by ways they have not known, along unfamiliar paths I will guide them; I will turn the darkness into light before them and make the rough places smooth. These are the things I will do; I will not forsake them.*
*Isa. 42:16, NIV.*

# Unexpected Paths

Our lives sometimes change course in unexpected ways. Most people have heard about Helen Keller, the blind deaf-mute who not only learned to speak and write, but graduated from Radcliffe College with honors and eventually learned to speak several foreign languages. But few remember Anne Sullivan, the young woman who led Helen out of her dark, silent prison into a useful life that blessed others.

Anne became partially blind early in life as a result of an eye infection. In 1876, when she was 10, her mother died and Anne was placed in an almshouse. After several years she was admitted to the Perkins Institution and Massachusetts School for the Blind, where she learned a touch-code system for communicating with blind deaf-mutes. She graduated from Perkins in 1886. In the meantime, doctors were able to restore her sight through a series of delicate eye operations.

In 1887 Anne was asked to take charge of Helen's education. Within two weeks her bright 7-year-old student learned 30 words spelled by the touch-code method. For the next 49 years Anne and Helen were inseparable. Anne accompanied Helen on lecture tours all over America, Europe, and Japan, raising funds for training the blind. In her later years Anne's blindness returned, and during the years immediately preceding her death in 1936, it was largely Helen who took care of her.

Sometimes our spiritual lives experience unexpected changes. Our verse tells us that God often leads us in ways we do not anticipate. Often He guides the sincere, yet spiritually blind, through "thorny paths" that ultimately lead to "a joyful end."

No matter how good we may think our spiritual perceptions are, we are all spiritually blind to one degree or another. Let us therefore thank God that He promises to turn our darkness into light as He leads us along unexpected paths.

*Let us not grow weary in well-doing, for in due season we shall reap, if we do not lose heart. Gal. 6:9, RSV.*

# Perseverance in Well-doing

In a certain sense, it is not always true that "if the blind lead the blind, both shall fall into the ditch" (Matt. 15:14). Take the case of Louis Braille, a French farm boy who lost his eyesight as a small child. By age 18 he had perfected the raised-alphabet writing system that bears his name and that has led blind people out of their darkened lives into a bright new day.

Little is known about Louis's early life. About 1812, at age 3, he was blinded while playing with an awl in his father's saddle shop. When he was 10, he was put in the Institution Nationale des Jeunes Aveugles (National Institute for Blind Children) in Paris, where he learned to read the embossed letters of the Roman alphabet. The problem with this system was that it was almost impossible for the unsighted to write with it.

At 14, Louis lost his father and mother. The same year, his best friend at school and the school's director died. These were painful blows for the young man, and several times he became so discouraged that he ran away from school. Yet he returned, and eventually became a teacher at his alma mater.

In the meantime Louis heard of a system of writing used in the French Army. It consisted of a series of holes punched in cardboard, which could be read at night. This sparked an idea. Within three years Louis developed a simplified system of writing based on this principle. However, when he demonstrated it before the Royal Academy in 1832, it was turned down.

Louis lived for another 20 years. Plagued by tuberculosis, he finally succumbed to the disease in 1852. He did not see the beneficial fruits of his labors in his lifetime, but 80 years after his death his system, with modifications, was universally adopted for use by the blind.

Rewards for well-doing are not always reaped in one's lifetime. Sometimes, as in the case of Louis Braille, they are not reaped until many years after the "do-gooder's" death—and sometimes the reward does not come until the great hereafter—but this should not hinder us from persevering in well-doing.

*God is opposed to the proud, but gives grace to the humble. James 4:6, NASB.*

# Pride and Humility

While picking pole beans this morning, I observed that the plants that had the most abundant foliage, promising the most fruitage, had the least number of pods. Those with below average number of leaves usually had the most pods.

It occurred to me that those plants with their pretentious foliage represent professed Christians who try in their own wisdom and strength to develop fruit of the Spirit—"love, joy, peace, longsuffering, gentleness, goodness, faith, meekness, temperance" (Gal. 5:22, 23).

Jesus, our great exemplar, counsels us that the very first step we must take when we begin to follow in His footsteps is self-denial. Jesus "said to them all [and this includes you and me], If any man will come after me, let him deny himself, and take up his cross daily, and follow me" (Luke 9:23).

Until we take this step and recognize our utter helplessness and dependence on Christ, looking wholly to Him, we can do nothing. But if we wholeheartedly follow His plan instead of our own, we discover that "there is no limit to the usefulness of one who, by putting self aside, makes room for the working of the Holy Spirit upon the heart, and lives a life wholly consecrated to God" (*The Desire of Ages,* pp. 250, 251).

Humans tend to rate sins of the flesh, such as murder, adultery, stealing, etc., as more grievous than sins of the spirit—pride, covetousness, egotism, etc. However, those sins that men are disposed to look upon as small frequently are the very ones Heaven accounts the greatest transgressions. No sin, however "small" in our sight, is small in God's sight; any sin that is unconfessed and unforsaken, and hence unforgiven, can keep a sinner out of heaven.

"The drunkard is despised and is told that his sin will exclude him from heaven, while pride, selfishness, and covetousness go unrebuked. But these are sins that are especially offensive to God" (*Testimonies,* vol. 5, p. 337).

*I am . . . unfit to be called an apostle, because I persecuted the church of God. But by the grace of God I am what I am, and his grace toward me was not in vain. On the contrary, I worked harder than any of them, though it was not I, but the grace of God which is with me. 1 Cor. 15:9, 10, RSV.*

# The Meaning of Grace

John Newton, the author of the beloved hymn "Amazing Grace," went to sea in 1736 at the age of 12. When he was 17, he was impressed into the British Navy and led the life of a typical sailor. Because of harsh treatment he tried to desert but was caught and flogged so mercilessly that he escaped at his first opportunity. In 1747 he became captain of a slave ship and sank to the lowest depths of degradation imaginable.

In 1748, during a terrible storm, he called upon the Lord for deliverance, promising to give up his sinful life and dedicate himself to the service of God. His prayer was answered and he became a Christian. Yet strangely enough, for the next seven years he saw nothing wrong with continuing in slave trading. It was not until 1755 that he began to see that slavery was wicked. He gave up slave trading and became a minister, and the remainder of his life was one of upward progress.

Two or three years before his death in 1807, Newton and a fellow minister were having breakfast together. It was their custom to read a verse of Scripture after the meal and comment on it. The verse they chose that morning was our verse for meditation. After a few moments of meditation, Newton's comment to his friend went something like this: "I am not what I ought to be. I am not what I wish to be. I am not what I hope to be. But, by the grace of God, I am what I am."

Grace is often defined as "unmerited favor"—undeserved condescension shown us by God, who died for our sins on Calvary in the person of Jesus Christ. But it is more than this. Accepted into our lives, it is God's enabling power to accomplish His will. This is why Paul says, God's "grace toward me was not in vain. On the contrary, I worked harder than any of them, *though it was not I, but the grace of God which is with me."*

Let this grace work in you today in doing God's good pleasure.

*None of these things move me, neither count I
my life dear unto myself, so that I might finish
my course with joy, and the ministry, which I
have received of the Lord Jesus, to testify the
gospel of the grace of God. Acts 20:24.*

JULY

12

# Total Dedication

The August 20, 1957, issue of *Look* magazine carried a story about Colonel William Draper, whose job was to oversee the safety of the *Columbine III*, the aircraft used by the presidents of the United States in the late 1950s and early 1960s. A 33-man crew worked under Draper. Ordinary aeronautical precautions were not enough for this man. An oil leak, for instance, had been known to keep the crew up all night until it was repaired.

The 36-year-old pilot was always available at a moment's notice. When on trips he slept, not with one alarm clock but two—in case one failed. When someone asked what it was like to have the responsibility for the president's life in his hands, he replied, "I believe it demands a special kind of dedication. Everyone in the crew down to the newest mechanic must have it."

This is the kind of dedication you and I must have as Christians—total dedication.

Many years ago during a worship service a small boy tugged on the sleeve of an usher who was taking up the offering. The lad whispered, "Please put the offering plate on the floor." The usher thought it a bit crazy but, noticing his earnestness, complied. Stepping onto the plate, the boy said, "I give my whole life to You, Lord."

The boy was Robert Moffat, who became a great missionary to Africa.

What if this were to happen in your church? Would the people think it a bit crazy? Would they laugh? Or would they be moved to dedicate their lives to God? How would you react?

Some thought the apostle Paul was mad, or crazy. You remember, as he stood before Governor Festus and King Agrippa and gave his testimony, "Festus interrupted with a shout, 'Paul, you are mad! And your great learning is driving me mad!' " (Acts 26:24, NAB).

What if the world thinks total dedication to God is crazy? The important thing is what Heaven thinks about it.

*As for me, I came so close to the edge of the cliff! My feet were slipping and I was almost gone. For I was envious of the prosperity of the proud and wicked. Ps. 73:2, 3, TLB.*

# Spiritual Mountain Climbing

When I was in my mid-teens I listened to a broadcast on the British Broadcasting Company network telling about three young Germans, just a few years older than I, who had lost their footing while climbing in the Austrian Alps. Two of them, unable to stop their fall, plunged over a cliff to their death. The third man managed to check his descent and, although injured, was clinging precariously to a narrow ledge. Later broadcasts told how a rescue team tried desperately to save him. But icy conditions on the slippery slope slowed their efforts to reach him, and in the end their effort failed.

One of the cardinal rules of mountain climbing, as all alpinists know, is always to have at least two hands and one foot, or two feet and one hand, set securely on handholds or footholds on the face of the rock one is climbing. Another rule is to keep looking up. Looking down from vertiginous heights can be fatal.

Charles B. Williams' translation of Philippians 3:13, 14 suggests that the Christian life is an "upward" climb. In the psalmist's ascent of the godly life he suddenly discovered that he was losing his footing. Instead of keeping his eyes looking upward, he began looking around to see how those around him were faring, and noticing that the ungodly seemed to be doing quite well, he came close to falling to his ruin.

Unlike the young German alpinists, the psalmist tells us that his "backsliding" was checked when he "went into the sanctuary of God; [for] then understood I [the] end" of the ungodly (Ps. 73:17). Do you wonder why?

Remember, the psalmist's feet began slipping when he looked around and noticed the seeming prosperity of the wicked. Remember, too, that the sanctuary was the place where the priests ministered before the Lord. Hebrews 8:1, 2 tells us that Jesus is our high priest and that He ministers in God's sanctuary above. So long as we continue to cling to the Rock and keep looking up to Him, not to those around us, we are safe.

*He was oppressed and He was afflicted, yet He opened not His mouth. Isa. 53:7, NKJV.*

JULY

14

# Cure for Rabidity

The ancient people of Egypt, Greece, and Rome thought rabies, also called hydrophobia, was caused by evil spirits, because animals that ordinarily were docile suddenly became, without any apparent cause, aggressive and vicious.

Up to 1885 there was no known cure for the disease. But in 1882 Louis Pasteur, a French microbiologist, began experimenting on what he hoped would be a remedy for this terrible and usually fatal illness.

He discovered that by passing the rabies virus through a succession of some 100 rabbits and drying the infected tissue between inoculations, he was able to obtain a weakened form of the infective agent that made animals resistant to the sickness. He found, for instance, that dogs he experimentally infected with the "street variety" of rabies, which were treated with the attenuated virus before the onset of symptoms, were resistant to the disease. Early in the summer of 1885 a 9-year-old French boy named Joseph Meister was badly bitten by a rabid dog. On hearing about Pasteur's experiments, the boy's mother took him to Paris and implored the great scientist to inoculate him. Pasteur hesitated. He had never before tried the new vaccine on a human being. But then, he reasoned, if dogs could be immunized over a two-week period, the long incubation interval observed in humans might permit immunity to be induced in the boy, since as yet he showed no symptoms of the disease. So, on July 6, 1885, Joseph was inoculated. His body resisted the illness, and he survived.

In some ways an evil temper is like rabies. Have you ever known someone who was ordinarily docile but who suddenly became "rabid" under the least provocation? You probably have. But have you ever seen such a person "inoculated" with Christ's spirit—the Christian spirit? Remember, when Jesus "was reviled, [He] did not revile in return" (1 Peter 2:23, NKJV).

The secret of overcoming this spiritual illness is in being "inoculated" with the spirit of Christ, *before the onset of the "disease"*—right now, for instance. Then, when the "disease" strikes, you will be prepared to resist it.

**205**

# 15

*When someone becomes a Christian he becomes a brand new person inside. He is not the same any more. A new life has begun! 2 Cor. 5:17, TLB.*

# Christian "Evolution"

When Charles Darwin, called the father of organic evolution, first visited Tierra del Fuego on the southern tip of South America in 1832, he met a race of human beings so primitive that he judged them to be "below the level of domestic animals and incapable of being civilized." Recording this opinion in his journal, he said: "The Fuegians are in a more miserable state of barbarism than I have ever expected to have seen any human being."

Thirty-six years later Darwin revisited Tierra del Fuego. In the meantime the Patagonians had come under the influence of the gospel, and the lives of many of them had changed for the better. This time Darwin admitted: "I certainly should have predicted that not all the missionaries in the world could have done what has been done. It is wonderful and it shames me, as I have always prophesied a failure. It is a grand success."

Whatever we may think of the theory of evolution, at least Darwin was honest in admitting his mistake. This is more than some professed Christians are willing to do. However, Darwin's honesty does not mean that therefore his theory was correct, and it goes without saying that organic evolution has never produced a moral change for the better. Only the gospel—"the power of God unto salvation" (Rom. 1:16)—can bring about such a change in a soul that surrenders itself to Christ. No wonder Darwin was surprised.

The most powerful argument in favor of the gospel is the evolution that takes place when a person is "in Christ" (2 Cor. 5:17). Paul speaks of this transformation in our verse. This change does not take place over eons of time but within a single lifetime—and the power that brings it about does not arise naturally from within man, but supernaturally, from outside of him.

The ideal "evolution" of the Christian life is described in Proverbs 4:18: "The path of the just is as the shining light, that shineth more and more unto the perfect day." Open your heart and mind today and let this "evolution" take place in your life.

*I have run the great race, I have finished the course, I have kept the faith. And now there awaits me a garland of righteousness which the Lord, the righteous Judge, will award to me on the great day. 2 Tim. 4:7, 8, REB.*

# Vindictive Verdicts Reversed

When Paul wrote these words, Nero, a monster of cruelty, had recently sentenced him to death. The apostle had little hope of seeing the sentence overturned.

In 1912 James Francis Thorpe, a Native American, won gold medals in both the pentathlon and decathlon events of the World Olympics—a feat never duplicated before nor since. Hugo Wieslander, of Sweden, who competed against Thorpe in the pentathlon, declared him to be "the greatest athlete in the world." James Sullivan, U.S. commissioner to the Olympic Games, eulogized him as "unquestionably the greatest athlete that ever lived."

Seven months after Jim Thorpe received his medals he was stripped of them because of a technicality—at one time he had played in bush-league baseball for $2 a game, unaware that this was against Olympic rules. The judges refused to take that fact into consideration.

Thorpe bore the injustice stoically, but soon after his death in 1953 his children appealed to International Olympic Committee (IOC) president Avery Brundage to restore their father's medals posthumously. Brundage refused. Brundage had competed against Thorpe in the 1912 pentathlon—and lost—and apparently never forgave Thorpe for besting him.

Brundage's biographer, Heinz Schobel, in *The Four Dimensions of Avery Brundage,* states that among his character traits were "narrow-mindedness, [and] jealousy." These may have been accompanied by a good dose of vindictiveness as well, for Brundage, who became president of the IOC (1952-1972), never relented in his refusal to restore Thorpe's medals.

But in January 1983, almost 30 years after Thorpe's death, a more "righteous judge," Juan Antonio Samaranch, president of the IOC, restored Thorpe's medals to his descendants.

Many unjust judgments are not overturned in this life. But do not lose courage. Soon the Lord, the righteous judge, will overturn every vindictive verdict (see James 5:9).

# 17

*I count everything sheer loss, because all is far outweighed by the gain of knowing Christ Jesus my Lord, for whose sake I did in fact lose everything. Phil. 3:8, NEB.*

# **Would You Rather Have Jesus?**

George Beverly Shea, celebrated singing evangelist, took voice training in New York City as a young man. After completing his courses, he was auditioned by a radio station and offered a job. When he asked if he could sing gospel songs on the program, he was told that he might include one occasionally, but that mainly he would be singing worldly songs.

One Saturday night George's mother, who had been praying for him to make the right decision, placed the poem "I'd Rather Have Jesus" on the piano where George usually practiced. When he read it in the morning, his heart was touched and he turned down the contract! Later he composed the beautiful song with the same title as the poem his mother had put in his path. Not long after this, he met Billy Graham, the famous evangelist, and became the song leader of his crusades.

Paul is believed to have been a member of the Sanhedrin, the body that governed the religious life of the Jewish nation, before becoming a Christian. One reason for this assumption is that, under the authority of Rome, the Sanhedrin had the power of life and death, and Paul says that when Christians were put to death, "I cast my vote against them" (Acts 26:10, NIV).

If he was indeed a member of this august body, Jewish law required that he be married. Yet the New Testament makes no mention of his having a wife. Consequently, some have conjectured that when he accepted Christ, his wife left him. If so, Paul lost much in becoming a Christian, but he gave up far more—he says he gave up *everything* for Christ.

Becoming a Christian involves giving up everything. Often, however, God lets us keep some of the things we cherish. But when He does, we are merely stewards, and whenever He asks us to surrender them, we should gladly give them up. The problem is that after a while some of us begin to feel that the things God lets us keep are really ours. This is a mistake.

Would you rather have Jesus than anything else?

*Let it be your ambition to . . . work with your hands, as we told you, so that you may command the respect of those outside your own number, and at the same time never be in want.*
*1 Thess. 4:11, REB.*

JULY

18

# Money and Effective Witnessing

One day (it must have been in the first half of 1931) our family heard that Charles A. Lindbergh, famous airplane pilot, and his wife, Anne, were going to land their seaplane at Funchal, the capital of Madeira, where we were living at the time. My father and I went downtown to watch them come in. Presently we heard the distant hum of an airplane engine high up in the sky. We caught a brief glimpse of the colonel's plane as it roared overhead. But the Lindberghs didn't land. We were disappointed, of course. Later we learned that the pilot had not landed because the ocean was too choppy.

To many, Lindbergh had a baffling personality. Just four years before his flight over Madeira he had been the first man to fly nonstop alone across the Atlantic. When he returned to America he was welcomed as a hero, but these honors did not faze him in the least. Offers of money came from everywhere. One person estimated that he could have made $5 million in one week if he had accepted the hundreds of offers to sign testimonials.

William Randolph Hearst offered him a half million dollars if he would star in a film about aviation. A vaudeville company offered him a contract worth a million dollars. A movie magnate offered him another million-dollar deal. He firmly but graciously turned them all down. Money was sent to him as gifts. He returned it all. A friend summed up his reason for so doing this way: "Lindbergh won't take money he hasn't earned."

Although undoubtedly there are exceptions, it is a good rule not to accept money that is not earned. It is a biblical principle, as our text suggests.

Many years ago I read about an old Italian who lost his job during the Great Depression and had to go on the public dole. Instead of doing nothing, he bought a broom and began sweeping the streets of his town—because he didn't believe in getting something for doing nothing.

A Christian's witness is usually more effective when he does productive work for remuneration received.

**19**

# You Are Good for Something

Willie Rugh, a young crippled newsboy, lived in a suburb of Gary, Indiana. In the autumn of 1912 the doctors recommended that one of his legs be amputated, since it was useless. Soon after this recommendation was made, a girl, Ethel Smith, was badly burned. Her chances of survival were poor unless she received a skin graft. So the doctors asked Willie if he would let them use skin taken from his yet-to-be-amputated leg for grafting onto the burned areas on Ethel's body. The boy agreed without hesitation.

Willie survived his operation and did well for a while, but then pneumonia set in. In those days there were no antibiotics, and in spite of all the doctors could do, Willie's condition deteriorated. Finally he had to be told he would not recover. When he heard this discouraging news, rather than bemoaning his misfortune, Willie said, "I'm glad I've done it, Doctor. Tell Ethel I hope she gets well real soon. I guess I'm good for something after all." Courageous words!

The story of Willie's selfless act was published in the nation's papers. The city of Gary went into mourning. Public offices and businesses closed their doors for the day. A band and a police escort accompanied his casket to the cemetery, and the mayor declared in eulogy, "The name of Willie Rugh should be remembered in Gary as long as the city lasts."

Some people feel they are good for nothing because their physical condition or appearance may not be all they could wish for. But no matter what our condition, we are good for something. This "something" may not be what we would like it to be, but it is "something" God has in mind for us. It is for us to seek with a humble spirit to find out what this "something" is. *We are all good for something!*

*This is the day which the Lord has made; let us rejoice and be glad in it. Ps. 118:24, RSV.*

JULY

20

# This Is the Day

Too many of us live in the past or the future while neglecting the present.

Now, there is nothing wrong with occasionally thinking about the past. After all, the past is what we have been, what we have experienced. There can be great value in gleaning from our past lessons that we can apply to the present and the future. But dwelling on past mistakes, things we cannot change, can ruin the present—and the future.

Old Mac was an inmate in a rest home in Lodi, California. I used to visit him and the others there from time to time in an endeavor to bring them a little hope and happiness. Old Mac was close to 90 when I knew him back in the early 1950s. He said he had been a member of the Jesse James gang and had known Jesse personally. Now in his old age, all he could talk about was his misspent youth and the vain regrets he had about the wicked things he had done. I never visited him but what he brought up his past.

Others dwell on the future. One man who worked in the same institution where I worked as an editor had it all figured out what he would do when he turned 65. Again, there is nothing wrong with planning ahead; in fact, I think it is an excellent idea. The problem with this individual was that, when he finally retired, he found it was a lot less fun than he had imagined it would be. Reality didn't measure up to his expectations. He had never learned to enjoy the present.

"We live, and move, and have our being" (Acts 17:28), not in the past or the future, but in the present. Let us make the most of it. Life is a journey, not a destination, and happiness is not there—somewhere in the past or the future—but here. Today is a parenthesis between yesterday and tomorrow. Good things should happen, can happen, *will* happen today, if we approach the present in the right spirit with God as our partner.

"This is the day which the Lord hath made" (Ps. 118:24). Yesterday is dead; tomorrow hasn't yet been born; today, this moment, right now, is all you really have. Rejoice and be glad in it!

211

*Aware of [the disciples'] discussion, Jesus asked, "You of little faith, why are you talking among yourselves about having no bread? Do you still not understand? Don't you remember the five loaves for the five thousand?"*
*Matt. 16:8, 9, NIV.*

# Great Faith, Great Gain

John McNeil, a minister in the British Isles, reports that he once pastored a church that was heavily in debt. This worried him, and he prayed a lot about it. One day a stranger came to his office and said he was aware of the church's indebtedness and offered to help. Then, laying a blank check on the pastor's desk, he told him to write in whatever amount was needed, and promised to return later and sign the check.

The pastor couldn't believe his senses. After the man left, he began to rationalize: "This can't be true. Does this man realize that our debt runs into thousands of pounds? I doubt he would pay it all—if he knew. And yet he told me to make it out for the full amount. No, that would be taking unfair advantage. I'll put down only half." And that is what he did.

When the stranger returned, he signed the check without hesitation. He obviously meant what he said. The church's benefactor was a well-known philanthropist. When the pastor realized that the man was fully capable of paying off the debt, he wished he had written in the full amount the church owed.

This story purports to be true, and I have no reason to believe it is not, yet some reading this illustration may be saying to themselves, "This can't be true. Who would be that generous?" And they may be right, but it does illustrate an aspect of God's character.

When God promises something, He keeps His word. He invites us to come to Him "in faith, *nothing wavering"* (James 1:6), and promises that "if we ask any thing according to his will, he heareth us," and "whatsoever we ask [with this submissive attitude], we receive" (1 John 5:14 and 3:22). The least we can do is test Him, complying with the conditions He lays down.

What a great God we serve! But remember—little faith, little gain; great faith, great gain.

*I resolved to know nothing while I was with you
except Jesus Christ and him crucified.*
*I Cor. 2:2, NIV.*

JULY
22

# Paul's Blind Spot

Although there is no reliable description of the apostle Paul, an ancient document known as The Acts of Paul and Thecla describes him as "baldheaded, bowlegged, strongly built, a man small in size, with meeting eyebrows, with a rather large nose, full of grace, for at times he looked like a man and at times he had the face of an angel." Fascinating but not exactly prepossessing, wouldn't you say? And yet, with the exception of Christ, Paul was the most dynamic personality of the first century of the Christian Era. He played a large part in transforming Christianity, so to speak, from a mere sect of Judaism into a universal religion.

Paul visited many lands in the eastern Mediterranean and saw many scenes in different countries. Whenever he was able, he wrote letters, or epistles, to the people he had visited or intended to visit. Much of what we know about Christians of the first century comes from his writings or from the writings of Luke, who accompanied Paul on some of his journeys. But did you ever notice that there is not a single line of descriptive scenery of the countries through which he traveled? Not one verse tells about the wonders of the architecture of his day. There is not the least hint regarding the customs of the people of the Roman world.

*Paul had a blind spot!* As he traveled about on his missionary journeys he was blind to everything but Jesus Christ. This willful blindness is reflected in our verse for meditation. He says that he determined to know nothing but Jesus Christ and Him crucified.

When did this blindness begin? On the way to Damascus, when he met the Lord Jesus Christ and was physically blinded by the vision of His glory. This physical blindness was healed three days later when God restored his physical sight. But it was during this very time that a "spiritual" blindness set in—a blindness that lasted for the rest of his life. From that time on, Paul could see nothing but his Lord.

The same thing can happen to you and me when we catch a vision of Jesus Christ.

*In our union with Christ [God the Father] has blessed us by giving us every spiritual blessing in the heavenly world. Eph. 1:3, TEV.*

# Cargo Cultists

During World War II the American military frequently used the islands between Australia and Indonesia as staging areas from which to launch their drives on New Guinea. White men came in large, noisy "birds" bearing cargo—and gifts. Through these unexpected visitations the inhabitants of the islands became acquainted with civilization.

To their amazement, planes would swoop down from the skies, land, disgorge their cargo, and take off—leaving behind such marvels as boxes that talked, things that produced instant fire, and monsters that trampled down the jungle and constructed airstrips. They saw for the first time power tools, modern weapons, and many varieties of food. They were entranced—and concluded that the White men must be gods.

After the soldiers left, the islanders built shrines for the cargo gods—shaped like hangars and radio towers, but fashioned from bamboo. Years later, some of these islanders still prayed for cargo from every plane that flew overhead. In their shrines they worshiped cigarette lighters, eyeglasses, and ballpoint pens left behind by the Allied Forces. Later yet, when White missionaries arrived to preach the gospel, they received an enthusiastic welcome—at first. The islanders were sure this was the "second coming." You can imagine their disillusionment when they realized that instead of cargo the missionaries were offering the gospel. The missionaries found it almost impossible to penetrate the materialism that had become the essence of the islanders' religion.

We smile at these people's naïveté. But really, don't we reveal a cargo cult mentality in the way we sometimes pray? When we are more desirous of receiving material blessings for which we pray than the spiritual blessings of the heavenly world our heavenly Father offers, do we not reveal ourselves to be "cargo cultists" at heart?

Why not "seek . . . first the kingdom of God, and his righteousness" (Matt. 6:33) rather than making material things first?

*Arise, and go down to the potter's house, and there I will cause thee to hear my words. Then I went down into the potter's house, and, behold, he wrought a work on the wheels. And the vessel that he made of clay was marred . . . : so he made . . . another vessel. Jer. 18:2-4.*

JULY

24

# Let Your Life Be Repaired

When my wife and I were missionaries in Boa Vista, Rio Branco territory (now the state of Roraima), Brazil, we led out in the building of a mission school. One day I hired an oxcart and went with my two boys to a brickyard where clay vessels were made, as well as bricks. I noticed in one corner of the yard a sizable pile of potsherds. While waiting for the oxcart to be loaded, I asked the owner of the yard what caused so many of the vessels to fracture. He said that the clay had not been allowed to dry thoroughly before firing, and the moisture in the clay had turned to steam, causing the clay to shatter. These shards, he said, were worthless except to fill potholes—to be trodden under feet of men, no doubt.

Keeping large objects of clay or metal from cracking during manufacturing can be difficult. For example, Big Ben, a bell that hangs in Westminster Palace tower and is probably the most famous bell in the world, was cracked before leaving the foundry. It was sent back for repairs, and these repairs were so successful that it has chimed out the time virtually uninterrupted since it was installed almost 140 years ago.

Unlike the broken vessels I saw in Boa Vista, there was hope for the ruined vessel Jeremiah saw in the potter's shop. The clay had not been fired, so the potter simply made it over. However, once a clay vessel is kilned, it is impossible to make it over. In a similar way, it is impossible for us to be made over after the fire of the last day has done its work.

Paul says that "the quality of each person's work will be seen when the Day of Christ exposes it. For on that Day fire will reveal everyone's work . . . and show its real quality" (1 Cor. 3:13, TEV).

Now is the time for you to let the Master Potter remake you into "a vessel for honor" (2 Tim. 2:21, NKJV).

*Oh, that you would choose life; that you and your children might live! Deut. 30:19, TLB.*

# Choices

Jobs were scarce in the 1930s. Fay West, a machinist in San Francisco, California, put in long hours to support his wife, Emily, and their seven children. Then, just when it looked like they were going to succeed in eking out an existence, the doctor informed Emily that child number eight was on the way.

Completely ignoring the fact that it takes a father as well as a mother to produce a child, Fay, not a Christian at the time, ranted, "We can't afford another kid! I can't get enough work now to feed the kids we have! Do something about it!"

Emily understood what that meant. In those days there was no such thing as legal abortions. As she wrestled with the problem, someone arranged for "someone a friend knew" to take care of the situation. The day of the abortion found Emily crying out in agony for divine guidance. Before she got up from her knees she determined not to keep the appointment. It was then that she heard an audible voice say, "She will be a comfort to you in your old age." Startled, Emily looked around. She was alone in the room. The voice repeated, "She will be a comfort to you in your old age." (Notice, the voice said "she," not "he.")

That eighth child was born, and grew up believing she was Fay's favorite daughter. She never tired of hearing about how her mother chose life or the angel's promise. Eventually, Fay became a Christian, and I had the privilege of baptizing him. And his "baby," later my Vesta, did indeed become a comfort to her mother *and her father* in their old age.

The abortion issue is like opposite areas between two intersecting lines. They have a midpoint, but no common ground for compromise. Thus, the issue is amicably unresolvable in human terms. All I can say is that I am eternally grateful for Emily's choice.

Every day we face choices, some of them easy, some extremely difficult. We may not always hear an audible voice saying "This is the way, walk ye in it" (Isa. 30:21), but if we daily and sincerely commit our lives to God, He promises to guide us in the way that we should go.

*These who are wise will shine like the brightness of the heavens, and those who lead many to righteousness, like the stars for ever and ever. Dan. 12:3, NIV.*

JULY

26

# As the Stars Forever and Ever

This morning when I stepped out under the starry heavens, what a glorious celestial scene greeted my eyes! Without a cloud to obscure their witness, what a message these myriads of twinkling, shining celestial bodies conveyed to me!

I imagined they were saying, "Each one of us has been shining for untold ages, because of the light imparted to us by the Great Light of the universe!" And then the assurance, "You too can shine forever and ever if you will reflect His light, if you will cooperate fully with Him, placing yourself in complete harmony with His plan for your life."

"[As] every shining star which God has placed in the heavens obeys His mandate, and gives its distinctive measure of light to make beautiful the heavens at night; so let every converted soul show the measure of light committed to him" (*The SDA Bible Commentary,* Ellen G. White Comments, vol. 4, p. 1153).

Among the host of the redeemed in the hereafter there will not be two who will have experienced the saving, transforming grace of their Redeemer in exactly the same way. Nor will this distinctiveness be lost in eternity beyond. Each one will have his or her special way of revealing that unspeakable love, that love that will be the subject of study of the redeemed throughout the endless ages of eternity. How grateful, then, should we be to Him from whom "flow life and light and gladness, throughout the realms of illimitable space" (*The Great Controversy,* p. 678).

The shining orbs we see in the heavens ever testify to the love and power and wisdom of their Creator. "The love of our heavenly Father in the gift of His only-begotten Son to the world is enough to inspire every soul, to melt every hard, loveless heart into contrition and tenderness; and yet, shall heavenly intelligences see in those for whom Christ died, insensibility to His love, hardness of heart, and no response of gratitude and affection to the Giver of all good things? . . . Shall the Sun of Righteousness shine in vain?" (*Fundamentals of Christian Education,* p. 198).

Only you and I can answer this question.

# 27

*For you who obey me, my saving power will rise on you like the sun and bring healing like the sun's rays. You will be as free and happy as calves let out of a stall. Mal. 4:2, TEV.*

## Glorious Sunrises and Sunsets

How glorious the sun appeared this morning as it peeped over Bogus Basin through red and golden sunlit clouds. My wife and I enjoyed it on our usual morning walk on the country road not far from our house. As we walked along, there opened to me a scene so glorious and indescribable as will remain indelibly impressed on my memory. The rays of the rising sun filtered through the trees, seeming to touch every branch and twig with a magic wand, transmuting the droplets of dew into nuggets of gold! I suddenly felt as if I were a multibillionaire. Some of the other sunsets we have seen in Idaho have been just as gorgeous and rich, but in a different way.

Ellen White, who frequently traveled through the Western states, must have viewed such a sunset on one occasion, for she wrote: "We were favored with a sight of the most glorious sunset it was ever my privilege to behold. Language is inadequate to picture its beauty. The last beams of the setting sun, silver and gold, purple, amber, and crimson, shed their glories athwart the sky, growing brighter and brighter, rising higher and higher in the heavens, until it seemed that the gates of the City of God had been left ajar and gleams of the inner glory were flashing through. For two hours the wondrous splendor continued to light up the cold northern sky—a picture painted by the great Master-Artist upon the shifting canvas of the heavens" (*My Life Today,* p. 337).

How grateful we can be that our Creator is a lover of the beautiful, that "by his spirit he hath garnished the heavens" (Job 26:13), but above all, that He shares the beauties of His creation with His earthly children.

"God makes His sun to shine on the just and on the unjust, and this sun represents Christ, the Sun of Righteousness, who shines as the light of the world, giving His blessings and mercies, seen and unseen, to rich and poor alike. This principle is to guide our conduct toward our fellowmen" (*Testimonies to Ministers,* p. 280).

*I give you a new command, "Love one another." Just as I have loved you, so you should love one another. By this everyone will recognize that you are My disciples. John 13:34, 35, MLB.*

# The Eleventh Commandment

One time before James Ussher became well known for his biblical chronology, he was shipwrecked on the coast of Ireland, but he managed to swim to shore. Virtually naked, he went to the nearest house and knocked. A man answered his knock. Ussher explained that he was a clergyman and asked for help. It so happened he had knocked at the home of the parish pastor. Wary of being duped, and perhaps wanting to have a little fun, the pastor decided to test Ussher with a Bible question before rendering assistance. "How many commandments are there?" he asked.

"Eleven," replied Ussher, detecting a note of derision in the pastor's voice.

"Wrong!" chortled the pastor. "There are only 10."

"There are 11," Ussher insisted. "I think you've forgotten the one that says, 'A new commandment I give unto you, that ye love one another.' "

Did the pastor eventually help Ussher? I don't know. I hope he did, and I hope he showed the next stranger who came to his door greater kindness, with greater promptness, than he showed Ussher.

Some years ago I heard a sermon illustration that made a deep impression on me. A Roman Catholic priest was driving from northern New York State to New York City, and saw a young man thumbing a ride. He stopped to pick him up. The hitchhiker was a homely young man whom everyone in town called "Satan Smith" because of his looks. Discouraged in his futile attempts to find a job, Smith had decided to turn to crime, but the priest, through kindness, was able to turn his life around.

If we always lived as close to the Lord as we should, is it not possible that the Lord would impress us when to help those in need? In this day and age it is not always wise to pick up hitchhiking strangers. But think of the Ethiopian eunuch who was seeking for truth and was impressed to pick up Philip the "hitchhiker" (see Acts 8:26-39). Is it not possible that, if we live close to the Lord, He would impress us with whom to help and whom to avoid?

**219**

*My heart stands in awe of Your words.*
*Ps. 119:161, Amplified.*

# The Bible's Proper Place

Across the street from where my wife and I lived in Bangkok, Thailand, was a Muslim school. In that country 4 percent of the population are Muslims, more than 90 percent are Buddhists, and less than 1 percent are Christians.

The Koran, the Muslims' holy book, is a bit shorter than the New Testament. Although it has been translated into other languages, Muslims do not regard these as authoritative. Only the Arabic version is considered to be the Word of Allah. Good Muslims never touch their holy book with unwashed hands; never lay it on the floor; never carry it below the waistline.

Perhaps we Christians could learn something from our Muslim friends about respecting our Sacred Book. Although we respect the Bible, we do not regard the Bible as an object of near-worship. On the other hand, I am sure many of us could show more reverence for God's Book than we do. In many so-called Christian homes the Bible is allowed to sit on a shelf or table year after year unnoticed, unopened, and unread. Often, ordinary books and magazines are piled on top of it.

During my early teenage years our family lived in Europe, and I can remember hearing that it was customary in certain countries over there to put other books on top of the Bible. People did this, I was told, because to them the Bible was "the foundation." Thus, apparently, it was perfectly proper to place other papers and books on top of it. In our home, we were taught that "nothing should be allowed to supersede" the Bible. Thus, even now, many years later, I feel uncomfortable at seeing other things piled on top of God's Word.

While no one can be dogmatic and say that some particular way of placing the Bible is right and all the other ways are wrong, yet the place we give the Bible physically probably reflects the place we give it mentally. One thing, however, is beyond dispute: Giving the Bible's teachings the central place in our lives is far more important than precisely where we place the physical Book.

*There are "friends" who pretend to be friends,*
*but there is a friend who sticks closer than a*
*brother. Prov. 18:24, TLB.*

JULY

# 30

# Closer Than a Brother

One day when Marjorie, our oldest daughter, was 4 she found a couple cockleburs clinging together. She quipped, "Two little cockleburs lovin' each other."

We all laughed. But burrs are no laughing matter when you have to pick them off your clothes. My mother used to say they were like a friend "who sticks closer than a brother."

But believe it or not, burrs have served a useful purpose. In 1948 George de Mestral, a Swiss alpinist, returned from a mountain climb, his pant legs covered with burrs. Examining them closely, he noticed that the burrs had little projections, each of which had a tiny barb at the end. It was by these that the burrs clung to his clothes.

From this observation Mestral and a French textile weaver invented Velcro, a very useful material. It consists of two strips of nylon, one with little hooks, the other with a woollike surface to which the little hooks cling.

The Holy Spirit is like Velcro—or burrs. He is a friend who sticks closer than a brother. David describes His "stick-to-itiveness" thus: "Whither shall I go from thy spirit? Or whither shall I flee from thy presence? If I ascend up into heaven, thou art there: if I make my bed in hell, behold, thou art there. If I take the wings of the morning, and dwell in the uttermost parts of the sea; even there shall thy hand lead me, and thy right hand shall hold me" (Ps. 139:7-10).

Just think of what would have happened to David if this persistent Friend had let him go after he sinned with Bathsheba. How thankful we can be that this Friend loves us so persistently. He never leaves us nor forsakes us—unless, of course, we leave Him.

*"[Ahaziah,] why did you send messengers to Baal-zebub, the god of Ekron, to ask about your sickness?" Elijah demanded. "Is it because there is no God in Israel to ask?" 2 Kings 1:16, TLB.*

# Go Not to the God of Ekron

Ahaziah, king of Israel, was the son of Ahab and Jezebel. His name means "Jehovah has grasped [my hand]." As heir apparent to the throne, he probably was present on Mount Carmel the day Jehovah revealed Himself as the true God and exposed Baal as a false god (see 1 Kings 18:19-39). Ahaziah's name may even suggest that he professed to be a follower of the true God.

In all probability, Ahaziah knew about Elijah's prophecies concerning his parents' violent deaths and had seen these predictions literally fulfilled (see 1 Kings 21:19; 22:34-38; 21:23; 2 Kings 9:33-37). And yet, in the face of all this evidence, at heart he followed Baal (see 1 Kings 22:51-53).

Some two years after his father's death, Ahaziah fell from an "upper chamber" (2 Kings 1:2) window and was hurt so seriously that he feared for his life. However, instead of sending for one of God's prophets to ask whether or not he would recover, he sent messengers to inquire of Baal, "the god of Ekron."

There are many today—even professed Christians—who act in much the same way as did Ahaziah. Consider the person who faces a life-threatening health problem, to whom this present life is more important than eternal life. Such a person likely will not care whether God or Satan answers his prayers for healing. He forgets that while God can heal any and all diseases, it is not always His will to restore the sick to health.

It is at this point that Satan steps in with his miracle-working power and, operating through his so-called "ministers of righteousness" (2 Cor. 11:15; cf. Matt. 7:21, 22), deceives, if possible, "the very elect" (Matt. 24:24). Revelation 16:14 says he can perform miracles, and he uses this power to ensnare souls.

God does not work this way. When He heals, it is not merely to prolong life but because He has a plan in mind for the life He prolongs. So instead of going to the god of Ekron, seek to discern God's plan for your life and freely submit to His will.

*And it shall come to pass in that day, that the Lord will set His hand again the second time to recover the remnant of His people.*
*Isa. 11:11, MT.*

AUGUST

1

# A Second Chance

At the Battle of Bunker Hill, fought June 17, 1775, the forces under Col. William Prescott showed conspicuous bravery in the face of the British regulars. Thus, when Prescott ordered his men to hold their fire until they could "see the whites of their eyes," many were obedient unto death. But not all the Americans that day were so brave. After the battle Captain John Callender of the Massachusetts Militia was charged with "cowardice in the face of the enemy."

After George Washington took command of the Continental Army at Cambridge, Massachusetts, on July 3, 1775, one of his first duties was to court-martial Captain Callender. At the end of the unpleasant ordeal, Callender was stripped of his commission and expelled from the army in disgrace.

But this was not the end of the story. Callender reenlisted as an ordinary private, and a year later, during Washington's perilous withdrawal following the Battle of Long Island, showed such outstanding valor that the general publicly revoked his sentence and restored him as an officer in his army.

When we fail our divine Commander in the battle against the forces of evil, we can be thankful that He does not reject us out of hand. Although He cannot condone "cowardice in the face of the enemy," He holds out hope. If we humbly acknowledge responsibility for our wrongdoings, accepting a lower position if necessary, He pardons us and accepts us back into His army.

Our verse for meditation refers to the experience of God's chosen people in Old Testament times. After shameful episodes of apostasy preceded by warnings, God finally permitted His people to be taken captive to Babylon.

During the 70 years that followed, the Jewish people seemed to be cast off. However, in reality God was simply permitting the bitter experience to persuade His people of the folly of their ways.

Amid the painful consequences of wrongdoing, it is our privilege to heed God's call and renew our allegiance to Him.

*[Christ] is able also to save them to the uttermost that come unto God by him, seeing he ever liveth to make intercession for them. Heb. 7:25.*

# "He Is Able"

Abraham is called the father of the faithful (Gal. 3:7-9), not because he never doubted God's promises, but because he overcame his doubts and reached the point where he "staggered not at the promise of God through unbelief; but was strong in faith, . . . being fully persuaded that, what he had promised, he was able to perform" (Rom. 4:20, 21).

Have you ever been tempted to think that God was able to fulfill His promises to Abraham and other ancient worthies, but for some reason He can't or won't fulfill them to His children in this day and age—to you, for instance?

When a friend of mine got up one morning, he found a little plaque his wife had placed on his desk. On it were written these words: "He is able." Only three words, but how reassuring! The words, taken from our memory text, assure us that God *is* (present tense) able to help us. He has helped His people in the past and He can help us *now!*

My friend kept this little plaque on his desk to remind him that God keeps His word. We need to have God's promises indelibly impressed on our minds and never forget that "God is . . . a very *present* help" (Ps. 46:1).

A very present help does not mean that we will always discern immediately the fulfillment of God's promises. It does mean that as soon as we present our needs and claim a promise He has made, He begins to shape circumstances toward the fulfillment of that promise. As a matter of fact, before we call He has already, in His foreknowledge, begun to act on our behalf (Isa. 65:24).

We alone can frustrate the fulfillment of God's promises by giving up our faith or by seeking our own selfish way rather than His. When our prayers are not answered, we should wait patiently, knowing He *will keep His word*—but it will be *in His own good time and way.*

How thankful we can be that "our God whom we serve is able" (Dan. 3:17)!

*I was in prison and you came to visit me. . . . I tell you in truth, whatever you did for one of the least of these brothers of mine, you did for me. Matt. 25:36-40, NIV.*

# Freed From Spiritual Imprisonment

In his book *Just for Today,* James Keller tells how one afternoon in January 1951, Sakuichi Yamada, a young Japanese Christian girl, approached the superintendent of a prison in one of the smaller cities of Japan. She handed him a little parcel that carried her return address, and asked that he give it to some condemned criminal. Then she quietly left.

The packet contained Christian books and a comforting letter from the girl. The letter ended with these words: "In the eyes of God a criminal is His child." It was signed simply, "From a schoolgirl."

The prison superintendent handed the package to a murderer who had been condemned to execution for wiping out a family of three. When the doomed man read the books and the letter, he was deeply touched and wrote Yamada. He confessed he was a vicious criminal and acknowledged that he had been afraid to die, but that since reading the books and her letter his fear had greatly diminished. He concluded his letter, "How great is the mercy of God to me, this sinner. . . . May God bless you."

Having spent 37 months in internment, facing the possibility of being killed, I can empathize, at least to some degree, with this prisoner on death row. During those three years our family received no mail except one letter from my uncle Ira. It reached us more than a year after it had been mailed. I still have that letter. What a comfort it was to know that we had not been forgotten, that somebody cared.

Being deprived of one's liberty is bad enough, but finding oneself incarcerated also in the prison house of sin is far worse. It is to these latter prisoners especially that Jesus addressed these words of the first sermon He ever preached: "The Spirit of the Lord is on me. . . . He has sent me to proclaim freedom for the prisoners" (Luke 4:18, NIV).

If the Holy Spirit were to impress you to follow Yamada's example, would you obey?

*Jesus wept. John 11:35.*

# Tears

This is the shortest verse in the English Bible, but what an insight it gives us into the humanity of our Saviour.

Recently I read an article that stated that chemical analyses of tears have shown that they contain minute quantities of waste products from the brain. These products are believed to result from certain emotional states—anger, fear, the shock resulting from sudden sorrow, a beautiful wedding, and so on.

Dr. Sandor Feldman, associate professor of psychiatry at the University of Rochester, has concluded from a recent study that one never weeps for sheer joy—behind supposed tears of joy there is always a hidden element of sorrow.

Soldiers, or at least commanding officers, are not supposed to weep. But in his book *They Fought Alone,* John Keats tells how Col. Wendell W. Fertig, a leader of the Allied resistance forces in the Philippines, suddenly burst into tears as his *banca* (Filipino sailboat) neared the shore at Tangub, Mindanao and he heard the people singing "Somewhere Over the Rainbow," a song popular before World War II. The song somehow reminded him of his wife and children, from whom he had been separated when they were sent home to America before the war broke out.

Some people seem to be unable to weep—my father and my wife, for example. Only once did I see my father weep, and then only for a few seconds. That was when my youngest sister died. At the funeral, which he conducted, he was totally stoical and dry-eyed. I have never seen my wife weep, but this morning as I discussed this reading with her, I learned for the first time that occasionally she does weep—in private, when she is reading a particularly poignant story, for instance. In general, as we get older we seem to have less control over our tears.

I'm glad Jesus wept. I can't help believing that, after the last judgment, when the lost are cast into the lake of fire, God will weep, for God takes no pleasure in the death of the unrighteous (Eze. 33:11). The Bible declares that when the reign of sin is over, God will wipe away tears from all eyes (Rev. 21:4), *His own included,* I am convinced.

*Blessed be God the Father of our Lord Jesus Christ, who has blessed us with all the spiritual blessings of heaven in Christ. Eph. 1:3, Jerusalem.*

AUGUST
5

# How to Count Your Blessings

Have you ever had someone glibly say to you, "Count your blessings"? People who say this mean well, but I have to admit that sometimes when they have said it to me, I've found it hard to follow their advice. Perhaps you've had the same experience. But, you know, there's another way to look at things.

Our verse speaks of "spiritual [not material] blessings," and it is all these that God assures us He has blessed us with. So, while it is pleasant to enjoy material blessings, it is far more important to recognize and count our spiritual blessings.

The other day I was repairing something for my wife, when a small but important screw slipped out of my hand and fell on the floor. Because the carpet and the color of the screw were so nearly alike, I could not find it. I was frustrated. Then, suddenly, an idea popped into my head. I got a magnet, passed it over the carpet, and soon found the object of my search.

The next time I find it difficult to count my blessings, I'm going to put my "spiritual magnet" to work—the "mind . . . which was . . . in Christ Jesus" (Phil. 2:5), "who for the joy that was set before him [your salvation and mine] endured the cross" (Heb. 12:2).

Can you imagine anyone finding joy in a cross? Jesus did—because looking beyond it, He saw you and me drawn to it.

The lack of material blessings can blind us to spiritual blessings that lie beyond—if we let it. It goes without saying that "no 'chastening' seems pleasant at the time." But never forget: "When it is all over we can see that it has quietly produced the fruit of real goodness in the characters of those who have accepted it" (Heb. 12:11, Phillips).

So learn to look beyond the immediate present and try to see the spiritual blessings that are sure to come if you accept your seeming lack of blessings at the moment.

*Cast thy bread upon the waters: for thou shalt find it after many days. Eccl. 11:1.*

# After Many Days

In 1568 when Mary, Queen of Scots, fled to England she took with her a necklace of rare black pearls. Nineteen years later, when she was executed, the ornament disappeared. The British government ordered a search, but the necklace could not be found. After considerable time and effort, the search had to be called off—but it was not forgotten.

More than 350 years later, two American women touring Great Britain went into an old pawnshop looking for a cheap souvenir to take back home. The shopkeeper showed them a string of dingy black beads that he offered to sell for a shilling. The women bought them and took them to a jeweler to have them cleaned.

Several days later, when the women went to pick up their souvenir, a representative of the British government informed them that the beads were Queen Mary's long-lost necklace. To recover it, the government paid the women £5,000 sterling.

Just like the search for the necklace was not immediately successful, so our search for souls may not produce immediate results. But this should not discourage us from witnessing for Christ. While my father was a soldier in World War I, he witnessed by giving his buddies copies of *Steps to Christ.* He saw no immediate results from his efforts, but 44 years later he learned that one of the men in his unit, John Casner, had accepted Christ as the result of reading the booklet.

Just because the harvest seems long delayed should not deter us from sowing the gospel seed at every opportunity. "Proclaim the message, press it home on all occasions, convenient or inconvenient" (2 Tim. 4:2, NEB), urged Paul. Solomon further admonishes us: "In the morning sow thy seed, and in the evening withhold not thine hand: for thou knowest not whether shall prosper, either this or that, or whether they both shall be alike good" (Eccl. 11:6).

No, God's word never returns unto Him void (see Isa. 55:10, 11)—but sometimes it takes "many days" before we see the results.

*Son of man, I have appointed you a watchman to the house of Israel; when you hear a word from My mouth, you shall give them warning in My name. Eze. 3:17, MLB.*

AUGUST

7

# The Sleeping Sentinel

It is a sentinel's responsibility to remain alert and sound the alarm if he sees the enemy coming. Because the lives of so many of his fellow soldiers depend on his wakefulness, the usual penalty for sleeping at his post is death by a firing squad.

One night after the Battle of Arcole (November 15-17, 1796), Napoleon Bonaparte made the rounds of the sentry posts circling his camp and came upon one of his sentinels sleeping. Stealthily removing the soldier's weapon without waking him, the general took over his duty until almost time for the man's relief to arrive.

Near the end of his watch the soldier woke up. Horrified at seeing his commander doing the duty with which he had been charged, and knowing that the penalty for sleeping at his post was death, he exclaimed, "I am a lost man!"

"Be at peace," shushed Napoleon, handing him his gun. "The secret is between you and me."

In the great invisible conflict going on between the forces of good and evil, our divine Commander has set you and me as sentinels with the duty of giving God's warning if we see the enemy approaching. In the metaphor used in our text, God says: "If you refuse to warn the wicked when I want you to tell them, You are under the penalty of death, therefore repent and save your life—they will die in their sins, but I will punish you. I will demand your blood for theirs. But if you warn them and they keep on sinning, and refuse to repent, they will die in their sins, but you are blameless" (verses 18, 19, TLB).

Ours is a solemn responsibility. If "the protector of Israel never dozes or sleeps" (Ps. 121:4, TEV), if in His compassion He watches in our place and forgives us for our negligence, this is no reason we should presume on His mercy.

By God's grace let us do all we can to arouse, in clear yet appealing ways, those who are living sinful lives and in danger of eternal damnation. If we do our part we shall, at the end, hear the words "Well done" from the Captain of our salvation.

*My son, . . . reject not of your mother's teaching. Prov. 1:8, RSV.*

# Maternal Influence

I was 20 the spring of 1944, when Herbie Swick and Richie Green escaped from Camp Holmes to join guerrilla forces. Always a realist, I had a feeling that when the Americans liberated us internees, our captors would shoot those who were of military age to keep us from becoming soldiers against them. So, soon after Swick and Green escaped, I teamed up with Sonny Woodson, who knew the country well and spoke Ilocano (the local language of northern Luzon). We began laying plans to escape.

We discovered we could get out of camp by crawling through the sewage overflow ditch behind the men's barracks. Secretly we made knapsacks and began saving up a portion of our rice ration. Our big problem was boots. After two and one half years in prison camp our shoes were in tatters. But Sonny had an idea. There were men in camp who, before the war, had been gold miners. They had good boots; Sonny got them to "lend" us their boots for a skit we young people were supposed to put on.

The time for our escape was set for September 10, 1944. Up to a few hours before our planned departure we had maintained absolute secrecy. Not even Ralph Longway, my best friend, knew of our plans. Soon after roll call that evening I went to bid my mother goodbye. I was sure she would be shocked. Instead, she looked me in the eye and said, "If you go, the Japanese will kill your father and your brother. Don't go!"

When I heard that, I knew I couldn't go. Having to tell my friend I wasn't going was one of the hardest things I ever had to do. Since I wasn't going, Sonny decided not to escape, either.

Thirty-two years later I met Herbie at an internees' reunion in San Francisco. I asked him what our chances would have been if we had escaped the camp. "You wouldn't have stood a chance," he said. "We would have shot you because you had had no prior communication with the guerrillas. You could have been spies, dupes for the Japanese. When Richie and I escaped, we had that advance communication and orders to go."

Mothers have a powerful influence over their children. May it always be on God's side.

*We who are strong in the faith ought to help the weak to carry their burdens. We should not please ourselves. Rom. 15:1, TEV.*

AUGUST

9

# The Helping Hand

Some years ago a friend of mine had surgery on his left hand to correct a condition known as Dupuytren's contracture. The operation impaired the blood circulation in that hand. As a consequence, he found that when the weather turned cold his right hand seemed to automatically take his left hand to warm it up.

This is the kind of cooperation on the spiritual level that Paul is talking about in our memory text. In several of his Epistles the apostle compares Christ's church to a body, and its various parts to the members of the church (see Rom. 12:4-6; 1 Cor. 12:13-27; and Eph. 4:11-13).

Applying my friend's experience to Paul's analogy, we find that if we see the love of one member beginning to cool (Matt. 24:12), we who are spiritually healthy will do everything in our power to "warm" that member up. Why? Because the warmth of God's love "is shed abroad in our hearts" (Rom. 5:5) and we love to share with others its "healing" rays (Mal. 4:2). The problem is that all too often, instead of aiding the healing process of those who are hurting spiritually, the members of Christ's body add to the hurt. Instead of encouraging, we discourage. Does this make sense? "Consistency, thou art a jewel rare."

In Psalm 133:1 David exclaims: "Behold, how good and how pleasant it is for brethren to dwell together in unity." This is how God wants His children to live. Rather than hurting one another, He wants them to help one another.

What a "spectacle" it would be "unto the world [Greek, *kosmos*, the universe], and to angels, and to men" (1 Cor. 4:9) if selfless, loving ministry were to characterize every action of every member of Christ's body.

John 17 records a prayer Jesus prayed a few hours before His death. In verses 21 and 23 the Saviour expresses the thought that unity among His followers is the crowning proof of His Messiahship. You and I can help answer Jesus' prayer by helping our brothers and sisters rather than hurting them.

*Just as you trusted Christ to save you, trust him, too, for each day's problems; live in vital union with him. Let your roots grow down into him and draw up nourishment from him. See that you go on growing in the Lord, and become strong and vigorous in the truth you were taught. Col. 2:6, 7, TLB.*

# Put Your Roots Down Deep

A tree absorbs water and nourishment through its roots. By sending forth innumerable hairlike processes, each branching of the root system increases its absorbent surface. These rootlets are covered by a kind of "skin" especially designed by the Creator to absorb vital elements dissolved in water, much as a blotter soaks up ink.

Some trees not only take up moisture and nutrients for growth, but store these up for future use. One tree in Madagascar develops sausage-like swellings that serve as reservoirs, retaining water for the tree during the dry season.

Although it is only a low, shrublike tree, the tamarisk puts down its taproot as much as 100 feet! On the other hand, a giant cactus tree may put down a three-foot taproot, but supplements it with a root system that spreads out horizontally for as much as 90 feet in all directions. Both root systems are seeking moisture and nourishment. It has been estimated that a single tuft of Kentucky bluegrass puts out in one growing season more than 80,000 rootlets to which are attached a million root hairs.

It is only by means of its root system that a plant can take in the essential elements needed for life and growth. So, too, in the Christian life. We receive spiritual life from Christ when we are born again. This is justification. But we don't stop there. We grow up in Christ. This is sanctification. This process results in a character change that continues as long as life lasts.

Growth in the spiritual life is not something that we accomplish on our own. It is accomplished by Christ in us—we in Him, and He in us (see John 15:4-7). Christ works in us to will and do of His good pleasure.

As you dig daily into God's Word your spiritual roots will go down deeper and deeper. As you do this you will find the water of life and spiritual nourishment flowing into you, bringing vitality and growth to your soul.

*When [King Uzziah] grew powerful his pride led to his own undoing: he offended against the Lord his God by entering the temple of the Lord to burn incense on the altar of incense.*
*2 Chron. 26:16, NEB.*

AUGUST
11

# The Perils of High Position

For most of his life, King Uzziah "did that which was right in the sight of the Lord" (verse 4), but "when he grew powerful his pride led to his . . . undoing." Because he was king, he assumed he could perform the duties of a priest. So he "went into the temple . . . to burn incense upon the altar" against the protestations of the priests. As a consequence he was smitten with leprosy (verses 16, 19, 20).

When our family lived in Maryland, our neighborhood was covered with oak trees. One morning, after an especially severe thunderstorm, we came upon a giant oak that had been felled by the wind. It blocked our way to work, and we had to make a detour. Looking at it one could see that in spite of its majestic appearance it was rotten within. What was true of that oak tree is frequently true of people—even those in high positions.

But not all trees that fall in a storm come down because they are rotten within. In Camp Holmes internment camp there grew a perfectly healthy pine tree. One night, during a terrible typhoon, it was uprooted and hurled completely over the top of the camp workshop. It landed on the other side of the shop without so much as touching it. As I surveyed the area nearby I discovered that it was not the only tree that was down. Higher up the mountainside, where the winds were even stronger, many more trees had been felled by the storm.

It is not surprising to find this to be true in the natural world. But we sometimes forget that it is equally true in the spiritual realm. "In the valley of humiliation, where men depend on God to teach them and to guide their every step, there is comparative safety. But the men who stand, as it were, on a lofty pinnacle, and who, because of their position, are supposed to possess great wisdom—these are in gravest peril. Unless such men make God their dependence, they will surely fall" (*Prophets and Kings,* p. 60).

This is good counsel for all of us.

*See that no one pays back wrong for wrong,
but at all times make it your aim to do good to
one another and to all people.
1 Thess. 5:15, TEV.*

# Noble Revenge

One day an army officer struck a young soldier who was noted for his martial arts. The blow was unjustified, but military regulations forbade that he retaliate; besides, he was a Christian.

"I shall yet make you repent of this," said the soldier with a smile.

Some time later the soldier's company was hotly engaged in battle, and he saw a wounded officer trying desperately to crawl back to his lines. The young soldier recognized him as the officer who had struck him. Risking his life, he went to the wounded man's assistance and helped him back to an aid station.

As the officer lay on the ground waiting for the medics to give him first aid, he took the soldier's hand, stammered an apology, and expressed his gratitude. Squeezing the officer's hand, the young soldier gave him a friendly grin and said, "I was sure someday you'd repent." From that day on the two became friends.

During World War II, Private First Class Desmond T. Doss, a Christian noncombatant soldier from Lynchburg, Virginia, was ridiculed for his faith, even by some of his officers. During the Okinawa campaign one of these officers was seriously wounded. Doss risked his life to save him. He also saved the lives of many other wounded men, some of whom no doubt had earlier poked fun at him. In recognition of his valor a grateful nation awarded him the Congressional Medal of Honor, the highest decoration for bravery awarded by the United States—and the first such medal ever given a noncombatant.

Those who are true to Christian principles are not always recognized and honored by earthly societies. But this, after all, is not what Christianity is all about. A Christian lives by principle, and no matter how badly he is treated by his fellowmen he looks for ways of returning good for evil.

Today, as a soldier of the cross, look for ways of doing good to those who may not like you.

# If You Want to Have Friends

Several years ago, while I was serving as a local elder on a church board, our pastor brought to a board meeting a letter he had just received from a new church member. The writer stated that ours was the coldest, most unfriendly church he had ever attended. For more than a month no one had so much as greeted him. Even the pastor's handshake at the door at the close of the divine service was described as "perfunctory." The man concluded his letter demanding his name be dropped.

Have you ever felt this way?

Of all people, Christians should be the friendliest. The members of our particular church, myself included, should have manifested warm, Christian sociability toward this brother, regardless of what we might think of his attitude. But in the light of our verse, is it not possible that in his case he bore, at least in part, a measure of responsibility for the very situation of which he complained?

Christian sociability should be sincere, spontaneous, and *appropriate.* This implies that some manifestations of friendliness may be inappropriate. Let me give you an example.

While I was pastoring a church in a certain city, I received a postcard asking me to visit a man who had expressed interest in joining the church as a result of watching a television broadcast. When I called at his home, he threw his arms around me and greeted me like a long-lost brother. The first time this happened, I accepted it as a genuine expression of Christian brotherhood.

But his "bear hugs" didn't stop. Every time I called on him I experienced an effusive outpouring of affection, so much so that I became uncomfortable with his repeated physical demonstrations of brotherly love. After much prayer, I wrote him what I hoped would be a tactful letter suggesting we confine our greetings to a friendly handshake. He accepted the suggestion, and I later had the privilege of baptizing him.

Never forget: If you want to have a friend, be a friend—sincerely, spontaneously, *appropriately.*

*You will open the eyes of the blind, and release those who sit in prison darkness and despair. Isa. 42:7, TLB.*

# Enduring Unjust Duress

Not long ago I was watching the evening news on TV and saw two men released from prison who had spent 17 years behind bars for a murder they didn't commit. What a miscarriage of justice! After being pronounced innocent, one of them said, "Seventeen years of my life wasted!" They needn't have been.

In the former Soviet Union millions of innocent people were exiled to prison camps in Siberia, and countless thousands were sent to mental hospitals for "crimes" against the state—such as complaining about intolerable living conditions. Some were even administered drugs to break down their willpower.

We don't expect injustices of this kind to exist in a free society—and yet they do. Several years ago a woman was unjustly committed to a mental hospital by narrow-minded relatives. Some would have given up in despair—but not this woman! Listen to her courageous words written from her "prison cell":

"There is a 'still small voice' which assures me that the prayers in my behalf are being answered. There is a language which is stronger than words, and the closer I lean on divine love, the better I am able to understand. I stick to my belief that what is God's will cannot be out of place. Man power could have given me physical freedom long ago, but all the good in me must be thoroughly tried and its depth and genuineness proved. . . . Maybe [those who are physically free] are not experiencing as much joy as I am in this apparent restraint. In here I have learned how much we ourselves are responsible for the amount of joy, or the lack of it, we have in our lives."

> Stone walls do not a prison make,
> Nor iron bars a cage;
> Minds innocent and quiet take
> That for an hermitage.

How often those of us in our Japanese concentration camp used to recite these lines by the English poet Richard Lovelace. You and I do not know what the future holds, but a mind fortified by the divine presence can endure any kind of duress.

*Do not return evil for evil or reviling for reviling; but on the contrary bless, for to this you have been called. 1 Peter 3:9, RSV.*

AUGUST

15

# Return Good for Evil

I first read about Jacob de Shazer in the San Francisco *Chronicle* in the fall of 1945 or early 1946. This was just a few months after I had been liberated from internment camp.

De Shazer was one of General James Doolittle's raiders who bombed Japan on April 18, 1942. During the raid De Shazer's plane was hit by antiaircraft fire. He was forced to bail out and was captured. After he landed, he saw two of his companions executed by a firing squad. He felt sure he would be executed also, but apparently God had other plans.

At the time he was captured, De Shazer was an atheist, but during his months of imprisonment he began to ponder the question of why he hated his captors and why they hated him. As he searched for answers, he thought back on what he had learned about Christianity. One day he asked his guards for a Bible. At first they only laughed, but in May 1944 a guard finally flung a Bible at him, saying he could keep it for three weeks, no more.

Sure enough, three weeks later they took the Bible away from him, but in those three weeks De Shazer's life was changed. I remember reading in the *Chronicle* how he intended to return to Japan as a missionary. His decision influenced me to want to go to Japan as a missionary too, but God had other plans. However, in De Shazer's case, he did return as a missionary in 1948. By so doing, he returned good for any evil that may have been done to him. He showed the true spirit of a Christian.

Although I can truthfully say I never hated the Japanese, I cannot say I actively loved them while I was interned. Not so with Christ. He actively loved all men "with an everlasting love" (Jer. 31:3)—even those who cursed and abused Him and crucified Him (see Luke 23:34). His life and death are a living example of how we should behave toward those who mistreat us (see Matt. 5:44).

"Let this mind be in you, which was also in Christ Jesus" (Phil. 2:5).

*If your enemy is hungry, feed him; if he is thirsty, give him a drink. You will make [his conscience] burn with shame, and the Lord will reward you. Prov. 25:21, 22, TEV.*

# The Best Way to Treat an Enemy

The typical Japanese soldier of World War II is remembered for his ruthless disregard for human suffering. As a former prisoner, I know. I have come to realize, however, that these men were victims of the satanic system under which they served, for they were as insensitive to the sufferings of their own wounded as they were of their enemy's.

And yet not all Japanese soldiers were unfeeling. I well remember how late one night one of our guards at Camp John Hay tiptoed through our barracks and tenderly covered internees who had gotten uncovered. I also heard that Lieutenant Tomibe Rokuro, our commandant for a time, wept when he saw how the Kempeitai (secret police) had tortured some of our men.

There were also examples of compassion shown by Allied POWs. In Thailand, where my wife and I served as volunteer missionaries from 1990 to 1992, we heard about a trainload of British World War II POWs that was shunted onto a siding for a lengthy delay. The POWs heard the moans of Japanese wounded in another train nearby. Some of them went to investigate and found these men in a shocking state of neglect. Without a word, and over the protestations of "No good *ka*" by a Japanese guard, they shared their water and rations, and cleansed and bound up the wounds of the poor wretches as best they could. As they left, the grateful enemy soldiers called out, "*Arigato* [thank you]."

An Allied officer who observed the scene berated the good Samaritans for "giving aid and comfort to the enemy." He was reminded, however, that the original good Samaritan had helped an enemy (cf. John 4:9 with Luke 10:33), so why shouldn't they?

If someone considers you his or her enemy, treat this person with Christian kindness. Your acts of love may make his or her conscience "burn" and alter his or her behavior—but don't count on it, for this should not be our motive for doing good to our enemies. We should do good because we are followers of Christ, and this is how He acted.

*I will take from you your hearts of stone and give you tender hearts of love for God, so that you can obey my laws. Eze. 11:19, 20, TLB.*

AUGUST

17

# An Inside Job

Some of the greatest and most successful robberies have been so-called "inside jobs." These robberies are carried out with the help of someone working within the target institution. For example, a bank employee. The celebrated Brinks bank robbery is said to have been committed this way.

Because the expression "inside job" has usually been associated with criminal activity, it has acquired an unsavory connotation. But today let us consider the expression in a better sense. Let us think of it as the work God can do within us when we allow Him to have total control of our lives.

There is a species of religiosity that presents an attractive exterior but leaves the inner being unchanged. Jesus was speaking of this kind of religion when He said to the scribes and the Pharisees, "You are like tombs covered with whitewash; they look well from outside, but inside they are full of dead men's bones and all kinds of filth" (Matt. 23:27, NEB).

The apostle Paul alluded to the same kind of religion when he wrote of "men who preserve the outward form of religion, but are a standing denial of its reality" (2 Tim. 3:5, NEB). This kind of religion is worse than worthless. Those who practice it are nothing but polished instruments of Satan.

When I was a child I enjoyed watching my mother make bread. One of the ingredients she needed was yeast. Yeast is separate and distinct from the flour, but in order for it to work, it must be mixed in with the flour. Only then can it make dough rise.

Like yeast or leaven (see Matt. 13:33), divine grace is something that comes from outside ourselves. God must put it within us in order for it to work; only then can it bring about a lasting change in our behavior and transform our characters. But God will not do this without our consent.

Is God speaking to your heart today? Let Him do an "inside job" on you.

AUGUST

18

*On the last and greatest day of the Feast, Jesus stood and said in a loud voice, "If a man is thirsty, let him come to me and drink."*
*John 7:37, NIV.*

# If Anyone Is Thirsty

The worst place in the world to get thirsty is in a desert. I remember seeing pictures in *Life* magazine years ago showing two couples who had gone for a picnic in the desert somewhere in Egypt and had been marooned. The first pictures showed them enjoying their lunch. Later shots showed them suffering from thirst. The final picture, apparently taken by the last survivor, showed the others dead. The camera and pictures, along with the bodies, were found by a search party.

It is said that anciently when Arab caravans ran low on water they would send a rider ahead to find an oasis. After a bit a second rider would be sent out, then a third. As soon as the first man reached water he would shout to the rider nearest him, "Come!" That rider in turn would shout to the next man, "Come!" and he would repeat the shout to the caravan. Thus encouraged, the men and animals would press forward in hope of soon quenching their thirst.

The greatest thirst in the world is not a physical thirst for water. It is thirst for that water that only Jesus can give. Many suffering from this thirst sense something is missing, but they don't know what. What they need is the water of life Christ offers.

But have you ever noticed that in His appeal to thirsty sinners, Jesus speaks concerning you and me? Immediately after our verse He says that "rivers of living water shall flow from the inmost being of anyone who believes in me" (verse 38, TLB). That includes you and me, doesn't it?

As believers we are Christ's bride (see 2 Cor. 11:2). It is through us that He dispenses the water of life. But this is a work that we cannot do alone. That is why Revelation 22:17 says: "The Spirit and the bride say, 'Come!' And let him who hears say, 'Come!' Whoever is thirsty, let him come; and whoever wishes, let him take the free gift of the water of life" (NIV).

*Zacchaeus stood up and said to the Lord, "Look, Lord! Here and now I give half of my possessions to the poor, and if I have cheated anybody out of anything, I will pay back four times the amount." Luke 19:8, NIV.*

AUGUST

19

# Restitution

Forgiveness involves the principle of restitution whenever amends are possible. There are some wrongs for which total restitution can be made; there are others for which partial restitution can be made; but there are still others for which no restitution can ever be made. Some can be very complex.

In one case I know of, a church member defrauded a brother in a business deal. The injured party complained to their pastor. The pastor called the parties together and listened to their accounts. It was established beyond doubt that the one brother had defrauded the other. The proper solution would have been for the defendant to make restitution as soon as possible. In this case, however, the pastor said to the offending party, "Go and sin no more." You may be sure the injured party was not happy with this solution.

In a case in which a person wrongfully takes the life of an individual who has no living relatives, it is obviously impossible to make amends of any kind. But take the case of a man who commits adultery with a married woman and a child is born. How does the adulterer make restitution to his wife? To the injured husband? To his own children? To the child born of the adulterous union? Cases like this are difficult to resolve.

What is the solution? Should people go around for the rest of their lives feeling guilty because they can never fully atone for a wrong? Or is it enough for them simply to say, "The Lord has forgiven me, and that is all there is to it; I have no further obligation"? Or shall they, after asking God's forgiveness and the forgiveness of the parties involved, put matters in the Lord's hands, willing to do what—and when—He directs? I think the answer is obvious. But doesn't this principle apply to all cases in which people wish to make restitution?

*The stone which the builders rejected as worthless turned out to be the most important of all. This was done by the Lord; what a wonderful sight it is! Mark 12:10, TEV.*

# The Rejected Stone

For millennia a stone lay untouched by human hands in a North Carolina creekbed. One day a man picked up the stone, noticed that it was unusually heavy, and decided to use it for a doorstop at his home. There it lay for years. One day a geologist passed that way and noticed the stone. His practiced eyes recognized it as a gold nugget—the largest lump of native gold found east of the Rocky Mountains.

An ancient rabbinic tradition says that when Solomon's Temple was built, the massive stones for the walls and foundation were hewed out of the living rock and shaped at the quarry, after which they were hauled to the Temple mount. According to the story, one unusually large stone was wrestled to the site, but the workers could find no place for it, so they let it sit unused. As they continued working on the foundations, this stone always seemed to be in the way. For a long time it remained neglected, if not rejected.

Then one day the workers reached the place where the cornerstone was to be laid. In order to support the tremendous weight of the Temple proper, this stone had to be of enormous size and strength. Several stones were tried, but none was suitable. At last attention was drawn to the long-rejected stone. Exposed to the elements for all these years, it revealed no cracks or defects, and when brought to the corner site, it was found to be an exact fit.

The psalmist in our text alluded to this tradition, and the rabbis recognized it as having reference to the Messiah.

The question that comes to you and me is: Will we, like the geologist in the story, recognize the great worth of Jesus, the neglected stone? Or, like the Temple builders, cast Him aside? Many people acknowledge Christ's value as a great teacher—but fail to give Him His proper place in their lives.

Let us recognize Christ as a precious stone and make Him the cornerstone of our soul temple (see 1 Peter 2:4, 5).

*I trusted well in thee, O Lord: I said, Thou art my God. In thy hand are my destinies. Ps. 31:14, 15, Leeser.*

AUGUST
21

# You Are Safe in God's Hands

In the Metropolitan Museum of Art in New York City stands one of French sculptor Auguste Rodin's famous masterpieces. As you approach it, it seems to be merely a large block of white, unhewn marble. But as you come closer, there seems to emerge from the rough stone a huge, beautiful, shapely hand. The hand seems to grow right out of the marble—a characteristic impression Rodin liked to give some of his works.

As you come closer still, you see that the hand is holding two human figures—the half-formed bodies of a man and a woman. Upon close examination you notice at the base an inscription that reads, "The Hand of God." When I first saw these words they reminded me of the Old Testament verse that says, "Look to the rock from which you were cut and to the quarry from which you were hewn" (Isa. 51:1, NIV).

In Psalm 74:11 Asaph addresses God with the complaint: "Why withdrawest thou thy hand, even thy right hand?"—as though heretofore God has protected him but now for some reason He has "pulled the carpet out from under him." Is it any wonder Asaph almost irreverently urges God to "pluck" His hand out of His "bosom." It is as though Asaph is saying, "Come on, Lord. Do something!"

All of us at times have probably felt this way. The urgency of the moment seems to demand that God do something right now. What we need to remember is to look beyond the temporal to the eternal (see 2 Cor. 4:18)—and remember, nothing can separate us from the love of God (see Rom. 8:38, 39).

Every human being owes his or her existence and happiness to a loving Creator—a faithful heavenly Father who holds him or her in the hollow of His hand (1 Peter 4:19, NKJV). When trials and difficulties press upon us, we are prone to lose sight of this fact. Just as with Rodin's "Hand of God," we cannot clearly discern His presence—"though He is not far from each one of us" (Acts 17:27, NKJV).

When this happens to you, look by faith to the Rock from which you were cut, the Quarry from which you were hewn.

243

*If anyone is caught doing something wrong,
you, my friends, who live by the Spirit must
gently set him right. Look to yourself, each one
of you: you also may be tempted.
Gal. 6:1, REB.*

# How to Approach a Wrongdoer

Walter B. Knight, author of the *Master Book of New Illustrations,* relates that a church member committed a grievous sin and it fell the pastor's duty to deal with the problem. He took it to his church board. Everyone agreed that the sin was heinous. One board member huffed that this was one sin she never would be guilty of committing. All the other board members, except one, agreed—they would never be caught dead committing that particular sin. The one exception stated that, if he had been tempted, he might have fallen even lower.

When the board talked about visiting the fallen brother and confronting him with his wrongdoing, the pastor chose to take with him the board member who admitted he might have sinned even more grievously. Said the pastor, "You seem to be the only one of us who has the right spirit to call on our sinning brother and restore him to fellowship and acceptance with the Lord."

When we read Galatians 6:1, it is obvious that all too frequently in our dealings with sinners, we fail to follow the principle and manifest the spirit called for in our text. "But," objects someone, "how can you reprove sin when you admit you might have done worse? You must at least be above that particular sin; otherwise, you have no moral authority."

This may be true, but going to a sinner with this holier-than-thou attitude (see Isa. 65:5) will only drive the person away. If anyone ever had a right to approach sinners in this spirit, it was Jesus, who never sinned. But He never used that approach! (See John 8:3-11.)

But now, suppose a fellow sinner (and that includes all of us, doesn't it?) puts himself or herself in the sinner's place and realizes that, but for the grace of God, he or she could fall into that same sin—*or some other sin!*—and approachs the wrong-doer in that spirit. Would that person not be much more likely to win the erring brother back to Christ?

Next time you and I are tempted to jump on the bandwagon and condemn a wrongdoer, let us try this approach.

*Let my counsel be acceptable unto thee, and*
*break off thy sins by righteousness. Dan. 4:27.*

AUGUST
# 23

# Breaking Off With Sin

One of the mementos my father left me is a little notebook he kept as a teenager. On one page appear these words in a script not his own: "I promise to quit smoking as soon as my tobacco pouch dreens [drains?] out. (Signed) Cecil Taylor."

I once asked Dad if Cecil kept his promise. He said apparently he did—for a short time. He then said that a week or two later he saw Cecil with a little sack of Bull Durham in his shirt pocket. When asked why he carried it around, Cecil joked, "I keep it just in case I'm tempted."

Humerous? Perhaps. But quitting evil is no laughing matter. There can be eternal consequences. When it comes to sin, it is best to make a clean break, not try to "taper off."

Not long after trying to get Cecil to quit smoking, Dad ran away from home, took up the ways of the world, and acquired the smoking habit himself. I'm glad that God in His mercy didn't give up on him. Ten years later Dad attended some gospel meetings and by God's grace broke with the habit—once for all.

Before this, Dad had tried many times to "taper off." He was not successful. Now, this is not to say that God cannot use the tapering-off method with some people. I believe He can and does. In fact, I believe He even helps those who claim to have "kicked the habit cold turkey"—and then boast that God had nothing to do with it. How can they be so sure God had nothing to do with it? After all, who is to say that behind the scenes God in His mercy didn't help them? In any case, Daniel's inspired counsel strongly suggests that God's preferred method is to "break off" with sin, not "taper off."

Are you struggling with a sinful habit from which you would like to be free? It can be done by placing your will on God's side—not later, but right now. Having done this, believe that He can replace your evil habit with a good one (see Rom. 12:21)—and go about your work thanking Him for helping you do it. "He who promised is faithful" (Heb. 10:23, NIV). He *can* "keep you from falling" (Jude 24) as you reaffirm your decision to keep your will on His side. Will you do your part?

**24**

*The brothers at Rome . . . came as far as Appius' Market and the Three Taverns to meet us, and as soon as Paul caught sight of them, he thanked God and took courage.*
Acts 28:15, Williams.

# Courage in the Face of Defeat

When Luke wrote these words concerning Paul, the latter was on his way to Rome, where he faced possible execution at the hands of a capricious and brutal emperor—Nero. Yet Paul was not dismayed by this prospect. Instead, looking at the firstfruits of a bountiful harvest of souls, *he thanked God and took courage.*

The world needs more courageous souls like Paul.

During the dark days of June 1940, Winston S. Churchill, prime minister of Great Britain, flew to the temporary headquarters of the French government at Tours and endeavored to inspire his faltering ally to continue resistance to the German juggernaut. His efforts proved fruitless. The French army was in a shambles, the government on the verge of collapse, and the future looked hopelessly dark.

Returning to England, Churchill reported to his cabinet on the gravity of the situation. He painted no pretty picture, but he concluded with these memorable words: "We now face Germany completely isolated. We are alone." Then looking around defiantly, he added, *"I find it rather inspiring!"* His courage in the face of overwhelming odds and almost certain defeat was contagious. It galvanized the British people into action and, as we all know, they went on to ultimate victory.

In the great, ongoing conflict between the forces of good and evil, the forces of good have not always been victorious. There have been temporary setbacks—but the Captain of our salvation has never failed nor been discouraged (see Heb. 2:10 and Isa. 42:4). Rather, He has turned these reverses into brilliant victories. Calvary is the most outstanding example of this. What appeared to be an overwhelming victory for the forces of evil turned out to be a catastrophic debacle for Satan and his minions. The same can be true of us in this ongoing conflict. Jesus can turn apparent defeats into signal victories—if we let Him. When we see our "defeats" from this perspective, we can, like Paul, thank God and take courage.

*I assure you that anyone who gives you a drink of water because you belong to me will certainly receive his reward. Mark 9:41, TEV.*

AUGUST
25

# Sharing Our Blessings

Some years ago, Sam Foss, a writer and traveler, came to a little rustic house in England situated at the top of a hill. Nearby was a signpost that read: "Help yourself to a cool drink." Not far away he found a spring of ice-cold water. Above the spring hung an old-fashioned gourd dipper, and on a bench nearby was a basket of summer apples and another sign inviting the passersby to help themselves.

Curious about the people who showed such hospitality to strangers, Foss knocked at the door. An elderly couple answered, and Foss asked them about the well and the apples. They explained that they were childless. Their little plot of ground yielded a scant living, but because they had a well with an abundance of cold water, they just wanted to share it with anyone who happened by.

"We're too poor to give money to charity," said the husband, "but we thought that in this way we could do something for the folks who pass our way."

The unselfish gesture by this elderly couple is said to have inspired the poem "The House by the Side of the Road."

It is not large gifts presented with ostentation that Heaven esteems most highly, but the "little, nameless, unremembered, acts of kindness and of love" (William Wordsworth) that Heaven values most.

When the heavenly court sits, the "Judge of all the earth" (Gen. 18:25) is described as saying to the righteous, "I was hungry and you gave me something to eat, I was thirsty and you gave me something to drink, I was a stranger and you invited me in" (Matt. 25:35, NIV). But did you ever notice what the righteous say?—"Lord, when did we see you hungry and feed you, or thirsty and give you something to drink? When did we see you a stranger and invite you in?" (verses 37, 38, NIV).

Are these words just an act the righteous are putting on? *No!* They are simply recognizing that whatever they have done was God's doing, and hence they can claim no credit for it!

**Hatred stirs old quarrels, but love overlooks insults. Prov. 10:12, TLB.**

# How Love Deals With Hatred

Aaron Burr, an American soldier and political leader, was gifted, capable, and personable, but he also had a vengeful streak, which led to his downfall.

In the national election of 1800 Thomas Jefferson ran for the presidency of the United States as leader of the Republican (today we would call it Democratic) Party with Aaron Burr as his vice presidential running mate. Because of a blunder in the electoral process, Burr received as many electoral votes as Jefferson. As a result, the election was thrown into the House of Representatives. There, Burr proceeded to encourage the representatives to elect him president instead of Jefferson. Jefferson was wise enough to say nothing. But Alexander Hamilton, a Federalist opponent, who intensely disliked Burr, and, apparently, understood Burr's character flaws better than did Jefferson, persuaded the House to elect the latter rather than Burr. Burr never forgave Hamilton for this.

Again in 1804, when Burr ran for governor of New York, Hamilton threw his influence against him, and Burr again lost. Smoldering resentment now flamed into open hatred. Burr challenged Hamilton to a duel. Hamilton accepted. The two men met at a deserted spot near Weehawken, New Jersey. Burr's pistol shot killed Hamilton. Revenge may have seemed sweet, but it ended Burr's political career. Long afterward he admitted he would have been wiser to have buried his hatred. Had he done so, he might eventually have succeeded in becoming president of the United States. Instead, he lost everything he had hoped to achieve and died an embittered old man. Hatred, ultimately, is self-defeating.

Christians do more than simply not hate. They actively seek opportunities to "do good to them that hate [him/her]" (Matt. 5:44) in acceptable ways. They do this, not to gain the admiration of the crowd, or even the favor of their enemies (although in some cases it may have this result), but because it is the right thing to do. The love of Christ constrains Christians to act in this manner.

*My people have done two evil things: They have forsaken me, the Fountain of Life-giving Water; and they have built for themselves broken cisterns that can't hold water! Jer. 2:13, TLB.*

AUGUST
27

# Broken Cisterns and Life-giving Water

Some years ago I had the privilege of going with a group on a tour of the Bible lands. On one of our side trips we visited Petra, the ancient capital of the Edomites. The citadel of these people was situated on a colorful, sandstone mesa, the top of which sloped toward a sharp declivity. Little channels had been cut in the sandstone to conduct rainwater into several cisterns that had been excavated near the drop-off. These reservoirs were bone-dry, unable to hold water—whether from earthquakes or age, I do not know.

In our verse, water represents truth. The people in Jeremiah's day had abandoned God, the source of truth, and replaced Him with false gods and the religious practices associated with them. Jeremiah's messages were intended to awaken the people to their need of the true God.

Many years ago a house near Bucyrus, Ohio, was struck by lightning. Faster than it takes to tell it, the bolt burned a path down the eaves of the house, through the rain gutter, and into the cistern. Luckily the house was not set afire. Not long after the storm, one of the children was sent to fetch a pail of water and discovered that the cistern was dry. Examination showed that the bolt had burned a hole in the bottom of the cistern, causing the water to leak out.

When the father went down to plug the leak, he heard the sound of gurgling water. Investigating further, he discovered an under ground stream. A well was dug where the cistern had been, and from that day on the family had an abundance of cold, clear, pure water. They lost a cistern but gained a never-failing source of the life-giving beverage.

Why must God strike people with a figurative "bolt of lightning" to bring them back to Him when they could accept His gracious invitation, "Come, everyone who is thirsty—here is water" (Isa. 55:1, TEV)? Only we can answer that question.

*The [Lord] said to [Paul], "My grace is sufficient for you, for my power is made perfect in weakness." 2 Cor. 12:9, NIV.*

# How to Deal With Tragedy

In September 1858 Henry Fawcett, a young Englishman, was blinded in both eyes when his father accidentally discharged his shotgun while they were hunting.

Before the tragedy, Henry had been a bright, ambitious young man with a great future before him. Following the accident, he was filled with despair. But one thing saved him. He loved his father deeply and knew his father was nearly out of his mind with grief at what had happened to his son.

The only way Henry found to preserve his father's sanity was to choose hope over despair. He pretended to be cheerful when he was not. He pretended to take an interest in life when he felt like giving up. When despair clutched at his heart he pretended to have hope that he could yet be a useful citizen.

Then a strange thing happened. Pretense became reality! It was as if by an act of will Henry had exorcised an evil spirit. He pursued his chosen career, was elected to Parliament, and later, at the request of Prime Minister Gladstone, was put in charge of the British postal and telegraph systems. In this latter position he was instrumental in bringing about significant improvements in the mail and telegraph services of his country.

In the verses preceding our verse for meditation the apostle Paul speaks of having "a thorn in the flesh" (verse 7). He doesn't tell us what that thorn was, but Bible students have speculated that it had to do with his eyesight, because elsewhere he says, "If you could have done so, you would have torn out your eyes and given them to me," and later on in the same Epistle he says, "See with what large letters I have written to you with my own hand" (Gal. 4:15, NIV, and 6:11, NKJV).

Perhaps it is a good thing we do not know with absolute certainty what Paul's thorn in the flesh was, for there are tragedies even worse than loss of eyesight. But the wonderful thing is that, by assuming a positive attitude, God's grace can enable us to triumph over tragedy.

*I will answer them before they even call to me. While they are still talking to me about their needs, I will go ahead and answer their prayers! Isa. 65:24, TLB.*

AUGUST
29

# Before They Call

Dr. William Moon, noted for inventing a raised alphabet for people blinded as adults, and for founding the Moon Society, was himself blind. As a young man he dedicated his life to work for the sightless. In the summer of 1852 his organization found itself in financial straits because of a debt of £22 sterling that he had contracted in connection with his work.

A few hours before the payment was due, he prayed that the way would be opened for him to repay his obligation on time. His prayer seemed to go unanswered. But at 4:00 in the morning of the due date a blind woman living in Brighton couldn't sleep and, to pass the time, began to read Psalm 34 by Dr. Moon's raised alphabet. In verse 6 she read these words: "This poor man cried, and the Lord heard him."

Suddenly she felt impressed that Dr. Moon needed money to carry on his work. As soon as it was light, she dressed, went to her cashbox, and took out a £5 note. She was then struck by the thought that this was not enough, so she took out three more £5 notes. These she put in her purse, which contained two sovereigns, and went to Dr. Moon's house.

After being guided to his study, she asked him if he was having financial difficulties in connection with his work. Prior to this visit, Dr. Moon had determined not to tell anyone except the Lord about his problem. So when the woman put this question to him, he was reluctant to answer. She then held out her purse and told him that its contents were for him to use as he saw fit. We can imagine Dr. Moon's surprise when he discovered that her purse contained the exact amount needed to pay his debt that day.

It is gratifying to read about prayers God has answered in a definite, exact, or unexpected way. However, God knows what is best for us. So if your prayers aren't answered in some dramatic fashion, or in exactly the way you would wish, don't become discouraged. More often, He answers us in less-striking ways.

*For God who said, "Light shall shine out of darkness," has shone within my heart to illuminate men with the knowledge of God's glory in the face of Christ. 2 Cor. 4:6, Moffatt.*

# Blind Beauty

In his book *Let Me Illustrate* (p. 156), Donald Grey Barnhouse relates an incident that casts light on our text.

A young officer was blinded, apparently in one of the world wars. While convalescing, he was cared for by a nurse with whom he fell in love and later married. One day he overheard some people talking about him and his wife. The cruel conversation went like this, "Lucky for her he is blind. He probably would never have married such a homely woman if he had had eyes."

Walking toward the voices, he said, "I happened to overhear what you said, and I thank God from the depths of my heart for the blindness that might have kept me from seeing the marvelous worth of the soul of this woman who is my wife. She has the most noble character I have ever known. If the conformation of her features is such that it might have masked her inward beauty, then I am the great gainer for having lost my sight."

What a rebuke! But more important, what a testimony!

Fallen human nature tends to go for the pretty face, the shapely figure, the handsome features, the athletic build—and overlooks character, the "inner self, the unfading beauty of a gentle and quiet spirit" (1 Peter 3:4, NIV).

When the second person of the Godhead became the incarnate Son of God, Isaiah tells us that "He had no beauty or majesty to attract us to him, nothing in his appearance that we should desire him" (Isa. 53:2, NIV). I believe God had a purpose in ordaining it thus. He did not want human beings to be attracted to His Son because of His physical appearance, but rather because they appreciated the beauty of His character.

As you and I study the life of Jesus as revealed in the Bible, a transformation can take place in our spiritual eyesight—"the things of earth . . . grow strangely dim in the light of His glory and grace" (Helen H. Lemmel). As this happens, Christ leads us poor, spiritually blind sinners in ways we know not, in paths we have not known.

*Look at my Servant. See my Chosen One. He is my Beloved, in whom my soul delights. . . . He does not crush the weak, or quench the smallest hope. Matt. 12:18-20, TLB.*

AUGUST

31

# Sparing the Sensitive Soul

Rearing four young children while keeping up with regular housework is a challenging chore. Add to this the care of an invalid sister and a husband too busy earning a living to lend a helping hand, and you have the prescription for a crushed spirit. Such was the life of Phoebe Hinsdale Brown, a young Connecticut housewife in the early nineteenth century. Yet in spite of her crowded routine, Phoebe determined to spend time alone with God.

Not far from her home lay the estate of a wealthy woman in which was a secluded flower garden. In the evenings Phoebe would slip away to this bower for a few moments of prayer and meditation. Thinking the owner would not object, she did not ask permission. One day the gardener discovered her presence and reported it. Suspicious that she had evil intentions, the owner confronted the frightened woman, demanding to know what she was doing on her property and insinuating that sneaks were not welcome!

A shy, sensitive soul, Phoebe was crushed, for she had meant no harm. The next evening she wrote a note of apology and asked forgiveness. The note took the form of a poem. Holding her youngest child on her lap, she wrote "An Apology for My Twilight Rambles." Here is the first verse of her poem:

I love to steal awhile away from every cumbering care,
And spend the hours of setting day in humble, grateful
    prayer.
I love in solitude to shed the penitential tear;

And all His promises to plead, where none but God can hear.

We don't know the wealthy woman's reaction to the note, but Phoebe's poem found its way into our old *Church Hymnal* (No. 317).

It is so easy to misjudge others and lash out at them when we don't know all the facts. Christ was always careful in this regard. "He was never rude, never needlessly spoke a severe word, never gave needless pain to a sensitive soul" (*The Desire of Ages,* p. 353).

What a lesson for us!

*The angel of the Lord appeared unto [Moses] in a flame of fire out of the midst of a bush: and he looked, and, behold, the bush burned with fire, and the bush was not consumed. Ex. 3:2.*

# Do You Feel Like a Burning Bush?

Originally the Bible was not divided into chapters and verses as we find them today. In former times a passage of Scripture was usually referred to by a key word. In the story of Moses at the burning bush, for instance, the passage was referred to as "The Bush," or simply "Bush." This is the way Jesus referred to it. Mark 12:26 reads: "Have you not read in the book of Moses, in the account of the bush . . . ?" (NIV).

A desert bush on fire normally burns up very quickly, but the bush Moses saw burning did not. Although it appeared to be burning up, God kept it from being consumed. There is a lesson here for us.

"Those who are suffering reverses are represented by the bush that Moses saw in the desert, which, though burning, was not consumed. The angel of the Lord was in the midst of the bush. So in deprivation and affliction the brightness of the presence of the Unseen is with us to comfort and sustain" (*The Ministry of Healing,* p. 212).

What a thought! The Angel of the Lord is with His faithful children in the midst of the burning! Although He permits fiery trials to test them, although they may think they are about to be consumed, God will not permit them to be destroyed by the flames.

Are you being tested? Does it seem as if the fires of affliction are about to consume you? Remember, God will not permit you to be tested above what you are able to bear. His grace *is* sufficient (see 1 Cor. 10:13).

God promises: "When thou walkest through the fire, thou shalt not be burned; neither shall the flame kindle upon thee" (Isa. 43:2). The fires of affliction will never be permitted to consume the trusting children of God, for His Angel, Christ, is with them while the fire burns (see Isa. 63:9). The only thing He permits to be consumed is the dross!

*Our brothers won the victory over [Satan] by the blood of the Lamb and by the truth which they proclaimed; and they were willing to give up their lives and die. Rev. 12:11, TEV.*

SEPTEMBER

2

# Faithful Unto Death

Dedication to a cause, especially in the face of death, is a rarity these days. However, there are outstanding exceptions. During World War II an air raid warden advertisement appeared in British newspapers calling for volunteer messengers. It read: "Boys, 16 and over, to run messages—apply A.R.P. Warden."

Derrick Belfall, only 14, felt called to do something for his war-ravaged country and offered his services. He was turned down because of his age. Undeterred, he applied again and again until he was finally accepted. He was assigned the job of delivering messages to air-raid wardens in various parts of the city. It was his custom, after returning from an errand, to say respectfully, "Derrick Belfall reporting; I've delivered the message."

One day as he returned from a mission he passed a building that had recently been demolished by a bomb. Rescue workers were working frantically to clear away the debris. Derrick heard a child's cry and offered his help. It was accepted. He climbed down into the cellar and, finding the child, handed it up to the other rescuers. Before he could extricate himself, a wall collapsed on him, hopelessly pinning him. When asked if he wanted to send a last word to anyone, he replied, "Just say 'Derrick Belfall reporting; I've delivered the message.' "

By joining in the war against evil, we too have volunteered to serve in a cause—and all ages are accepted; no one is turned down on account of being too young or too old. Many of the volunteers before us have won the victory over Satan by the blood of the Lamb and the word of their testimony.

"The word of their testimony." What does this mean? It means bearing our personal witness to others concerning the good news of salvation, telling people what Christ has done for us by His sacrifice on Calvary. This is the message entrusted to us to bear to a dying world. May we be faithful in delivering it, even if it means losing our temporal life in so doing.

*As Paul, the aged, and now also a prisoner of Christ Jesus—I appeal to you [Philemon] for my child, whom I have begotten in my imprisonment, Onesimus, who formerly was useless to you, but now is useful both to you and to me. Philemon 9-11, NASB.*

# Reclamation Projects

Sewage, once deemed worthless waste, has been found to be a useful commodity. A certain species of algae that can be grown in sewage can turn it into an edible product. One tablespoon of this algae, when dried, has food value equal to one ounce of steak—with all the essential vitamins except vitamin C.

This single-cell plant, known as Chlorella, when grown in liquid waste at a temperature of 105° F, doubles its dry weight every two and a half hours. A single Chlorella plant multiplies to 10,000 new plants every 24 hours. The sewage from a city with a population of 100,000 has been made to yield 10 tons of dry algae every 24 hours, and in addition supply 10,000 gallons of irrigation water.

If our astronauts ever travel to distant planets in our solar system, it is quite likely they will put formerly useless waste to good use. But coming down to earth, this transformation has the potential of feeding a hungry world.

Similar transformations from uselessness to usefulness have taken place in human beings. Take Onesimus. He was the slave of a Christian master named Philemon. Around A.D. 62 he escaped from his master, who lived in Colossae, Asia Minor, and made his way to Rome, where he met Paul, who was in prison. Under the latter's ministry, Onesimus was converted to Christ, and now Paul is returning the runaway with Tychicus, who bears a letter to Philemon.

In the letter Paul makes an interesting play on words; he assures Philemon that the one who was once "useless to you . . . now is useful" (verse 11, NASB).

If we just looked around us, there are many useless slaves of sin who could be transformed into useful servants of Christ—if someone took a genuine and abiding interest in them. That someone could be you or me.

*It will be with barbarous speech and strange tongue that this people will hear God speaking, this people to whom he once said, "This is true rest; let the exhausted have rest. This is repose," and they refused to listen.*
*Isa. 28:11, 12, NEB.*

# Not the Grammar, but the Message

The most effective soul winners have not always been the most polished preachers. Sometimes God has chosen humble, uneducated men and women to proclaim His message.

Our verse speaks of those who would "refuse to listen" to God's message, because the speech of His messenger was "barbarous" and "strange." Such persons lose much because they assume this attitude. Could it be that they belong to that class of people about whom Paul speaks, who "surround themselves with teachers who tickle their ears" (2 Tim. 4:3, NAB)?

In the early days of his ministry, a critic took the great evangelist Dwight L. Moody to task because his grammar was faulty and his diction left much to be desired.

"Mr. Moody," carped his critic, "you oughtn't to speak in public until you've perfected your grammar. You make so many grammatical mistakes, it's a shame."

"I lack a great many things," conceded Moody, "but I'm doing the best with what I've got." Then turning tables on his critic, he asked, "My friend, you've got good grammar. What are you doing for Jesus?"

So far as I know, the critic never answered the question.

On the other hand, just because God sometimes uses persons who are not cultured speakers to proclaim His message, that is no reason for cultivating slovenly habits of speaking. I think all would agree that a humble, consecrated speaker who uses good grammar and syntax, and draws attention to God and His message rather than to his own faulty diction, can serve God more effectively than one who speaks slovenly.

But simply because our speech is imperfect is no excuse for hiding our light under a bushel basket. By permitting the Holy Spirit to use us, we can be effective agents in winning souls, even if we "cannot preach like Paul."

*Don't forget to be kind to strangers, for some who have done this have entertained angels without realizing it! Heb. 13:2, TLB.*

# Kindness Pays

Late one night many years ago an elderly couple trudged up to the night clerk in a third-class hotel in Philadelphia. The husband pleaded, "Sir, do you have a room where we could spend the night? We have been all over the city looking for a place to stay, and haven't been able to find any. Please don't tell us you don't have a room where we can spend the night."

"Well," replied the clerk, "I don't have a single room available, but you can have my room. It is not as nice as some other rooms, but it's clean, and I'll be happy to have you as my guests."

"God bless you," sighed the wife.

Next morning at breakfast the husband asked one of the waiters to call the night clerk. He wanted to see him about some important business. When the man came in, the husband thanked him for his kindness and asked him to sit down. "I'm John Jacob Astor," he said. "You are too fine a person to spend the rest of your life as a night clerk in a third-class hotel. How would you like to be the general manager of a big, beautiful, luxurious hotel in New York City?"

"It sounds wonderful," stammered the night clerk.

And so the kindness of an obscure night clerk was rewarded by his becoming the general manager of the famous Waldorf-Astoria Hotel.

Our verse alludes to the hospitality Abraham showed to three wayfarers who turned out to be angels. Yes, kindness pays. But the pay isn't always received in this life. In many cases payday doesn't come until the day the Lord Jesus says, "Come, you blessed of My Father, inherit the kingdom prepared for you from the foundation of the world: for I was hungry and you gave Me food; I was thirsty and you gave Me drink; I was a stranger and you took Me in; I was naked and you clothed Me; I was sick and you visited Me; I was in prison and you came to Me" (Matt. 25:34-36, NKJV).

*Do not take revenge on someone who wrongs you. If anyone slaps you on the right cheek, let him slap your left cheek too. Matt. 5:39, TEV.*

SEPTEMBER

6

# Turning the Other Cheek

When John Selwyn, celebrated missionary to the South Sea Islands, attended university, he was noted for his boxing skill. Years later, while serving in the South Pacific, it fell his duty to rebuke one of the islanders for a serious misdeed. The man became angry and struck Selwyn on the cheek with his clenched fist. Selwyn could have easily overpowered his assailant. Instead, he folded his arms and meekly turned the other cheek. Surprised by the missionary's behavior, the islander fled into the jungle.

Years later the man came to Selwyn's successor and asked to be baptized. After determining that his conversion was genuine, the missionary asked the islander how he wanted to be known as a Christian. "John Selwyn," he replied. "He taught me what Jesus was like." What a testimony!

But have you ever heard someone say "It may be all right to turn the other cheek under certain circumstances, but if someone threatens my life or my wife and children, I will maim my assailant and, if necessary, kill him"?

The problem with this philosophy is that what we determine to do in advance of a crisis is what in all probability we will do when the emergency arises. Thus, if we have decided to rely on the arm of flesh (Jer. 17:5), we will most likely do "the works of the flesh" (Gal. 5:19-21). But if we are resolved to obey the counsel of God's Word, He promises to make "a way to escape" (1 Cor. 10:13).

Recently I heard about a mother and daughter who passed through a life-threatening experience that shows how God can work when we let Him. One night the women were surprised by an intruder intent on rape and murder. They prayed silently for protection and were impressed to tell the man he could not harm them unless God permitted. Although he ranted and threatened, the man could do nothing, and finally left the women unmolested.

When we trust God and obey His Word, He will do on our behalf more than we will ever gain by taking matters into our own hands.

*Ye shall receive power, after that the Holy Ghost is come upon you. Acts 1:8.*

# Divine Transforming Power

Rural electrification for Boa Viagem, a suburb of Recife, Brazil, where I lived as a boy, began in the fall of 1929. I well remember the workers from the power company heaving and straining as they erected heavy cement power poles, to which they later strung wires. I also remember hearing the mothers in the neighborhood (mine included) warning children never to touch those wires. We could get hurt, even killed.

One day before the job was done, one of the little neighbor boys picked up a live wire and couldn't let go. I can still see him in my mind's eye. In spite of all of his screaming, the current held him fast. His mother became frantic. Every time she tried to pull him away, she received a shock. It wasn't until his wise old grandmother wrapped a towel around his middle and yanked that he was pulled free.

On the road where I now live are high-tension wires. Although they carry many more volts than the wires with which I was familiar as a child in Brazil, I have often seen birds perched nonchalantly on those wires without suffering the least harm. Why? Because the birds aren't grounded. Were you or I to touch those same wires while we remained in electrical contact with the earth, we would be killed.

God is a God of power. At His word worlds were brought into existence (Ps. 33:6, 9). But His power manifests itself in other ways, among them the power to transform lives. This power is not to be trifled with.

Have you ever noticed how "impossible" it is to "renew" people who "were once enlightened, and . . . tasted . . . the powers of the world to come," but have fallen away—because they tried to hang on to the world and God at the same time? (See Heb. 6:4-6.) If such people ever again come to life spiritually, it is because God in His great mercy has given them another chance.

The only safe way to handle divine transforming energy is to let go of the things of earth and let God's power surge through us in doing His will.

*Lend without expecting repayment. Then will your recompense be great. You will rightly be called sons of the Most High, since he himself is good to the ungrateful. Luke 6:35, NAB.*

# Unrequited Love

On September 8, 1860, a terrible storm swept over Lake Michigan and threatened to sink the passenger steamer *Lady Elgin*. On shore, watching the tragedy unfold, were some students who had come from nearby Garrett Biblical Institute. As the ship began to break up, one of the students, Edward W. Spencer, noticed a woman clinging to a piece of wreckage. Unable just to stand by and watch her drown, Spencer threw off his coat, plunged into the raging surf, swam to the sinking vessel, and brought her safely to shore.

Again and again he swam out and brought back someone, until his strength was gone and he collapsed on the beach from exhaustion. As a result of his efforts, 17 lives were saved, but it almost cost Spencer his life. He never fully regained his health.

After his death some years later, someone wrote his wife and asked if it were true that not one of those who had been rescued thanked her husband. Here is her reply: "The statement is true. Mr. Spencer never received any thanks from anybody he succeeded in saving, nor any recognition from any one of them." Then, in an admirable spirit of magnanimity, she went on to blame the seeming lack of gratitude on the general confusion and exhaustion of the rescued as well as the rescuer.

She closed the letter with these words: "My husband always took this view of the situation and never manifested any feeling of resentment, and I am sure he felt none. He did his best, with no thought of reward or appreciation."

And yet one would think that, after the confusion and exhaustion were over, at least one of those who had been rescued would have sought him out and thanked him. His experience reminds us of the 10 lepers whom Jesus healed. In that episode only one returned to thank Him, and he was a Samaritan (see Luke 17:16).

But what an admirable attitude on Mr. Spencer's part. Divine love expresses itself in a similar way. God does not demand expressions of gratitude, yet thankfulness is the proper response by one who has been saved from the stormy sea of sin.

*Let us walk honestly, as in the day; not in rioting and drunkenness, not in chambering and wantonness, not in strife and envying. But put ye on the Lord Jesus Christ, and make not provision for the flesh, to fulfil the lusts thereof. Rom. 13:13, 14.*

# Character

When I attended college, Walter B. Clark was dean of men. One evening when conducting worship, he said, "Character is what you are in the dark." He might have added, ". . . and what you are in the daytime—when you think nobody is looking."

Several years ago John Gosson was heading for an auto repair shop in Syracuse, New York, on his motorcycle. He had seen an advertisement for a Honda Accord and wanted to look it over and possibly buy it. However, before he reached the shop the wind blew open the snap of his jacket pocket in which he was carrying $7,500—his savings of the past seven years.

The money was soon scattered all over the highway. Passing motorists stopped and helped themselves to the "windfall." One honest motorist who gathered up $3,120 returned it to Gosson. Another, however, added insult to injury not only by keeping the money he had picked up, but by sending the unfortunate man an offensive card in which he gloated over his "paid vacation" to California. His card read: "It was like seventh heaven, picking up and gathering loose change on the highway, which, as I found out, was from you."

What would you have done, what would I have done, if we had been one of those motorists? Would we have followed the "multitude to do evil" (Ex. 23:2), or would we have done what the lone motorist did who returned the money he picked up?

It is quite possible that Joseph could have gotten away with adultery with Potiphar's wife, but he did not try, because he loved God supremely and his neighbor (in this case, Potiphar) as himself.

If we would always bear in mind that a faithful record is kept in heaven of all that we do and say, I am sure that many of our thoughtless acts would remain undone. But this is not the best motive for doing good. Why not do right because we love God supremely and our neighbor as ourselves?

*Lord, I look up to you, up to heaven, where you rule. As a servant depends on his master, and a maid depends on her mistress, so we will keep looking to you, O Lord our God.*
*Ps. 123:1, 2, TEV.*

# Looking Upward for Guidance

Many years ago in one of the Southern states, a city-bred woman and her country cousin were traveling in a horse-drawn chaise through a dense forest when darkness overtook them. There was no moon, only a bit of starlight. Soon it was impossible to see the road. The city dweller became a bit frightened when she thought they had lost their way, but her country cousin seemed unconcerned. She stopped the horse, stepped to the ground, walked around a bit, and came back, saying she had found the road. She got back into the chaise, and they continued on their way.

As they went along, the city dweller noticed by the dim starlight that her companion, instead of looking down at the ground, was looking up. "Why," she asked, "are you looking up when the road is below us?"

"Because," her friend explained, "that is the only way I can tell where the road is. The trees have been cleared to make way for the road. On a night like this it is impossible to see the road, but by looking up I can tell where the road is by the stars in the open sky."

This is the way it is on the road of life. As we travel along, there are times when trials and perplexities close in around us as black and impenetrable as the darkness in a dense forest on a moonless night. At such times many lose their way—but this need not happen!

When the "downlook," and even the outlook, are dark and forbidding, never forget that the uplook is bright. Take comfort in the fact that "the darkness and the light are both alike" to God (Ps. 139:12). He can see when we can't see a thing. Even when the sun is shining and everything seems bright and clear, it is always wise to look to heaven, where God rules, for no road is safe unless He is guiding.

263

*When you stand and pray, forgive anything you may have against anyone, so that your Father in heaven will forgive the wrongs you have done. Mark 11:25, TEV.*

# The Proper Posture for Prayer

During my freshman year in college, I heard that one of my schoolmates, a sincere and devoted Christian, always "lifted up his eyes" in prayer. When I asked why he prayed this way, I was told that he quietly answered that this was the way Jesus prayed, and made reference to John 11:41. I watched the student to see if the story were true. It was. I also noticed that I was not the only one who was watching and smiling. I can speak only for myself, but I can assure you I received no blessing from the prayer that was being offered.

Years later I visited a church where one of the members insisted that kneeling was the only proper posture for prayer. He not only put his conviction into practice; he convinced others, including the young pastor, that no other stance was appropriate. Some of the members objected, citing today's verse. Others asked if someone who was bedfast had to kneel to pray (see Ps. 4:4).

Whatever the merits of kneeling for prayer, this division of opinion confused visitors and divided the church. Sincere as our brother may have been, most Christians would agree that his practice was unwise because of its effect on the church and especially the visitors, who didn't know whether to stand or to kneel.

Insisting on a divisive issue such as this seems to be a violation of the principle of unity, as supported by the admonition "God is not the author of confusion" (1 Cor. 14:33). Further, most would agree that by making himself conspicuous by his practice, our brother was probably drawing more attention to himself than he was to Christ.

The Bible prescribes no single posture for prayer. While kneeling is certainly appropriate and shows reverence, it would seem that the important thing is not so much our physical posture as our mental attitude. May we ever bear this in mind.

*If you fail to [keep your vow], you will be sinning against the Lord; and you may be sure that your sin will find you out.*
*Num. 32:23, NIV.*

# Convicting Evidence

In the days when freebooters and buccaneers plied the Spanish Main, the British warship *Sparrow* suspected the brig *Nancy* of carrying contraband and stopped it off the coast of Haiti. An examination of the latter's papers and cargo yielded only circumstantial evidence. Nevertheless, the captain of the *Sparrow* deemed this sufficient for him to tow the *Nancy* into Kingston, Jamaica, and charge the captain and crew with transporting illegal cargo.

Meanwhile, the officer in charge of a tender of the British frigate *Abergavenny*, which happened to be cruising in the same waters, noticed a school of sharks feeding on a dead bullock. He decided to see if he could catch one of the predators for sport and ordered his ship to pull up alongside the dead animal. The sailors succeeded in hooking one of the sharks.

Hauling the shark aboard, they opened it up and discovered in its stomach a bundle of papers. Examination showed that these belonged to the *Nancy*. Convinced that they might serve a useful purpose, the captain set sail for Kingston.

The *Abergavenny* arrived in port not long after the case of the *Nancy* came up for trial. The latter's captain and crew, and even her lawyers, were sure the case would be thrown out of court for lack of evidence. But what must have been their consternation when they were suddenly confronted with the papers found in the shark's belly. Instead of being acquitted, they were convicted.

"All [of us] have sinned" (Rom. 3:23). We all know this. We also know that there is plenty of evidence to convict us. No matter how well we may think our wrongs are concealed, unless they are confessed, forgiven, and forsaken, they will someday find us out—if not in this life, then in the day of judgment (see Eccl. 12:14).

In making things right, let the Lord be your guide. Neither be hasty nor tardy, but rather, let Him direct you step by step.

*Behold, I come as a thief. Blessed is he that watcheth, and keepeth his garments, lest he walk naked, and they see his shame. Rev. 16:15.*

# The Need to Be Clothed

Ever since Adam and Eve ate the fruit of the forbidden tree, human beings (generally speaking) have felt ashamed of appearing naked in public. Even those who have had little or no contact with civilization usually wear some kind of loincloth to cover themselves.

Have you ever dreamed of appearing naked in public? Most of us have. Recently a friend of mine had a dream in which he seemed to be standing naked in a classroom. We can imagine his embarrassment. His professor looked him straight in the eye, called him by name, and asked him what the lesson was about. When he said he didn't know, he was unceremoniously dismissed.

My friend says he knows how the man in Jesus' parable of the wedding garment must have felt when the king came in and found him improperly attired (Matt. 22:2-13). It was his own fault, for the king had provided robes for all.

Revelation 3:17-20 pictures Christ knocking at a door. Those inside the door are described as ones who claim to be "rich, and increased with goods, and [in] need of nothing." The reality, however, is that they are "wretched, and miserable, and poor, and blind, and *naked.*" The condition of such individuals do not correspond to their profession. They pretend to need nothing, yet in their heart they know they are stark naked. We can understand their reluctance to open the door, and yet the solution to their problem lies in the One who seeks admission.

In his dream, my friend seemed to have no way of altering his predicament. But thank God, while the day of salvation lingers, sinners can accept the "white raiment" that the heavenly Guest offers, "that thou mayest be clothed, and that the shame of thy nakedness do not appear" (verse 18).

Today, even now, Jesus stands at the door of your heart and knocks. He offers you the robe of His righteousness. If you have never accepted it, why not let Him cover you with it—not someday, but *now!*

*Two men will be in the field; one will be taken and the other left. Two women will be grinding with a hand mill; one will be taken and the other left. Therefore keep watch, because you do not know on what day your Lord will come.*
*Matt. 24:40-42, NIV.*

# One Taken, the Other Left

On the night of April 14-15, 1912, the White Star liner S.S. *Titanic*, with more than 2,000 passengers on board, struck an iceberg south of Newfoundland and sank with the loss of 1,513 lives. When news of the sinking reached England, the scene outside the steamship office was indescribable. Relatives of passengers on the ill-fated vessel packed the street in front of the main entrance, and all traffic came to a standstill.

On either side of the doorway two large billboards were hammered up in place. Above one was printed in oversize capitals: "KNOWN TO BE SAVED." Above the other, in equally large letters: "KNOWN TO BE LOST." From time to time a man would emerge from the steamship office carrying a piece of cardboard on which was printed the name of one of the passengers.

A deathlike stillness would sweep over the crowd as the people watched, emotions strained to the breaking point, to see which way the man would turn. Would he pin the name up on the side of the saved or the lost? In the end, each passenger would end up in one group or the other—either *saved* or *lost!*

In the case of the *Titanic,* it is possible that many who were listed as "lost" will ultimately be saved in God's kingdom, and many who were listed as "saved" will ultimately be lost; for it is not the first death that determines one's ultimate destiny (see Heb. 9:27). It is in the judgment that this determination is made, and this determination is eternal—irrevocable! There is no second chance. This is a solemn thought.

This being the case, "what sort of persons ought you [and I] to be in lives of holiness and godliness" (2 Peter 3:11, RSV)? Behold, today is "the day of salvation," "now is the accepted time" (2 Cor. 6:2). Tomorrow could be too late.

This morning I reaffirm my commitment to Christ. Why don't you do the same, and make sure your name is "posted" among the saved?

# 15

*To the Jews I became as a Jew, that I might win Jews. 1 Cor. 9:20, NKJV.*

# A Burden for the Chosen People

Although Paul was a Jew, he is known as the apostle to the Gentiles because he carried the story of salvation to the non-Jews of the Mediterranean world. And yet he was not unmindful of his own people. He had a burden for his Jewish brethren. Notice how in Romans 9:1-3 he exclaims in an agony of spirit, "Oh, Israel, my people! Oh, my Jewish brothers! How I long for you to come to Christ. My heart is heavy within me and I grieve bitterly day and night because of you. Christ knows and the Holy Spirit knows that it is no mere pretense when I say that I would be willing to be forever damned if that would save you" (TLB).

Moses felt the same way, for after the Israelites worshiped the golden calf, he said, "Oh, these people have sinned a great sin, and have made themselves gods of gold. Yet now if you will only forgive their sin—and if not, then blot *me* out of the book you have written" (Ex. 32:31, 32, TLB).

What a burden for God's chosen people these men had!

Richard Wurmbrand, author of *Tortured for Christ,* although a Jew by birth, was an avowed atheist before he became a Christian. Unbeknownst to him, a Christian carpenter who lived in the Carpathian Mountains of Romania began praying that God would help him win a Jew to Christ before he died.

One day the carpenter was irresistibly drawn to the village in which Wurmbrand lived. When he learned that Wurmbrand was a Jew, he made friends with him. But he did more than just make friends. He spent hours alone in prayer, seeking ways to lead Wurmbrand to Christ. As the Holy Spirit worked through the carpenter, Wurmbrand's interest was aroused. The carpenter gave him a Bible. Conviction led to conversion, and the erstwhile atheist became a follower of the lowly Nazarene. Subsequently, Wurmbrand was instrumental in winning many others to Christ.

Perhaps you have a Jewish neighbor who does not know Yeshua as God's Messiah. Why not make friends with that person and ask the Lord to give you not only a burden for him or her, but to also show you ways of winning this soul to Christ?

*Thus says the Lord God, "Although I have cast them far off among the Gentiles, and although I have scattered them among the countries, yet I shall be a little sanctuary for them in the countries where they have gone."*
*Eze. 11:16, NKJV.*

SEPTEMBER

16

# A Little Sanctuary

A sanctuary is a place where God dwells. When God gave Moses instructions for building the tabernacle, He said, "let [My people] make me a sanctuary; that I may dwell among them" (Ex. 25:8). Later, in Solomon's time, a much larger structure built of stone replaced the tentlike dwelling of Jehovah.

As a priest Ezekiel must have been familiar with the first Temple and its services, as well as the fact that in the Holy of Holies dwelt the Shekinah glory—the visible manifestation of God's presence. However, because of apostasy and rebellion, the Jewish people were taken into captivity, the first Temple lay in ruins, and Ichabod!—"the glory had departed."

Now living in a strange land, many of these captives had begun to think about the shameless way they had treated God. Had He left them forever? Was there still hope? It is at this juncture that the God of mercy, through Ezekiel, assured His erring people that He had not abandoned them entirely. In the quaint expression used in our verse, He assures His people that in the faraway land of their captivity He will be to them "a little sanctuary." What a comfort this must have been to Ezekiel and his fellow exiles.

Some 56 years later, the chosen people were restored to the Promised Land, and eventually the Temple and its sanctuary were rebuilt. But again the Jewish people backslid into apostasy and went so far as to reject the Messiah. As a consequence, their "house" was "left unto" them "desolate" (Matt. 23:38).

No longer is there on earth a special sanctuary where the presence of God is manifest visibly. Yet God has not abandoned His people. Even now He can be "a little sanctuary" to you and me. It matters not whether we live in a palace, a humble home, or a prison cell, or have no shelter at all, God promises to be with us "alway, even unto the end of the world" (Matt. 28:20).

How thankful we can be that He will still be "a little sanctuary" to us!

# 17

*Take heed to yourself, and diligently keep yourself, lest you forget the things your eyes have seen; and lest they depart from your heart all the days of your life. And teach them to your children. Deut. 4:9, NKJV.*

# The Power of a Father's Influence

Some years ago five young men from Pennsylvania left home and went to the Northwest to make a living. When they arrived there, they discovered freedoms they'd never known before. Temptations abounded on every side. They found work, made money, and after a few years returned home. Four of them were much the worse spiritually for the experience. But one was different. He came back physically, mentally, and spiritually stronger. When asked why he did not go the way of the others, he said, "Because I carried a picture with me."

You might suppose it was the picture of a fiancée he had left in Pennsylvania. When asked what it was, he said, "It was the picture of my last morning at home. We were all sitting around the breakfast table, Dad at one end and Mom at the other, with the kids sitting around. There wasn't much talk that morning. We all realized the family circle was breaking up.

"After breakfast Dad took down the old family Bible, as was his custom, and began to read. But he didn't get far. His voice broke, and he couldn't go on. Then we knelt for prayer, and again his voice broke. This was the mental picture that saved me from falling into evil ways. During the time I was away, I could not bear the thought of breaking my father's heart."

The home in which I grew up was a happy one. While my mother's influence on me was profound, the most powerful influence on my life was that of my father. Fathers who take time to teach their children to choose good over evil will empower those offspring to make right decisions—decisions that will stand them in good stead in years to come. Whether they use this instruction to best advantage is another matter. But even though such instruction cannot guarantee success, it enhances the chances that the outcome will be favorable.

*He . . . brought me up out of a horrible pit, out of the miry clay, and set my feet upon a rock, and established my steps. Ps. 40:2, NKJV.*

SEPTEMBER

18

# Rescue From a Horrible Pit

A few years ago Tommy Stage, a 7-year-old boy, accidentally fell into a 275-foot well shaft. In the fall he suffered multiple fractures of his legs. Fortunately, his father was not far away and saw the accident happen.

When he saw Tommy fall, Mr. Stage raced over to the wellhead and heard his son cry out, "Daddy, get me out of here!"

"Don't worry, son," his father called down. "Don't be scared. We'll pull you out as soon as we can. Now, listen. I'm going to phone for help and will be right back. Push against the sides of the pipe so you don't sink any deeper."

A rescue team arrived and lowered a rope to Tommy. The boy's father gave him specific instructions on how to run the rope around behind him and under his armpits, then how to tie it securely in front of him in a knot. The boy obeyed and was lifted to safety some 45 minutes after he had fallen in.

Later reporters asked Mr. Stage how his boy could follow instructions so faithfully at such a young age. He replied simply, "Tommy has always been good at obeying orders."

All of us, because of our sinful natures, have fallen into the horrible pit of sin. Some of us have sunk into it deeper than others—often because of our own foolishness. Bruised and broken, we cry out, "Get me out of here!" and our heavenly Father comes "running" (see Luke 15:20) and says, "Fear not, child. Just follow My instructions, and I'll soon get you out of your difficulty."

The quicker we follow our heavenly Father's instructions, the quicker He can get us out of the "scrape" in which we find ourselves. "The way will be opened for you to disentangle yourself from embarrassment and difficulty" (*The Desire of Ages,* p. 329). What a God! A heavenly Father who not only lifts us out of the horrible pit in which we find ourselves but who also sets our feet on solid ground and establishes our steps! Yes, what a God!

**19** *I drew them with cords of a man, with bands of love, and I was to them as one who lifts up and eases the yoke over their cheeks, and I bent down to them and gently laid food before them. Hosea 11:4, Amplified.*

# The Right Way to Lead

Hosea's description of how the Lord leads is one of the most moving in the Old Testament, perhaps in all the Bible. Note that God draws; He does not drive or compel—He attracts. He puts His love for us in human terms—He draws us with the "cords of a man, with bands of love." This is something we humans can understand and appreciate.

General Dwight D. Eisenhower was chosen to lead the Allied forces in the invasion of Europe during World War II largely because of his ability to persuade others to follow. On one occasion he used a piece of string to demonstrate the art of leadership to a group of officers. He placed the string on a table and said, "Pull it and it will follow you wherever you lead it. Push it and you can't make it go anywhere. It is just that way when it comes to leading people. They will follow a person who gets out in front and leads by example." At another time he said, "You do not lead by hitting people over the head—that's assault, not leadership."

In the graphic picture of the most loved of all the psalms, Psalm 23, the Lord is depicted as leading, not driving, His sheep—"he leadeth me beside the still waters" (verse 2). Pastors and church officers can learn from His divine example.

They are not to lord it "over those entrusted to [them], but [be] examples to the flock" (1 Peter 5:3, NKJV). Altogether too often those in positions of leadership try to drive instead of lead. Driving people may work for a while, but ultimately it is counterproductive.

What is true of church leaders is equally true of parents. Although some children may learn from a parent who says "Do as I say; not as I do," this method of leading is never as effective as leading by example. Incidentally, this principle of drawing instead of pushing is applicable to courtships as well.

*God forbid that I should glory except in the cross of our Lord Jesus Christ, by whom the world has been crucified to me, and I to the world. Gal. 6:14, NKJV.*

# Glorying in the Cross

A few months ago my wife and I, accompanied by our daughter DeDe, flew from Bangkok to Hong Kong. While there, we decided to visit Macao, a Portuguese enclave a few miles away, where I hoped to be able to use the language I had grown up speaking. I was disappointed. More people speak English than Portuguese in Macao.

But one thing did not disappoint me. As we traveled around the city by bus we noticed on the hill overlooking the harbor a cathedral built by the early colonists. Several centuries ago a raging typhoon proved stronger than the works of man, and the structure collapsed, except for the front wall. High atop that façade, defying the elements, stood the great bronze cross I had read about prior to our visit.

In 1825 Sir John Bowring, an Englishman, visited Macao and was impressed by the same sight that greeted my eyes. As he looked, he was moved to write the words to a familiar hymn—

> In the cross of Christ I glory,
> Towering o'er the wrecks of time,
> All the light of sacred story
> Gathers round its head sublime.

The cross, in which many people glory today, has not always been an honored symbol. Paul alludes to this fact when he says in 1 Corinthians 1:18: "The preaching of the cross is to them that perish foolishness." In verse 23 he enlarges on this: "We preach Christ crucified, unto the Jews a stumblingblock, and unto the Greeks foolishness." The Jews looked forward to a conquering Messiah, not a crucified Saviour; to the Greek mind, worshiping a God who had died a death reserved for criminals was the height of absurdity.

The cross Paul is talking about is not of wood, such as Jesus' cross, but "the power of God unto salvation" (Rom. 1:16), which that cross represented. The centuries may come and go, but this cross endures, and with the apostle, we glory in it!

*Even a child is known by his actions, by whether his conduct is pure and right.*
*Prov. 20:11, NIV.*

# Parental Influence

One of the most remembered maxims of Jesus is "By their fruits ye shall know them" (Matt. 7:20). We are accustomed to judging adults by this rule, but what about children, and above all, what can their good example teach adults?

At the unusually early age of 4, Nikolaus Ludwig, Count von Zinzendorf (1700-1760), Moravian religious and social reformer, was converted to Christ. Although his father died when he was only an infant, his mother told him about his father's devotion to Jesus. Her quiet talks made a deep impression on his young mind. A bit later the words "Thou art our dear Father, because Jesus is our Brother," which he heard sung in a hymn, also had a profound influence on his life.

"These words," Zinzendorf's biographer quotes him as saying, "impressed me very much during my fourth and fifth years: for I thought, that accordingly everyone had a right to talk with the Saviour as a brother." His biography also related how as a child he would write letters to Jesus and send them fluttering out the upstairs window of his home, fully confident that his Saviour would receive them—and read them. And who is to say these letters, or at least their content, didn't reach their intended destination and were read? (See Matt. 18:10 and 2 Kings 19:14.)

When only 22, Zinzendorf opened his estates in Saxony to the persecuted Moravian Brethren and helped them found Herrnhut Colony on his property. Later he joined them in their beliefs. In 1736 he was ordered to leave Saxony because of his religious activities. For many years thereafter he traveled about, spreading the beliefs of the Moravian Church. His theological tenets exerted a marked and beneficial influence on nineteenth-century Protestantism, much of which can be traced to his training as a child.

Adults in general, and parents in particular, have a great deal to do with whether or not a child's conduct is pure and right. May God help us who are fathers and mothers always to exert our influence on the side of good.

*Do not let anyone look down on you because you are young, but be an example . . . in your speech, your conduct, your love, faith, and purity. 1 Tim. 4:12, TEV.*

# How to Win Respect

Many adults find it hard to endure the scorn and contempt of other adults, but it is doubly difficult for an adolescent to endure scorn and contempt from their fellow teenagers.

As Leo Buscaglia was leaving school one day, a gang of rowdies muscled in on him and began hurling epithets at his Italian ancestry. Humiliated and in tears, he broke through the circle of tormentors and ran home. There he locked himself in the bathroom and wept bitterly.

His father overheard him crying and asked what the matter was. When Leo told him, he expected Dad would take immediate action—either beat up the troublemakers or at least tell their parents and demand the boys be punished. His father did neither. Instead he pointed out some things about Italians that Leo could be proud of.

But this didn't appeal to the boy. "I don't like being different," he protested. "I want to be like everyone else."

"Like everyone else? You mean, you'd like to be like those boys who insulted you?" his father asked pointedly.

"No!" Leo roared back.

"Then be proud of what you are," his father advised. "After all, everyone is different from everyone else."

How true! Even Leo's tormenters were different—although they pretended that only Italians were singular. Would that all teenagers—and adults—could remember that.

But Paul's advice to young Timothy goes beyond the advice Leo's father gave his son. By being a model Christian one can win the respect of others.

Now let us look at the problem from another angle. When you and I take a stand for the right instead of going along with the crowd, we may be ridiculed, but people respect those who do what they believe is right, those who have the courage of their convictions. Try it next time "a multitude [tempts you] to do evil" (Ex. 23:2). It works!

*Blessed are the peacemakers; they shall be called God's children. Matt. 5:9, REB.*

# Breaking the Cycle of Hostility

A few months ago a woman wrote to advice columnist Ann Landers. She signed herself "Daughter, Everywhere, U.S.A." The writer described her mother as "the world's lousiest parent." She told how her mother criticized her as far back as she could remember, making her feel worthless and stupid.

Fortunately, the writer had married a peacemaker—the kind of person Jesus was talking about when He pronounced the seventh beatitude. The woman's husband helped her see that her mother was the product of her upbringing and encouraged her to imagine what her mother's early life must have been like, because *her* mother had been critical, selfish, and unapproachable. The writer remembered her grandmother very well.

She accepted her husband's suggestion and had no trouble picturing what her mother's childhood must have been like. It must have been at least as bad as her own.

As the letter writer began to view matters in this light, her attitude toward her mother began to change. Compassion replaced hostility. And although her mother had not basically changed at the time of writing (perhaps this was too much to expect), the writer had changed—and this was the important thing!

But in addition, her relationship to her mother improved to the point where she could overlook her critical remarks. In turn, she found her mother throwing fewer barbs at her. She even hoped that someday she and her mother could be friends.

What an admirable example of peacemaking! Would that more Christians were like that husband—and that daughter!

If we would just remember that behind the hostility abroad in the world stands the archtroublemaker of the universe, Satan, it might help us view those who have fallen victim to his deceptions in a more compassionate light. It is he who initiated the cycles of hostility and hatred we see in the world today; thus, his victims are not altogether to blame for their behavior.

By letting God change you and me into peacemakers, He can use us as His agents in breaking these cycles of hostility.

*Your wife will be like a fruitful vine in your home, and your sons will be like young olive trees around your table. Ps. 128:3, TEV.*

SEPTEMBER

24

# Child Training

Samuel Taylor Coleridge, author of "The Rime of the Ancient Mariner," was talking one day with a woman visitor who advocated the philosophy that children should not be given religious instruction—they should be left to grow up "naturally." In this way they would make more "mature" and "rational" decisions, because they could better understand what they were doing. This philosophy sounds plausible, but something may sound plausible and yet be fallacious.

Coleridge listened to the woman expound her point of view, but said little. After a while he invited her to take a look at his garden. He led her out to a place in his backyard where only weeds were growing.

"How do you like my garden?" asked the poet tongue in cheek. "Isn't it beautiful?"

"Garden? You mean you call that a garden? I call that a weed patch," observed the woman.

"Well," explained Coleridge, "I decided some time ago not to infringe on the right of these plants to grow up as they pleased—until they reached maturity."

His visitor got the point.

I once had some relatives who subscribed to this woman's *laissez-faire* philosophy. Not surprisingly, their children adopted no religion after they grew up. These parents have long forgotten that they once held—and practiced—this philosophy. Today they bemoan the fact that their children pooh-pooh religion, have no moral scruples, and rebel against all authority.

Instilling Christian principles in children does not guarantee they will adopt them as their own. After all, human beings were created with the power of choice, and some, unfortunately, make the wrong choice (see Joshua 24:15 and Rom. 14:12). But proper training does increase the probabilities. If in spite of Christian home training children still go wrong, parents can at least have the satisfaction of knowing that they did the best they could.

*Ye have not chosen me, but I have chosen you.*
*John 15:16.*

# I Have Chosen You

Wilfred Grenfell, Labrador's celebrated missionary doctor, met a young woman on shipboard while he was on his way to the mission field. He fell in love with her almost immediately, and within a very short time he declared his intention to marry her. Taken aback, her not surprising reply was, "Why, young man, you don't even know my name." (She meant her surname.) Quick as a flash Grenfell responded, "I may not know your name, but I know what it is going to be."

The young lady liked Grenfell's repartee. In time she accepted his proposal, and their romance blossomed into a happy marriage. They spent many challenging years in service for God.

Some years ago I read about a young man who was attending a boarding college in the West Indies. One day while standing in line for lunch, he expressed in a novel way his choice of a young woman who had been spurning his attentions. He passed her a note on which he had scribbled the words of our verse. He too was successful.

But it doesn't always turn out that way. After all, human beings have the power to choose, and when it comes to romance and marriage, man proposes—but woman disposes!

All morally responsible beings have the power of choice. When we are born again we choose Christ, but in reality we are merely affirming a choice He made. Before we chose Christ, He had already chosen us. Ephesians 1:4 tells us that God made this choice in Christ "before the foundation of the world." This choice included everyone. "God shows no partiality" (Acts 10:34, RSV). He "wants everyone to be saved" (1 Tim. 2:4, TEV).

However, not everyone will be saved, because we can reject the choice God has made. He could, of course, force us to accept His choice, but He will never do this because He desires only the service of love. After all, this is the only kind of service that is worth having.

Today God invites you to ratify the choice He made concerning you before the foundation of the world, when He chose us to be His sons and daughters.

*Be ye all of one mind, having compassion one of another, . . . not rendering evil for evil, or railing for railing: but contrariwise blessing; knowing that ye are thereunto called.*
**1 Peter 3:8, 9.**

SEPTEMBER
26

# You Determine How You Act

Christians are called to live the golden rule—regardless of how others treat them. This is contrary to fallen human nature, but one who has become a partaker of the divine nature is enabled to live by this principle.

One evening several years ago, Sydney Harris of the Chicago *Daily News* and a Quaker friend walked up to a newsstand. The Quaker bought a paper, then thanked the vendor politely. The vendor didn't so much as acknowledge his thanks.

"Sullen fellow, isn't he?" Harris remarked.

"I've been buying my papers from him for years, and he never responds," the Quaker quietly replied.

"Why, then, do you continue to be polite to him?" Harris asked.

The Quaker's answer was revealing. "Why should I let him determine how I act?"

When you stop to think about it, there is real wisdom in that philosophy. Those who let others determine how they are going to act are among the most miserable people in the world. We have all met them.

Some people resemble amphibians. The body temperature of amphibians, a family of creatures that includes frogs and newts, is determined by the environment. When the temperature around an amphibian rises, its body temperature rises; when the surrounding temperature falls, its body temperature falls.

Have you ever known someone, for instance, who stopped attending church because the church members seemed cold? If it is true that the church is cold, such people have taken on the temperature of their environment.

I once read about two men who lived near a swamp. Neither liked the swamp. One of them moved out. The other drained the swamp and made it habitable! Ask yourself, as I ask myself, Which of these two men am I more like?

*[Peter] was terrified and began to sink. "Save me, Lord!" he shouted. Instantly Jesus reached out his hand and rescued him.*
*Matt. 14:30, 31, TLB.*

# A Friendly Hand

Many years ago the schooner *Thomas M. N. Stone* sank off the east coast of the United States. Captain Newcomb and his crew of six escaped in a lifeboat. They were picked up a few days later by the bark *Africa,* which deposited them in New York.

Newcomb filed a complaint with the marine authorities in which he stated that a black-hulled, single-funnel steamer had passed within a mile and a half of their lifeboat without stopping to help. The steamer's crew had obviously seen their internationally recognized distress signal (an oar with a blanket attached), for the steamer blew three blasts with her whistle— but kept on going. Said Newcomb, "If I knew the name of that steamer and her captain, I would tell the world."

I wonder if we always realize that many castaways on the sea of life are like the ignored captain and his crew.

My wife and I recently visited our son, Doctor Don, and his family in Paradise, California. I had been a young ministerial intern in that very town 40 years before. As my wife and I drove to places familiar to me, I pointed out the spot where some parishioners (I'll call them the Foxes) had lived. When I visited them, Mrs. Fox asked me to call on her 19-year-old son, who lived in a little cabin nearby. She said he was friendless, never went anywhere, and was just wasting his life away.

When I knocked and the cabin door opened, I was met by the saddest face I think I have ever seen. Moments into our visit the boy burst into tears. I didn't know what to do. I read a verse of Scripture, offered a brief prayer, and left. Because a short time later I was moved to another parish, I never followed up on that initial visit, but that was really no excuse for neglecting the boy. I could have at least written him a letter of encouragement. Inexperience should not be used as an excuse for failure to reach out to those in need.

All around us are people like that young man. They need a friend. Someone who cares. Someone who will lead them to Jesus, who never fails to reach out His hand to save. You or I can be that friend.

*Can a man carry fire in his bosom and his clothes not be burned? Or can a man walk on hot coals and his feet not be scorched? Prov. 6:27, 28, MLB.*

# Playing With Fire

Have you ever heard of fire walkers? They are people who walk on red-hot coals and don't get burned. Perhaps you have seen, as I have, movies of Hindus walking on beds of live coals, seemingly negating Solomon's adage. I am not sure how they do it; however, I believe they are aided in some way by the great deceiver.

Fred Hardin, a fellow classmate of mine at Potomac University, once witnessed a fire walking ceremony in Ceylon, which validates Solomon's observation. He and a missionary of another denomination watched some fire walkers step onto some sizzling hot coals without apparent damage to their feet. Hardin's companion decided to try his hand at it—or perhaps I should say, foot.

He may have presumptuously claimed the promise "When thou walkest through the fire, thou shalt not be burned" (Isa. 43:2; cf. Lev. 18:21). He removed his shoes and socks, strode into the fiery pit—and the next instant he was hot-footing it out, his feet badly burned.

Solomon's metaphors in our verses refer to illicit sex. We know this because in verse 29 he speaks of the man "who commits adultery with his neighbour's wife" (REB).

In one of the countries where I once lived, in which prostitution was rampant, one of the missionary men felt that God had especially called him to minister to fallen women. He was warned about the danger of getting involved, but he ignored the caution—and for a time seemed to have great success. From time to time he would report to his wife on the souls he was winning and the wonderful victories he was gaining. She pleaded for him to stop, but in vain. Eventually he had to leave the mission field because of having fallen into temptation.

No, Solomon is right. One cannot play with the kind of fire he is talking about without getting burned—eventually. The best course to follow is to stay as far away as possible from this kind of "strange" fire.

*In the night I remember my song; with my heart I meditated and my spirit made diligent search. Has the Lord rejected me for ever? Ps. 77:6, 7, MLB.*

# Changed by a Hymn

A song can have a powerful effect upon the spiritual life of a person. An example of what it can do happened one night many years ago in Macao, a Portuguese enclave on the coast of southeastern China. Colonel Russell H. Conwell, an American tourist who was visiting the colony, walked through one of its famous casinos. He paused as he passed a table where two of his countrymen were gambling. As the older of the two men began dealing a hand, the younger man began idly humming the tune of the familiar hymn "One Sweetly Solemn Thought," by Phoebe Cary.

Suddenly the older man stopped and asked, "Harry, where did you learn that hymn?"

"In Sunday school," the younger man replied.

Dashing the deck of cards to the table, the older player exclaimed, "I've played my last game! This is it!"

The older man had won about $100 from Harry. Pulling his winnings from his pocket, he pushed them over toward the other player and said, "There, Harry. That's what I won from you. Take it and do good with it, and I shall do the same with my money. I'm sorry I have misled you."

The colonel, who later became a well-known pastor in Philadelphia, was so impressed by the sudden change brought about by a hymn that he kept track of the two men for years and reported that the reformation they experienced that night was permanent.

Not long ago a church leader was invited to speak to a congregation on one of the islands in the South Pacific. His talk was preceded by a song service consisting largely of so-called gospel rock. When he stood up to speak he uttered no words of censure about the type of music, but simply began singing an old gospel hymn in his rich baritone voice. The message was inescapable, its effect on his audience palpable.

Music has tremendous power for good—or for evil. It can stir the human heart as nothing else can. Thank God for songs that can change lives permanently for the better!

*Like a refiner of silver [the Lord] will sit and closely watch as the dross is burned away. He will purify the Levites, . . . refining them like gold or silver, so that they will do their work for God with pure hearts. Mal. 3:3, TLB.*

# Sterling Character

Most of us have seen the word "sterling" stamped on the back of objects made of unusually pure silver, and you've probably heard people speak of someone as having a "sterling character." But have you ever wondered how the word sterling originated?

According to Walter de Pinchebek, who lived about 1300, some years before his time there was a mercantile firm in Hanse, north Germany, named Easterling. The partners of this firm were recognized as being so upright in their dealings that they were granted special banking and trading privileges. Merchants in the London branch of this firm were allowed to coin money in their own name. These coins were stamped with the word "Easterling." These coins consisted of 92.5 percent silver and less than 8 percent alloy (the latter was necessary to keep the silver from wearing out too quickly). Eventually the word Easterling was shortened to sterling, and from that day all silver meeting these specifications is marked "sterling."

In our verse for today the Lord is portrayed as the refiner of precious metals. Refiners of gold and silver in Bible times are depicted as sitting before a furnace, intently watching the purification process lest any of the precious metal be lost (see Isa. 1:25). For best results, the refiner applied neither too much nor too little heat. After the ore was brought to the melting point, the dross was skimmed off without injuring the precious metal.

God frequently uses trials that seem "fiery" to refine our characters. As the psalmist puts it: "You have purified us with fire, O Lord, like silver in a crucible. . . . But in the end, you brought us into wealth" (Ps. 66:10, 12, TLB). The wealth the psalmist is talking about is not material wealth, but rather spiritual wealth—wealth that makes our work for God spring from a heart with pure motives.

What sterling is to silver, Christian should be to character.

*Whatever a person is like, I try to find common ground with him so that he will let me tell him about Christ and let Christ save him.*
*1 Cor. 9:22, TLB.*

# Throw Out the Lifeline

Around 1875 the trawler *Gertrude* was caught in a violent storm some 40 miles east of Lowestoft off the coast of England. Five seamen, as well as everything movable on deck, were swept overboard. Only a sailor and the cook remained alive. The trawler *Alfred,* from Ramsgate, ventured out to see what it could do to help. Time and again the men of the *Alfred* threw lines to the *Gertrude,* but every cast either fell short or the survivors, numbed by the cold, could not hold on.

Night fell. The *Alfred* kept in touch with the stricken ship by means of flares. As morning dawned, Alfred Freeman, an 18-year-old apprentice seaman, volunteered to go to the vessel. Alone in the raging storm, he sculled his rowboat to the *Gertrude* and boarded her. But the next wave smashed his little craft against the side of the ship. In a final, desperate attempt, the *Alfred's* crew threw one more line. Freeman caught it and the men were saved.

Some have thought that the hymn "Throw Out the Lifeline," by Edward S. Ufford, commemorates this incident. Actually Ufford received his inspiration from seeing a wrecked ship on the shore near his home in Westwood, Massachusetts, although he may have been influenced by the rescue made by the *Alfred.*

Paul, who wrote the words of our verse, traveled a great deal by sea. On his way to Rome his ship was caught in a storm and wrecked. But, storm or no storm, he witnessed for his Lord. Even as the storm raged, he testified: "Last night an angel of the God whose I am and whom I serve stood beside me and said, 'Do not be afraid, Paul. . . . God has graciously given you the lives of all who sail with you.' So keep up your courage, men, for I have faith in God that it will happen just as he told me" (Acts 27:23-25, NIV).

Do you know souls on the "sea of life" in danger of making shipwreck of faith (see 1 Tim. 1:19)? Why not speak words of hope and encouragement to them—today?

*The tongue is a . . . world of iniquity . . . that
. . . defileth the whole body, and setteth on fire
the course of nature; and it is set on fire of hell.
James 3:6.*

OCTOBER

2

# If Your Tongue Offends

Many years ago, when my parents were missionaries in the Madeira Islands, my father saw a postcard that caught his fancy. (It is now in my possession.) It depicts a husband, with hammer in hand and a look of grim satisfaction on his face, nailing his wife's oversized tongue to the kitchen table. She is kneeling, hands tied behind her back.

It so happened that at the time this cartoon came to my father's attention, our church in Funchal was having problems with gossipers—*bilhardeiras,* they were called. Dad didn't usually make mistakes, but he did this time. He thought that tacking up the cartoon on the church bulletin board would stop the gossiping. It didn't. It inflamed matters. The chief gossip apparently recognized herself in the cartoon and took it as a personal attack on her character.

By coincidence, soon after this we began receiving a newspaper called *The Oregonian.* One issue made an indelible impression on my mind; it showed a woman holding a towel over her mouth; she was in obvious pain. The accompanying story stated that she was a nurse who had decided to cure herself of gossiping by literally carrying out the instructions given in Mark 9:43-48. She had cut off the tip of her tongue. I do not know if her action had a salutary effect. And no, Dad didn't post this clipping.

Some men seem to think that only women gossip. They are wrong! I have known men (myself included) who gossiped—only we called it "sharing." Somehow the name change made it almost sound good.

The Bible condemns gossiping (see Lev. 19:16), and a true follower of Christ will overcome this habit. If you find that you have this tendency, the secret of overcoming is not in physically cutting off your tongue or nailing it to the kitchen table, but in letting the spirit of Christ so control your tongue that it blesses rather than injures others. Read James 3:7-11.

*A soft answer turns away wrath, but a harsh word stirs up anger. Prov. 15:1, RSV.*

# A Soft Answer

Not long ago I read about a pastor who moved into a new parish and discovered he had a church member who seemed to be determined to find fault with everything he did. At first the pastor tried to disregard the criticism, but the man would not be ignored. One day the minister received an especially vitriolic letter, replete with accusations. Most of these were false, and the others were completely out of proportion to the facts.

The pastor could no longer ignore his critic. He realized he faced a problem that must be resolved. He knew he could refute every one of the man's libelous charges, but before responding he prayed for heavenly wisdom. He was impressed to write his critic a four-word letter: "Please pray for me."

The effect of this simple request was nothing short of miraculous. It touched the critic's heart and completely altered his attitude. From that time on he became one of the pastor's staunchest supporters.

Let us consider the pastor's reply for a moment. Its tone is conciliatory, yet in no way does it capitulate to the critic's charges. But it does acknowledge that, if the accusations were true, the pastor needs his critic's help.

Coming from some men, such a reply might be interpreted as condescension, even sarcasm. But evidently this critic knew in his heart that this pastor was made of different stuff. Was it because of the pastor's patient attempts to ignore the criticism? I don't know, but I do know that most human beings are willing to help someone who asks for help.

Now, we don't need to think for a moment that when Solomon said that a soft answer turns away wrath he meant that it works every time—especially if we have gotten caught up in responding to our critics with words that stir up anger. But even if this is the case, if we sincerely ask God to put a right spirit within us, praying that He will give us a soft answer, He will begin doing for us that which He otherwise could not do "did we not thus ask" (*The Great Controversy,* p. 525).

*The word of God is living and powerful, and sharper than any two-edged sword, piercing even to the division of soul and spirit, and of joints and marrow, and is a discerner of the thoughts and intents of the heart.*
*Heb. 4:12, NKJV.*

# God's Word Is Powerful

We may not always realize it, but there are tremendous reserves of power all around us. For instance, it is estimated that the average lightning bolt releases about a billion watts of power in every discharge. In recent years, scientists have begun to understand how this release comes about.

Electric charges begin building up in cumulanimbus clouds when hot, moist air comes in contact with cold, dry air. This interaction produces an imbalance of electrical charges. The bottom of the thunderhead becomes negatively charged, whereas the earth is positively charged. The charges accumulate and attract each other, every "feeler" coming a little closer to the cloud. When the point is reached at which air resistance is overcome, an enormous charge of electricity leaps through the path prepared by the feelers, and we see it as a flash of lightning.

Scientists have calculated that lightning bolts strike the earth about 16 million times each year—approximately once every two seconds. The greatest concentration of these powerful discharges occurs in Indonesia, where electrical storms occur an average of 222 out of 365 days a year.

God is a source of infinitely greater power than any lightning strike, and yet most of the time we are not aware of this power. By His word "were the heavens made; and all the host of them by the breath of his mouth. . . . For he spake, and it was done; he commanded, and it stood fast" (Ps. 33:6-9). Not only is God's spoken word powerful; His written Word is equally powerful.

Just as the cloud has a role in the release of electric power, so we have a role in experiencing the spiritual power reserved in God's Word. As we search that Word and "feel after" God (see Acts 17:27), His transforming power manifests itself in transformed lives.

*Amaziah [king of Judah] said to the man of God, But what shall we do for the hundred talents which I have given to the army of Israel? And the man of God answered, The Lord is able to give thee much more than this.* **2 Chron. 25:9.**

# Much More Than This

Amaziah had raised an army of 300,000 men to fight Edom, then he had hired an extra 100,000 mercenaries from the kingdom of Israel for 100 talents of silver. Today this much silver would be equivalent to about US$1 million—not much in terms of military expenditures at the present time, but a sizable fortune in those days.

But then a "man of God," a prophet, came with a message. If Amaziah went to war with his Israelite mercenaries as allies, the Lord would cause him to "fall before the enemy," because "the Lord is not with Israel" (2 Chron. 25:8, 7). Amaziah stood to lose the hundred talents as well as the support of the Israelite army. What should he do?

The other day I visited a publishing house manager who faced a similar dilemma. He had been accepting advertisements for a certain brand of toothpaste from a local businessman and placing them in his health journal. Clearly there is nothing wrong with toothpaste, and the extra money was helping pay overhead expenses.

Then, without thinking, our friend accepted an ad for another product from the same company, a product that was inconsistent with the objectives and health principles of his magazine. Soon he realized his mistake and explained to the businessman that he could not run the new ad. The businessman began to argue and threatened to pull out all of his advertising. I'm glad to say our friend chose to give up "the hundred talents" rather than get involved in something that was leading in the wrong direction.

Have you ever faced a similar dilemma? Have you ever, for example, innocently invested means in something that promised large returns but later proved to be a questionable deal? In such situations, it is better to go into the kingdom minus your "right eye" or your "right hand" (Matt. 5:29, 30), than "gain the whole world, and [perhaps] lose" your own soul (Matt. 16:26).

*Be gentle and ready to forgive; never hold grudges. Remember, the Lord forgave you, so you must forgive others. Col. 3:13, TLB.*

# In Spite of Spite

In the July 1990 issue of *Guideposts,* Carol A. Virgil tells how Teresa, her teenage daughter, came home from school one day fighting back tears as she tossed a new book she had just bought into her mother's lap. Inscribed inside the back cover Carol read, "I hate you, you're ugly and you're scum." Teresa said they were written by Brooke, one of the school bullies.

"I can't imagine what I've done to make her hate me so," lamented Teresa, tears brimming in her eyes.

The impulse to get even with her daughter's tormentor surged in Carol. Peer approval is so important to 13-year-old girls. What could she say to help her daughter? Perhaps she should have taught her children to be more aggressive.

Carol and her daughter began to think of cutting remarks they could invent to put Brooke in her place. "And how about a daily 'Brooke report'?" Carol snidely suggested.

About a week later Carol came across her kindergarten diploma and began to reminisce. Suddenly she remembered saying "I hate you!" to Rebecca, a homely schoolmate and a slow learner. Her teacher, Mrs. Lidke, overheard her make this cutting remark. She said, "Carol, I'm surprised. I expected so much more from you." Taken aback and embarrassed, Carol apologized.

Now as she reflected on why she had treated Rebecca so shamefully, she realized that she had done it to gain peer approval. She at once decided to put an end to the "Brooke reports." She wrote out the verse for today's meditation and placed it in a prominent place on Teresa's bed. Later she told her daughter how she had treated Rebecca and why.

"I never thought of it that way," admitted Teresa. "I guess I can be nice to Brooke." Then both mother and daughter knelt and asked God to give them the grace to forgive Brooke—and He did!

At the time of writing, Brooke hadn't changed, but Carol and her daughter had! And that is the important thing.

*About dates and times, my friends, we need not write to you, for you know perfectly well that the Day of the Lord comes like a thief in the night. I Thess. 5:1, 2, NEB.*

# Like a Thief in the Night

Have you ever had a thief sneak into your house while you were asleep and make off with your valuables? If you have, you can appreciate the feeling of being taken unawares.

When I was an infant, my parents lived in a place called Engenho de Dentro, a suburb of Rio de Janeiro, Brazil. My brother was born there. Each evening Dad placed a glass of water on a chair in the corner of my bedroom so I could have a drink if I got thirsty during the night. One night Mom and Dad were awakened by the rattling of a spoon in that glass. Dad was about to get up and investigate when Mom persuaded him it was probably "just a mouse," so they went back to sleep.

Next morning when Dad picked up his trousers he discovered that his gold watch and his wallet with a month's salary in cash had been stolen! Further investigation disclosed that a lot of other things had been taken as well—some of them irreplaceable. You can imagine their chagrin.

Unpleasant as such experiences are, they can help us better understand the bitter disappointment of the unrepentant sinners when the day of the Lord overtakes them unexpectedly. These experiences can also encourage us to be ready for that day.

We usually think Paul's words apply to the dismay of those caught unawares by the Second Coming. However, they seem more appropriately to describe those who expect the Second Coming yet are caught unprepared by the close of human probation.

Notice these words: "Silently, unnoticed as the midnight thief, will come the decisive hour which marks the fixing of every man's destiny, the final withdrawal of mercy's offer to guilty men" (*The Great Controversy,* p. 491).

No Christian need be caught unprepared by this event. As our verse for meditation says, "Ye, brethren, are not in darkness, that that day should overtake you as a thief" (verse 4). We are "children of the light" (verse 5), and we continue to be children of the light as long as we stay near the Light of the world.

*[Satan] will completely fool those who are on their way to hell because they have said "no" to the Truth; they have refused to believe it and love it, and let it save them, so God will allow them to believe lies with all their hearts.*
*2 Thess. 2:10, 11, TLB.*

# Keep Abreast of Truth

In 1608 John Robinson, known as "the pastor of the Pilgrim Fathers," left England because of his love for truth. A year later, he and about 100 followers moved to the city of Leiden in Holland, where his ministry flourished and his congregation increased to about 300. Speaking concerning this group of Christians, William Bradford, governor and historian of the Plymouth Colony, described them as having such "true piety, humble zeal, and fervent love toward God [as to come nearer than any other group] to the . . . pattern of the first [Christian] churches."

Shortly before September 16, 1620, when the ship *Mayflower* sailed for the New World with 100 passengers, 35 of whom were members of his congregation, Robinson spoke these memorable words:

"I charge you before God that you follow me no further than you have seen me follow the Lord Jesus Christ. If God reveals anything to you by any other instrument of His, be as ready to receive it as you were to receive any truth by my ministry, for I am verily persuaded that the Lord hath more truth yet to break out of His holy Word."

These are courageous words. Frequently religious leaders forbid their followers to accept anything beyond that which they have taught them. But revealed truth is not static; it is progressive. By the same token new truths do not annul old truths; they build on them. James Russell Lowell, an American poet, speaks of the progress of truth in his poem "The Present Crisis," in which he commends those who "keep abreast of Truth."

How can we avoid, on the one hand, saying no to new truth and at the same time keep from being blown "about with every wind of doctrine" (Eph. 4:14)? There is only one way. We must approach that Word that "is true from the beginning" (Ps. 119:160) with a humble and teachable heart, and sincerely pray for "the Spirit of Truth" to "guide [us] into all truth" (John 16:13).

*Foreigners shall serve me and shall quickly submit to me when they hear of my power.*
*2 Sam. 22:44, 45, TLB.*

# God Desires Prompt Obedience

Jenny, a Norwegian girl in her early 20s, worked as a hairdresser in New York City in the mid 1970s. She lived with a married man in an apartment close to the beauty shop where she was employed. In the same apartment complex lived a Brazilian girl, a Christian, named Carmo. Carmo became friends with Jenny and began sharing her faith with her. Before long Jenny accepted Jesus as her Saviour.

One day Carmo told Jenny it was sinful for her to live with a married man. Up to that moment Jenny had never considered she was doing anything wrong, but as soon as the Holy Spirit convicted her that what she was doing was sinful, she terminated the liaison immediately. The separation was painful, but she was determined to serve God wholeheartedly at all cost.

Not long after she ended her illicit affair, I met Jenny in upper New York State at a weekend retreat at which I was one of the speakers. During my off hours I studied the Bible with her and answered her questions. Seldom have I met a person more determined to give up sin at once than was Jenny. Later, I heard she returned to Norway and, in spite of opposition from her family, became a Bible worker.

The last time I saw Jenny was in England in 1982. She told me during the brief visit we had together that she had terminal cancer and had only a short time to live. Not long after this, I heard she had died, faithful to her Lord to the end.

The Holy Spirit convicts of sin (see John 16:8, NKJV). But few of us act as quickly as Jenny did. Conviction leads to repentance, and repentance means sorrow for sin. But it means more than being sorry for sin. It also means turning away from it. While most of us are sorry for sin (especially when we get caught), how many of us are sorry enough to quit as soon as we are convicted?

The Lord is "longsuffering to us-ward, not willing that any should perish" (2 Peter 3:9). We can be thankful for that. But is He not better pleased when we quit sinning as soon as the Holy Spirit convicts us, rather than presuming on His mercy?

*Do not get drunk with wine, which will only ruin you; instead, be filled with the Spirit. Eph. 5:18, TEV.*

OCTOBER

10

# Drinking That God Approves

Several of my mother's brothers were construction workers in their later teen years. Because the building trade was depressed in West Virginia, where they lived, they usually worked in neighboring states during the week and returned home by train on weekends. One Friday afternoon as they traveled home, they noticed a young man board the train who appeared to be slightly intoxicated. His eyes were bloodshot and he swayed as the train jostled. He sat down across the aisle from the brothers.

The brothers decided to have some fun. They made joking remarks about drunks, then laughed uproariously. The young man ignored them, but some of the passengers were disgusted.

A little later another passenger boarded the train and sat next to the young man. They began to talk. In the course of the conversation my uncles overheard the young man say that he had just buried his wife. The joking stopped. Did the boys apologize? I don't know, but at least they told the story on themselves, and apparently regretted what they had done.

The ironic thing is that several of those brothers later died as alcoholics. They were sure they knew how to handle their liquor, and no one could persuade them otherwise. But as a Japanese proverb says: "First a man takes a drink, then a drink takes a drink, then a drink takes a man."

Some professed Christians drink alcoholic beverages and justify their practice by claiming that in Bible times the drinking of liquor was condoned. Perhaps the best answer to this argument is that "the times of this ignorance God winked at" (Acts 17:30)—just as He "winked" at the practice of slavery. But "now," today, in the face of mounting evidence that even moderate drinking damages our body's cells, the imbibing of alcoholic beverages is certainly "not wise" (Prov. 20:1).

Without question, the drinking of alcoholic beverages can lead to ruin. Not so with the "beverage" our verse for meditation recommends. Those who "rise up early" (Isa. 5:11) and drink deeply of this "wine" are built up and strengthened to resist evil.

# 11

*Do not be ashamed . . . of testifying to our Lord, . . . who saved us and called us with a holy calling. 2 Tim. 1:8, 9, RSV.*

# Never Be Ashamed of Your Saviour

In certain countries it is customary for families to have a coat of arms. Many of these escutcheons bear the figure of some "noble" animal—a lion, a horse, an eagle. But the coat of arms of the Fitzgeralds of Ireland bears the likeness of a baboon—and they are proud of it! Here is the reason.

During the conquest of India, a British officer named Fitzgerald was sent to fight in one of the campaigns. He left his wife and infant son in the care of some Indian retainers. While he was away, the enemy attacked his home and everyone fled for safety—and forgot the baby. Their pet baboon, however, apparently noticed the omission and ran into the house. The animal took the child from its crib and, holding it in one arm, climbed to the top of the abbey. After the attack had been repulsed, the baboon descended and returned the baby to its mother.

When the head of the family returned home and learned what the baboon had done, he felt he owed it a debt of gratitude. As a token of appreciation he had the likeness of a baboon carrying a child emblazoned on the family's coat of arms.

Today most people are proud to be called Christians. However, when Paul wrote his Second Epistle to Timothy, apparently there were some who were ashamed to be known as followers of Christ, and no wonder. It must have been difficult for a Christian to explain to his neighbors that he worshiped a God who had been crucified as a criminal. Little wonder Paul says that the preaching of "Christ crucified, unto the Jews [was] a stumbling-block, and unto the Greeks foolishness" (1 Cor. 1:23).

There are people who profess to be Christians, yet, like Peter, are ashamed to confess it under certain circumstances (cf. Matt. 16:16 and 26:69-74).

If the Fitzgeralds were not ashamed to display to the world on their coat of arms a baboon that saved their child, why should Christians be ashamed to confess to the world the One who not only saved them but gave His life in so doing?

*New wine is found in the cluster, and one says,*
*"Do not destroy it, for a blessing is in it."*
Isa. 65:8, NKJV.

OCTOBER

12

# New Wine and God's Macedonias

Many years ago young Charles E. Welch and his wife, accepted a call to a mission field in Africa. However, during the wife's physical examination, it was discovered she could not stand a hot, humid climate without endangering her health. The appointment was canceled. Disappointed but determined to serve the Lord in some other capacity, the husband began looking for ways to earn money that he and his wife could contribute toward spreading the good news of salvation in foreign lands.

Prior to their disappointment, Thomas B. Welch, the young man's father, a dentist and a teetotaler, had been experimenting with ways to keep grape juice from fermenting. He believed that the use of wine in the Communion service was inconsistent with the biblical teaching concerning the drinking of alcoholic beverages. Charles took over his father's experiments and devoted his time and energies to furthering the project. In time he succeeded beyond all expectations. The Welches contributed thousands of dollars toward foreign missions from the sale of Welch's grape juice.

Someone has said that disappointments are God's appointments. This was certainly true of the Welches. It was also true of the first missionaries who took the gospel to Europe. You remember, Paul and Silas decided to go to Bithynia, a region situated in what is now northwestern Turkey, but when they tried to go, "the Spirit did not permit them" (Acts 16:7, NKJV). We may never understand all the reasons the Holy Spirit had for preventing them from going to Bithynia, but then, when one considers the harvest of souls reaped in Macedonia because they obeyed the Spirit's promptings, perhaps we can begin to understand.

Have you ever had plans fail, which to all appearances were in harmony with God's will, only to discover that He had something else in mind? It has been said, "Often our plans fail that God's plans for us may succeed" (*The Ministry of Healing*, p. 473).

Yes, we may have our Bithynias, but God has His Macedonias.

## 13

*I will set My eyes on them for good. . . . Then I will give them a heart to know Me, that I am the Lord; and they shall be My people, and I will be their God, for they shall return to Me with their whole heart. Jer. 24:6, 7, NKJV.*

# Change of Heart

In 1849 Jenny Lind, the famous "Swedish Nightingale," was singing in an opera house in London when a drunk wandered in unnoticed. In the middle of the program he made his way unsteadily up to the stage, exclaiming, "My Jenny, my little Jenny! Speak to me and tell me you remember."

"Put him out! Put him out!" shouted the audience, annoyed at the interruption.

A bouncer rushed on stage and had already laid his hands on the drink-befogged man when Jenny intervened. "Please don't throw him out. Let me hear what he has to say."

Turning to the inebriate, she asked, with tender compassion, what he wanted. Then suddenly she recognized him and exclaimed, "Max Bronzden, my first and truest friend!"

She explained to the audience that it was Bronzden who first planted in her heart the desire to become a singer.

"It is not too late, my friend," she encouraged him. "Be no longer a vagabond, but a man worthy of my friendship."

Bronzden never forgot that night. Years later, speaking of the audience's reaction to Jenny's words, he said, "The [opera] house . . . [became] as silent as death; then it suddenly burst into tumultuous applause. . . . I left that place a new man, with new aspirations and courage, and in all the years since that night I have been, by God's help, a conqueror of sin."

What a wonderful testimony! What a change God can produce in a life led by His Spirit. But just as marvelous is the fact that God oftentimes uses human beings—you and me—as catalysts in bringing about this change.

A catalyst is an agent that brings about a significant change that otherwise might not take place. Today we may meet a soul needing to change his or her life. Will God find us ready to be catalysts in His hands to bring about this transformation?

They stoned . . . Stephen. . . . He fell on his
knees and cried aloud, "Lord, do not hold this
sin against them," and with that he died.
Acts 7:59, 60, REB.

OCTOBER

14

# What God Did for Stephen

In the early 1850s, Charles Haddon Spurgeon (1834-1892), while still a young man, was called to pastor the New Park Street Chapel in Southwark, England. One evening as he was preaching about Stephen's martyrdom, a cynic interrupted. "What did God do for Stephen when he was stoned to death?" he bellowed.

Instantly Spurgeon retorted, "He helped him pray, 'Lord, lay not this sin to their charge!' "

The skeptic was silenced.

God always answers our prayer—but not always in the way we think He should. In Stephen's case, He didn't turn the stones aside; He didn't spirit him away to some safe place; He didn't even strike his assailants dead—but He gave him grace to endure the pain—and manifest the same spirit of forgiveness toward his murderers that Jesus showed toward those who crucified Him.

When I was a pastor, more than once I had a parishioner tell me that his or her prayers seemed to rise no higher than the ceiling. One woman told my father, when he was her pastor, that she seemed to hear her prayers bounce back like a mocking echo. Of one thing we can be absolutely certain, it was not the voice of God that was mocking her prayers. If anything, it was the voice of the great deceiver and adversary of souls.

But many times the problem lies with us. "We do not know how to pray as we ought" (Rom. 8:26, RSV), and the reason is that we pray for the "wrong purpose" (with "selfish motives," perhaps?) (James 4:3, Amplified). God cannot say yes to such prayers and still be true to Himself. Were He to answer these prayers as *we* want them answered, it would not be for our ultimate good. So in His infinite wisdom, He says no.

If we want positive answers to our prayers, we need to ask according to God's will—and timing. When we pray with this submissive spirit, and He still doesn't answer immediately, He may be simply saying, "Be patient; not just now" (see Heb. 10:36).

*God knows how I miss you all, loving you as Christ Jesus loves you. Phil. 1:8, Jerusalem.*

# An Earnest Concern for Souls

In our verse Paul declares that he had as much love for the souls of the Philippian believers as Christ did. You and I need more of that kind of love for souls.

On one occasion in the early days of the Society of Friends, a Quaker was riding across a moor when he heard the sound of hoofbeats behind him. In a moment a highwayman drew abreast and, pointing a pistol at him, demanded, "Your money or your life!"

Without a moment's hesitation the Quaker pulled out his purse and handed it to the man.

"That's a fine horse you have," observed the robber. Then he ordered, "Get down! I'm taking him."

Calmly, without a word of protest, the Quaker dismounted, and the robber changed horses. As the robber was turning the horses around to ride off, the Quaker stepped in his path and, taking hold of the bridles, began to talk to him.

"How can you," he asked with quiet earnestness, "a man made in the image of God, be happy living a life of crime and violence? Repent, my friend, before it is too late!"

The robber drew his pistol and pointing it at the Quaker's head, snarled, "How dare you preach to me, you . . . Another word and I'll shoot you where you stand."

The Quaker never flinched. "Friend," he smiled, "I know you could kill me. I wouldn't risk my life to save either my purse or my horse, but I would gladly lay it down if I could save you from eternal damnation!"

Without a word, the robber returned the pistol to its holster, sprang off the Quaker's horse, and returned it to him with his purse. Then, mounting his own horse, he rode off, saying, "If you're that concerned for my soul, I'm not taking anything."

We can hope, but can't be sure, that the robber's change of mind led to a change of heart. We *can* be sure that if we showed as much concern for a soul as the Quaker showed, we would see many more miracles of grace than we do.

*If a stranger dwells temporarily with you in your land, you shall not suppress and mistreat him. But the stranger who dwells with you shall be to you as one born among you; and you shall love him as yourself.*
*Lev. 19:33, 34, Amplified.*

# Kindness to Strangers

It was Sunday night, December 29, 1946. The first edition of the Miami *Herald* had just gone to press. Timothy Sullivan was getting ready to go home and get a well-deserved night's rest when his telephone rang and a woman's voice pleaded, "Please help me! My husband is bleeding to death!"

The dying man was Rudy Kovarik, of Dearborn, Michigan. He and his wife were vacationing in Florida when his stomach ulcer began to bleed and he was rushed to the Biscayne Hospital. A bleeding ulcer is not necessarily life-threatening. However, the fact that Kovarik had rare AB Rh-negative blood and this type was unavailable anywhere in the area made the situation critical. Unless a donor with this type of blood could be found very soon, doctors feared Kovarik would not last until morning.

What could a city newspaper editor do? But a man was dying. Sullivan had an idea. He called radio station WCBS, a few blocks away, and asked to speak to newscaster Walter Winchell, who was to go on the air in a few minutes. The operator at the station reluctantly let him speak to Winchell. In a few minutes Winchell broadcast the news about Kovarik, giving the name of the patient and the telephone numbers of the hospital, the local police station, and the Miami *Herald* editor's office.

Within minutes these telephones were swamped with calls from all over the nation offering to donate blood. One offer came from a soldier on leave who was staying in a hotel only a couple blocks from the hospital. Within minutes his life-giving blood was flowing into the veins of the stricken man. Kovarik's life was saved. A few weeks later, Sullivan got his reward when the now-recovered Kovarik walked into his office and thanked him—no longer a stranger, but a friend.

Sometimes we are rewarded for showing kindness in this life, but don't count on it. Be kind to others, not because there may be a reward, but because Christ's love constrains you to do so.

*I will give you a new heart—I will give you new and right desires—and put a new spirit within you. I will take out your stony hearts of sin and give you new hearts of love.*
*Eze. 36:26, TLB.*

# A New Heart

On December 3, 1967, Dr. Christiaan N. Barnard, a South African heart surgeon, performed on Louis Washkansky the first human heart transplant in medical history. Some time after this, Dr. Barnard performed another heart transplant, this time on a Dr. Philip Blaiberg. What made this latter operation unique was that soon after Dr. Blaiberg awoke from the anesthetic, Dr. Barnard walked into his room, gowned and muzzled to prevent infection, carrying in his hand a small transparent plastic box. Holding it up, he said, "Dr. Blaiberg, this is your heart. Do you realize that you are the first man in history to look at his own dead heart?"

Not long after this, Dr. Blaiberg received a visit from the wife of the man who, in losing his life, had given him another chance at life. He was taken by surprise by the visit, and apparently didn't express his "undying" gratitude in quite the way he would have liked to, for later he mused, "What does one say in such circumstances?" Then he added feelingly, "She lost a life; I gained one."

Something similar happens when God, who so loved the world "that he gave his only begotten Son" (John 3:16), offers us new spiritual hearts. He lost a Life; and you and I each gain a life that is eternal. How thankful we can be that He loved us so much!

God has been doing spiritual heart transplants ever since the human race became afflicted with that fatal heart disease called sin. Those beset by critical heart problems frequently face imminent death unless they receive new hearts. With sinners, eternal death is more certain. We "shall all likewise perish" (Luke 13:5) unless we let God transplant in us new spiritual hearts.

When we allow this spiritual operation to be performed, new desires, a new spirit, a new way of thinking, is implanted in us. No longer do we live for self. Now, with undying love for the One whose heart is now in us, we live for Him.

*How long, O Lord, have I cried to thee, unanswered? I cry, "Violence!", but thou dost not save. Why dost thou let me see such misery, why countenance wrongdoing?*
*Hab. 1:2, 3, NEB.*

 OCTOBER

18

# Why?

My mother used to say that when I was a child I almost drove her to distraction asking, "Why?" She would no sooner answer one why than I would come back with, "But why?"

Children aren't the only ones who keep asking why. Adults keep asking it too. The prophet Habakkuk, the author of our verse, was one of them. Many people read his little book and miss its great message. Its central theme is the question Why?

Habakkuk lived in a time of apostasy. As he surveyed the spiritual condition of his people, he was appalled and wondered why God let them "get away with it."

Before long he got an answer. "The Lord replied, 'Look, and be amazed! You will be astounded at what I am about to do! For I am going to do something in your own lifetime that you will have to see to believe' " (verse 5, TLB). I can imagine Habakkuk must have felt considerably relieved to learn that at long last God was going to do something about Judah's wickedness!

However, when the Lord revealed what He had in mind, Habakkuk was more perplexed than ever. God said, "I am raising a new force on the world scene, the Chaldeans, a cruel and violent nation who will march across the world and conquer it" (verse 6, TLB). God was going to use a nation more wicked than Judah to punish His people! Why? No wonder Habakkuk was more perplexed than ever.

God never answered all of Habakkuk's whys, but the prophet finally came to a realization that "the Lord is in his holy temple." God was on His throne; He was in control, and because He was in control, Habakkuk could say, "Let all the earth keep silence before him" (Hab. 2:20). Knowing that the God of infinite wisdom and power was in control was answer enough.

Do you ever keep asking why without seeming to get a satisfying answer? Remember, "The Lord is in his holy temple." Appearances to the contrary, *God is in control*, and for you and me that is answer enough—for now. Final, complete answers will come when we get to heaven.

*Is it by your wisdom [Job] that the hawk soars and stretches her wings toward the south [as winter approaches]? Job 39:26, Amplified.*

# Lessons From the Birds

Bird migration is an example of God's arrangement for optimum living conditions and food supplies. It has been estimated that some 10 billion birds each year engage in migratory flights. Here are a few notable examples: Alaskan curlews fly over thousands of miles of open ocean to reach the Hawaiian Islands. A Baltimore oriole was reckoned to have taken a trip to South America and returned to the same elm tree in a town in New York. The golden plover flies 2,500 miles from Newfoundland to Colombia each autumn. One species of shrike wings its way 3,500 miles from Central Asia to Central Africa.

The arctic tern has one of the longest migration patterns of all birds. It flies from the Arctic to the Antarctic late each summer, a distance of some 11,000 miles. It retraces its flight from the Antarctic to the Arctic the following spring, spending approximately two months going each way.

Jeremiah speaks of several other kinds of birds that have migratory instincts. He says, "The stork knows the time of her migration, as does the turtledove, and the crane, and the swallow. They all return at God's appointed time each year; but not my people! They don't accept the laws of God" (Jer. 8:7, TLB).

Human beings have few instincts of nature that birds have. But the Creator has implanted in us something He has not given the birds or any other animal—the power of moral choice. The reason He did this was so that our love for Him might arise freely from our appreciation of His character of love. Only this kind of love is worth having.

Israel made a tragic mistake by refusing to accept God's law of love. You and I can profit from their mistake.

*Throw away your gold; dump your finest gold in the dry stream bed. Let Almighty God be your gold, and let him be silver, piled high for you. Job 22:24, 25, TEV.*

OCTOBER
20

# Let God Be Your Gold

Idaho, the state in which I live, is popularly known as the "Gem State" because of its rich mineral deposits. In 1860 Captain E. D. Pierce discovered gold in Orofino Creek. News of the rich strike started a gold rush into what was then part of the Oregon Territory. Two years later more gold was discovered in what is now called Treasure Valley.

In 1896 William W. Priestly, an enterprising prospector, invented a novel way of recovering gold and used it successfully on the Snake River. It had long been known that large quantities of gold particles were washed down the creeks and rivers from the gold-yielding mountains and deposited in the gravel bars and mud flats of the various streams in Idaho. Priestly fitted suction pipes, operated by steam engines, to barges that he plied back and forth across the river. The pipes sucked up sand and gravel onto the deck. The material was then run through a sluice, and the gold-bearing gravel was diverted over tables covered with burlap and copper plates. There the precious ore was amalgamated with mercury and later extracted. The coarse stones and larger rocks were returned to the river.

Men have gone to extraordinary lengths to gain gold, sometimes sacrificing their very lives in the process. Gold, or what it represents—material wealth—exerts a kind of hypnotic spell on many minds causing them to act irrationally. Two young forty-niners were prospecting near Placerville, California. They were blood brothers and had always gotten along well, but one day they both spotted a gold nugget at the same instant. Both grabbed for it. A fight ensued and they ended up killing each other.

No earthly thing is worth losing your life over—and eternal life even more so. If material wealth is exerting an inordinate fascination on you, heed Eliphaz's counsel—dump it back into the stream and let God be your gold.

*You are to be a witness on behalf of [Christ] before all men, a witness of what you have seen and heard. Acts 22:15, Moffatt.*

# Faithful Witnessing

Dr. J. Wilbur Chapman, a celebrated evangelist of an earlier time, relates that, while studying for the ministry at a Christian college, he roomed for almost two years with a young man who did not profess to be a Christian. Tragically, during that entire period Chapman never once talked to his friend about spiritual things.

At the end of this time, having completed his course, Chapman went to tell his roommate goodbye. We can imagine his surprise when his roommate asked, "Why didn't you ever talk to me about becoming a Christian?"

Chagrined, Chapman tried to justify his failure by saying he didn't want to foist religion on someone who wasn't interested.

Said his friend, "You didn't know it, but I chose you as my roommate because I knew you were a Christian and hoped you would speak to me about what it means to follow Christ. I hesitated to bring up the subject, but not a day passed that I wouldn't have been happy to talk about it, if *you* had brought up the matter."

Chapman tried to lead his friend to Christ in the few minutes he had left. However, later events seemed to indicate he was not successful. Said he, "My failure to witness to my friend at the opportune time is one of the greatest regrets of my life."

Christ counts on each of His followers to witness to those closest to them concerning the salvation of their souls. Such witnessing is part of the Great Commission to preach the gospel (see Mark 16:15, TLB). Those who fail to fulfill this injunction may be saved, but they will suffer loss (see I Cor. 3:12-15).

How much better for you and me faithfully to witness to others, and at last hear our Master say: "Well done, thou good and faithful servant: thou hast been faithful over a few things, I will make thee ruler over many things: enter thou into the joy of thy lord" (Matt. 25:21).

*[Jesus] called his disciples together and said to them, I tell you that this poor widow put more in the offering box than all the others. For the others put in what they had to spare of their riches; but she, poor as she is, put in all she had—she gave all she had to live on."*
*Mark 12:43, 44, TEV.*

# Dedicating All to God

During the Nazi blitz of London in 1940, Matthew Sands received a telegram from the British War Office, stating that his son, David, had been reported missing and was believed dead. The report proved true. Heartbroken, Sands wrote on the back of the telegram: "All that I have and all that I am, I give to God for His service."

Not long after he received the terrible news, someone telephoned Sands to remind him he had an important engagement coming up. On his way to his appointment, he walked by an old abandoned church and noticed a sign that read, "For sale by auction." He entered the building to pray before going on, and was impressed to buy it and restore it as a house of worship. Unbeknown to him, another man, Andres Jelks, had also seen the sign and decided to buy the building and convert it into "Andy's Amusement Arcade."

On the day of the auction, both men showed up. Sands had prepared a letter with a formal bid for the property, but in his grief and confused state of mind he inadvertently handed in the wire from the War Office instead of the bid.

The auctioneer silently read the telegram as well as Sands's message dedicating his all to God's service. Finally, when all the bids were in, he announced that the church had been sold to Matthew Sands, the highest bidder. Asked why, he read the words on the back of the telegram. Those present agreed with the auctioneer's decision.

God calls for total dedication. In Mark 12:30 this complete dedication is put in these words: "Thou shalt love the Lord thy God with all thy heart, and with all thy soul, and with all thy mind, and with all thy strength." This is quite comprehensive. It encompasses all that we have and are. Nothing less is acceptable. May this be the character of your dedication and mine.

*I am well content with weaknesses . . . ; for when I am [physically] weak, then I am [spiritually] strong. 2 Cor. 12:10, NASB.*

# Infirmities Can Be an Advantage

Physical infirmities can sometimes be an advantage.

On the night of February 5, 1945, I, along with 468 internees and some 800 survivors from Bataan and Corregidor, was evacuated from Old Bilibid prison to Ang Tibay shoe factory, on the outskirts of Manila. The battle for the liberation of the city from the Japanese was on; the city was ablaze, and the fire was creeping inexorably toward our compound.

As we sat on the floor in the dark at Ang Tibay, I became acquainted with some of the survivors of the death march. For a month my group had been separated from them by a 15-foot wall; this was my first opportunity to talk with them. I learned that many of the comrades of these men had been shipped to Japan as slave laborers; the last boatload had left Manila in mid-December, and that ship had been torpedoed by an American submarine. Many on board had died.

In the group that night was a soldier who had been scheduled to go on that ship but had been left behind because of a physical disability. I shall never forget how, with tears in his voice, he told us that his life had been spared because he had been incapacitated on Bataan.

Anyone who has looked carefully at pictures of President Theodore Roosevelt knows he was nearsighted. During his 1912 presidential campaign he was shot by a maniac named Schrank, but he survived the assassination attempt. The doctor who examined Roosevelt after the incident told him his life had been spared by a pair of steel-rimmed spectacles he had in a case in his vest pocket.

"Isn't that strange," commented Roosevelt. "I've always considered it a burden to carry around two pairs of glasses because of my nearsightedness, and here the spare spectacles I had in my pocket have been the means of saving my life."

We may not realize in this life why God permits us to suffer physical afflictions. But in some cases we can be sure He permits them because He knows that, like Paul, we are spiritually stronger when we are physically weak.

# Blessed Are the Merciful

Tamatoe (Ta-ma-TOE-eh), king of Huahiné, an island about 80 miles west northwest of Tahiti, became a Christian in 1818 as a result of the labors of missionaries from the London Missionary Society. Some of Tamatoe's heathen neighbors on a nearby island hated Christianity and determined to burn Tamatoe to death, along with those who had become Christians with him.

However, the plot was discovered by the Christians, and a band of them hid near the landing site. As their enemies leaped from their canoes in the dark, they were disarmed without receiving any physical harm. Now weaponless, the heathen were sure they were going to be put to a cruel death. We can imagine their surprise when Tamatoe and his fellow Christians treated them kindly because, as they explained, Jesus taught His followers to be kind to their enemies.

But the Christians went further. They prepared a sumptuous feast and invited their erstwhile enemies to partake of it with them. At the end of the repast one of the heathen chiefs stood up and said that because of this unexpected kindness, he had decided to become a follower of Christ. Others joined him, and within days every heathen idol on their island was destroyed and the people became Christians.

The mercy that our text says will be shown the merciful is not necessarily the mercy others show us in return for the mercy we show them. Frequently the "tender mercies" of others turn out to be quite "cruel" (Prov. 12:10). So a better translation of our text probably is: "Happy are those who are merciful to others; God will be merciful to them" (Matt. 5:7, TEV).

This is the kind of unmerited favor we all need; for in a sense we are all "enemies" of God (Rom. 5:10), and He shows us mercy to the same degree that we show mercy to others. This is the same principle as God forgiving us "the wrongs we have done, as we forgive the wrongs that others have done to us" (Matt. 6:12, TEV). The Christians of Huahiné had learned and subsequently put in practice this principle.

*Judge not, that you be not judged. For with the judgment you pronounce you will be judged, and the measure you give will be the measure you get. Matt. 7:1, 2, RSV.*

# Human Judgments Are Fallible

*The Living Bible* translates the first part of this verse: "Don't criticize, and then you won't be criticized." This may be generally true, but there are exceptions. Some people who never indulge in criticism of others are criticized by others just the same. The *Good News Bible* renders the verse: "Do not judge others, so that God will not judge you." This is closer to the truth, I believe, but I think the Revised Standard Version says it best.

One of the most incredible cases of misjudgment I have ever heard of was made by Honoré de Balzac, a prolific French novelist. Besides novel writing, he fancied himself an expert in graphology—the study (no, it isn't a science) of handwriting to determine a person's character and personality.

One day a woman brought a notebook to the great writer that had some childish scrawlings in it. She asked him to analyze it.

After carefully scrutinizing the script, the learned man concluded that the child was mentally deficient; yet he wanted to be diplomatic, so he asked, "Are you the child's mother?"

"No, I am in no way related to him," she replied.

"Good."

Balzac's forehead furrowed. He was pondering: *How can I be kind and yet tell the truth?* Candor won out.

"This child's handwriting gives every indication of imbecility. I fear he will never amount to much, if anything."

"But, sir," protested the woman, "these are your scribblings. Don't you recognize your own handwriting? This was your notebook when you attended the *collége* (elementary school) of Vendôme."

Apparently, Balzac couldn't recognize his own script!

I have seen graphologists make fascinatingly shrewd "guesses"—and be right. But I have also seen them be wrong. Human judgments are fallible—and this is especially true respecting motives. Only God can read the heart; you and I cannot (see I Sam. 16:7). Is it any wonder that when we try to judge others in matters in which we are not competent, we condemn ourselves?

# Convincing Proof

When I was a teenager I decided to make my mark in the world as an artist. My father had recently purchased a three-volume set of the Bible, illustrated by Paul Gustave Doré, and these drawings had an important bearing on my decision.

Doré gained his fame by his sketches of religious and historical characters. I spent hours studying his techniques, and although my interest in art waned as time went on, I still have vivid mental images of his drawings.

On one occasion while traveling in Europe, Doré lost his passport. When he reached the next checkpoint a guard asked him for his travel documents. Doré tried to explain what had happened. "I am Paul Gustave Doré," he said, "and I have lost my passport. I hope you will be kind enough to let me pass. I have some important appointments I must meet."

"Don't try to fool us," snapped the guard. "You're not the first person to claim he lost his passport and try to pass himself off as some distinguished individual."

Doré pleaded for understanding, but in vain. Finally an officer took charge and said, "If you are indeed Doré, take this pencil and paper and sketch that group of peasants over there."

Within minutes the great artist produced a striking likeness of the group. Even before he finished, the officer, convinced he was the famous artist, allowed him to enter the country.

Some people today try to pass themselves off as Christians, but lack the brotherly love Jesus said would characterize His followers. The early Christians lived in an age when practicing their religion could mean martyrdom, yet they demonstrated their brotherly love by risking their lives to help their persecuted brethren—and in some instances won the grudging admiration of their persecutors. Tertullian, a Christian writer of the second and third centuries, quoted one pagan official as saying, "See how these Christians love one another."

Brotherly love is not a cloak "put on" to convince unbelievers, but a quality that springs naturally from a heart of love.

*People will hide in caves in the rocky hills or dig holes in the ground to try to escape from the Lord's anger . . . , when he comes to shake the earth. Isa. 2:19, TEV.*

# Where Will the Lord Find You?

My freshman year in high school was spent in a small Christian boarding academy in the hills of western North Carolina. A fellow student told me one day that up on the mountain behind the school was a cave in which a Confederate deserter had hidden out during the Civil War. My friend gave me directions for finding the place, and one day I went up there alone and actually located the cave.

I had imagined it would be a light, large, comfortable cavern, with an abundant water supply. It wasn't. The roof was barely high enough to stand up under, and it was dismally dark. But there was evidence of human habitation. How, I puzzled, could this troglodyte survive in such primitive conditions? Later I was told that there was a natural spring not far from the cave, and that the man raided the local farms at night for food and other necessities.

Besides this nameless soldier, there were others who deserted during the Civil War. Two such men hid out in a valley in the same general area—and didn't know that the war was over until two years after hostilities had ceased.

The Bible tells us that when Christ comes the second time there will be two classes of people: those who hide themselves in the dens and caves of the earth because they are unprepared to meet Him, and those who look up into the heavens and say with gladness, "Lo, this is our God; we have waited for him, and he will save us: this is the Lord; . . . we will be glad and rejoice in his salvation" (Isa. 25:9).

The way you and I live today will determine in which group we will find ourselves on that tomorrow. We can be either among the "spelunkers," who hide "themselves in the dens and in the rocks of the mountains," and cry out "to the mountains and rocks, Fall on us, and hide us from the face of him that sitteth on the throne, and from the wrath of the Lamb" (Rev. 6:15, 16), or among those who meet the Lord in peace. The choice is ours.

*As lawlessness spreads, the love of many will grow cold. But whoever endures to the end will be saved. Matt. 24:12, 13, REB.*

# How to Keep From Growing Cold

In 1776 James Cook, famed British naval captain and explorer, was commissioned by his government to lead an expedition that would settle the question of whether or not there was a navigable passage between the Pacific and Atlantic oceans via the northern coast of Canada. The expedition set out from Plymouth, England, July 12, 1776. Among its members was Dr. Solander, a Swedish naturalist, whose assignment was to make scientific observations of the flora and fauna encountered along the way.

In the fall of 1779 the expedition searched the area around Bering Strait. There a party, under the command of a Lieutenant Hodder and including Dr. Solander, set up a camp and moved inland. An early winter storm caught the men by surprise far from their encampment and threatened them with death by freezing. Because of his experience with cold weather in his native Sweden, Solander called the men together and cautioned them against the dangers of hypothermia.

"We must resolutely set our faces to get back to camp with never a stop," he warned. "Our great danger is falling asleep and never waking up."

"I suppose we shall get horribly tired," commented Hodder.

"Of course we shall," said Solander. "As their blood grows cold, the men will beg to be allowed to rest. Do not permit them to stop for a moment. Urge them on with blows—with bayonets, if necessary. To give in to the desire to sleep will be fatal."

The members of Hodder's party heeded the doctor's admonition and made it back to their camp without the loss of a man.

Jesus has warned that as we approach the end of the age, iniquity, or lawlessness, will increase, and the love of many of His followers will grow cold as they absorb the spirit of the world around them. We see this happening today—Christians falling asleep as they conform more and more to the world.

What can we do individually to avoid this fate? Resolutely set our faces Zionward, meanwhile encouraging others along the way by our example.

*[Abraham] made his home in the promised land like a stranger in a foreign country; he lived in tents. . . . For he was looking forward to the city with foundations, whose architect and builder is God. Heb. 11:9, 10, NIV.*

# The City With Foundations

A few years ago the producers of the famous Rand McNally maps surveyed living conditions in all the larger cities of the United States and came to the conclusion that Yuba City, California, had the worst living conditions. Pittsburgh, Pennsylvania, was rated the best. The Yuba City people were understandably unhappy with the survey, perhaps justifiably so.

Not long ago I read that cities all over the world are deteriorating rapidly in a physical way. In New York, for instance, the pipes conducting water into the city are in such bad shape that, should they break, the city would be faced with a major catastrophe. Replacing them would be so expensive it has virtually been ruled out as a viable solution.

But the cities are not merely degenerating physically. They are declining morally and spiritually as well—and unfortunately, this deterioration is also infecting smaller cities. According to a divine survey made of the major cities of earth many years ago, not one of them is an ideal place in which to live—and the counsel given is to move out of them as quickly and judiciously as possible (see *Country Living*, by Ellen G. White).

Notice these words of counsel and warning in this book: "Our cities are increasing in wickedness, and it is becoming more and more evident that those who remain in them unnecessarily do so at the peril of their soul's salvation" (p. 9).

The city Abraham looked forward to living in had "foundations." This is seen as a reference to the New Jerusalem (see Rev. 21). God's Word assures us that "there shall in no wise enter into it any thing that defileth, neither whatsoever worketh abomination, or maketh a lie: but they which are written in the Lamb's book of life" (Rev. 21:27).

What a pleasure it will be to live in that city. Our sojourn here on earth is a preparation for becoming dwellers in that grand metropolis.

*Just as a father has compassion on his children, so the Lord has compassion on those who fear Him. For He Himself knows our frame; He is mindful that we are but dust.*
*Ps. 103:13, 14, NASB.*

# God's Solution for Despondency

If anyone ever had good reasons for feeling on top of the world, it was Elijah. At his word rain had not fallen for three and a half years (see James 5:17). In answer to his prayer, lightning flashed from a cloudless sky and consumed his sacrifice. He prayed, and it rained again (see verse 18 and 1 Kings 18:36-39, 45). Exuberant with success, he ran ahead of Ahab's chariot from the summit of Carmel "to the entrance of Jezreel" (verse 46).

But soon after his mountaintop experience, Elijah found himself wallowing in the slough of despondency. How can we account for this mood swing? Is it possible that after the Lord had worked so mightily through him he had begun to think that the power given him to do these things was his in his own right? Or was he simply experiencing a natural reaction to his physical exertion in running from Carmel to Jezreel? Or could it have been a case of self-pity because of Ahab's and Jezebel's ingratitude?

Whatever the reason, I like the way God dealt with His despondent servant. You remember, He spoke to Elijah on Mount Horeb in a still, small voice.

I can imagine God putting His arm around Elijah and saying, "What are you doing here, Elijah? You've been trying to do My job instead of letting Me handle it. Leave Jezebel and her wicked followers for Me to take care of."

And I can hear Elijah answer, "Lord, I've been very zealous for You, and I'm the only faithful one left in all Israel, and look, they are trying to kill me!"

Then I can hear God responding, "What you don't realize, Elijah, is that I still have 7,000 left in Israel who have not bowed their knee to Baal. My son, forget yourself. I have much work left for you to do."

Have you ever felt like Elijah? Isn't it wonderful that we have a heavenly Father who knows our frame and treats the despondent with compassion?

*Remember the words of the Lord Jesus, that He said, "It is more blessed to give than to receive." Acts 20:35, NKJV.*

# Treat Rather Than Trick

A young high school student took a walk one day with one of his teachers who was noted for his fairness in dealing with the young people in his classes. As the two walked along, they came across a pair of old shoes lying alongside the path. Seeing a laborer working in a nearby field, they assumed the shoes belonged to him. The man was just ending his day's work.

Turning to his teacher, the student chuckled, "Let's play a trick on the old duffer. Let's hide his shoes, conceal ourselves behind these bushes, and watch his bewilderment when he can't find them."

"Do you really think we should do that?" asked the teacher. "Let me make a different suggestion. Why not surprise the old fellow by putting a silver dollar in each shoe, then watch his reaction when he finds the money?"

The student wasn't exactly enthusiastic, but he went along with the idea.

When the poor man finished his work and slipped his shoes on, he felt something hard inside. Surprised, he looked at the coins, then fell to his knees and thanked God for providing money he desperately needed for his family.

"Don't you feel happier," whispered the professor, "for having helped the old fellow rather than playing a trick on him?"

The student had to agree.

This evening many children in America will go out trick or treating. Usually they go in groups from house to house soliciting fruit or candy. Some of these children will show their displeasure at what they get by doing "dirty tricks." And, sad to say, in some cases, adults have been known to do "dirty tricks" on the children, such as slipping razor blades and even poison into the food they give them.

As Christians let us remember not only that it is more blessed to give than to receive, but also to do unto others as we would have them do unto us.

*Faith is the assurance (the confirmation, the title-deed) of the things [we] hope for, being the proof of things [we] do not see and the conviction of their reality—faith perceiving as real fact what is not revealed to the senses.*
*Heb. 11:1, Amplified.*

# Seeing the Unseen

Even before there were telescopes powerful enough to see the planet Pluto, Percival Lowell, an American astronomer, believed that such a planet existed in our solar system. He arrived at this conclusion more than 15 years before the planet was discovered by Clyde W. Tombaugh on February 18, 1930.

Lowell's belief was no haphazard guess. He arrived at his conclusion through systematic observation and careful calculation of the orbits of Neptune and Uranus. The perturbations he observed in their orbits convinced him that there must be a trans-Neptunian planet. So confident was Lowell of its existence that he gave the first two letters of the name of the yet-to-be-discovered planet the initial letters of his name—P and L. He also predicted that the planet would be found near the star Delta Geminorum. His belief was confirmed after his death when Tombaugh photographed and studied the Geminorum region of the sky and discovered the predicted planet.

Faith in the reality of heaven, like Lowell's belief in the existence of Pluto, is not a haphazard guess. It always rests on the underlying "assurance" of sufficient evidence to warrant confidence in what is not seen. *Hupostasis*, the Greek word translated "assurance" in *The Amplified Bible,* is used in the ancient papyri to mean a legal document by which a person proved ownership of a piece of property. In other words, a title deed.

By exercising faith, you and I can consider ourselves already in possession of the wonderful things that God has promised. This enables us not only to claim promised blessings to come, but to receive and enjoy them now. In this way, that which the natural eye cannot perceive (1 Cor. 2:14) is visible to the eye of faith.

# 2

*We were as gentle with you as a nurse caring for her children. Our affection was so deep that we were determined to share with you not only the gospel of God but our very selves.*
*1 Thess. 2:7, 8, REB.*

# Needed: "Aunt Hannahs"

Shortly after the turn of the twentieth century, a sociology class at Johns Hopkins University made a study of the children of the worst slum section of Baltimore. The students in the class visited the homes of these children, noted the good and evil influences surrounding them, and tabulated their findings on cards. Two hundred of these cards were marked "Headed for jail." The cards were then filed for future reference and study.

Twenty-five years later another class at the same university was looking for a study to do and came across these cards. They decided to find these people and discover what had happened to them. Finding them was not an easy job, but they were able to locate every one. They were stunned by what they found. Only two of the 200 had spent time in jail! How, the students of the second class wondered, could the students of the first class have been so wrong?

Aunt Hannah was the reason. This woman was an elementary school teacher in Baltimore's slum section who took a personal interest in her pupils. Time after time the testimony of those she influenced was the same: "I was headed for jail, no doubt about it, but Aunt Hannah got hold of me and started me in the right direction, and that made all the difference."

When asked to account for her success, Aunt Hannah modestly replied, "Oh, I just loved them as if they were my own children. You see, I never had any boys and girls of my own, so they were all mine, in a way."

What a noble spirit!

Today, almost a century later, America's children are in deep trouble. And not only American children—worldwide, delinquency among the underprivileged, and even among the well-to-do, is on the rise. Modern "Aunt Hannahs" could make a difference. Is it possible that God is calling you to this kind of work? If He is, would He find you willing to share yourself with these children?

*I bear them witness that they have a [certain] zeal and enthusiasm for God, but it is not enlightened and according to [correct and vital] knowledge. Rom. 10:2, Amplified.*

NOVEMBER

3

# Zeal Not According to Knowledge

For a couple years my father, when he was in his early 20s, worked as a desk clerk in a large hotel in New York City. One night while he was on duty someone apparently dropped some smoldering material into a trash can containing paper. Suddenly these materials caught fire and threatened to set the building ablaze. Dad phoned the fire department at once, but one of the guests, a man old enough to know better, whipped off his coat and began flailing the flames, scattering the fire in every direction. In a few moments the lobby turned into a raging inferno.

Fortunately the fire department responded promptly and was able to put the fire out quickly—but not before it had done far more damage than it would have if the man had simply waited and let the fire fighters do their job. As for the zealous patron, he not only ended up with a ruined coat, but received a lecture from the fire chief for his efforts. Here was a man who demonstrated "zeal . . . , but not according to knowledge" (Rom. 10:2, NKJV).

There are some professed Christians who seem to be inspired by great zeal for God yet fail to exercise good judgment when they speak. Doubtless you have seen and heard such individuals. In a meeting they speak to an issue with such intemperate language that it sets passions ablaze and damages a good cause—perhaps the very cause for which they stand. Frequently such people never seem to recognize their own shortcomings.

James speaks to this point in his Epistle: "The tongue proves a very world of mischief among our members, staining the whole of the body and setting fire to the round circle of existence with a flame fed by hell" (James 3:6, Moffatt). In this connection, the wise Solomon gives good counsel: there is "a time to keep silence, and a time to speak" (Eccl. 3:7). To the last phrase he might have added, "with good judgment."

If you sense that you lack wisdom and good judgment, one of the best places to find these is in God's Word.

*The share of the man who stayed with the supplies is to be the same as that of him who went down to the battle. All will share alike.*
*1 Sam. 30:24, NIV.*

# Holders-on Reward

A book on labor conditions in British shipyards mentions two classes of workmen; the first are known as "riveters," and the others as "holders-on." We all know who the riveters are. The ear-splitting blows of their pneumatic hammers ring out from every new vessel under construction. The holders-on, whose pincers grip the red-hot steel bolts and hold them steady for the riveters are less dramatic, less acclaimed.

The two classes of workers are similar to Christians who labor in the Lord's cause. Some, like the riveters, seem to work in the limelight and receive all the glory. Others, like the holders-on, make no fuss, but are absolutely essential for getting the work done—yet get little or no credit.

In the parable of the laborers, the workmen who were hired in the morning agreed to work in the vineyard for a denarius—an ordinary day's pay. Those who were hired later in the day, even the eleventh-hour laborers, were promised they would be paid what was right. At the end of the day, when the landowner paid his men and gave the latecomers the same pay as those who had worked all day, those who worked longer complained that they should have been paid more. This parable, Jesus explained, represents "the kingdom of heaven."

Now, we are not to suppose that on the day when rewards are given out those who have labored more without receiving special consideration or, to change the figure, have been the "holders-on," will complain that eternal life is not enough, that they should receive more "pay," or credit. After all, parables were not intended to "walk on all fours." The point is that everyone who is saved will receive the same reward—eternal life. I suppose that anyone dissatisfied with this reward would probably not even be around to receive it. All of us, I am sure, will be happy just to realize that we have been eternally saved. If some in this life seem to have gotten more credit than others, what is that compared to the "eternal weight of glory" that will be the reward of the faithful (2 Cor. 4:17)?

# Are You Afraid to Witness?

Jeremiah was an "ochlophobe." He feared facing crowds. So it is not surprising to learn that he didn't want to be a prophet. Being a prophet meant witnessing to people. He pleaded that he was too young and suffered from ochlophobia.

My mother once told me about the worst case of stage fright she ever saw. One of the requirements for a college speech course was to give a talk before the class. When one young man's turn came, he strutted up to the lectern, seemingly full of confidence, but suddenly he panicked. He never got a word out. He turned deathly pale and fled from the classroom in humiliation. Everyone was embarrassed for him. Then someone quipped, "If Bob had gone up the way he came down, he might have come down the way he went up." That broke the tension.

David Livingstone, famous missionary-explorer of Africa, is remembered for his courage in the face of danger. But did you know that as a young man he suffered from ochlophobia?

On one occasion, after agreeing to preach in a little kirk, he was seized with such panic that he left town. When his friends discovered his absence, they went looking for him. They finally found him, but he refused to return. Then one of them reminded him of Jesus' promise: "I will never leave thee, nor forsake thee" (Heb. 13:5). Taking these words of assurance personally, Livingstone returned and spoke with such convicting power that several of those present were converted.

Are you like Jeremiah? Have you ever passed up an opportunity to witness for Christ because you had ochlophobia? Take heart. Here are some things you can do to overcome stage fright: (1) prepare carefully, (2) tense and relax your muscles several times before facing your audience, and (3) take some deep breaths before speaking.

But there are two other things you can do that are even more important: (1) become so wrapped up in witnessing for God that self is *forgotten*, and (2) *remember* that God promises never to leave you nor forsake you. When you stand before people in this frame of mind, you will "not be afraid of their faces."

*I cried unto the Lord with my voice, and he heard me out of his holy hill. Ps. 3:4.*

# Things Wrought by Prayer

Have you ever heard someone say (or perhaps said it yourself) "I can pray only when I feel like it"? To say this is to misunderstand the purpose of prayer. It bases prayer on feelings, and feelings change. They are unreliable. They frequently fluctuate with the weather, the news, our state of health. Our prayer life must rest on a more secure foundation than feelings. Prayer can so align our will with God's will that He can open channels through which to work that otherwise would be closed. So we need to pray more earnestly when we don't feel like it than when we do.

Dr. Alexis Carrel, French-American surgeon and Nobel laureate (in 1912 he won the coveted prize for physiology), has left the following testimony respecting the power of prayer:

"Prayer is the most powerful form of energy that one can generate. The influence of prayer on the mind and body is as demonstrable as that of secreting glands. Its results can be measured in terms of increased buoyancy, greater intellectual vigor, moral stamina, and a deeper understanding of human relationships.

"Prayer is indispensable to the fullest development of personality. Only in prayer do we achieve that complete harmonious assembly of mind, body, and spirit. . . . When we pray, we link ourselves with the inexhaustible motive [power] that spins the universe."

What a challenge!

In his poem "Morte D'Arthur," Tennyson states: "More things are wrought by prayer than this world dreams of." But the greatest change brought about by prayer is not in God, for He never changes (Mal. 3:6); rather, it is in us. Although God sometimes intervenes directly in human affairs in miraculous ways, He usually brings about change by altering our spiritual outlook. According to Dr. Carrel, our altered spiritual outlook actually changes our mental condition and, in turn, our physiological processes in remarkable ways.

As you pray today, link yourself with the inexhaustible Source of power that spins the universe.

*He who goes forth weeping, carrying seed for sowing, shall doubtless come again with joy, carrying his sheaves. Ps. 126:6, MLB.*

NOVEMBER

7

# Joy at Harvesttime

Thomas Johannes Bach, an engineering student, was walking down one of the streets of Copenhagen one day when a teenager approached him and held out a gospel tract. "Would you accept this little leaflet?" asked the boy. "It has a message for you."

Glancing at the tract, Thomas saw that it was religious. He wasn't interested and bristled at the idea of someone stopping him on the street and offering him a tract. "Why do you bother people with your religion?" he demanded. "I'm quite able to take care of myself."

When the boy continued to hold out the tract to him, Thomas snatched it from his hand, tore it up, and stuffed it in his pocket. The boy turned and walked sadly away. But now Thomas couldn't take his eyes off the boy.

Stepping into a doorway, the teenager bowed his head. As Thomas watched he saw tears course down the boy's cheeks. Thomas's heart was touched. Here was someone who cared enough for his soul to offer him a tract, and he had rejected it. From that moment on, Thomas's life took a different course. Instead of becoming an engineer, he became a missionary.

Some, reading about this boy's method of witnessing, may fault him for "foisting" his religion on others—and maybe he was! Some may conclude that the boy shed tears because his feelings were hurt, not because he was concerned about Thomas's soul—and they may be right! And some may see in the boy's tears a genuine concern for souls who will someday cry, "The harvest is past, the summer is ended, and we are not saved" (Jer. 8:20)—*and they may be right!* But why not give the boy the benefit of the doubt?

Witnessing for Christ should be winsome and inoffensive, and tears, if shed, should be out of concern for souls, not self. But who can gainsay that the Holy Spirit used this boy to win a soul to Christ? Are you and I doing as much for Him?

I can't help believing that in the great harvest day at the end of the world (see Matt. 13:39) this boy will come rejoicing, bringing with him his "sheaf" of souls.

*Evening, and morning, and at noon, will I pray, and cry aloud: and he shall hear my voice. Ps. 55:17.*

# Calls to Prayer

It seems apparent from the above verse that the psalmist made it a practice to pray three times a day.

When I visited Egypt some years ago, I learned that Muslims pray five times a day. One day our tour group visited a mosque in Cairo. When it came time for prayer, a muezzin high up on the balcony of one of the mosque's minarets called the faithful to prayer in a high-pitched, quavering voice. In response, the followers of "the prophet" stopped whatever they were doing and laid out their prayer mats. Facing toward Mecca, they bowed in prayer. Out of respect, our group paused and at least some of us prayed.

As I stood there meditating, the thought struck me: *These Muslims put us Christians to shame. Most of us don't pray even as often as the psalmist did.* And then the thought: *Can Christians afford to pray less often than the Muslims?*

No, surely we cannot. This doesn't mean that every time we pray we have to unroll a prayer mat and genuflect, but it surely would be well if we directed our thoughts heavenward three, five, or even more times a day.

Have you considered that every circumstance in a Christian's life is a call to prayer? Not only should we pray in times of crisis; we should especially pray when everything seems to be going well—perhaps too well. It is at these times that we tend to forget to depend on God. It is also at these times that Satan surreptitiously usurps that place in our hearts that rightfully belongs to the Lord.

No, we need not physically bow every time we pray, but if we want to maintain our spiritual health we must live in an attitude of prayer.

"We may commune with God in our hearts. . . . When engaged in our daily labor, we may breathe out our heart's desire, inaudible to any human ear; but that word cannot die away into silence, nor can it be lost. . . . It rises above the din of the street, above the noise of machinery. It is God to whom we are speaking, and our prayer is heard" *(Gospel Workers,* p. 258).

*The Lord's arm is not so short that he cannot save nor his ear too dull to hear; it is your iniquities that raise a barrier between you and your God, because of your sins he has hidden his face so that he does not hear you.*
*Isa. 59:1, 2, NEB.*

# Why God Doesn't Always Hear

Soon after I began dating Vesta, now my wife, we stopped at her grandmother's place in Lodi, California. During our visit, Grandma Sanford served us some of her delicious homemade, whole-wheat bread. Next time we called, Grandma was sick abed. We talked to her for a while, then went into the kitchen, where my mouth got to watering for a piece of her tasty bread. I quietly asked Vesta where she kept it, hoping I'd be offered a slice.

"It's in the earthenware jar under the cupboard by the sink," I was startled to hear Grandma say.

I could not believe it. I had spoken in an undertone, and Grandma, some 25 feet from us, two rooms away, heard!

"Can she hear us?" I mouthed the words to Vesta.

Vesta nodded Yes.

Next time we visited Grandma and went to her kitchen, I took the precaution of whispering my "needs" to Vesta. Well, Grandma couldn't make out what I said, but she heard me whisper. She called out from her bedroom, "Don, if it isn't worth saying out loud, it's not worth saying!"

Sometimes when my prayers haven't been answered, I've wondered if God's hearing isn't somewhat less acute than Grandma's. Have you ever felt that way?

Does God really hear our prayers? Of course He does! "He that planted the ear, shall he not hear?" (Ps. 94:9). Why, then, doesn't He always answer us?

When God doesn't seem to hear and answer our prayers, there are two reasons: either our prayers are "hindered" by cherished sin (see 1 Peter 3:7), or we ask with the wrong motive (see James 4:3). In other words, we ask, but not according to *God's* will (1 John 5:14).

So if you want God always to hear and answer your prayers, confess and forsake known sin and submit your will to His will, realizing that He knows best.

*Teach me to do thy will, thou art my God;
guide me by thy good Spirit on a straight
road. Ps. 143:10, Moffatt.*

# Line Up the Lights

One dark and starless night many years ago, Dr. F. B. Meyer was crossing St. George's Channel from Dublin to Holyhead Harbor in Wales when he began to wonder how a vessel traveling on such a night could possibly make it into port without losing its way. The captain was standing nearby, so he asked him.

"Do you see those three lights?" returned the captain.

"Yes," replied Dr. Meyer.

"Well, the pilot must line up the ship so that those three lights appear as one. When they do, we know the exact position of the harbor's mouth."

Something similar is true in the spiritual realm. When we ask God to answer prayer, three things must always "line up": 1. Is our prayer in harmony with God's will as revealed in His Word? 2. Will the answer to our prayer bring glory to God? 3. Are we willing to wait for God to answer our prayer in His own good time and way? When these three "guiding lights" line up, we can rest in the assurance that our prayers will always be answered to our best and eternal good.

The Bible speaks of those who pray "amiss" (James 4:3). I recently read of an incident that illustrates this point. A young, unmarried pastor had been praying for the perfect wife when he came across an article in a Christian singles magazine written by a woman. Thoughts began stirring in the young man's head. The author seemed to fit his ideal perfectly. He wrote a letter to the magazine's editor, stating that he was sure the author of the article was God's answer to his prayer, and asking for the woman's address. You can imagine his surprise and chagrin when he read the editor's reply—the woman was already married!

This young pastor was apparently sincere. But sincere or not, he had failed to follow the guidelines for effective prayer. Is it any wonder God could not answer his prayer? When you and I ask God to answer our prayers, we must always make sure (before we launch out on a foolish course of action) that we are lined up with His three guiding lights.

# Prayer, the Breath of the Soul

I can almost hear someone say, "It is impossible to pray without ceasing."

Well, in certain parts of Europe and Asia there is a spider called *Argyroneta aquatica,* which spends a considerable part of its life under water. That's where it "makes its living." From time to time it comes to the surface, breathes in some fresh air, a bubble forms about it, and it returns to the bottom of the pond or stream, where it remains for a period of time. When it again comes to the surface, it is perfectly dry and clean. Although it spends most of its time at the bottom of the stream or pond, it remains untouched by the water and mud around it. Why? Because it is enveloped in a capsule of air from above!

Air from above!

Observe that after the little spider has taken a breath of fresh air and becomes surrounded by air, it continues to breathe the atmosphere in which it is enveloped. Even so in the spiritual life. When we direct our thoughts toward heaven the first thing in the morning and breathe in its atmosphere, we need to become surrounded by it. This means more than taking a quick gulp of spiritual air. It means communing with God until our spiritual life is charged with vitality. Then throughout the day we continue to breathe the air with which we have become surrounded. This "air" is the breath of the soul. It needs to be replenished periodically.

Just as our physical life depends on breathing, so our spiritual life depends on praying. One surrounded by spiritual air breathes it as naturally as he breathes physical air. This is what is meant by praying without ceasing.

We live in a world filled with spiritual and moral corruption, but just as the spider does not become contaminated with the mud that surrounds it, so the Christian, surrounded by the atmosphere of heaven, remains uncorrupted by the world.

Breathe deeply of heaven's pure air in the morning and continue to breathe it from time to time throughout the day from the spiritual atmosphere that surrounds you.

*Let us not give up meeting together, as some are in the habit of doing, but let us encourage one another—and all the more as you see the Day [of Christ's coming] approaching.*
**Heb. 10:25, NIV.**

# Church Attendance

Michael Faraday, a great British scientist who made several important discoveries in the field of magnetism, was an earnest Christian who placed attendance at the services of his church above attendance at any other meeting. In one of these "other" meetings he held an audience spellbound with a demonstration of the properties of a magnet. He brought his lecture to a close with an experiment so novel, so fascinating, so thrilling, that for some time the lecture hall reverberated with enthusiastic applause.

When the clapping subsided, the prince of Wales stood and proposed a toast to Faraday, but the great man was not around to respond. Finally, one of Faraday's associates rose and explained that the physicist had left for prayer meeting at the little Sandemanian church—a congregation that never boasted more than 20 members—where Faraday was an elder.

What an example of faithful attendance at prayer meeting! What a witness for Christ!

It has been said that the spiritual health of a church can be accurately gauged by attendance at prayer meeting. If this is true, churches with low attendance are on the verge of spiritual death, and others that have given up prayer meeting altogether may have already crossed over the great divide.

What can you do, what can I do, to arouse Christians from this deadly lethargy? What can we do to "strengthen the things which remain, that are ready to die" (Rev. 3:2)?

Our verse for meditation suggests that the greatest motive for faithful attendance at church services is the fact that "the day" of Christ's coming is "nearer than when we first believed. The night is far spent, the day is at hand" (Rom. 13:11, 12, NKJV). The signs of the times tell us so!

In view of the nearness of Christ's coming and the admonition to be faithful in church attendance, how inconsistent it would be for one who professes to believe in the Second Advent to be careless about his church attendance.

*For preaching the good news I claim no glory, for I am under compulsion to do so. It is woe to me if I do not preach the good news.*
*1 Cor. 9:16, MLB.*

NOVEMBER

13

# A Compulsion to Preach the Gospel

Most people are probably familiar with the fact that some 75 years after the sinking of the S.S. *Titanic,* its wreckage was discovered at the bottom of the North Atlantic and photographed. It was not in the location it had been believed to be for all those years. As I write, it has just been announced on the radio that a recently completed investigation shows that the claim made by the captain of the S.S. *Californian* that his ship was "too far" from the *Titanic* to rescue its passengers was false. If that conclusion is true, what an awful example of crass indifference. But, thank God, not all were as unconcerned as this captain for the 1,500 souls that perished that night.

Four years after the *Titanic* went down, a young Scotsman stood up in a meeting in Hamilton, Ontario, and said, "I am a survivor of the *Titanic.* As I was drifting alone, clinging to a spar, the currents brought John Harper, the preacher from Glasgow, close to where I was. 'Man,' he asked, 'are you saved?'

" 'No,' I replied, 'I am not.'

" ' "Believe on the Lord Jesus Christ, and thou shalt be saved," ' he urged. Then we drifted apart.

"But strange to say, a little later the waves brought us together again, and he asked, 'Are you saved now?'

"I had to answer, 'No, I cannot honestly say that I am.'

"He simply repeated, ' "Believe on the Lord Jesus Christ, and thou shalt be saved." '

"Soon after this we were separated for the last time. It was after this that, alone in the night, I accepted Jesus Christ as my Saviour. I am John Harper's last convert."

This is the kind of burden for souls that Paul had when he said, "Woe is me if I do not preach the gospel!" (1 Cor. 9:16, NKJV). This is the kind of burden all Christians should have. It is true that we have not all been given the same talents, but we are all to use the talents that have been given in helping to save others.

*It is God who avenges me, . . . He delivers me from my enemies. You also lift me up above those who rise against me; You have delivered me from the violent man. Ps. 18:47, 48, NKJV.*

# The Real Rebel Caught

In the latter half of the sixteenth century, during what was known as "the killing time" in Scotland, John Welsh (or Welsche), a Covenantor preacher and son-in-law of Scottish reformer John Knox, was pursued mercilessly by those who wished to take his life. For a long time he managed to elude his pursuers, but finally there seemed to be no safe place to go. He prayed, and believed God gave him a plan to outwit his enemies.

That night Welsh knocked at the door of a man who was well known for his bitter opposition to the so-called field preachers, a man who was seeking to arrest Welsh but who had never met him. Unrecognized by the householder, Welsh was received with kindness. During the evening the conversation turned to the hated Welsh. His host complained bitterly that he had not been able to apprehend this man whom he considered a rebel and an agent of Satan.

"I have been commissioned," said Welsh, "to apprehend these people. I know where Welsh is going to preach tomorrow. If you like, I will put him in your hands."

"Nothing could please me better," said his host.

The next day Welsh and his host walked to the place where the Covenantors had agreed to meet. Welsh invited his host to sit in the only chair available—one Welsh had especially provided for him. Then he began to preach about God's love for sinners. He spoke with such persuasive power and pathos that his enemy's heart was melted.

At the close of the meeting Welsh said, "Sir, I am Welsh. Take and arrest me, and do whatever you wish."

His former enemy, now his friend and convert, declined!

"When in faith we take hold of [God's] strength, He will change, wonderfully change, the most hopeless, discouraging outlook. He will do this for the glory of His name. God calls upon His faithful ones, who believe in Him, to talk courage to those who are unbelieving and hopeless" (*Christian Service*, p. 234).

These words should encourage us when the outlook seems dark.

*Moab from the first has lain at ease, never known exile afar, lain like wine on the lees, never poured from jar to jar, that tastes the same as ever, and its scent mellows never.*
*Jer. 48:11, Moffatt.*

NOVEMBER

15

# Have You Been Decanted?

From time immemorial vintners have endeavored to improve the "bouquet" of wines by decanting them—pouring them from one vessel into another in order to discard the lees, or sediment. Unremoved, these dregs are said to give the wine a bad taste. So it is in the Christian life. God permits us to be decanted, not to harm us, but to improve our characters.

Years ago when our family lived in the Azores Islands, I observed a method the local wine makers had of improving their so-called *vinho de cheiro* (literally, "wine that smells"). They filled casks with new wine and suspended them by chains attached to the undercarriage of a horse or bullock cart. As the vehicles jostled along the rough cobblestone streets, the sloshing back and forth of the spirits within the casks was supposed to improve the flavor of the potion. After this it was decanted.

Having never sampled the product of this process, I cannot vouch for any improvement in flavor, but I can assure you that its *aroma* could be detected "a mile away."

Our verse brings out the thought that the Moabites, having never learned dependence on God by being disturbed, did not give off a fragrance that was pleasing to Him. Trying experiences by themselves do not make us acceptable to God. It all depends on how we relate to them. J. B. Phillips puts it this way in his paraphrase of Hebrews 12:11: "No 'chastening' seems pleasant at the time: it is in fact most unpleasant. Yet when it is all over we can see that it has quietly produced the fruit of real goodness in the characters of those who have accepted it."

Have you ever wondered why you were being jostled and decanted by trials over which you had no control? There is nothing unusual or "strange" about this (see 1 Peter 4:12). But the question is How did you relate to these adversities? By viewing them in a positive light, they can teach you greater dependence on God.

*God keeps faith, and he will not allow you to be tested above your powers, but when the test comes he will at the same time provide a way out, by enabling you to sustain it.*
*1 Cor. 10:13, NEB.*

# God Knows Your Plimsoll Mark

I first noticed the Plimsoll mark on the sides of British ships in the harbor of Funchal, Madeira Islands. It was many years, however, before these markings took on significance. These curious lines and circles, as you may know, indicate a ship's safe load capacity in waters of various temperatures and salinity.

Samuel Plimsoll, who devised this mark, was a British politician and social reformer. He was especially concerned with unseaworthy, overloaded vessels known as "coffin ships." In 1875 a bill was introduced into Parliament, which he considered inadequate but which he went along with until something better could be arranged. However, when Prime Minister Disraeli dropped the bill from consideration, Plimsoll thought that was too much and he called the members of Parliament "villains." Plimsoll lost that round, but the country shared his views and the shortly thereafter Parliament passed a bill requiring ships to carry his mark.

God has placed a "mark" on each one of us similar to the Plimsoll mark. The trials and temptations He permits us to bear may sometimes seem to overload our little ship, but He knows our limitations and does something no Plimsoll mark could ever do. When our load is too heavy, He invites us to cast our burden upon Himself, with the assurance that He will sustain us (see Ps. 55:22; cf. Deut. 33:27). What more could one ask? Listen:

"He is watching over you, trembling child of God. Are you tempted? He will deliver. Are you weak? He will strengthen. Are you ignorant? He will enlighten. Are you wounded? He will heal. . . . 'Come unto Me,' is His invitation. Whatever your anxieties and trials, spread out your case before the Lord. Your spirit will be braced for endurance. The way will be opened for you to disentangle yourself from embarrassment and difficulty" (*The Desire of Ages,* p. 329).

Yes, God knows your "Plimsoll" capacity, and remember: "Underneath are the everlasting arms" (Deut. 33:27).

*A good man takes care of his animals, but
wicked men are cruel to theirs.
Prov. 12:10, TEV.*

NOVEMBER
17

# Cruelty Will Be Recompensed

When I was about 9 years old, our family lived in the Madeira Islands. The streets of Funchal, the capital, were paved with cobblestones (they still are), and much of the transportation in the island was done on sleds dragged over these stones. The sleds had long steel runners and were drawn by horses or mules. The drivers of these sleds reduced the friction on the runners by greasing them periodically with beef suet wrapped in gunny sacks.

One day as I walked along one of the streets of the city, I came across a crowd watching a man with a team of horses and one of these sleds trying to move a large shed that was sitting on the cement sidewalk. I stopped to watch also. The driver had attached long, heavy ropes from the collar harnesses to the sled and was beating his horses unmercifully. My heart went out to those poor creatures. Strain as they might, they could not budge the load.

While the driver considered his next move, the ropes slackened momentarily. The driver turned and began to step across the ropes, apparently to lash one of the horses he thought was malingering. His movement startled the animals. They lurched, pulling the ropes taut. Quick as a flash the man was hurled into the air. The image of him coming down headfirst is indelibly etched in my memory. He landed on his head and was badly injured. I winced, but I must confess that, in my childish mind, I also was pleased that he had gotten a taste of his own "medicine."

A Christian should never rejoice at another's misfortune— even if it is the person's own fault (see Prov. 24:17). After all, vengeance belongs to God. But on the other hand, abusing animals is wrong, and God holds those who practice it accountable. If a sparrow does "not fall on the ground without" our heavenly Father's notice (Matt. 10:29), surely He notices the way we treat His other creatures.

But if this is true, should we not treat with kindness our fellow beings who "are of more value than many sparrows"? (verse 31).

331

*Conduct yourselves as citizens of Christ that are worthy of the Gospel, . . . standing firm in one spirit and one mind, as you are joined in conflict for the faith of the Gospel, not for a moment intimidated by the antagonists.*
**Phil. 1:27, 28, MLB.**

# The Cost of Conscientious Convictions

Sam Houston, Texas statesman and general, was known for defending unpopular causes, even when it cost him dearly. At a time when it was unpopular to defend American Indians, he went to Washington as member of a Cherokee delegation to complain to the government about the corrupt practices of Indian agents. He opposed slavery at a time when it was unpopular to do so. On March 18, 1861, he was deposed as state governor because he opposed secession and refused to swear allegiance to the Confederacy.

Two weeks later, in a speech to a mob clamoring for his blood, he stated: "It has always been the invariable rule of my life never to form an opinion or verdict upon any great public question until I have first carefully and impartially heard and considered all the evidence . . . , and when I have thus formed my verdict, no fear of popular condemnation can induce me to modify or change such verdict. I have never permitted popular clamor, passion, prejudice nor selfish ambition to induce me to change an opinion or verdict which my conscience and judgment has once formed and tells me is right. . . .

"The *vox populi* is not always the voice of God, for when the demagogues and selfish political leaders succeed in arousing public prejudice and stilling the voice of reason, then . . . can be heard the popular cry of 'Crucify Him, crucify Him!' The *vox populi* then becomes the voice of the devil."

These were courageous words, but note that before Houston took a conscientious stand he always made an effort to be in the right.

Standing for what is right frequently arouses opposition and persecution. Today it is popular to be a Christian, but it may not always be so, and the question comes to you and me, Are my conscientious convictions right; are they in harmony with God's Word? If they are, hold to them, no matter what the cost!

*I will give you treasures hidden in the darkness,*
*secret riches; and you will know that I am*
*doing this—I, the Lord, . . . the one who calls*
*you by your name. Isa. 45:3, TLB.*

NOVEMBER
19

# The Treasures of Darkness

In the early 1950s I pastored a small church in Cloverdale, California. On the north side of town was a unique railroad tunnel. What singled out this tunnel as special was the fact that, according to Robert Ripley's *Believe It or Not,* it was the only tunnel in the world that ran under a cemetery.

Tunnels are constructed for a definite purpose. They are not dead-end excavations that lead nowhere. The Simplon Tunnel, for instance, was blasted out of solid granite in the Swiss Alps to facilitate transportation between Switzerland and Italy. It is 12.25 miles in length (the longest tunnel in the world) and saves travelers scores of miles and hours of travel time. In 1980 my wife and I and DeDe, our youngest daughter, traveled through this tunnel from Switzerland to Italy.

A much longer tunnel is being constructed under the English Channel to connect Great Britain with the mainland.

Long tunnels are in some ways similar to the Christian life. Unless lighted, they are black as midnight. Similarly, spiritual tunnels are dark unless illuminated by Christ, the Light of the world. Again, just as tunnels lead somewhere, so in our "tunnel experiences" God is leading us to a glorious destination. As tunnels shorten travel time, so tunnel experiences can shorten the learning time of our spiritual pilgrimage if we view them from the right perspective.

The reason our heavenly Father permits us to go through tunnel experiences is to give us "treasures hidden in the darkness; secret riches" that will enhance our soul's worth.

Are you going through a tunnel experience? Don't think it strange (see 1 Peter 4:12). All of us go through such experiences from time to time. But remember, we best benefit from them as we accept them in the right Light.

## 20

*Prepare to meet thy God, O Israel. Amos 4:12.*

# Preparation Day

In the Bible the millennium, that 1,000-year period that interposes between the second and third coming of Christ, is also spoken of as "the day of the Lord"—the "day" on which God intervenes directly in human affairs (see Zeph. 2:1, 2; 1 Thess. 5:2-4). God's redeemed will spend that day in heaven in fellowship with Him, with the angels, and with unfallen beings of other worlds. Satan and his evil angels will be bound on this earth, and the land will experience a 1,000-year sabbatical.

"The great controversy between Christ and Satan, that has been carried on for almost six thousand years, is soon to close" (*Signs of the Times,* May 8, 1884). When it does close, the day of the Lord begins. Thus, at present we are, in a sense, living in the "preparation day," awaiting the millennial "Sabbath," when we shall meet our God face-to-face.

One Friday afternoon not long ago, after I had finished my chores and was preparing to welcome the Sabbath, I sat down in a lawn chair on my back porch to enjoy the sunset. As I looked at the westering sun, the thought suddenly struck me that not only was it late Friday afternoon of the literal week but that it was also late Friday afternoon in the history of the world. As the two concepts blended in my mind, I thought, *Surely it is high time to be ready to meet our Lord in peace.*

Have you ever seen the illustration that appears in some of our older publications that depicts a farm boy on the run, jiggling a pail of milk, trying to make it home before the sun dips below the horizon? If I remember rightly, the picture is captioned, "Rushing to get ready for Sabbath."

Times have changed. Most milking these days is done by machine, so it is not likely that many of us experience this particular kind of lack of preparedness for welcoming the Sabbath hours. However, there may be other ways in which we come up to Friday sundown unprepared.

In view of the fact that we face the sunset of the world, should we not be prepared to meet our God on His special day when it comes to us this Friday evening?

*All I did was just and honest, for righteousness was my clothing! I served as eyes for the blind and feet for the lame. Job 29:14, 15, TLB.*

NOVEMBER
21

# Eyes to the Blind

In Job's day, to serve as eyes for the blind and feet for the lame meant to lead the blind around by the hand and bodily transport the lame from place to place. Today, of course, one can sometimes accomplish these acts of mercy through organ transplants.

Stacy Goetze, of Orlando, Florida, related in Ann Landers' advice column how a corneal transplant had dramatically altered her life.

Five years earlier an eye disease deprived Stacy of her eyesight. A college student with a bright future, her world was plunged into darkness. Up to then it had never crossed her mind to become an eye donor, but now her chance of ever seeing again depended on receiving a corneal transplant from someone else.

Just when everything seemed most hopeless, a family suffering the agony of losing a loved one reached out and touched Stacy's life. "Today," Stacy wrote, "I work for the Medical Eye Bank of Florida in Orlando. I help bring others like myself the gift of sight." She continues:

"Though I will never know the donor or the family who made my miracle possible, each morning as I awake and see the sunrise, I smile and think of [them]. . . . However, many others will never get a chance to experience a beautiful sunset or see a rainbow without the generosity of an organ donor."

Several years ago when I renewed my driver's license I was presented with a form asking whether I would donate my organs for the benefit of others. I signed the form. I have no burden to urge others to make the same choice, but I think it is a wonderful opportunity to be of benefit to someone else.

But there is another way of interpreting our verse. Because of sin, people are born spiritually blind, and we who have spiritual eyesight have the privilege of offering them hope. If the opportunity presents itself to you today, bring a soul the joy of spiritual enlightenment by your witness.

*"I am carrying on a great project and cannot go down. Why should the work stop while I leave it and go down to you?" Neh. 6:3, NIV.*

# The Way to Answer Critics

This verse relates to the building of the walls of Jerusalem after the Babylonian captivity. The arduous task was accomplished in an astonishing 52 days, women working alongside the men! (See Neh. 6:15 and 3:12.)

Daniel had prophesied that "the wall . . . [would be built] in troublesome times" (Dan. 9:25, NKJV). So Nehemiah probably wasn't too surprised when some critics came around and tried to stop his work. Nehemiah says that "Sanballat the Horonite, Tobiah the Ammonite official, and Geshem the Arab . . . laughed us to scorn" (Neh. 2:19, NKJV). One day one of his critics scrutinized the wall and snorted, "Even a fox could knock it down" (Neh. 4:3, TEV). But Nehemiah refused to stop the work God commissioned him to do and argue with his critics. This is a good way to answer cavilers.

When Colonel George W. Goethals was building the Panama Canal, he faced problems that would have daunted a lesser man. But the worst part was that he had to endure captious comments from carping critics from his own country. They were sure he would fail. After all, hadn't Viscount de Lesseps, the famous builder of the Suez Canal, given up on the project? But Goethals ignored the cavilers.

One day an exasperated subordinate asked him, "Aren't you going to answer your critics?"

"Yes, in time."

"Well, when and how?"

"With the canal."

What a superb answer!

When my father began missionary work in the Azores, he laid out a plan for soul winning. It involved going from door to door with tracts and returning each week with a new tract that was exchanged for the old one. Some doubted the plan would work. Dad never argued the point; he simply went out with Mother and us boys and showed that it could be done.

If the work you are doing is approved of God, don't stop to argue with your critics. Let the results speak for themselves!

# Thank God for Everything?

Does God expect us to thank Him for *everything*—even the misfortunes that befall us? Some people seem to think so.

I remember reading a report in a popular news magazine some years ago about a religious organization that taught its adherents literally to thank God for *everything* that happened to them—good or bad. As an example, the magazine cited the case of a service station attendant who was mugged by a gang of hoodlums. The attendant was knocked senseless and robbed, but fortunately, not killed. When he regained consciousness, instead of bemoaning his misfortune, he exclaimed, "Thank God!"

I could be wrong, but I think that the man was thanking God for sparing his life, not for getting beaten up. But suppose he *was* thanking God for his misfortune; does God really expect us to thank Him for the bad things that happen to us?

Apparently Job thought so. When his wife urged him to "curse God, and die," he replied, "What? shall we receive good at the hand of God, and *shall we not receive evil?*" (Job 2:9, 10). Job believed that evil as well as good comes from God, and, since it is proper to thank God for the good He bestows, it must be equally proper to thank Him for the evil He sends.

Although Job apparently never knew it, he was mistaken. Unlike us, he was never taken behind the scenes and shown that Satan, not God, was the cause of his afflictions. It is Satan, the originator of sin, who is ultimately responsible for all suffering, and surely no sufferer owes him thanks for misfortunes.

But notice that Paul does not say "Thank God *for* everything," but "*In* everything give thanks"—and this makes all the difference in the world. It means that we should maintain a thankful attitude at all times: in prosperity as well as in adversity. In prosperity because we know that all blessings come from God; in adversity because we know that God can bring something good out of something bad—a blessing out of what seems to be a curse.

*I will go about Your altar, O Lord, that I may proclaim with the voice of thanksgiving, and tell of all Your wondrous works.*
Ps. 26:6, 7, NKJV.

# Thanksgiving Day

The custom of setting aside days of thanksgiving is not of recent origin. It was a common practice among the people in Old Testament times. However, the custom of setting aside an annual special day of thanksgiving for God's blessings did originate in modern times in America.

On December 26, 1620, the *Mayflower*, with Captain Christopher Jones in command, dropped anchor in Plymouth Bay. The perilous crossing from the Old World had taken two months—a long time by today's standards. Before stepping ashore, the 41 men on board signed the famous Mayflower Compact. By signing this document, the fidelity of these earnest Christians took on visible form. They not only thanked God for His providences; they also renewed their dedication to a principle—faith. Faith had prompted them to set out on their voyage, faith had sustained them on the way, and faith now constrained them to raise their voices in praise and thanksgiving to God for bringing them safely "unto their desired haven" (Ps. 107:30).

During the winter that followed, almost half the passengers and crew perished. Yet when spring came and Captain Jones offered free passage to anyone who wished to return to the old country, not a soul accepted his offer!

The faith of these Pilgrims, who might have returned to the Old World, is reminiscent of the steadfast faith of Abraham, Isaac, and Jacob. They "confessed that they were strangers and pilgrims on the earth. . . . Truly, if they had been mindful of that country from whence they came out, they might have had opportunity to have returned." But they didn't return! Why? Because they "desire[d] a better country, that is, an heavenly" (Heb. 11:13-16).

You and I are also strangers and pilgrims on this earth. As we thank God today for our material blessings, let us also thank Him for the heavenly country He has prepared for the faithful of all ages (see verses 39, 40).

*There is a judge for the man who rejects me and does not accept my words; the word that I spoke will be his judge on the last day.*
*John 12:48, NEB.*

NOVEMBER
25

# Judged by the Word

It is reported that several years ago two American tourists were looking at a famous painting in one of the great museums of Europe when one of them sneered, "I wouldn't give a nickel for that painting." A guard, overhearing the remark, stepped over to the critic, tapped him on the shoulder, and said, "Sir, these paintings are not on trial. But you are."

Another class of critics likes to put the Bible on trial. Many years ago when I was earning my way through college as a Christian book salesman in San Francisco, an older man engaged me in conversation as I was returning home on the streetcar. He wanted to know what I did for a living. I told him I sold Bibles and other religious books. I shall never forget his reaction: "The Bible is one of the filthiest books known to man." Perhaps I should have challenged his statement, but I didn't. I simply ended our conversation.

There are people who seem to enjoy downgrading the Bible. Some of them even profess to be Christians. These people apparently study the Bible, not to gain spiritual understanding, but to display their intellectual acumen. The Bible describes them as people who are "above what is written" (1 Cor. 4:6, Sharpe). They presume to sit in judgment on God's Word. What they don't realize is that someday the Word will judge them.

The Word will judge them? How can that be? Notice:

Students of the mind tell us that everything of which we become conscious is stored in memory and needs only the proper stimulus to be recalled. The Holy Spirit stands by every student of Scripture, whether a sincere seeker of truth or a quibbler, and brings conviction to conscience. These convictions stored in memory will rise at the last day to condemn the caviler and commend the sincere seeker of truth.

How important, then, that we obey the convictions the Holy Spirit brings to our minds as we study the Bible. And remember, these convictions will always be in harmony with God's Word.

# 26

*I [have not] gone back from the commandment of [God's] lips; I have esteemed the words of his mouth more than my necessary food.*
**Job 23:12.**

# What Is God's Word Worth to You?

Around the turn of the nineteenth century a poor Welsh girl named Mary Jones distinguished herself in Sunday School by her eagerness to memorize and repeat large portions of Scripture. Bibles were scarce in those days. The nearest person who owned a copy lived two miles from her home. Mary's great desire was to possess her own Bible someday. In order to do this, she denied herself many things. She also set aside what little money she could spare from the wages she earned as a weaver in her father's shop.

After several years she scraped together enough money to buy a Bible. Bala, the nearest town where she could buy the precious Book, was 25 miles away. Undeterred, she set off, walking barefoot, carrying her shoes in a bag to save wear and tear on them. When she reached the home of Thomas Charles, the local Bible salesman, she learned that he had only two Bibles on hand, both of which had already been spoken for.

When he told Mary he had no Bibles for sale, tears welled up in her eyes. Mr. Charles was so touched by her disappointment that he sold her one of the Bibles, knowing that he could replace it.

In December 1802 Charles laid before the committee of the Religious Tract Society the pressing need for Welsh Bibles. A resolution was passed at the meeting that eventually led to the founding of the British and Foreign Bible Society, an organization that has promoted the sale of Bibles at affordable prices all over the world.

Since then the Bible has been the world's best-seller year after year. It can be found in most homes throughout the Western world. Unfortunately, in many of these homes it lies on a shelf gathering dust.

In Job's day there were no Bibles as we know them today, yet he esteemed God's spoken words above his necessary food. Should we not value God's Written Word at least as highly?

# Hide God's Word in Your Heart

In his book *In the Presence of Mine Enemies,* coauthored with his wife, Phyllys, Captain Howard Rutledge tells how he discovered the preciousness of the Bible in a North Vietnamese prisoner-of-war camp, where he spent seven years. Here are a few excerpts from his book:

"I had completely neglected the spiritual dimension of my life. It took prison to show me how empty life is without God. . . .

"I tried desperately to recall snatches of Scripture, sermons, the gospel choruses from childhood, and the hymns we sang in church. . . .

"How I struggled to recall those Scriptures and hymns! . . . Regrettably, I had not seen the importance of memorizing verses from the Bible or learning gospel songs. I never dreamed I would spend seven years (five of them in solitary confinement) in a prison in North Vietnam or [that] thinking about one memorized verse could have made a whole day bearable. One portion of a verse I did remember was, 'Thy word have I hid in my heart.' How often I wish I had really worked to hide God's Word in my heart" (pp. 34-38).

Having spent three years interned as a prisoner of war during World War II, I can empathize with Captain Rutledge's feelings. In the very early days after our captivity and the very last days before liberation, when death and famine stalked the land, the Word of God was very precious to me. I can remember memorizing Psalm 33:18, 19: "Behold, the eye of the Lord is upon them that fear him, upon them that hope in his mercy; to deliver their soul from death, and to keep them alive in famine."

The Bible warns us that days are coming when there will be "a famine in the land, not a famine of bread, nor a thirst for water, but of hearing the words of the Lord" (Amos 8:11). How precious then will the Word of God seem to us. How important, therefore, that in these days of relative peace and prosperity we store His Word in our hearts.

*If the disease has spread in the walls of the house, then the priest shall command that they take out the stones in which is the disease and throw them into an unclean place outside the city; and he shall cause the inside of the house to be scraped round about, and the plaster that they scrape off they shall pour into an unclean place outside the city. Lev. 14:39-41, RSV.*

# Biblical Criticism

Bible critics of the early nineteenth century had a field day ridiculing some of the health laws mandated by the Mosaic code, among them the practice of removing the plaster from the houses of leprous patients. Although we do not have all the answers to the whys and wherefores of these regulations, we don't hear that particular ridicule made anymore—and there's a reason.

About 100 years ago, before Pasteur's germ theory was clearly understood, doctors observed that surgeons performing amputations at the Bellevue Hospital in New York State were losing an alarming number of patients to infections. They also observed that the same surgeons performing the same kinds of operations at the newly constructed Roosevelt Hospital in the same state were having a high success rate.

From these statistics the doctors concluded that, although great care was being taken to sterilize surgical instruments and the operation theater, somehow the plastering and floors of the old hospital building must be harboring germs. These were finding their way into the wounds of the amputees, causing them to develop sepsis. As a consequence, Dr. H. B. Sands introduced a resolution that thenceforth no major surgical operations be undertaken at Bellevue.

Science has subsequently confirmed this part of Moses' Levitical law. Today some of the germs that have become resistant to antibiotics, such as *Staphylococcus aureus,* continue to be a menace to patients because they lurk in the plaster and floors of hospitals.

What can we learn from all this? That, although we may not be able to give a rational explanation for everything the Bible says, it behooves us not to be "above what is written" (1 Cor. 4:6, Sharpe). The future may yet bring additional discoveries that will add to the authenticity of the Bible.

# God's Word Is True in Its Entirety

In 1880 William M. Ramsay, an English scholar and admirer of Julius Wellhausen (the father of higher biblical criticism), went to Phrygia in Asia Minor to disprove Luke's history as recorded in his gospel and the book of Acts. He was first awakened from his illusion by a study of Acts 14:6, which states that one passes from the frontier of Lycaonia in going from Iconium to Lystra.

Luke's statement ran counter to the opinion of the most authoritative modern geographers and appeared to be contradicted by ancient writers. But as Ramsay studied the inscriptions, he came to realize that the author of Acts knew more about the ancient geography of Phrygia than the modern critics did. In all other statements of fact in Luke's history, Ramsay found such surprising accuracy that in 1915 he declared that "Luke's history is unsurpassed in respect to its trustworthiness." So convincing was the evidence Ramsay discovered that he became a Christian and a staunch defender of the Bible.

What Sir Ramsay discovered with respect to Luke is essentially true of the rest of the Bible—*God's Word is true in its entirety.* In the light of archaeological discoveries, the late William F. Albright, regarded by many as the preeminent Near Eastern archaeologist of his time, acknowledged that "archaeological and inscriptional data have established the historicity of innumerable passages and statements of the Old Testament; the number of such cases is many times greater than those where the reverse has been proved or has been made probable." In those few instances in which scholars think the Bible is incorrect, the Christian can afford to hold suspended judgment. The spade is still confirming the Book.

Some critics like to point out that the manuscripts of the Bible contain some 50,000 variants. The vast majority of these are minor, such as variations in the spelling—and not a single one of these affects our salvation. The overwhelming evidence is that, for all practical purposes, the Bible is true in its entirety. The Bible may seem "imperfect" by human standards, but it is perfect for its purpose—"even the salvation of [our] souls" (1 Peter 1:9).

*Although the Lord warned Manasseh and his people, they refused to listen. So the Lord let the commanders of the Assyrian army invade Judah. They captured Manasseh . . . and took him to Babylon. In his suffering he became humble, turned to the Lord his God, and begged him for help. God accepted Manasseh's prayer. 2 Chron. 33:10-13, TEV.*

# The Uses of Adversity

The nut of the wine palm, a native of the tropics, takes as long as three years to sprout and sometimes does not sprout at all. Various methods have been tried to decrease the sprouting time. It has been found, for instance, that if the seed is immersed in water until it swells and then is dried, it will never germinate. But if it is subjected to freezing cold for a couple of days, then thawed by pouring boiling water over it, then immersed in water for 10 hours, it will sprout in a few short months. The harsh treatment actually proves to be beneficial.

Manasseh, son of Hezekiah, failed to learn dependence on God and obedience to His will under the sun of temporal prosperity. But under the harsh treatment meted out by his Assyrian captors, the knowledge of God, which had lain dormant for nearly a lifetime, germinated and produced the fruits of righteousness at last.

Samson's experience was similar. Born to deliver his people from Philistine oppression, he failed to develop the kind of dependence on God that should have characterized his life. Yet, buffeted by adversity, deprived of his great strength, his liberty, and his eyesight, he diligently sought and found that God is the source of all power (see Judges 16:21-28; cf. Heb. 11:32, 33).

When God created man He didn't intend adversity to be necessary for the development of a righteous character. Rather, He placed our first parents in a beautiful garden surrounded by every conceivable blessing. But when Adam and Eve chose to be disobedient, they were banished from Eden and a curse was pronounced upon the ground. And yet this very curse, accepted in the right spirit, was designed to be a blessing. As in the case of the nut of the wine palm, life's trying experiences can lead to the germination of righteousness and often become the source of our greatest blessings.

*Jesus said, "Father, forgive them; for they know not what they do." Luke 23:34, RSV.*

DECEMBER

1

# What Forgiveness Can Do

Wilfred T. Grenfell, famous medical missionary to Labrador, was born in 1865. In 1892, while still in his 20s, he dedicated his life to the people of the eastern seaboard of Canada, where he served his Lord until five years before his death in 1940. Once, when asked what influenced him to devote his life to Christian humanitarian work on the cold, forbidding coasts of Newfoundland and Labrador, he said that, one night a woman was brought into the emergency room of the hospital in which he worked. It was evident that she had no hope of living. According to the testimony of witnesses, her husband had come home drunk, and in a rage had hurled a lighted kerosene lamp at her. Neighbors called the police, and the now half-sober husband, accompanied by an officer, arrived at her bedside. The officer leaned over and asked the woman exactly what happened. At first she refused to say anything, but he insisted. Finally she said simply, "Sir, it was only an accident." She died soon after.

Grenfell said that if love could forgive a wrong of that magnitude, he wanted to follow Jesus' example and dedicate his life in ministry to others. Did this woman's example have a similar effect on her husband? I do not know, but let us hope so.

Forgiving those who wrong us, who from a human point of view do not deserve our forgiveness, can have a powerful effect for good. When Jesus forgave those who crucified Him, it made a deep impression on many of those responsible for His death. Acts 6:7 says that subsequently "a great many of the priests were obedient to the faith" (RSV).

Something similar may have happened when Stephen forgave those who stoned him to death (see Acts 7:58-60). It's not unlikely that Saul's conversion stemmed from that experience.

When you and I do as Jesus did, and freely forgive those who have wronged us, it *may* have a similar effect on them—*but don't count on it*. After all, our goal in life as Christians is to follow Christ's example, not to make others feel sorry for the wrongs they've done *us*.

2

*Another reason for right living is this: you know how late it is; time is running out. Wake up, for the coming of the Lord is nearer now than when we first believed. The night is far gone, the day of his return will soon be here. So quit the evil deeds of darkness and put on the armor of right living. Rom. 13:11, 12, TLB.*

# High Time to Wake Up!

I have a digital wristwatch that has given me good service until this morning. Its battery has gone dead, and, accustomed as I am to regulating my activities by it, I miss it very much.

There is another timekeeper, however, that is of infinitely greater importance to us. Without it we would be hopelessly disoriented as to where we are in the stream of time. I refer, of course, to Bible prophecy—God's great prophetic time clock (see Galatians 4:4). Were we deprived of it, we would not understand the meaning of events we see happening all around us. We would be in ignorance as to how to prepare for the greatest event of the future—the return of our Saviour as King of kings and Lord of lords.

Christ has warned, "Be ye also ready: for in such an hour as ye think not the Son of man cometh" (Matt. 24:44). Only those who regulate their lives by God's great timepiece will be found ready to go with Jesus to the "heavenly" country (Heb. 11:16) He has promised to those who love Him. Listen to this:

"The coming of the Lord is nearer than when we first believed. The great controversy is nearing its end. Every report of calamity by sea or land is a testimony to the fact that the end of all things is at hand. Wars and rumors of wars declare it. Is there a Christian whose pulse does not beat with quickened action as he anticipates the great events opening before us?

"The Lord is coming. We hear the footsteps of an approaching God, as He comes to punish the world for its iniquity. We are to prepare the way for Him by acting our part in getting a people ready for that great day" (*Evangelism,* p. 219).

If ever there was a time to be awake, it is now. The signs of the times tell us that Christ is coming very soon!

*O God, save me; for the waters come up to my lips; . . . I have come to deep waters and a flood overwhelms me. I have cried until I am exhausted. Ps. 69:1-3, MLB.*

DECEMBER

3

# Rescue the Perishing

I shall never forget January 13, 1982. Our family was living in Beltsville, Maryland, at the time. It had been snowing for hours when we turned on our television for the weather forecast for Washington, D.C., and vicinity. Suddenly, the broadcast was interrupted with the startling announcement that an Air Florida passenger plane had plunged into the Potomac River after taking off from Washington National Airport. We didn't see what followed, but we learned about it later.

Lenny Skutnick, a 28-year-old man, was watching people in a helicopter trying to rescue stewardess Priscilla Tirado, who was struggling in the water and in danger of drowning. Twice she lost her grip when a rope was dropped down to her. Noticing that her strength was ebbing, Skutnick shed his coat and boots, jumped into the icy water, and swam 30 yards to reach her and drag her to safety.

After the rescue, the media asked Skutnick what had motivated him to risk his life to save Ms. Tirado. Skutnick answered modestly, "It could have been anybody. I just happened to be there. I had been there all the time and nobody was getting in the water. . . . It is something I never thought I would do, but on looking back, I guess I did it because I didn't think about it. Somebody had to go into the water, and I happened to be the one."

The psalmist, struggling on the sea of life, felt his courage failing and cried to God for help. He who sees the sparrow fall heard that cry. "His heart of love is touched by our sorrows and even by our utterances of them. . . . There is no chapter in our experience too dark for Him to read; there is no perplexity too difficult for Him to unravel" (*Steps to Christ*, p. 100). Is it any wonder that in concluding David ends on a triumphant note? "I will praise the name of God with a song, and will magnify Him with thanksgiving" (verse 30, MLB).

What a wonderful God we serve! Frequently He saves struggling sinners by using us as instruments to accomplish His purpose.

*May the favor of the Lord our God rest upon us; establish the work of our hands for us—yes, establish the work of our hands. Ps. 90:17, NIV.*

# Rebuilding Ruins

When Thomas Carlyle, English essayist and historian, finished his first volume of *The French Revolution,* he handed the manuscript to John Stuart Mill for critiquing. Mill read the manuscript, then lent it to a friend. The friend left it lying on a study table one night after reading it. Early the next morning the housemaid, groping around for something with which to start a fire, found the loose mass of papers and, thinking it was discarded trash, used it for kindling. What had taken Carlyle years to write was gone!

When Mill, white as a sheet, reported the devastating news to Carlyle, the latter was so staggered by his loss that he could do nothing for weeks. Then one day, as he sat by his open window, brooding over his terrible loss, he noticed a mason rebuilding a brick wall. Patiently the man laid brick upon brick, all the while whistling a happy tune.

*Poor fool*, thought Carlyle, *how can you be so merry when life is so futile?* Then suddenly another thought struck him. *Poor fool*, said he of himself, *here you sit at your window whining and complaining while that man rebuilds a house that will last for generations.*

Rising from his chair, Carlyle went to work on his second draft of *The French Revolution.* According to his own account and those who had had an opportunity to read both versions of his work, the latter was a better product! The destruction of our cherished dreams does not have to be the end of the world. It could be the beginning of something better!

Carlyle has been an inspiration to many to begin over after they have seen their lifework destroyed. It is unlikely, however, that the humble bricklayer who gave Carlyle his inspiration to begin again ever knew that he had a hand in re-creating a literary masterpiece.

Our unconscious Christian example can be just the encouragement someone needs who has made a failure in life.

*Take the girdle . . . and go at once to Perath
and hide it in a crevice among the rocks. So I
went and hid the girdle. . . . After a long time
the Lord said to me: Go at once to Perath and
fetch back the girdle. . . . So I went to Perath
and looked for the place where I had hidden it,
but when I picked it up, I saw that it was spoilt.
Jer. 13:4-8, NEB.*

# What God Desires

In the spring of 1943, while my good friend Ralph Longway and I were interned in Camp Holmes (now Camp Dangwa), we decided to sneak out and hide some of our war souvenirs under a limestone outcropping on top of the mountain behind the camp. Among our "treasures" were a bandolier, an aluminum canteen cup, some Springfield rifle ammunition clips, and some .3030 rifle slugs.

Some time in December of that year we sneaked out of camp again and retrieved some of these objects. By then the bandolier, which was made of cotton, was badly deteriorated. We reburied the bandolier, together with some of the ammunition clips, under a limestone slab about 10 inches wide, 20 inches long, and 2 inches thick; we took the other things with us back to camp.

On March 26, 1991, almost a half century later, I returned to Camp Dangwa. Accompanied by two Filipino sergeants, I located the rock formation. Pointing to the spot, I told the soldiers the cache was under a slab, and gave the dimensions. We dug down about 8 inches, and *there was the slab!* We searched for the bandolier, but it no longer existed, nor were we able to find even a trace of the ammunition clips. But I did crack off an end of the rock slab and bring it back with me, so now I proudly own "a piece of the rock" (apologies to Prudential Life Insurance Company).

The burial and exhumation of Jeremiah's girdle was an object lesson for God's ancient people as well as for us today. In Jeremiah's acted parable, the rotted girdle represented the pride of Israel and Judah (see Jer. 13:9). They thought that because they were the chosen people, they were invulnerable. But Jeremiah's parable showed the worthlessness of such prideful presumption. It is humble obedience, not pride, that is of great value in God's sight (see Micah 6:8).

*I write you these things so that you may not sin, and if anyone does sin, we have a counsel for our defense in the Father's presence, Jesus Christ the Righteous One. 1 John 2:1, MLB.*

# Counsel for the Defense

The other evening I telephoned Steve, our second son, who is an attorney in northern California. In the course of our conversation I asked what sort of cases he had had recently. He said that a few days before, he had served as counsel for a defendant involved in a car sale. The plaintiff chose to be his own counsel. Steve concluded by repeating the old saw "He who acts as his own counsel has a fool for a client." It is better to have someone else plead your case than to try to plead it yourself.

One of the most poignant pleas in all history is Judah's plea on behalf of Benjamin. You remember, Judah had been the instigator of the plot to sell Joseph into slavery, but in the intervening years he had been converted. Now, standing before Joseph, whom he does not recognize, he pleads for him to let Benjamin return to his aged father (Gen. 37-45).

At the climax of his speech he says, "My lord, it was I who went surety for the boy to my father. I said, 'If I do not bring him back to you, then you can blame me for it all my life.' Now, my lord, let me remain in place of the boy as my lord's slave, and let him go with his brothers. How can I return to my father without the boy? I could not bear to see the misery which my father would suffer" (Gen. 44:32-34, REB).

What a change in Judah! What a "change" in Joseph—because of Judah's plea! "Joseph was no longer able to control his feelings" (Gen. 45:1, REB). While testing his brothers, Joseph "seemed" stern. But having passed the test, he revealed his love for his brothers openly—a love that had been there all along.

The Father, before whom our Advocate pleads our cases, may seem stern, even as did Joseph. Justice must be done; but we are assured that the Father Himself loves us (see John 16:27). Even so, at the end of the last judgment, having *satisfied the demands of justice before the universe, He displays His love openly for those who have passed the test* (see Rev. 20:11-21:5).

*The kingdom of heaven is like a merchant seeking beautiful pearls, who, when he had found one pearl of great price, went and sold all that he had and bought it.*
*Matt. 13:45, 46, NKJV.*

DECEMBER

7

# The Pearl of Great Price

Some time ago in the Philippines occurred the tragic death of a young Filipino pearl diver off one of the southern islands. The young man was only 18. He had dived into the sea and somehow a giant clam had closed its shell over one of his feet, holding him fast until he drowned. When his body and the clam were pulled to the surface, the clam was opened, and inside was discovered the largest pearl that had ever been found. It undoubtedly sold for a fabulous price—but its price must be calculated in more than money. It cost a man his life!

The pearl of great price in our verse represents Christ and His kingdom. In order to purchase it, we must give up our very life. Jesus put it this way: "If you cling to your life, you will lose it; but if you give it up for me, you will save it" (Matt. 10:39, TLB). This seems contradictory, but it really isn't. Jesus was using "life" in two senses: (1) this earthly life, with its pleasures, human relationships, and rewards, and (2) the life of happiness in the hereafter that will have no end.

On another occasion Jesus declared, "Everyone who has left houses or brothers or sisters or father or mother or children or farms for My name's sake shall receive many times as much, and shall inherit eternal life" (Matt. 19:29, NASB). Mark in his Gospel teaches that even in this life there are advantages in giving up the pleasures, human relationships, and rewards of this world for the sake of Christ and His kingdom—peace of mind, and new and better friends, for instance. But the greatest reward is living with Jesus forever in the great hereafter (see Mark 10:28, 29).

Be willing to give up everything, even this present life if need be, for the Pearl of great price. It's worth it!

**8** *Whenever Moses raised his hands Israel had the advantage, and when he lowered his hands Amalek had the advantage. But when his arms grew heavy . . . Aaron and Hur held up his hands, one on each side, so that his hands remained steady till sunset. Thus Joshua defeated Amalek. Ex. 17:11-13, NEB.*

# Supporting God's Cause

The battle our verses describe was fought more than 3,000 years ago in Rephidim, a rocky valley on the Sinai Peninsula. I visited Rephidim in 1959 with a Bible Lands tour group. Some of us climbed to the top of a ridge overlooking this site. Someone asked me to sit on a rock, Moses-like, while two of our group held up my hands and others snapped our picture.

It is generally true that for an enterprise to succeed, there must be support by those who do not play a "heroic" role. Without this backing many undertakings fail.

An example of such failure happened a few years ago off the coast of Nova Scotia. A vessel had been caught in a terrible storm and dashed to pieces, with dreadful loss of life. A lone survivor, clinging to flotsam, could be seen by the anxious people who had gathered on the shore.

A young man who was noted as a powerful swimmer tied one end of a rope around his waist and instructed the people to hang onto the other end while he swam out to rescue the survivor. He battled his way to the imperiled man and, after taking hold of him, signaled the people to pull them in. Just at that moment the people raised their hands with a roar of triumph—and, for just an instant, let go of the rope! Before they could grab hold again, the rope was swept out to sea, and both the rescuer and survivor perished! For just a moment the rescuer's supporters forgot the vital importance of their "unglamorous" role!

In our text, notice that Israel "gained the upper hand" whenever Moses' arms were raised, and the advantage passed to Amalek when he lowered them. This was an acted parable designed by God to teach Israel—and you and me—that although our role may seem unglamorous, the leaders of God's cause, as well as the "fighting troops," need our support in carrying on His work.

*This stone which I [Jacob] have erected for a memorial pillar shall become a house of God. Moreover I will without fail give Thee a tithe of all Thou shalt give me. Gen. 28:22, MLB.*

DECEMBER
9

# Returning the Tithe

Many years ago when candy manufacturer John Huyler set up his business, he made Jacob's pledge his own. Going to the bank, he opened an account, which he identified by the initials "M.P." Into that fund he regularly deposited a tenth of his income. When people asked what the initials stood for, he would say, "My Partner."

Keeping God uppermost in his mind in his business transactions, he was blessed by the Lord, and his company prospered phenomenally. Each week the Lord's work received increasingly larger sums of money. The size of these gifts became so large that it amazed his business associates.

Interestingly, these contributions were always accompanied with the request that the donor not be thanked, but that the recipient offer praise to God alone. "After all," Mr. Huyler would say, "the money isn't mine; it's the Lord's."

Most of us have eaten Quaker Oats at one time or another, but few of us remember who founded the company or the history of its prosperity.

More than 100 years ago Henry P. Crowell contracted tuberculosis and was told he could never achieve his ambition of becoming a preacher. After hearing a sermon by Dwight L. Moody, he prayed, "Lord, I can't be a preacher, but I can be a good businessman. If You will let me make money, I will use it in Your service."

A doctor advised young Crowell to work outdoors. He followed this advice and at the end of seven years had regained his health. He then bought the little run-down Quaker Mill in Ravenna, Ohio. His business prospered, and, true to his promise, he paid a faithful tithe. Within 10 years Quaker Oats was a household name. For the next 40 years Crowell faithfully gave *from 60 to 70 percent of his income to God's cause!*

Other examples of the benefits of faithful tithing might be cited. But the greatest advantages that come to those who return a faithful tithe and contribute liberal offerings are not material benefits but spiritual blessings.

353

*My people and I cannot really give you anything, because everything is a gift from you, and we have only given back what is yours already. 1 Chron. 29:14, TEV.*

# Not 10, but 100 Percent—Plus

A young couple that had recently moved to a new locality wanted to join a church close by and invited the pastor to visit them and acquaint them with his church's teachings. A lay member heard about the couple's interest and decided to "help" the pastor by giving the wife a phone call.

"Has the pastor told you about tithing yet?" the parishioner asked.

"No," the wife replied.

"Well," the parishioner volunteered, "he's going to tell you that before you can join, you have to agree to pay 10 percent of your income to the church."

When the pastor called at the couple's home, the first thing the wife asked was, "Is it true that we will be required to give 10 percent of our income to the church before we can join?"

The pastor breathed a quick prayer for wisdom. Maintaining his composure, he replied, "I'm sorry, but you have been misinformed. Actually you are going to be asked to give 100 percent—and yourselves, besides. The Bible teaches that all things are God's by creation, so whatever we return to Him was His to begin with. Turn with me to 1 Chronicles 29:14."

Then he continued, "God tests His children by instructing them to return one tenth of their increase to His 'storehouse' [Mal. 3:10]—the church treasury. This is called the tithe. But in addition, He invites us to give freewill offerings. But this isn't all. He appeals to us to give ourselves as living sacrifices to be used in His service as He sees fit."

"Oh," said the wife, "I want to belong to a church that expects so much of me."

Her husband agreed. Eventually the couple was baptized and became pillars in the church.

When we come to the point of recognizing that all we have and are belong to God, faithful obedience to His requirements becomes a pleasure.

*Unto [Jesus Christ] that loved us, and washed us from our sins in his own blood, and hath made us kings and priests unto God . . . ; to him be glory and dominion for ever and ever.*
**Rev. 1:5, 6.**

DECEMBER

11

# Training for Royalty

Many think of royalty in terms of the great privileges that attend that class. But many also forget that to be a member of royalty often entails special training.

Queen Elizabeth II and her sister, Princess Margaret, were not in the direct line of succession when their father, King George VI of England, was called to the throne upon the abdication of his brother, King Edward VIII, in 1936. And yet these two girls had been trained from childhood for the responsibilities they might have to assume one day as reigning monarchs.

Just as members of a royal family are carefully trained over a period of time to fill their high position in a royal court here on earth, so the Christian is granted a probationary period in which to train for heaven's royal courts.

We are told that "Adam was crowned as king in Eden" (Ellen G. White, in *Review and Herald,* Feb. 24, 1874). God bestowed upon him and Eve dominion, or kingship, over all the earth (see Gen. 1:28). But by selfishly choosing their own way instead of God's way, our first parents forfeited their right to royalty—and not only for themselves, but for their descendants as well. Since that time the only way that we can attain to the high honor of belonging to God's royal family is by adoption. And to prepare for a place in the kingdom of peace, we must humbly and gladly submit to training here on earth.

In order that we might have a pattern to go by in this training, the Sovereign of the universe sent His only-begotten Son to earth to show us how a member of heaven's royal family comports himself. In addition, God gave us a Guidebook that clearly lays down the principles and precepts for those who wish to become members of heaven's royal house.

In view of this fact, here are some questions you and I should ask ourselves: Am I daily preparing to be a member of God's royal household? Is every thought I think, every word I speak, every act I do, fitting me to be a member of heaven's royalty?

*Jesus answered, and said to her, "If you knew the gift of God, and who it is who says to you, 'Give me a drink,' you would have asked Him, and He would have given you living water." John 4:10, NKJV.*

# The Candid Coquette

It is noon, probably late December A.D. 28 or early January A.D. 29. Jesus, who has been traveling on foot with His disciples, has chosen an old well curb on which to sit. While He rests, His disciples go into the nearby village of Sychar to purchase food. Jesus is alone. As He looks across the valley toward the village, He sees a woman coming with a water pitcher on her shoulder.

Women of the Middle East don't usually come for water in the heat of the day. Perhaps she comes at noon because she is less concerned about the hot rays of the sun than about the withering looks of her more respectable sisters.

When she arrives at the well, Jesus asks her for a drink of water. Her response is a bit cheeky, perhaps even flirtatious: "How is it that You, being a Jew, ask me for a drink since I am a Samaritan woman?" (John 4:9, NASB). If she is playing the coquette, Jesus doesn't fall for it. Instead, He raises the issue to a spiritual plane.

"If you only knew the gift of God . . ." Jesus uses this expression in a cryptic sense to pique the woman's curiosity. What He means is, If you only knew Me. After all, He is God's Gift to the world (see John 3:16). His ploy works! The woman's interest is aroused. Then, little by little, Jesus carefully reveals the secrets of her shameful life.

The woman tries to sidestep the embarrassing revelations by turning the conversation into a theological discussion, but Jesus raises the issue to a higher level. Back on track, the woman acknowledges, "I know that the Messiah will come, and when he comes, he will tell us everything" (John 4:25, TEV). This is Jesus' golden opportunity. Going right to the point, He says, "I who speak to you am He" (verse 26, NASB).

The woman believes! The candid coquette is converted.

What a lesson in soul winning! Don't get sidetracked in a theological discussion; raise the issue to a spiritual plane.

*When you are invited [to a wedding reception], go and take your seat in an inconspicuous place, so that when your host comes in he may say to you, "Come on, my dear fellow, we have a much better seat than this for you."*
*Luke 14:10, Phillips.*

# Taking a Lower Position

Several years ago our family went on an excursion in which the tourists rode in cars, caravan-style. We visited many interesting places. At the end of each day we would pull into a motel for sleeping accommodations. It was rather amusing to watch certain individuals in our group "jockey for position" as we lined up to register. It almost appeared as if they wanted to make sure they got a room that fittingly reflected their station in life. Fortunately, not everyone in the world sets such a "shining" example.

When Sammy Morris, a Kru boy from Africa, came to America to attend Taylor University, he did not ask for the best dorm room. Rather, when President Thaddeus C. Reade asked him which room he would like to have, he replied, "If there's a room nobody wants, give it to me."

Commenting on this incident, President Reade said, "In my experience as a teacher, I have had occasion to assign rooms to more than a thousand students. Most of them were noble, Christian young ladies and gentlemen, but Sammy Morris was the only one of them who ever said, 'If there is a room nobody wants, give it to me.' "

It frequently happens that those who set aside their own interests and humbly make it their business to help others come to the attention of others and are honored by them. Why? Well, apparently, we admire humility—*in somebody else!*

But our verse is not speaking primarily of being honored by our fellow human beings. Jesus' primary emphasis was on spiritual things. The wedding represents both the kingdom of grace and the kingdom of glory. Those who in this life enter the kingdom of grace and learn the lesson of true humility will be honored by the heavenly Host in the kingdom of glory.

"Self-surrender is the substance of the teachings of Christ" (*The Desire of Ages*, p. 523). This may mean occupying an inconspicuous position in this life, but it results in occupying a position of honor in the hereafter.

*The Spirit clearly says that in later times some will abandon the faith and follow deceiving spirits and things taught by demons. Such teachings come through hypocritical liars, whose consciences have been seared as with a hot iron. I Tim. 4:1, 2, NIV.*

# Seared Consciences

One evening as I was stoking the fire in our fireplace insert, a hot baffle dropped down unexpectedly and grazed my hand, raising a blister. It hurt; I was sure the pain would keep me awake the rest of the night. Then I remembered something someone had suggested to me years before. I had been told that if I repeatedly held the burn close to the fire, it would hurt terribly at first, but if I were to continue to turn it toward the heat again and again, the pain would gradually subside. I tried the suggestion. It worked—at least, it did for me. (Before you try it you should check with your physician.) The next morning I could just barely feel pain in the affected area. The skin felt tough and insensitive.

I do not know the whys and wherefores of what happened to my burn, but I do know what happens when a person violates his conscience again and again. The first time we do something we know is wrong, our consciences hurt terribly, but repeated violations result in a diminishing sense of psychological pain until eventually we can sin and our consciences no longer bother us.

In the physical realm, desensitizing a painful burn by repeatedly putting it to heat may or may not work, but from the spiritual point of view, desensitizing the conscience is a most serious matter. It can result in committing the unpardonable sin (see Matt. 12:31, 32, RSV). It isn't that some sins are so bad that God won't forgive them. Rather, it is because those who sin willfully come to the place they no longer are able to hear the Holy Spirit speaking to them.

We can avoid committing this "great transgression" by allowing God to keep us from committing "presumptuous sins"—premeditated sinning in the expectation God will forgive (see Ps. 19:13).

*I shall count Rahab . . . among those who acknowledge me; . . . it will be said, "Such a one was born there." . . . The Lord will record in the register of the peoples: this one was born there. Ps. 87:4-6, REB.*

DECEMBER

15

# Rahab

Rahab was the harlot of Jericho who hid two Hebrew spies. According to Jewish tradition, she married one of these men after the fall of the city. If true, his name was Salmon (see Matt. 1:5, RSV).

It has been said that prostitution is the oldest profession. But that does not make it an honorable vocation. Most people regard it as a destroyer of the moral fabric of the family and society.

How does prostitution begin? Social studies have shown that the vast majority of girls who become prostitutes have been initiated into their careers as young children by men who were close relatives and took advantage of them—uncles, brothers, fathers, and even grandfathers! It is estimated that 75 percent of prostitutes were victims of such abuse as children.

It is hard to imagine God having anything to do with a house of ill fame, or Him cooperating with people who would use such an establishment as a hiding place. But this isn't all. Besides being a harlot, Rahab was a liar. She said she didn't know where the spies had gone when they left her place, when she herself had hidden them on the roof of her house (see Joshua 2:4-6).

But then comes a surprise. Unlike her fellow countrymen, she recognized Jehovah as "[the] God in heaven above, and in earth beneath" (verse 11). And then comes the biggest surprise of all—through the line of this former harlot came God's only begotten Son (see Matt. 1:1-16)!

If, without condoning sin (see Ex. 34:6, 7), God considers the circumstances that have shaped a person's life, can we not be more compassionate in our judgment of others? How thankful we can be that in the day of final reckoning a merciful heavenly Father takes into account the fact that "this one was born there." In Jericho, perhaps?

*When you give something to a needy person, do not make a big show of it, as the hypocrites do in the houses of worship. . . . [Rather,] do it in such a way that even your closest friend will not know about it. Matt. 6:2, 3, TEV.*

# How Love Gives

Sir Ernest Shackleton, famous British explorer of the Antarctic, was once asked what was the most terrible moment he experienced on the frozen continent. One might think he would tell about some horrendous polar blizzard, but he didn't. Instead, he said his most terrible moment came one night when he and his men were huddled together in an emergency hut and the last rations had been passed out.

After his men were snoring soundly, Shackleton remained awake, his eyes half-closed. Suddenly he noticed a surreptitious movement by one of his men. Squinting in the man's direction, he saw him stealthily reach over one of the other men and remove his biscuit bag from his pack. Shackleton was shocked! Up to that moment he would have trusted his life to this man. Now he had his doubts.

But then, as he watched, he saw the man open his own biscuit bag, take out his last morsel of food, quietly put it in the other man's bag, and replace it in his pack.

As Shackleton related the story, he said, "I dare not tell you the man's name. I feel his act was a secret between himself and God."

That is the way it is with the kind of love the Bible talks about. It does not perform good deeds in order to be seen of men. As Henry Drummond, a great British preacher, put it: "After love has gone out into the world and done its beautiful deed, it hides, even from itself."

The natural heart craves recognition. It does not want its good deeds to go unnoticed—and this is where many of us fall into Satan's trap! After God has worked in us "to do of his good pleasure" (Phil. 2:13), the tempter comes along and gets us to dote on the wonderful thing we have done.

What is the solution? *Never stop and dote.* Fix your mind on Jesus and continue to let God do His good pleasure through you.

*Oh the bliss of him whose guilt is pardoned,
and his sin forgiven! Oh the bliss of him whom
the Eternal has absolved, whose spirit has
made full confession! Ps. 32:1, 2, Moffatt.*

DECEMBER
**17**

# What Forgiveness Can Do to You

Two days before Christmas, Frank and Elizabeth Morris received a phone call telling them that 18-year-old Ted, their only child, had been in a bad accident. The caller instructed them to go to a large hospital in Nashville, Tennessee, as soon as possible. When they arrived, a neurosurgeon told them Ted had died.

Next day at the police station the Morrises learned that the other driver, Tommy Pigage, was only slightly injured. At the time of the accident his blood-alcohol level was three times the legal limit. He was charged with murder, but after he pleaded guilty the charge was reduced to second-degree manslaughter. Months later he was sentenced to only five years' probation, with the stipulation that, should he violate probation, he would have to serve a 10-year jail term. To say that the Morrises, especially Elizabeth, were enraged at such a lenient sentence is to put it mildly.

Later, at a meeting of Mothers Against Drunk Driving, Elizabeth heard Tommy tell how he couldn't stop crying when he heard Ted had died. Yet a few days after this he was caught drinking and was forced to serve his 10-year sentence.

In spite of conflicting emotions, Elizabeth, a Christian, began visiting Tommy in jail. One day as they talked, he begged to be forgiven.

"I forgive you," Elizabeth responded, then added, "and I'd like you to forgive me for hating you."

"Oh, Mrs. Morris, I do," he said with feeling.

On a subsequent visit Tommy told Elizabeth he wanted to stop drinking but couldn't. She assured him he could with God's help—and he did!

On January 12, 1985, Tommy was baptized. Later he was released on probation. The Morrises began taking him to their home and treating him like a son. Writing in the January 1986 *Guideposts*, Elizabeth said that after this she began to feel the peace that only God can give. And Tommy? He is a different person!

This is what can happen when we forgive—and are forgiven.

*When that day comes, the deaf will be able to hear a book being read aloud, and the blind, who have been living in darkness, will open their eyes and see. Poor and humble people will once again find the happiness which the Lord, the holy God of Israel, gives. Isa. 29:18, 19, TEV.*

# Hope for the Blind and Deaf-Mutes

In the book *There Are Sermons in Stories,* by William L. Stidger, the author tells about the first time he met Helen Keller; it was at a Chautauqua lecture. Earlier, she had learned to speak audibly, so, although she was deaf and totally blind, she delivered a speech to those assembled. At the close, there was a thunderous round of applause and Helen joined in the clapping with joyful exuberance.

It was evident that Miss Keller had somehow perceived the audience's enthusiasm. So after the applause died down, the chairman of the meeting asked her, through Ann Sullivan, who always accompanied her, how she was able to sense the applause when she could neither hear nor see.

"Through the vibrations in my feet," Helen explained.

Someone then asked her what her favorite book was, and she fairly shouted, "The Bible! It is the most wonderful book in the world."

In response to the question why the Bible meant so much to her, she replied, "It is because in my darkness, the Bible makes me see the Great Light!"

In Isaiah 9:2, the prophet says that "the people who walk in darkness shall see a great Light—a Light that will shine on all those who live in the land of the shadow of death" (TLB). The darkness Isaiah is talking about is spiritual darkness, and the great Light is none other than Jesus, who declared Himself to be the Light of the world (see John 9:5).

It is our privilege to be reflectors of the Light of the world, no matter what our vocation may be. As my wife and I have shared the Light from the Book with those who walked in darkness, whether in foreign countries or in the homeland, we have never ceased to be thrilled to see the light of joy come into the faces of new converts. This thrill can be yours too!

*You are a letter that has come from Christ,*
*given to us to deliver; a letter written not with*
*ink but with the Spirit of the living God.*
*2 Cor. 3:3, REB.*

DECEMBER

19

# Living Letters

Back in the days when Paul wrote these words, letters were usually written on papyrus, a writing material made from a reed that grew along the banks of the Nile. Our word "paper" is derived from papyrus. I have seen many of these letters in the great museums of the world, and perhaps you have too.

The quality of the handwriting indicates that most of these missives were written, not by the message sender, but by a scribe whose business it was to write letters. Scribes were needed in those days because few people could read or write. Some of these epistles are business letters, others deal with life and death matters, still others are love letters.

When I first began working as a ministerial intern in Santa Rosa, California, I was given an office and an old desk that had belonged to a previous pastor. It gave evidence of having been stored in an attic for a long time, and had not been cleaned for many years.

Soon after the desk was turned over for my use, I set about tidying it up. I pulled out all the drawers and was surprised at what I found. Some letters had fallen down behind one of the drawers. These were crushed and yellowed, and bore postmarks confirming their "great age."

Now, I am not in the habit of reading other people's mail, but I made an exception this time because I knew neither the writer nor the recipient of the letters. But I must confess that the contents of these letters (some never intended for other eyes) made me wish I knew these people. What insights they gave into the character of the correspondents!

In our verse for meditation the apostle Paul says that the Corinthian Christians were letters written by Christ and delivered to the world. We, too, are epistles "known and read of all men" (verse 2). How important, then, that the message our lives convey be one that corresponds with our profession.

## 20

*If a man has a hundred sheep, and one wanders away and is lost, what will he do? Won't he leave the ninety-nine others and go out into the hills to search for the lost one? Matt. 18:12, TLB.*

# Good Shepherds Never Give Up

Louis Pasteur, the famous French microbiologist who discovered that most diseases are caused by germs, was devoted to the pursuit of knowledge. Yet he maintained that there are spiritual values that transcend science.

In 1849 he married Marie Laurent, one of his lab assistants. They had five children. Three of these died in infancy. Nineteen years later he suffered a stroke from overwork and was left partially paralyzed.

When the Franco-Prussian war broke out in 1870, Pasteur's only son, Jean Batiste, was called to serve his country and was involved in the catastrophic defeat of French arms at Metz. Weeks passed without news from the boy, and Pasteur left his now-famous laboratory in Paris to find him. In spite of his partial paralysis, he headed northward in search of his son. The roads were clogged with defeated soldiers and stragglers. The journey was arduous, but after much inquiry, he located his son's unit. Then an officer told him the discouraging news: out of an original complement of 1,200 men fewer than 300 survived.

But Pasteur did not give up. He pressed on, picking his way along roads choked with dead horses and men suffering from freezing cold and gangrenous wounds. At last he came upon a soldier wrapped to his eyes in a greatcoat; he was hardly recognizable in his emaciated condition. It was his son! Father and son, too moved for words, embraced in silence.

In the war between the forces of good and evil, many a son, many a daughter, has suffered catastrophic defeat at the hands of the enemy of souls. Many, like Pasteur's child, are hardly recognizable because of the ravages of sin. Some professed Christians, perhaps even some parents, may pronounce such errant children beyond hope. But although "they may forget" (Isa. 49:15), the Good Shepherd, and the faithful parent, never forget!—even if at times they must administer "tough love."

# Reward for Liberality

Many years ago a young man traveling through one of the states in the Midwest on his way to Colorado came to a farm and asked for a night's lodging. The farmer gladly took him in. A little later another traveler and his wife stopped and asked if they could spend the night there. The young husband, who suffered from tuberculosis, explained that he had only $4 with which to pay for their lodging. The farmer invited them to stay the night free of charge.

The first young man, feeling pity for the sick man, offered to give up his bed and sleep in the barn, which he did. Next morning, as the sick man and his wife were leaving, the farmer put $100 in his hand and told him to use it and not to worry if he was never able to pay it back.

Twenty years passed. The first young man happened to be passing near the farm where he had stayed those many years before. He decided to see if the farmer still lived at the same place. He did. While they were renewing acquaintances another visitor knocked. By one of those once-in-a-lifetime coincidences, it was the other traveler! He had regained his health, and fortune had smiled on him. Recently he had heard that his generous host had suffered serious financial reverses. He had returned to repay his generosity.

"Friend," he said to the farmer, "you gave me $100 when I was destitute, and now I am repaying you $100 for each dollar you gave me."

I wish I knew the names of the people in this story, but I do not. All I know is that it was "told by the man who was the first guest at the farmhouse."

Generosity has its rewards—even in this life. Jesus said: "Give, and it will be given to you. A good measure, pressed down, shaken together, and running over, will be poured into your lap" (Luke 6:38, NIV). But don't expect it *always* to happen that way. Be generous because it is part of the golden rule—and look for spiritual blessings, not material ones.

*A child is born to us! A son is given to us! And he will be our ruler. He will be called, "Wonderful Counselor," "Mighty God," "Eternal Father," "Prince of Peace." Isa. 9:6, TEV.*

# The Prince of Peace

Jesus is often called the Prince of Peace, yet, paradoxically, countless wars have been fought in His name during the past 2,000 years.

A silver star used to hang in the Church of the Nativity in Bethlehem over Jesus' supposed birthplace. I visited this grotto in 1959, when I went on a tour of the Bible lands. I saw a star inset on the floor under the manger. However, I noticed no silver star hanging above it. It was only later that I heard that there had been a star there and that it had been removed 100 years before.

In 1853 this star became the focus of discord that led, in a short time, to the Crimean War. It all began when the clergy of the Eastern Orthodox Church decided to replace the star with a star of their own. The clergy of the Latin rite objected. The former were backed by Russia, the latter by France. When Turkey sided with France, Russia went to war with Turkey. France, Great Britain, and Sardinia in turn declared war on Russia. The war lasted three long years and resulted in the death and wounding of scores of thousands of soldiers. In the end, the allies won. But the ironic part of it is that, although two years after the war the center of contention, the silver star, was permanently removed, the war left a legacy of ill will that lasted for years.

Have you ever wondered why Christ has so often been linked with war and bloodshed when He is the Prince of Peace? Christ is not the one who causes these wars. They are caused by people who may *profess* to be His followers (see James 4:1, 2), but apparently have never experienced, and therefore do not reveal by their actions, the peace of which Christ is prince (see John 16:33).

This is the season of the year when the thoughts of many turn to the birth of the Prince of Peace. May it be a time when your thoughts turn to Him. May He be born anew in your heart, and may you always experience the peace He offers—peace "which passeth all understanding" (Phil. 4:7).

*[Mary] gave birth to her first-born son and wrapped him in swaddling clothes and laid him in a manger, because there was no room for them in the place where travelers lodged.*
**Luke 2:7, NAB.**

DECEMBER

# 23

# Caring, Not a Spectator's Sport

Callousness and indifference are not qualities confined to antiquity. They may also be seen in our day.

On December 6, 1964, a young mother gave birth to a child on the sidewalk of a busy intersection in Oklahoma City. A crowd of curious passersby stopped to watch but rendered no assistance. After a while a visitor from Tulsa took pity and called a taxi, but the driver refused to take the mother and child to the hospital because they would foul his vehicle. The helpful stranger called the police. They were too busy with more urgent problems.

About this time Bob Cunningham, a former state representative, chanced to pass that way and called the fire department for an ambulance. The call was never answered. Meanwhile, Cunningham asked a bystander to fetch a blanket from a hotel across the street, but the request was turned down. Finally Cunningham picked up the woman and child and placed them in his own car and took them to the hospital.

This unbelievable story is reminiscent of what happened to Jesus and His mother 2,000 years ago. But is it possible that we would have expressed the same indifference had we been the innkeeper of Bethlehem?

We live in an age when people are reluctant to get involved —especially if the person is a stranger or appears to be indigent. An example of this happened several years ago in New York City. Kitty Genovese was returning to her apartment late one night when she was attacked and stabbed many times. At least 38 people heard her cries for help. Eventually, some did raise their window sashes and look out to see what was happening. A few even yelled at her attacker, but *not one* called the police or offered assistance, and the unfortunate woman died.

When we go out of our way to help someone in need, we are actually doing it for Christ—for He said, "Inasmuch as ye have done it unto one of the least of these my brethren, ye have done it unto me" (Matt. 25:40).

# 24

*Here I stand, knocking at the door. If anyone hears me calling and opens the door, I will enter his house and have supper with him, and he with me. Rev. 3:20, NAB.*

## Royal Visitors

Late one afternoon around the beginning of the twentieth century, Edward VII of England was out in the country walking with his queen when she twisted her ankle and sprained it badly. In great pain and with considerable difficulty, she limped along, holding on to her husband's shoulder. Some time after dark they reached a cottage, and the king knocked on the door.

"Who is there?" a man's voice inquired from within.

"Edward, your king," replied the monarch.

"Enough of your nonsense!" shouted the angry cottager; then, "Be off!"

The king kept knocking. Finally the man demanded, "Who is there and what do you want?"

"I tell you, I am Edward, the king. Please let me in!"

"I'll teach you to torment a man trying to sleep," raged the cottager, rising from his bed.

Flinging open the door, he discovered to his great embarrassment that it was indeed the king. Apologizing profusely, he invited the royal couple in and immediately sent for help.

Years later, when he related the incident, the man observed, "And to think, I almost didn't let him in."

Two thousand years ago the parents of another King knocked at the door of a village inn and sought admission. When the innkeeper answered their knock, he must have noticed that the mother was in the late stages of pregnancy. At the very least, he could have offered his own room in the emergency. Instead, he offered them the stable, and there Jesus was born.

Today, at this very moment, this King, once the Babe of Bethlehem, now your heavenly Friend, stands at the door of your heart and knocks. He seeks admittance. He yearns to come in and commune with you, and He longs for you to commune with Him and learn to know Him better.

"Behold," says the King of love, "I stand at the door and knock." How could anyone turn Him away?

*When the fullness of the time had come, God sent forth His Son, born of a woman, born under the law, to redeem those who were under the law, that we might receive the adoption as sons. Gal. 4:4, 5, NKJV.*

# The Greatest Event of All Time

We can never be absolutely certain about the date of Jesus' birth. The fact that it gets quite cold in Palestine in late December, especially at night, yet shepherds were "living out in the fields, keeping watch over their flock by night" (Luke 2:8, NKJV), suggests a warmer season of the year. However, as one Christian writer notes, "Although we do not know the exact day of Christ's birth, we would honor the sacred event" (Ellen G. White, in *Review and Herald*, Dec. 17, 1889).

The true spirit of Christmas seeks admission to the inner sanctum of the soul, and awaits our invitation for it to enter. The spirit of Christmas may be all around us, and yet we may have insulated ourselves against the warm current of love that celebrates the event.

The spirit of the Nativity came that first Christmas Day only to such as were ready to receive the world's Redeemer. Although the priests in Jerusalem professed to be waiting for the Messiah, it was to the expectant shepherds in the fields of Bethlehem that the angels announced the Saviour's birth (see *The Desire of Ages*, p. 47).

Herod's pretentious palace stood nearby, but it was in a lowly stable that the Holy Child was born to a young mother— "because there was no room for them in the place where travelers lodged" (verse 7, NAB). There were many great and worldly-wise men in Rome, far to the west, but it was to Wise Men of the East, whose hearts sought for Him who was "born King of the Jews" (Matt. 2:2) that the star appeared.

The Incarnation is the greatest object lesson of love that the mind of infinite wisdom could conceive. In giving us His only begotten son, God gave to humanity all the treasures of the universe in one small bundle of life. Although the birth of our Lord 2,000 years ago was the greatest event of all time, its substance, spirit, and significance are lost if Christ be not born in us.

*Be the more eager, brothers, to ratify your calling and election, for as you exercise these qualities you will never make a slip.*
*2 Peter 1:10, Moffatt.*

# Confirm Your Reservation

Some time ago a friend of mine mistakenly boarded the wrong plane. He didn't discover his error until he was comfortably seated and the plane was ready to take off! Fortunately, he had time to get off and get to the plane he was supposed to be on.

In 1984 Michael Lewis, a student at Sacramento College (California), wasn't so fortunate. After a three-month visit to Germany, he was returning home to Oakland via Los Angeles. In Los Angeles, when an Air New Zealand attendant announced that the plane for *Aukland* was boarding, Lewis misunderstood *Oakland* and dashed aboard. After he was airborne he discovered his error, but by then it was too late for the plane to turn back. After returning to the States (courtesy of Air New Zealand, no less!), he explained that New Zealanders "talk different."

We smile at Lewis's error. Making such a slip is embarrassing, but making a mistake with respect to our eternal destination is no laughing matter. The Bible speaks of people in the judgment who thought they were "on board" for heaven only to discover that they'd arrived at the wrong place. We read about them in Matthew 25:31-46. These will protest, "Lord, Lord, have we not prophesied in thy name? and in thy name have cast out devils? and in thy name done many wonderful works? And then will [Christ] profess unto them, I never knew you: depart from me, ye that work iniquity" (Matt. 7:22, 23).

You and I can avoid making such a tragic slip by ratifying our calling and election now. This means checking on our destination and confirming our reservation each time God's Spirit speaks to our heart. It is the Holy Spirit who convicts us that the path we are taking is the wrong one, and, pointing to the right one, says, "This is the way, walk ye in it" (Isa. 30:21).

If you feel the Holy Spirit appealing to your heart just now, why not check your destination and confirm your reservation?

*While people are saying, "Peace and safety,"
destruction will come on them suddenly, as
labor pains on a pregnant woman, and they will
not escape. But you, brothers, are not in
darkness so that this day should surprise you
like a thief. 1 Thess. 5:3-5, NIV.*

# Don't Be Taken by Surprise

When our son, Steve, was born, Vesta and I were living in Manaus, 1,000 miles up the Amazon River. Our house was situated on the outskirts of the city. Bus service stopped at 10:00 p.m. and resumed at 4:00 a.m.—and there were no telephones nearby. As the time for Steve's arrival approached, I managed to locate three telephones about a mile from our house—just in case. And yet we were taken by surprise.

It wasn't because we had made no plans for Steve's arrival. We had. But he didn't arrive when we expected he would. The birth pains began about 1:30 a.m. I got up, dressed, and ran to the first phone as fast as I could. It was the home of a Barbadian midwife. I clapped, as is the custom in Brazil. When I persisted, some awakened neighbors informed me she was on vacation.

I ran up the street to a store that had a phone. It was closed! Just then I noticed a light shining through the transom of a bakery. I clapped, explained the emergency to the two workers, and asked permission to use the phone. They were sorry, but I would have to ask the *patrão,* who lived around the corner. I ran around the corner. My clapping must have engendered a foul mood in the boss, for when I explained my predicament and asked permission to use his phone, he told me in no uncertain terms that no one used his phone at that hour of the night, and he slammed the window shut.

By now I was desperate. Finally, I found some late-night drinkers nearby who had called a taxi. When I explained the situation, they graciously let me take the taxi they had called. By the time we reached the hospital, it was almost too late. Stephen was born five minutes after we arrived there!

Come when it may, Christ's second coming will catch most people by surprise. You need not let that happen to you if you are ready for His coming at all times (see Matt. 24:36-44).

# 28

*If the owner of the house knew when the thief was coming he would keep a watchful eye and not allow his house to be broken into. You must be prepared in the same way. The Son of Man is coming at the time you least expect. Matt. 24:43, 44, NAB.*

# Be Prepared

In March 1914 the British Imperial Antarctic Expedition left England under the leadership of Sir Ernest Shackleton with the intention of crossing the frozen continent from a base on the Weddell Sea to McMurdo Sound via the South Pole. However, their ship, the *Endurance,* was crushed in an ice pack. After drifting around on ice floes for five months, they managed to escape to Elephant Island in the South Shetland Archipelago. From there, Shackleton and five men sailed 800 miles in a whaleboat to South Georgia Island, where he obtained aid.

Three times Shackleton set out to rescue his stranded men, and each time was frustrated by the frozen sea. However, on his fourth attempt he found a narrow channel through the pack ice and at last reached them. When he arrived he was delighted to find them prepared to board ship without a moment's delay.

After the excitement of the men's rescue had eased, Shackleton asked them how they happened to be ready to board ship the moment he arrived. They told him that every morning the assistant leader he had appointed had rolled up his sleeping bag and said, "Get your things ready, boys. The boss may come today."

Christ's second coming is much more certain than was Shackleton's return to Elephant Island. Shortly before He left this earth and went to His Father, He promised, "I *will* come again" (John 14:3), no if's or maybe's about it.

When Jesus does return, all true Christians will be ready and eagerly waiting (1 Thess. 4:16, 17) "for the blessed hope—the glorious appearing of our great God and Savior" (Titus 2:13, NIV). Will I be ready, will you be ready for His coming? This is the important question that only we can answer.

Shackleton's men prepared every morning for the return of their leader. One of the best ways you and I can prepare for the return of our Leader is to study and meditate on His Word at the beginning of each day.

*"Write down clearly on tablets what I reveal to you, so that it can be read at a glance. Put it in writing, because it is not yet time for it to come true. But the time is coming quickly, and what I show you will come true. It may seem slow in coming, but wait for it; it will certainly take place." Hab. 2:2, 3, TEV.*

# A Sermon in Action

Jeremiah was a contemporary of Habakkuk. The Lord revealed to these prophets the bad news that their nation, Judah, would fall under the heel of the Babylonians. To Jeremiah He further revealed that the Jews should submit peacefully to the conqueror and go into captivity, yet He promised that after 70 years they would return to their homeland. This message was very unpopular, and most of God's professed people disbelieved it, to their sorrow.

Hanameel, Jeremiah's cousin, who apparently was one of the doubters, realized that the Babylonians would soon overrun his farm. He offered to sell it to Jeremiah at a bargain price.

Now, the last thing Jeremiah needed was a farm. In the first place, he was a prophet, not a farmer; in the second, he had no children to inherit it; in the third, he was so old that he had no prospect of living to settle on it 70 years hence. Yet he bought the farm, and not at Hanameel's panic price, either. He paid *its fair market value!* (See Jer. 32:6-15.) He went so far as to make the transaction a matter of public record. Why? Because he believed God's promise. His was a sermon in action.

Almost 2,000 years ago the Lord declared, "Surely I come quickly" (Rev. 22:20). Now, 2,000 years seems like a long time —and many of God's people today are saying by their actions, if not their words: "The days are prolonged, and every vision faileth" (Eze. 12:22).

How shall you and I relate to this seeming delay? Shall we say by our actions or our words "My lord delayeth his coming" (Matt. 24:48), or shall we, like Jeremiah, show that we believe the Lord's coming "is near, even at the doors" (Matt. 24:33)? After all, in the sight of the eternal God, 1,000 years are but "a watch in the night" (Ps. 90:4)!

# 30

*You are a building that rests on the apostles and prophets as its foundation, with Christ Jesus as the corner-stone; in him the whole structure is welded together and rises into a sacred temple in the Lord, and in him you are yourselves built into this to form a habitation for God in the Spirit. Eph. 2:20, 21, Moffatt.*

# Getting the Larger Picture

When Sir Christopher Wren, the famous British architect who designed St. Paul's Cathedral in London, walked through the edifice one day while it was under construction, he asked each workman what he was doing. One said he was laying bricks, another that he was putting stained glass windows in place, still another that he was doing carpentry. None of these replies was what Sir Christopher was hoping to hear.

As the great architect was leaving the construction site he came upon a man who was mixing mortar. He asked him the same question.

Looking up from his humble task, the workman answered with pride, "Sir, I am building a great cathedral."

What an answer! What vision! The average artisan saw no further than the particular job in which he was engaged, but here was a man who, although performing menial work, looked beyond the mixing of mortar and grasped the larger picture.

When I was a teenager, we sang a hymn entitled "Building for Eternity." The first verse went like this:

> We are building in sorrow or joy
> A temple the world may not see,
> Which time cannot mar nor destroy:
> We build for eternity.
> —N. B. Sargent

Whether or not we realize it, each of us is engaged in temple building. Our task may not seem important, but according to our verse, we are shaping our lives for a place in God's spiritual temple. Ask yourself as I ask myself: Am I like the average artisan building St. Paul's, or am I like the mortar mixer who caught a vision of the larger picture?

*This one thing I do, forgetting those things which are behind, and reaching forth unto those things which are before, I press toward the mark for the prize of the high calling of God in Christ Jesus. Phil. 3:13, 14.*

DECEMBER
31

# Back to the Future

Chinese ideograms have always fascinated me. Once Dr. William Mather, a scholar who had spent many years as a missionary in China, gave a lecture in which he stated that the way the ancient Chinese used the characters *yin* and *yang* (the two opposing forces) indicates that they were aware of positive and negative electricity long before the West discovered this phenomenon. He also said that the characters "dangerous" and "opportunity," when used together, mean "crisis." In other words, a crisis is a "dangerous opportunity." Quite a challenging thought!

But to me, one of the most fascinating concepts of the Chinese people is the way they conceive of the future. They think of themselves as walking backward into the future and facing the past. This may seem strange to us, but it makes excellent sense. The past lies in view. We can mentally "see" it. But the future is hidden from view as effectually as if it were behind our backs.

The Western idea of the future is diametrically opposite that of the Chinese. We speak of "facing the future." Reared in the Greco-Roman world, Paul obviously had the Western concept of the future when he spoke of "reaching forth unto those things which are before."

But maybe there is a point at which East and West meet. In his 1986 State of the Union address, President Ronald W. Reagan used the expression "back to the future." By this he meant that we've dwelt on the past long enough. It's time to consider the unknown "dangerous opportunities" ahead.

The curtain of time has rung down upon another year. God has brought us back to the land of beginning again. Whatever the future may hold, may your study of His Word this coming year help you ever to know Him better.

Keep pressing "on to know the Lord," whom to know is life eternal!

# SCRIPTURE INDEX

**377**

| | | | |
|---|---|---|---|
| 12:10 | Oct. 23 | | |

### GALATIANS

| | |
|---|---|
| 2:20 | Apr. 6 |
| 4:4, 5 | Dec. 25 |
| 6:1 | Aug. 22 |
| 6:2 | Mar. 23 |
| 6:9 | July 9 |
| 6:14 | Sept. 20 |

### EPHESIANS

| | |
|---|---|
| 1:3 | July 23 |
| 1:3 | Aug. 5 |
| 2:20 | Dec. 30 |
| 4:22-24 | Feb. 2 |
| 5:3, 4 | July 7 |
| 5:18 | Oct. 10 |
| 5:18, 19 | May 29 |
| 6:13 | Feb. 20 |

### PHILIPPIANS

| | |
|---|---|
| 1:8 | Oct. 15 |
| 1:17, 18 | June 20 |
| 1:27, 28 | Nov. 18 |
| 3:8 | July 17 |
| 3:10 | Apr. 3 |
| 3:13, 14 | Dec. 31 |
| 4:19 | Jan. 24 |

### COLOSSIANS

| | |
|---|---|
| 2:6, 7 | Aug. 10 |
| 2:13, 14 | Feb. 3 |
| 3:13 | Oct. 6 |

### 1 THESSALONIANS

| | |
|---|---|
| 2:7, 8 | Nov. 2 |
| 4:11 | July 18 |
| 5:1, 2 | Oct. 7 |
| 5:3-5 | Dec. 27 |
| 5:15 | Aug. 12 |
| 5:17 | Nov. 11 |
| 5:18 | Nov. 23 |
| 5:22 | May 6 |

### 2 THESSALONIANS

| | |
|---|---|
| 2:10, 11 | Oct. 8 |

### 1 TIMOTHY

| | |
|---|---|
| 4:1, 2 | Dec. 14 |
| 4:12 | Sept. 22 |
| 6:11 | Feb. 21 |
| 6:12 | Apr. 21 |

### 2 TIMOTHY

| | |
|---|---|
| 1:3 | Feb. 6 |
| 1:5 | Feb. 19 |
| 1:8, 9 | Oct. 11 |
| 1:12 | Jan. 3 |
| 2:3 | Jan. 15 |
| 3:16 | Jan. 9 |
| 4:7, 8 | July 16 |
| 4:11 | June 28 |

### TITUS

| | |
|---|---|
| 2:7 | Mar. 21 |

### PHILEMON

| | |
|---|---|
| 9-11 | Sept. 3 |

### HEBREWS

| | |
|---|---|
| 2:11 | June 7 |
| 2:18 | May 7 |
| 4:12 | Oct. 4 |
| 4:16 | Mar. 1 |
| 5:12 | May 27 |
| 6:10 | June 8 |
| 7:25 | Aug. 2 |
| 10:25 | Nov. 12 |
| 10:34 | Jan. 31 |
| 11:1 | Nov. 1 |
| 11:8 | May 22 |
| 11:9, 10 | Oct. 29 |
| 12:1, 2 | June 17 |
| 13:2 | Sept. 5 |
| 13:20, 21 | July 5 |

### JAMES

| | |
|---|---|
| 1:14, 15 | June 14 |
| 2:9 | Feb. 8 |
| 2:14 | Jan. 21 |

| | |
|---|---|
| 3:6 | Oct. 2 |
| 4:6 | July 10 |
| 5:6, 7 | Mar. 2 |
| 5:20 | Mar. 12 |

### 1 PETER

| | |
|---|---|
| 1:14, 15 | Jan. 23 |
| 1:18, 19 | Mar. 25 |
| 2:7, 8 | May 17 |
| 2:21 | Feb. 9 |
| 3:8 | Feb. 13 |
| 3:8, 9 | Sept. 26 |
| 3:9 | Aug. 15 |
| 5:7 | June 5 |

### 2 PETER

| | |
|---|---|
| 1:10 | Dec. 26 |
| 1:19 | Apr. 18 |

### 1 JOHN

| | |
|---|---|
| 1:6, 7 | Mar. 11 |
| 2:1 | Dec. 6 |

### JUDE

| | |
|---|---|
| 24, 25 | June 6 |

### REVELATION

| | |
|---|---|
| 1:5, 6 | Dec. 11 |
| 3:11 | June 29 |
| 3:20 | Dec. 24 |
| 5:9 | Apr. 8 |
| 12:11 | Sept. 2 |
| 14:13 | May 8 |
| 16:15 | Sept. 13 |

# Index of Anecdotes, Illustrations, and Allusions

**382**

## Criticism

**388**

394